Against
The Tide

# Against The Tide

## MY MEMOIR

WILLIAM D. GAIRDNER

Published in 2024 by
Kinetics Design, KDbooks.ca
ISBN 978-1-998351-07-7 (hardcover book)
ISBN 978-1-998351-06-0 (paperback)
ISBN 978-1-998351-05-3 (ebook)

Cover and interior design, typesetting,
online publishing, and printing by Daniel Crack,
Kinetics Design, KDbooks.ca
www.linkedin.com/in/kdbooks/

*Any dead thing can go with the stream,*

*but only a living thing can go against it.*

— G.K. Chesterton

*At a very young age I had my first philosophical experience*
*standing naked on one of those whaleback rocks*
*staring down through five feet of clear water ...*

# CONTENTS

# PART 1

## EARLY YEARS
## OF ADVENTURES
## AND MISADVENTURES

# EARLY YEARS, ADVENTURES, AND MISADVENTURES

*My life began suddenly.*
*And when the time comes, I hope it will end the same way.*

Mother was in end-stage labour. She moaned, struggled to peer over her imposing belly, and … there I was, her second baby boy. On October 19, 1940, in a small unassuming house on Douglas Avenue in Oakville, Ontario. I was named William after my father's best friend William Weis who, like my dad, had been a Royal Canadian Air Force pilot. Alas, he died during the invasion of Normandy on June 6, 1944, along with five crew members in the fiery crash of his Lancaster Bomber as it fell, screaming into the dark of a forest near the village of Bailleul, southwest of Paris … with a 500-pound bomb on board. Panic. Cries of terror in a spinning crescendo of screaming engines whining in smoke and flames. And gone. I'm not sure where my second name, Douglas, came from, but I'm hoping it wasn't that street.

Barely six years later, at Appleby College a boarding school in Oakville — the same school Dad and his friend had attended — I would wait anxiously with our choir beneath the balcony for the Sunday Evensong procession to begin. There, with sadness and curiosity, I would stare at the small stained glass panes of the memorial window dedicated to William by his family, "In loving memory." What was it like to fall from the sky to your death? How did Dad feel losing his best friend? "William" was both an honour and an absence; it felt strange to be named after a dead man. Of the 50 boys at Appleby old enough to fight in that war, almost half laid down their lives for their country.

My earliest years are a blank, except for what I see in old photos. Wee Billy, in a furry black winter cap sitting on Santa's knee at the Eaton's store in Toronto. Or with what looks very much like an oversized head, riding a tricycle in a white shirt and shorts, feet barely touching the pedals. After that I only remember being sick. A lot. In and out of bed, months at a time. In and out of school.

Ruthann Johnston, my mother, was a beautiful Toronto girl of high, sometimes prickly character, with a full laugh and acerbic wit, quietly merciless to those she thought foolish. Unofficially, she filled the role of local beauty when at her family's summer home overlooking sparkling blue Lake Ontario at the end of Park Avenue in Oakville, where she met my dad for the first time.

Word had gotten out. People supposed they would be a good match. He had a fetching and flashy grin, and the body of Adonis. The latest rumour was that he had climbed the 100-foot water tower on the Baillie property and done a handstand on the steel ball at the very top. One day, he wrote to ask if he could visit. He would like to drop by on Sunday. The gods were poised and arranging. He had been a very accomplished high school athlete and was in his second season with the Toronto Argonauts Football Club. My debutante mother got used to summertime visits at Park Lane from a lot of handsome, aspiring young men in white flannel trousers, blue blazers, and red-striped ties. Later in life she often said, "I could have married any one of them," with a bit of a laugh — and a hint of the rueful.

But Sunday came. The doorbell rang and there he was.

It was broad daylight and he was grinning, chewing on a green apple, dressed in a T-shirt and a pair of shorts he had cut with pinking shears from a pair of old blue jeans. Her whole life, she never could say why she let him in. It was the manliness she couldn't resist. Before the evening was out, they had talked of nearly everything in their lives that mattered. Especially about the recent death of his mother Norma when he was barely 18. The headmaster had come knocking at the classroom to break the tragic news. Just turned 42, she was sitting over tea with her sister Carol in a lovely sunroom at the Cox Estate in Oakville, overlooking the lambent green lawn and polo pony stables when suddenly, without the slightest hint of the darkness to befall her, she slumped forward, dead in her chair.

She had been an engaging woman, beloved by all, and Dad went into life-long shock, which we knew because he never mentioned her unless we asked. Which we didn't, to avoid giving him pain. After some difficulty in telling beautiful, damp-eyed Ruthann of this, he drew a finger along the thin scar she was wondering about that ran at an angle from the side of his nose along the crease of his cheek. That, he said, is where, as a 14-year-old (this, told with a shy smile), "I got kicked in the face by my own horse …"

That did it. So handsome. So brave. She was doomed. And so was he. Oakville was soon burning with the news of their romance, and they with the bliss of passion. Here they are in the sunny grip of their joyful, uncomplicated youth. I feel happy just looking at their happiness.

*Against The Tide*

But unbeknownst to them, this stage of their lives was set for calamity, a sudden turn of the wheel of fortune. Dad, still only 19, had recently finished high school (to Grade 13 in those days) and was happily riding his beat-up motorcycle to football practice in Toronto — free as a bird in the wind, fresh in love with the most beautiful girl in the world, everything ahead of him — when suddenly, a woman without a driver's licence pulled out from a parking spot and smashed into him.

"I only remember lying, stunned, crumpled on the road, my lower leg almost completely severed. It was there, beside me, hanging on by a twisted piece of skin and muscle. My boot and sock torn off. My toes facing backward, touching my knee. I just managed to grab my leg … and passed out."

He was in hospital for almost a year, suffering through multiple operations as surgeons tried to save what was left of his almost calf-less leg in a fight against decaying bone. Then, miraculously, just when they had given up and decided to amputate, a new Sulfa-based drug was invented which stopped the decay of bone. So he kept his leg until his late sixties, when they cut it off from the knee down.

Six months after the accident and back in hospital, his world already upside down, worries multiplied. In late April of 1938 a worried Ruthann told him she was pregnant. Oh my. I have a photo of them getting married. Him, in his hospital bed, smiling wanly — with a touch of embarrassment. Her, standing demurely beside him. My displeased and imposing grandfather — "Big Jim" as he was known to all — glowering in the background. To his mind, she had ruined the life of his prized eldest son, and I'm not certain he ever forgave her.

To make matters worse, the sabres of war were rattling. On September 1, 1939, a year and a half after the accident, with Dad barely six months out of hospital, Hitler invaded Poland, and the turn of events in just two years of their lives suddenly got more complicated. She had been a single, very desirable beauty with the world at her feet, but was now bearing the shame of what was called a shotgun marriage. He had been as free as the wind, a running back for the Argonauts in the full flush of youth, now a near-cripple getting about town with crutches while bombs dropped in Europe, his closest friends getting shipped out to defend the free world against evil Aryans. Brother Jamie arrived when they were barely 20 years old. I'm amazed when I think of the rapid-fire sequence of events in my dad's life: his beloved mother suddenly dead at 18; a leg mangled in a motorcycle accident at 19; a promising football career abruptly ended; his girlfriend pregnant; his marriage a shotgun wedding in the hospital, with news of WWII booming on the airwaves.

There were three of us kids before the war ended — a lot got done on leave — and four, eventually. Jamie, myself, and two younger sisters, Cassie and Norma. "But your dad never *had* to go to war. He never *had* to leave us. People *understood* he was crippled," Mom would sometimes cry mournfully, with the help of a little gin and bitterness … But he couldn't stand not going to fight alongside his friends. Vengeance was in order. The Army, foot-soldiering, was definitely not an option. But he could fly, couldn't he?

So, he applied to the Royal Canadian Air Force, and they kept rejecting his application. He could be trained to fly with a bad leg, but his eyesight was not good enough. So, he asked for re-testing, went straight home to wind a dark scarf over his eyes, and never took it off until Mom led him back to the doctor's office 24 hours later to stare at the numbers on the wall. Off came the scarf, and he passed the vision test. He was happy. She was not.

He soloed in a Harvard Mk II trainer after only four hours of training and went on to become an ace flight instructor at Trenton, and then Dunnville, until the war effort called up more pilots for active duty. Then he got posted to bases in England and then in Holland for a while, flying killer sorties into Belgium and France, while living mostly in a Quonset hut on a farm with a grass airstrip. By then, he had an ulcer. So, Mom sent him chocolate he could trade for milk and eggs with local farmers. He never told us war stories, except

Against The Tide

for the one about him diving his Spitfire at about 600 miles an hour to strafe what was purportedly a German troop train. He could see women with baby carriages on the platform. Fake women. Soldiers in skirts, he was told, planted to deter just such raids. He was never sure. But he did his strafing, and pulled up sharply, draining all the blood from his head with the G-force, and passed-out clean, heading straight up for the moon.

"Dad. Dad! What happened?" We just had to know.

"I was no war hero. But just as I got above the clouds at about 6,000 feet, I came to, and I saw two German Messerschmitts coming at me!" That got a "Wow" from us kids. "So, I just took 'er right back down below the clouds and got the hell out of there!"

Dad saw death and destruction up close enough to obliterate any deep convictions he otherwise may have been nursing about what some call the higher meaning of life. So, when it was over, he took to drinking, along with so many other survivors, and our young lives got filled with the weekend riot of post-war partying. Boisterous laughter, much dancing, and the smell of beer, scotch, cigarettes, and cigar smoke in a living room that looked like a train wreck the next day.

For the rest of his life, booze was his solace and a kind of personal existential response to what looked like a cruel and morally meaningless world. That was tough to live with, because in all other respects he was a happy soul, "a man's man", as people would say, who radiated a natural sense of command attractive to all who met him. They could easily imagine themselves fighting under his leadership or working hard alongside him. He was even a manly drinker (I was going to say, "a manly drunk", but couldn't bring myself to say that) who could down an entire bottle of rum in a day, and unless you knew him well, you couldn't tell. A born romantic, too. He hadn't looked at poetry since high school, but even late in life he could stand up at a party and with deep feeling recite whole sonnets and long passages from Shakespeare: "When in disgrace with fortune and men's eyes / I all alone beweep my outcast state / And trouble deaf heaven with my bootless cries / And look upon myself and curse my fate." His last recitation at the last gathering of the entire Gairdner clan at Minaki Lodge in Manitoba in 1987 was a three-minute piece from Tennyson's *Ulysses*, delivered with gravitas and charm, languid eyes damp with boozy emotion.

He and Mom had a kind of co-dependent marriage. Couples who go through wars or similar crises get welded together by adversity. Even then, she left him when I was 18, only to come back a year later. The whole time she was away, whenever her name came up, he had only nice things to say about her. He sent flowers on every special occasion, and sometimes for no reason at all. I got a sense of a gentleman's way I never forgot — how you should treat a lady. As the couple they were, they reminded me of the joke about the man who complained to a psychiatrist that he couldn't stand his wife anymore because she thinks she's a chicken. The shrink says: "So why don't you leave her?"

Husband: "I need the eggs."

As it happened, I walked my dad for the first time all wobbly into Toronto's Bell Clinic for alcoholism when he was forty. I carried him over the steps

Against The Tide

of the very same clinic for the last time, too hung-over and weak to walk, when he was seventy. He had no trouble getting sober. Six weeks later he went home all dried out, wrote a donation cheque to the clinic for $5,000 to thank them for curing his alcoholism, poured himself a rum and Coke, and kept on drinking until he died.

I still don't think I have reckoned fully what it meant to grow up with a dad who was a hero, but who still preferred the bottle to his family. It's hard to speak such a truth, even now. But it was true. It's true for all alcoholics. And although I lamented his boozing, I could never bring myself to judge him poorly, because I was never in his shoes. One night, near the end of his life, I asked him if he thought alcoholism was a disease. And I still admire his honesty. "No," he said quickly. And after a brief pause, "It's a weakness of character."

It took character to say that.

They did their best, in their personal circumstances, and who can ask more? And there was plenty of fun. Mom loved to party and would delight our teenaged friends with her love of dancing, wit, and sometimes off-colour jokes. She was what a close family friend who heard of her death described as "a high-octane goddess." To this child — to this sickly boy — she was the archetypal mother. Beautiful and caring. Engraved, embossed, planted in memory, is the image of Mom coming to my bedside to kiss me goodnight before she and Dad went out for the evening. He would stand by the door in his air force uniform, on guard, the eternal father, waiting impatiently for her to get on with her little ritual. Checking his watch. A doorway shadow over half his face. And she, wrapped in her mink stole, perfumed so sweetly I felt like swooning, her dark, soft, freshly washed hair touching my face, earrings dangling with a starry sparkle, would lean over and give a gentle kiss on my cheek and whisper something wonderful. The world stood perfectly still for a moment. When she was older, and became more difficult, we grew apart. But when she died, I was ambushed by the bliss of those memories and cried my heart out.

At about 70 she developed Lou Gehrig's disease, and soon became bedridden, but was mentally sound. Given just a few weeks to live, she wanted to end her own life, and she got her wish — but not without Dad's assistance, which he was willing to give but which I had begged her not to ask him for. I feared the aftermath. This still unmentionable event cast a pall over the whole family, and in the six years he lived following her death, whenever he spoke of it, he put his hand over his mouth like Job, wide-eyed, and said with a deeply-fearful look, "I played God."

The last time I saw him he was lying gaunt and half-upright in his bed, jaw set firmly against the cirrhosis that had him in its puffy grip, enjoying a small cigar along with a rum and Coke, the stump of his amputated leg peeking from under a white sheet. As I slipped tenuously out the door, I said, "You're having a party."

His face was set, and a little grim in his final cockpit: "You bet I am."

That was all I heard; maybe, very far away, the sound of a distant crowd cheering a touchdown, or the drone of a Spitfire soaring above the clouds.

## BIG JIM

My paternal grandfather, known to all as "Big Jim," was the patriarch of the Gairdner family and an intimidating presence in all our lives. At 17, after graduating from high school, he told his own father, a typesetter at Toronto's *Globe* newspaper (before it became *The Globe and Mail*), that what he really wanted was to be a doctor. But there was only enough money to help his sisters, not enough to send him to university. He would have to earn his own way. So, at once he set himself up as a merchant broker — a commissioned salesman. He could sell anything to anybody and loved it. He always said he wasn't *making* anyone buy something, he was just helping them realize they wanted it. After work, he trained as a runner, and was very fast. He achieved a time of 21.8" in the 220-yard race on the loose black cinders of the varsity track at the University of Toronto. This became a legendary spot for our family because he ran there, Dad played Argonaut football there, and I ran track races there — as have many of my children.

But WWI came crashing upon his world, and so instead of training for the Olympic Games, which had seemed like a fine and patriotic thing to do, he was soon a patriot in training for a brutal war. He became a commissioned officer quickly, trained, 1,000 men for battle, served bravely in the European theatre, and rose to the rank of major before coming back home.

Fifty years later, in 1963, having gone from broke to millionaire several times over and a little bent with illness and age, his chauffeur drove him from his home in Oakville to Varsity Stadium to watch me run a 120-yard high hurdles race. The field included Willie Davenport, a very fast American whose first Olympics (something neither of us could have known at the time) would be the same as mine: the Tokyo Olympic Games of 1964[1] — which I have thought of ever since as "the last happy Olympics" because there was no politics, no drugs, and no money paid to anyone.

I wanted Dad and Grandad to be proud of my race, partly because I knew their own hopes for higher athletic achievement — many of them worked up in this very stadium — had been dashed by war. So I ran hard, but was badly

Against The Tide

outclassed by Willie and another American. Here I am warming up over the hurdles just prior to the race. Big Jim is sitting in the stands in his hat just behind my left elbow.

After the meet, we invited Willie and his teammate Mel Pender, who eventually set many world sprint records, to the after-party at our home in Thornhill, a large 1803 colonial house we called "Cricklewood" that our family had bought for very little then rescued from 15 years of desuetude. It looked beautiful after two years of restoration.

There weren't many black track athletes in Toronto back then, and certainly none as good as Willie or Mel. That night, my high-octane mother put on a show of great food, wit, and dancing with the best of us until Dad gently danced her away to bed to let us party on down. None of my friends could believe I had a mother who was the life of the party. But then, I couldn't believe it either. She was the archetype of a certain kind of female — the kind that can charm and burn you at the same time, often before you know which is which. She laid my young man's template for what a real woman is. And, as I shall explain eventually, alas, of what a wife is. Here is a picture of her at her best, in the back yard of that restored house, with a large ceramic vase she made herself.

Those were my university years, which I prolonged as long as I could. Who wouldn't? After one very tough and lonely year at McGill in 1959–60, I transferred to American universities to escape snowy winters and run more serious track. First was the University of Colorado on a track scholarship and then, by sheer happenstance, Stanford University for post-grad work. I ran a lot of races in the USA along the way, and almost always got beaten. But whenever I bumped into Willie or Mel at, say, the Kansas Relays or the Modesto Relays, there were immediate smiles and shared memories of that party, and from them both: "How's your mom doin'?"

After writing these words, I browsed the Internet to see what has happened to them. Oh dear. At age 59, Willy was sprinting with his bag to catch a flight at Chicago's O'Hare airport when he dropped dead of a heart attack right in front of an astonished attendant just as he reached the gate. Sad to imagine an Olympic gold medallist like Fast Willy sprawled dead and crumpled in a heap on the floor of a busy airport, an ignominious end for a hero. I browsed for Mel, too, and found him. He's in his eighties, lives in Georgia, and runs a consulting firm. We had a warm chat on the phone, and guess what? The first thing he asked was: "How's your mom doin'?" before he checked himself and realized, correctly, that she was probably gone.

But back to Big Jim. When he got home from the war he went right back into sales again, and one night over cocktails, a friend said, "Jim, you should try selling stocks and bonds."

"What's a stock? What's a bond?"

He soon found out and went to work for the firm of Gundy & Co. (now CIBC Wood Gundy) in Toronto. He was a junior salesman placed on a team whose first job was to sell $10-million bonds issued by the City of Edmonton. After six months, Mr. Gundy, the owner and CEO, called him in to say that things were going to have to change.

"… Why, Sir?"

"Because you are our youngest employee. You've only been here six months, but you've already sold $5 million of the issue yourself, and you're making more money than me! So, we have to adjust your commission."

Big Jim was shocked, and told Gundy, "It's not fair. A deal is a deal. We shook hands." He would have to think about it. So he thought about it for a night, and the next day went out and created Gairdner & Company Stocks and Bonds. At its peak, a few decades later, the company had 450 employees in 22 offices across Canada, and he had become a millionaire a few times over — with lots of severe losses in between. He always said having a lot of money was not such a big deal. The high was, after losing it, figuring out how to make it back.

He was an inwardly kind man with a gruff, even scary demeanour, who by the mere bark of his voice could alarm all around him. When I was sent off to board at Appleby at age ten, very alone on weekends when all the other boys went home, I would sometimes take the Sunday bus to his home on the shore of Lake Ontario east of Oakville to have lunch with him and his second wife, "Aunt Kay". She became engraved in my memory because when I was about 12, she gave me an LP record of Neapolitan opera songs — "O Sole Mio" and all the other famous ones — by the Italian tenor Giuseppe Di Stefano. I loved it and played it for years (despite the ridicule of my friends, around whom I learned not to play it). Later, Mom introduced me to the incredible Joan Sutherland, whose sweet but powerful voice still pulls at my heart, and to Pavarotti. I still think their vocal purity and power is some kind of divine gift.

One Sunday, at Big Jim's home on the shore of Lake Ontario (now a heritage home owned by the City of Mississauga), I followed him and his two English Setters and two large French Poodles into the shed where he kept soft, beautifully coloured cooing pigeons.

He opened a cage and reached in, saying, "You know what a squab is?"

"No, Sir."

"Very tasty."

I had no idea what he meant.

Whereupon he pulled a young pigeon out of the cage. And there, proud, I am certain, to be exercising his grandfatherly duty of ensuring I would become a real man and not a sissy, he took the young bird by the head and twirled its body quickly with a flick of his wrist. Just as suddenly, its head came off, and he chucked it into a garbage pail even before that feathery body on its last flight smacked into the wall and fell limp and twitching onto his work bench, a thin trail of blood dripping down the wall. For a kid, that was quite a shock. But I guess for a major who had seen death and destruction up close in the trenches of WWI, he was just giving me some reality training.

At mid-life, he bought a lovely abandoned fix-up cottage on an island at the very north end of Georgian Bay where, among the whaleback granite rocks, wind-bent pines, and sparkling water. all of us fell in love with wild nature and the indelible feeling that this is where God lives. I still feel that way. There, he pursued his hobbies of oil painting and fishing for bass and pickerel. In a group of three or four boats he was usually the one pulling in the most fish. Sometimes he would take me out in his small motorboat, cast anchor, and paint while I watched. Much later, in my own mid-life, having taken up painting myself, it struck me as curious that he never once put a brush into my little hand. Nevertheless, something must have rubbed off. Here is a watercolour painting I did about 50 years after that day in his boat.

Against The Tide

Meanwhile, he had set up Trafalgar Investments as a family holding company and began his involvement with businesses that had nothing to do with stocks and bonds. Among them: Atlantic Sugar Refineries, Davis Leather Co., Bridge and Tank, Brantford Cordage, and … Chicken of the Sea — a large tuna-fishing company. He knew almost nothing about most of those businesses. But when they got into trouble, he knew enough to sell them at a profit and get the hell out as fast as he could. But until then, flush with cash and undaunted — *l'audace, toujours l'audace!* — he ordered several large tuna-fishing ships built and named them after family members. The photo below is of the *Atlantic Gairdner*, a 186-foot vessel of 1,455 tons that is still afloat, if under a different name now.

As a young man with no definite future in mind, I almost shipped out to work on it for six months to trawl for tuna off the lofty coast of Peru. For a youngster with no purpose in life, that was a romantic idea. But events took me in another direction …

Here is a picture of the *Atlantic Ruthann*, another fishing vessel built in 1967 that he named after my mother, found unloved in a South American port. I checked on July 30, 2023, and found this:

"The current position of *Atlantic Ruthann* is at South America East Coast reported 3 days ago by AIS. The vessel is sailing at a speed of 9.2 knots. The vessel *Atlantic Ruthann* is a Fishing Vessel built in 1967 (56 years old) and currently sailing under the flag of Uruguay."

The most significant and enduring achievement of Big Jim's eventful life, however, was in the realm of medicine. In later life, when he got very bad arthritis, he turned to his friend doctor Wallace Graham, and said, "Fix me." But the good doctor told him no one knew much about arthritis. So he talked Graham into forming the Canadian Arthritis and Rheumatism Society (now the Canadian Arthritis Society) and served as its first president from 1949 to 1952.

*Against The Tide*

He got the same reply from a cardiologist friend when he got heart disease and once again said, "Fix me." But no such luck. This medical ignorance is terrible, he concluded, and again decided to do something about it. So in 1957 he founded The Gairdner Foundation², the purpose of which was, and remains, to reward the finest medical scientists in the world for medical research and discoveries aimed at "the relief of human suffering."

By 2023, some 418 scientists from 40 countries had received this by now very prestigious Canadian award, and 96 of them afterwards won the Nobel Prize for Medicine. Not bad for a young man who longed to be a doctor but couldn't afford medical school!


## THE SICK YEARS

I was blessed with a lot of sickness as a child, which is an odd thing to say. But I think what seemed then like an endless succession of illnesses — exhaustingly painful repeat mastoiditis, scarlet fever, pneumonia, celiac disease, the lot — gave me a profound fear of weakness, and so, once I got healthy, just as profound a motive for getting and staying strong for the rest of my life. Only now while writing this memoir, old and feeling the expected weakness of age, do I see that motive so clearly.

My mother said that when I was a child, one of her friends stopped her as she wheeled me in a stroller along a shady Oakville sidewalk of a summer's day, and blurted in some embarrassment: "That's Billy? Why, I never thought he would —" and barely managed to stop herself saying the word "survive." In my earliest school years, it was bed for a month, then back at school, then bed for another month, and so on. Flunk a grade, skip a grade. God bless mothers. Mine taught me my times tables in bed and gave me a love of literature: *Gulliver's Travels, Treasure Island, and Tarzan, Lord of the Apes* — all with wonderfully coloured illustrations. My first attempt at art was a pencil drawing of Tarzan leaping from a tree onto the back of a lion, his menacing knife about to plunge into its back. I badly wanted to be Tarzan. I *would* be Tarzan. But not just yet. Barely able to get out of bed, it was enough that Mom liked my drawing.

Eventually, I ended up quarantined for ten days at Toronto's Victoria Hospital for Sick Children (which moved and became Toronto's Sick Kids Hospital in 1951), a place where pablum was invented and the fight led for the routine pasteurization of milk. Penicillin, the latest miracle drug, was delivered in a needle so big you could see the dark hole at the end very clearly. The nurse in charge asked me whether I wanted it in the arm or the leg? I figured my leg was bigger and could take more. About three times a day, and twice each night. I was brave enough in the daytime. But after about three days, just the sound of her heels clacking on the hard wooden floor in the dark of night on the way to stab me would start the tears flowing. I couldn't understand why I wasn't allowed to see anyone. Another boy was quarantined in the room beside me with a glass partition between us. After we got tired of our own comic books, we would hold them up to the glass and read each other's.

At the time, we had an Irish nurse we called Nanny, a kindly sweet woman who came to live with us after my maternal grandmother, for whom she had long been caring, passed away. Nanny was like a real granny, as loving and feisty as they come. And full of prejudice. She was afraid of Blacks and hated Germans, because they had killed her only love in WWI. She loved him so much that she died a virgin at 93. But just now, she didn't like the idea that her wee Billy was far from home in a city hospital. Under quarantine? No visitors? What?

While lamenting my outcast state, snow flurries flying by my hospital window in a wild wind, just longing to get out of there, who appeared suddenly at my fifth-floor window, grey hair blowing in the cold wind, but dear old Nanny, her face and bare hands pressed to the freezing glass. "Wee Billy, dear, how are you?" she cried. "Come home!"

Well, what a surprise! After rejection at the hospital reception — "Quarantined. Sorry. No visitors" — she had gotten mad and gone outside to find the fire escape, and at close to 70 years of age she had somehow managed to climb five floors all alone in a fiercely cold wind up that icy steel gangway to my window. I remember putting my cheek against the glass for a kiss. You never forget that sort of thing.

My maternal grandmother was born Ruth Pease to an American from Yipsilanti, Michigan quixotically named Peter Pindar Pease, who moved his family to Toronto. She was a beautiful young woman with a lovely voice who ended up studying opera for a while in Germany, where she met the already immensely famous artist Franz von Lenbach. He was especially renowned for his many exquisite portraits of the most influential Germans of his day, the most famous being the many portraits he did of Otto von Bismarck, the first chancellor of the German Empire from 1871–1890.

I don't know how Ruth Pease met von Lenbach, but I have always imagined that the great man fell in love with her, for he had an artist's eye for beauty. He named her "Miss P" on his portraits of her, and I have two of them — one in the most delicate pencil and conté crayon, the other in pastel. Here is his sketch.

Against The Tide

Alongside it I have included my very amateur sketch of my grandson Jonah.

I feel qualified by my inadequacies to say that his talent was something close to ethereal, and most lesser artists would give all their teeth to have half of it. On a 2018 trip to Europe, my wife Jean (about whom more soon) and I stopped in Munich for a few days, visited the HofBrau Haus where Hitler gave one of his first public speeches (and almost got assassinated), and visited the Lenbach Museum to see where the famous artist lived and worked. But there was nothing there comparable in beauty to the portraits he did of Grandma Ruth.

Two brief stories about her, and only her, because I never met my grandfather, who long predeceased her. I barely remember being about five years old and sitting beside a neatly groomed white-haired old lady on her piano stool in her south Rosedale, Toronto home as she played and sang quietly. The next morning, the sun just up, I heard the clip-clop-clip-clop of horseshoes on the street below as the milk wagon came by, the horse slowing so the milkman could run the milk up to grandma's door, then speeding up just a little once he got back on board, and on toward the next house, where the horse began to slow again. Then, suddenly, like an explosion, there was a riot of noise, people pouring into the street, sirens blaring, flags waving on every sidewalk and in every window to announce the end of World War II, though of course I had no idea what that was.

Nanny lived there and cared for Grandma in her last years. I would sit by Nanny as she ironed clothing in the darkish basement. I can still smell the steamy fresh dampness and starch from her hot iron and hear the stories she would tell about someone she called Joseph, who had a coat of many colours, and a man called David who killed a giant named Goliath. I loved those stories. Eight years later, at a Bible class at Appleby, our headmaster — "Rusty" to all who knew him, because of his flaming red hair — the same Rev. Dr. Bell who had told my dad of his mom's sudden death, and a fire and brimstone minister of the Anglican Church (long before it caved to the modern liberal gospel), one day began to read us stories about ... Joseph. And David. And Goliath! What? Immediate tailspin. "Hey! Those are Nanny's stories!" was my gut reaction to plagiarism. "Where did you get them, sir?" I felt a kind of deeply protective anger for my beloved Nanny, and it took a while to calm down when I found out she got them by memory from the Bible.

I never met my maternal great grandfather, Peter Pindar Pease. But Mom told me that when he died the family made him a special gravestone and upon it inscribed a little verse:


*Of Peter Pindar Pease,*

*Here Lies But The Pod;*

*His Soul Has Shelled Out,*

*And Gone To God.*


Years later, during a visit to San Francisco with my close friend Lowell, whom we will meet in a while, we walked past a Ripley's Believe It or Not museum, which had all sorts of amazing (and hardly believable) displays and sights on view. In the basement was a section for display of "famous gravestones." I told Lowell the story about PPP and said, who knows? We have to go see. Sure enough, there was a facsimile gravestone there of my great granddad with the verse chiselled on it about the pea and the pod.

Against The Tide

# THE BOARDING SCHOOL YEARS, 1951–59

At ten years of age I was sent away to Appleby College, where my older brother Jamie had already been boarding for two years. He only got to go home for holidays, and this was now my fate. Mom dropped me off on a crisp September day just before morning chapel service, and indelibly impressed in memory is the sight of my upset mother driving away hurriedly, a spiral of white exhaust twirling in the shape of a pig's tail from the rear of her car. I didn't know that I was never to be home again for any extended period. Ever.

Jamie was in charge of introducing me to the school and its routines. But within minutes he had dumped me into the hands of a boy my own age named Roger ("Gus") Carr, whom I still see on occasion these many years later. Everything was a whirl of new faces and places. I was shown to a long dormitory I would be sharing with 20 other boys. There were forbidding steel-railed army cots for beds, behind each of which was a curtained entrance to a tiny cubicle for clothing, toiletries, and so on. Then off to chapel we went. That night, the choirmaster went around the entire dormitory and spent a few minutes with each new boy. I was all washed up and sitting on my bed in this strange new home when he came by, plunked himself down on the end of my bed, and asked me to sing.

"Pardon, sir?"

"Just sing what I am going to sing." And he launched into a few lines of "Lighten our darkness, we beseech Thee, oh Lord, and by Thy great mercy, defend us …" This is a difficult little piece to sing on key, but as it happened — maybe thanks to Grandma Ruth — I managed to do it well enough that the next thing I knew I was dragooned into the school choir, where I became a soloist for the rest of my eight years at Appleby, and that was the occasion for some of the most spiritual moments of my life. So much so that I have seldom been to church since I left Appleby, except for weddings, Christmas, or funerals. And with the exception of singing in some of the great cathedrals of England and Scotland, which our choir would be doing during the coronation of Queen Elizabeth II in the spring of 1953, nothing compared to the Appleby Chapel for the feeling of closeness to God. Well, okay, pristine stillness lying on a hot Georgian Bay rock after a skinny dip in very cold water, under a timeless blue sky, is just as close for me. That's a baptism of its own.

But to that point I don't recall ever having been in a church and had never seen a Bible at home. But the Appleby College Chapel remains a holy space, a simple, warm house of worship in which a couple of hundred boys split up on each side of the Chapel sang rousing hymns at full throttle. I was being swept up in something far larger than myself: in sacred music that was to play a large role in my lifelong love of the beautiful — and also in my later intellectual life in the questions: What is beauty? Why is there beauty in the universe?

At Evensong that Sunday night I heard the pure sound of a boys' choir for the first time in my life, a sweet solo — and also, Mozart's "Ave Verum", I think it was — sung in Latin, which (again, the farthest thing from my mind), I would myself be singing within the year, and eventually, at one of the saddest funerals of my life. I had never heard or sung music that could make tears well up.

Two years later I sang Bach's "Ave Maria" with five other sopranos from our choir, accompanied only by a harpist, at "Timmy's All-Star Easter Show," an event hosted at Maple Leaf Gardens by the Society for Crippled Children and broadcast nationwide by the CBC. We were introduced to the crowd of 15,000 by our head prefect, Mart Kenney Jr., the son of a dad with the same name who at the time was travelling around with Canada's best-known jazz orchestra — Mart Kenney and His Western Gentlemen. This otherwise ordinary fact spurs me to say that life is full of retrospective surprises. What future events of any young life are unknowingly engendered right before our eyes?

As it happened, Mart Jr. eventually had a son named Jason, a son named Jason who, almost forty years after that night, when he was a third-year university student, wrote to tell me that his father had given him a copy of the first book I would publish: *The Trouble with Canada* (1990).

"When I began reading your book," he told me, "I was outraged. But by the end, I was converted." By which he meant that he was converted from a pseudo-socialist to a committed conservative. Who would have known? Jason went on to spend his entire career in politics, including some serious time as an advisor to Preston Manning, first Leader of the Reform Party of Canada (with whom I also ended up having an interesting relationship that I will speak about later), and then as a minister in former Prime Minister Stephen Harper's government. I also ended up knowing Harper casually, and who could have foretold that? Then, in April 2019, Jason got elected Premier of Alberta by a wide margin, from which post he resigned in 2022. Big steps along his way to perhaps becoming Prime Minister of Canada someday, as his wit, frankness, and guile determine. Some say all our future is written in our past. Omar Khayyam: "The moving finger writes / And having writ moves on / Nor all thy Piety nor Wit / Shall lure it back to cancel half a line / Nor all thy tears / Wash out a word of it."

But back to Maple Leaf Gardens. That huge sell-out crowd was staring at us and at crippled, crumpled Timmy, alone in his wheelchair at the front of the stage in a glaring spotlight, we five standing behind him in our blue cassocks with crisp white ruffled collars. We felt a strange power to hold such

*Against The Tide*

a large audience so still with only our voices. We felt the sadness of crippled Timmy's life as compared to our own. But at the end of that sublime piece, in the cavernous darkness, we saw thousands of white handkerchiefs daubing dampened cheeks. We got a taste for the evocative power of beauty, a beauty we were creating on the spot, to change people, to bring them to tears, right before our eyes. All this was a warm-up for a major singing adventure — unbeknownst to us — was just around the corner of our young lives.

## BEARSKIN HATS, CATHEDRALS, AND QUEEN ELIZABETH II

We never knew why, or thought we were good enough to deserve it, but in the fall of 1952, after winning the Kiwanis music festival prize for best boys' choir in Ontario, we were invited by the British Commonwealth Youth Movement to travel to England and Scotland the following spring on a six-week concert tour to help celebrate the coronation of Queen Elizabeth II. That was the beginning of our misery. We were to miss all sorts of sports and would endure endless choir practices. But on May 7, 1953, all decked out in our red coronation blazers we embarked on the 21,833-ton *Empress of Australia* in Quebec City and headed for Liverpool. Here is a photo of four of us — all aboard! I am second from the left, and brother Jamie is on the right.

This was the maiden voyage of our re-christened ship. It was formerly the French luxury liner *De Grasse*, which had been captured by the Nazis in WWII and used for naval cadet training and as a rest ship for German U-boat crews. We sang for the passengers, and we sang for the crew. And halfway across the Atlantic we ran into a five-day, force-9 gale with 50 mph winds. A lot of the boys got very sick. I remember seeing one of our boys puking over the rail in the wind. On its way down to the foaming sea the ejecta swirled onto the head of someone doing the same thing out of a porthole far below. A bad surprise.

Despite the rolling and pitching our choir practices continued at midships. As she rolled, we saw only water from the large windows on the port side, and only sky from the large windows at starboard. Then the ship would lurch back the other way: sky to water, water to sky. We were delayed an extra two days at sea, and it looked like we were going to miss a special Coronation Service planned for St. Paul's Cathedral in London for the day we arrived late in Liverpool. So the British government sent a special high-speed train to pick us up, and on the radio, we could hear what sounded like national alarm as announcers whipped up the public about whether or not "the Canadians" would get to St. Paul's on time for the service! Why, the train was rolling and jostling so fast you could hardly walk down the aisle, and all the while the nation watched our race against time. We got to London on time but got stopped dead in the worst stand-still traffic jam in English history. Nevertheless, the English press was out in force, snapping shots of us running up the cathedral steps.

# CHOIRBOYS ARRIVE WITH 23 min. TO SPARE

## EMPIRE SERVICE

DAILY TELEGRAPH REPORTER

Twenty-eight boys, in trim new crimson blazers and grey flannels, arrived at St. Paul's Cathedral with 23 minutes to spare yesterday before joining in the Empire Youth Sunday Service. They had won a race from Canada to be there on time.

They were the first group of 170 young people of the Commonwealth Youth Movement coming for the Coronation. Their ages range from 10 to 14.

The boys, all singers from Appleby College Chapel Choir, Oakville, Ontario, will watch the procession from seats outside Buckingham Palace. Their ship, the Empress of Australia, 21,833 tons, was late in arriving at Liverpool because of gales.

Customs men and British Railway officials co-operated in speeding them on their way. They were first to disembark and left by the first train, before the boat train.

### TRAIN SPECIALLY STOPPED

With their headmaster, Dr. J. A. M. Bell, his wife, and their conductor, Mr. E. Leslie Bott, they joined the Irish Mail at Crewe, which was specially stopped for them. Engineering works delayed the train, which was 60 minutes late at Watford. From Euston they finished their journey by coach.

The boys had had hardly any sleep on Saturday night. Mr. Bott said they were in a state of collapse when they boarded the train. Dr. Bell said only two or three had travelled in a train before. They joined in the service as part of the congregation and not the choir.

The Duchess of Kent and her daughter, Princess Alexandra,

attended the service. Nearly 3,000 people were present. A message from the Queen who is Patron of the Empire Youth Sunday Committee, was read by the preacher, the Bishop of Adelaide, Dr. Robin.

Sending her good wishes to "the young people of many lands" who were sharing in the observance of Empire Youth Sunday, the Queen asked them to pray: "That God may help me faithfully to fulfil the solemn vows which I shall undertake at my Coronation."

### AGE OF OPPORTUNITY

"We live in an age in which the boundaries of knowledge and power are rapidly extending and which offers great opportunities of adventure and discovery. It is my hope that the young members of our great Family of Nations will strive to fit themselves to use these opportunities with wisdom and courage and for the good of all.

"Thus we sha traditions of ch which have inspi laboured to cre wealth."

In his address "You would ha history of many centuries before sovereign who, a Throne, already of so many milli other peoples th as does Que Second." [Pictu

The Queen's l Mr. Attlee, Le tion, attended a Little Missenden said they had co cate themselves God's kingdom, near the Coron whose dedicatio called to mind.

The coronation itself was spectacular. In a day-long English rain we sat right outside the gates of Buckingham Palace on a high stand of wooden benches that ran the full half-mile length of the Mall, and the pageantry was astonishing. A moving fairy tale. Huge, beautiful, prancing black horses and white horses decked out in gold harness and white feather plumes passed us slowly by; knights in armour; the Queen's guard in tall black bearskin hats, ever so stern in their metal chinstraps, swords pointing skyward; shiny gilt carriages of every sort; then, more beautiful horses — this time of our own RCMP — stamping and snorting, but under complete control. Then came the black Queen of Tonga, who seemed immense, and immensely cheerful, in her sumptuous purple dress. Riding in an open carriage, black skin glistening wet, but smiling and waving, she drew the most cheers. Meanwhile, in the long pauses between carriages and horses, word got out that a Canadian choir was in the stands, and soon there was a clamour to have us sing for that soaking wet crowd. So we treated them to some down-home Canadian songs like "Jack the Sailor", "The Huron Carol", and then the beautiful "Goin' Home" adapted from Dvořák's melody, which really got them clapping. We felt like little ambassadors.

Three days later we sang in the majesty of Westminster Abbey at a special service for the new queen, and then were off on our tour of England and Scotland for a month. We sang nineteen concerts, did two BBC Radio Concerts and a half-dozen lunchtime concerts, after which ham was always on the menu. It had just come off post-war rationing, and so everywhere we went our hosts delighted in announcing that there would be "ham for lunch", at the sound of which, soon so sick of it, we nevertheless tried to smile graciously.

The impression made on us by singing, mostly unaccompanied, in places like St. Martin-in-the Fields, in 1,000-year-old cathedrals like Winchester, Chichester, and York Minster, of hearing our own pure treble voices echoing their way back to us solemnly from lofty stone arches and columns, while peering at stained glass so bright in the sun our eyes hurt, was never again to be, except in lifelong memory.

As for the fun of it? We ran excitedly up the countless stairs inside the columns of a lot of cathedrals, and once high above, we ran around excitedly among the bells and beams like Quasimodo in *The Hunchback of Notre Dame*, peering dizzily down from the apex at diminutive worshippers milling about like ants below.

We also played cricket against a half-dozen English schools and lost horribly every time but got to watch the English National Cricket team play at Lord's famous London grounds. Then, on the way to Sedbergh School in Cumbria in the hilly northwest of England, we watched an entire field outside our bus window suddenly lift and move away at a great pace, only to realize that what we were seeing was a living carpet of a million wild rabbits running from our bus.

Once settled at Sedbergh, flash rains came, and we were invited to try traditional hill-sliding in the rain. We were handed very thick felt shorts and ran with a few dozen Sedbergh boys up a 2,000-foot hill in the Yorkshire Dales in a crashing storm. Floods of water fell from the sky and laid down the long grass, creating a whole weave of rushing sluices down which we were told to run, whence, at high speed, we would surely fall on our bums, and slide down, down the whole mountain in those felt shorts, water spraying high between our legs from the speed, careening between rock piles and grazing sheep to the bottom, where we arrived with very numb bums indeed. But what fun. We left that school to go to Edinburgh, and as the bus pulled away we saw a man running after us in the pelting rain. But we didn't stop for him.

Fifteen years later, the man running after the bus — who, to my immediate surprise, called himself William Gairdner — showed up with his wife at our home in Thornhill, north of Toronto, to introduce himself to our family. I was upset to meet a man with my name. After all, it was *my name*. So how could it be *his*, too? It turned out that he had been a teacher at Sedbergh and happened to see our concert program with the Gairdner name on it, and went immediately into high alert, bolting after our bus to hail us down. A few years later he emigrated to Canada and took a job as a professor of French literature at the University of Winnipeg where, among other things, he translated and commented upon a fine book by the French philosopher Louis Lavelle.

Many years later I pieced it together that he was the son of William Henry Temple Gairdner. (What? Another "William Gairdner"? By now, I surely had to give up the illusion that mine was a unique existence.) This Gairdner had been an atheist in his youth at Oxford University. But his roommate fell so ill that no one knew how to help. So the atheist Gairdner looked after him, bringing soup every day and changing his fevered clothes until he got so weak that at the end of the school term he died in Gairdner's arms. So gracefully did he suffer and die that Temple Gairdner (as he was then known) became convinced there must be a God: else, how could anyone die with such grace? Thereupon he became a committed Christian. He was a very gifted fellow and a lovely writer, well-known in his day, but forsook a brilliant literary career in England to spend most of his life in the service of the British Church Missionary Society as the Canon of Cairo, where he died prematurely at 58 from a tooth infection at the height of his considerable powers. The Church

Against The Tide

of Jesus, Light of the World was immediately built in Old Cairo and dedicated to his memory.

I got his life story from a lovely biography discovered in my father's library after he died, by Constance Padwick, his secretary, entitled *Temple Gairdner of Cairo*. It's a moving story, and in rendering the essence of a life devoted to the spiritual care of others, it gives the sense that he was as close as an ordinary human can come to living as Christ wished us to live. He also had a lovely gift of language, gave sermons in Arabic within six months of arrival in Cairo, and published a number of books on literary and philosophical matters, including a bestseller called *The Reproach of Islam*. He was deeply persuaded that Islam, in which he was very interested but with which he found serious fault, had only arisen in the world as a rebuke to Christianity, which had not fulfilled its promise. This, along with the weekly journal he created in 1904 entitled *Orient and Occident* (which remained a going concern for more than half a century), was an effort to build mutual understanding between Christians and Muslims. Little could he have imagined — or did he? — that one day the World Trade Centre in New York would be attacked by radical Islamists, collapsing in an inferno of fire and twisted steel, and that terrorist organizations such as the Muslim Brotherhood would rise, as has happened so many times in history, to attack everything for which Christianity and Western civilization stands.

## CUBA, CASTRO, AND TARANTULAS

In the still dawn of a wintry Sunday morning that next fall, the peace of 20 boys sound asleep in our darkened dormitory was broken by sudden wild shouting. Half a dozen of us leapt from our beds and put noses to frosty glass to see the two Gomez brothers, Ricky and Guillermo, out on the frozen grass, laughing, whirling in their dressing gowns, tongues stuck out. Sent to Appleby from Cuba, they had never seen the magic of snow falling from the sky, and each was trying to catch more flakes on his tongue than the other, while the rest of us winter-hardened Canadians stood chuckling at their delight.

They were lonely, homesick foreigners, so for the rest of the school year Jamie and I invited them to our home in faraway Newmarket for the Thanksgiving, Christmas, and Easter holidays. Then, before school was out in spring of 1954, our parents received a letter inviting the Gairdner boys to Cuba for the month of August. "Okay," said Mom. "But you have to help pay your way." So after two months spent mopping floors, cleaning windows, painting, and the like for her while my brother worked on the farm next door, we flew to Cuba.

We arrived on July 26th and learned years later it was exactly a year after a notorious failed attempt by Fidel Castro and his small band of revolutionaries to storm a Cuban army outpost with machine guns to bring down the government of dictator Fulgencio Batista. Fidel got caught and was in jail when we arrived. But what he did affected the public mood, even at Gomez family meals, where there was anxious "what if" talk about the future that we didn't quite understand. Nevertheless, Cuba and Castro became a fleeting part of our lives. After we left he was set free, and five years after that he marched into Havana to turn Cuba into a brazen Communist enclave on the very doorstep of America.

Eight years after this trip I would be bent over my desk at the University of Colorado, listening in fascination as President Kennedy stick-handled the "Cuban missile crisis" of October 1962 when Russia's belligerent Nikita Khrushchev, shoe-banging on his lectern, tried to send Soviet missiles by sea to Cuba for his new bearded, cigar-chewing friend Fidel. The rest is now history, but at the time, everyone was wondering where to hide from a nuclear explosion. On the news we heard that one fellow in Chicago had built a bomb shelter in his back yard with a machine gun mounted on top … to keep his neighbours away. Weird times. And not long after writing this segment in the summer of 2021, there were freedom riots in the streets of Havana once again. Poor Cuba.

Meanwhile, I was fortunate enough to experience Cuba *libre*, and it was quite fascinating even from the limited perspective of a young boy, for the Havana of "Papa" Ernest Hemingway was in full swing. Rum punch and cold beer, roast pig, and other tasty Cuban morsels, including *granizado* — tooth-numbing, shaved-ice cones with wonderfully sweet, syrupy summer flavors — were sold on every corner of that colourful, somewhat seedy, but oh-so-vibrant Havana. Her narrow streets were restless with quick cash deals, seedy beggars, flamboyant tourists, and here and there, beautiful coffee-skinned girls barely a few years older than me, looking for customers, their perky breasts straining braless against nearly transparent blouses. That was a tantalizing shock. I had never seen a grown woman's breasts before, and at almost 14, in the fullness of sexual awakening, I got a sore neck from sightseeing.

The Gomez family lived in Miramar, a well-off suburb of Havana where Señor Gomez was a doctor. Their home, like the others nearby, was small but well-kept, on a sand and pebble lot shaded by tall banana trees, garlanded with red hibiscus. The first day we got introduced to black beans and rice, plantain, guava jelly, and chickpeas. It was very hot, so we slept with a door open to the outside, four boys in a bedroom for two.

Against The Tide

When I opened my eyes on our first morning I got a real fright to see a hairy brown tarantula on the bedsheet over my chest, staring, about a foot from my face, crawling slowly toward my mouth. Ricky! Help! With a memorable nonchalance, sleepy Ricky climbed out of his bed and swatted the tarantula so hard it flew right out the open door where, he said, it lives in a hole in the ground. Sure enough. This fellow was to be a regular visitor I never grew to like.

On those long hot days, we mostly headed straight to the beautiful Club Comodoro — a sports and social club for the well-off that got closed down by Castro's Marxist ideologues in their hunt to stamp out filthy capitalism and was eventually converted into the Hotel Comodoro — a run-down shadow of its former self. The original Club was a seaside paradise for which we made a beeline every morning to skin-dive in sun-drenched salty sea water, clarity 20 feet down, filled with coloured corals, waving fans, and fish of every imaginable shape darting all about, sometimes stopping to stare at us. Other times we fled larger fish, or they themselves were fleeing from the sudden appearance of a dangerous moray eel or two sizeable barracuda that swam with heads angled down, sunlight rippling colourfully on their scales. We were protected from roaming sharks by a large net that enclosed the area, but those barracuda slipped inside the net to watch us backing away respectfully.

Of course, I also fell in love at the club. Every day at noon we went for a sandwich and a Coke by the pool, where a beautiful, swarthy-skinned, dark-haired Cuban girl nicknamed Tica-Tica came to swim. To watch her frolic in the water with back rolls, her enticing water-beaded shape breaking the surface again and again, was mesmerizing. She and I would acknowledge each other with occasional furtive glances — and once, I was pretty sure, with a shy smile. We maintained our secret, silent friendship for weeks. But I never got up the nerve to speak to her, nor she to me. When we left Cuba, I could see the Club Comodoro through the airplane window, and I died for a few minutes imagining what might have been.

Halfway through our month we travelled with the Gomez family to Varadero Beach, a gorgeous reach of glimmering white sand 12 miles long, fringed with tall waving palms, lapped by the clearest blue water we'd ever seen. When I was a sickly boy, Mom gave me *Robinson Crusoe* to read, which certainly inflamed my imagination, and the year before this trip it was R.M. Ballantyne's *The Coral Island*, a story about boys my age getting shipwrecked in the South Pacific, drifting ashore unconscious, and waking to this very scene. And here was I, suddenly in this pristine paradise empty of other human beings, bananas, oranges, and coconuts for the taking, imagining I might see a footprint in the sand of my own Man Friday.

We swam a lot in a kind of watery translucent suspension, had a picnic lunch and with a machete hacked open a freshly fallen coconut for sweet milk and creamy flesh. When the adults slept in the shade, I went exploring inland along a dirt path that wound its way over roots and rocks through scrubby growth, shade palms, and pineapple plantings. After a while — and quite abruptly — I was shocked and alarmed by screaming like no other that penetrated straight to the heart, the memory of which chills me to this day.

I had no doubt this was the high-pitched screaming of a mortally terrified child, and without time for thought, my legs propelled me not away from but toward that horrible sound. But what was I rushing into? What violence might befall me? More winding trail. Louder screaming. Tripping over roots. Faster. Faster. The screams changed now to a final high and horrible panic. Higher still. Some small child being murdered … And suddenly, the trail ended, just as the screaming did, and I emerged from the darkness of trees.

There, on the other side of a small sandy clearing, among high grasses under more shade trees was a scene out of time: two small brown-skinned children running around naked by a thatch-roofed hut; a grisly, dark-faced, barefoot man in a floppy straw hat sitting on a stump with a bloody knife in one hand, holding a small piglet upside down by its hind feet with the other, throat freshly slit. Blood dribbled in a stream off the pig's pink nose onto the sand, splashing between the man's toes. My heart pounded loudly in the silence, fixed in his cold stare.

White boy intruder in his private, primordial world, backing away, disappearing from view.


## RUNNING: WHERE THE ROAD TO THE OLYMPICS BEGAN

I wasn't aware until I got into it, as the saying goes, that writing a memoir was going to raise so many questions. But it's only now that my life is much closer to its end that I realize how much of it has been spent running. And that has led me to ask: Who was that boy? Who was that man? What determined where running would take me — or where I would take myself running? I mentioned that I was blessed with a lot of sickness as a child. An odd thing to say, perhaps. But deep down, at least at the start, before it became part of a philosophy of life, I was running away from hated sickness. If you run hard enough you will never get sick again. It was that simple. It was not enough to be healthy, free of disease. I wanted to be strong and tough, fearless Tarzan leaping onto that lion's back though I could barely get out of bed by myself. In our years on Rural Route 3 (now Mulock Road) south of Newmarket, in the small log cabin home my dad built, and before leaving home for Appleby,

Against The Tide

and so before the coronation and the Cuba trip, I was slowly getting stronger. And whether with siblings or friends, a lot of time was spent in the woods. Running, sometimes half-naked, with spears we fashioned with our precious pocket-knives from saplings, so earnestly hunting for rabbits or squirrels that never seemed to stay still long enough to hit them. But almost. Here is a little poem I wrote much later in life about that experience:

## My First Rabbit

*I still see the hot sun,*
*shining pink and clear,*
*through the wary, red-veined ear*
*of my first rabbit on the run.*

*He stopped, in dreadful fear,*
*too close to breathe,*
*under an old oak tree.*

*Just him and me.*

*But I was unmanned,*
*by the delicacy,*
*the impossible perfection*
*of tiny hairs*
*bending quietly,*
*soft as silk,*
*in that gentle breeze.*

*I just hope God is aware,*
*it was my heart alone*
*that drove him to his lair.*

Our survival bailout was starting a small fire with dry twigs and leaves, cooking a sour green apple for lunch, and pretending it was tasty. Winter was skating and hockey 'til you drop on a frozen pond and, when there had been a flood of the woods from the little creek that ran through our property followed by a flash freeze, skating at night under the moonlight between the ghostly trunks and looming shadows of trees. We had a great childhood, free as the wind, summer and winter, roaming and running everywhere. Here is a set of four little poems I wrote about that time.

## THE FOUR SEASONS OF A BOY

### Spring

At melting-time we fell,
down the tumbleslippery
sweet and muddy hills,
all scraped
from chasing victory,
or was it vengeance?

We laughed along
the heartless, rushing dance,
the danger smell of wild floods
we knew could suck you under

and if you're lucky,
someone, by chance
a mile from here
will find you dead,
spinning face down
in your own private pool,

and that was enough to stop us
from ever wanting children.

### Summer

Always came too late,
but just in time for sour green apples
and purloined peaches,
sucked chin-dripping sweet
through fuzz that made it hard to concentrate
on the real work of braving things —
like dry summer thistle stings,
and other daily tests designed
to turn us into men,

earning the right to brush
by plan or accident,
against the pungent loins
of girls, who laughed

*to send us down the ladder*
*of our momentary sorrow.*

*But for warrior kings, girls*
*had no lasting meaning.*
*For we had capes, and wings*
*made of old sheets,*
*with bow and arrow, and saplings*
*spear-sharp to fling*
*in barefoot majesty,*
*at anything that moved*
*before tomorrow.*

## Autumn

*Meant the end*
*of milkweed parachutes*
*drifting in still air,*
*down to the valley of nowhere.*

*Meant all too soon*
*a prison of teachers,*
*and boots.*

*Meant frosty-fingered death*
*would come again,*
*without permission, to bend*
*the swooning grass of summer,*
*to laugh at the burning of our breath.*

*Meant an early drop*
*of darkening dew*
*chewy candies, too,*
*(snatched with deepest panic*
*from a black-witch treasure),*
*pulling, at fiercely-eager teeth*
*in sweet-and-sour pleasure.*

*Meant somersault*
*from an old fence-rail,*
*into golden leaves*
*and buried girls,*

*who prayed to be found*
*by the last boy hiding,*
*(betrayed,*
*by the happy wag*
*of a dog's tail).*

## Winter

*Rural route 3*
*where I grew up*
*is gone now,*
*except in words.*

*They fall through memory*
*like slow snow,*
*for those who know*

*the telltale carving sound*
*of a sharp blade,*
*on crack-black ice,*
*announcing,*
*as sure as your next breath,*
*a puck-slap on the boards.*

*How to sit*
*panting hard in the frosty air,*
*chopping the darkest hole*
*with a single skate-heel arc,*
*then kneel, with new invented holy words*
*and burning lips, to suck*
*the whole in streaking river up.*

*Mom said*
*that would freeze an over-heated heart.*
*Time to come home.*

*But she didn't know —*
*for a thirsty boy*
*that's no price to pay,*
*compared to bed.*

Almost the first thing I learned at Appleby was that where there are a lot of boys, there is a lot of bullying. A favourite move of the older ones was to form a fist into a knuckle-driver shape and punch the arm of a younger boy so that the knuckle met the upper arm at the exact point where there is bone but almost no muscle. It hurt for days afterward. But I quickly learned that if they wanted to bully me, they had to catch me first. It was a delight to outrun and outdodge an older, clumsier boy, at least most of the time. I had never had much in the way of organized sports at public school. But at Appleby, every afternoon after 3 o'clock was set aside for sports. No exceptions unless with a doctor's note. I loved it all. In football you could get tackled and roughed up pretty good. But they had to catch you first. So broken field running became my joy. Even if I couldn't outrun a couple of older tacklers because of the angle to the touchdown line, I loved trying to outsmart them. For example, to run straight at them, then suddenly change direction and run parallel to the goal line, forcing them to run sideways hard between me and the line. Then, I would slam on the brakes so fast they couldn't stop in time, and I would just walk across.

Two years later, I discovered "Sports Day," a week of track and field events measured out on a grass track. Sprints, middle distance, jumps, throwing events, the lot. On Saturday the finalists in every event vied for the junior, intermediate, and senior championships, and a crowd of parents, lovely, lightly perfumed Oakville girls dressed in spring finery, and prominent guests of the school showed up on the banks overlooking the field to watch. For all eyes to see, there was a white-clothed table with all the coveted awards: silver spoons, silver ashtrays, pewter beer mugs, and various almost sacred trophies such as the *Victor Ludorum*, Latin for "The Winner of the Games."

Dad's name was engraved on that trophy, twice. He won it in grade 12, and then again in grade 13. Twice! — as no other boy in the history of the school had ever. So, there was nothing I wanted more than to have my name on that cup one day, alongside his. On this particular day I won enough points for the junior championship and took home a lot of that silver. That's how my life of salvific running began.

The next big track event happened at night. It was always "lights out" on the floor after 10 p.m. But for my effort in winning I had been given a small English booklet on track and field by Mr. Bruce-Lockhart, one of our teachers, who also gave me a pair of old track shoes he had worn as a young-ster with embedded "spikes" such as we had never seen before. I couldn't wait to try them, my mind aflame with the thought of how much faster I could go without slipping on dewy grass. I had no idea at the time that he had played international rugby for Scotland, and that his father was at the time of our choir trip, the headmaster of … Sedbergh School! Which is surely why we ended up there, slid down that mountain, and got tracked down by the man running after the bus.

I was under my blanket with a small flashlight reading about the heroes of English track and field when I felt the pain of a sudden smack on my head: the master on duty had hit me with his flashlight and I heard: "Lights out, Gairdner." But the seed of track and field, my escape from the grip of sickness, was already planted in the soil of my life.

A few years later, Mr. Bruce-Lockhart's son Kim, six years younger than me, was sent back to England to Sedbergh School, after which he became an international-level squash player for Scotland. Then, sadly, he died of a sudden heart attack during a national title squash match at only 33 years of age. I only found this out when I organized our Coronation Choir Reunion in 1983 and wrote to his dad, by then retired in Scotland, inviting him to attend. He sent back a most moving letter to express regret that he couldn't attend and spoke of his profound sadness over Kim's death. Included was a small, badly faded photo of Kim winning a foot race in the same spikes I had returned when I outgrew them.

Running has played a very large part in my life in ways I could never have imagined, leading to international travel, the Olympic Games, career changes, and even to marriage and family. But in the sense of how a young man develops a self-conception, it really began in the mind, as I shall now relate.


## RUN FOR YOUR LIFE!

Appleby had a cross-country running course that wound for a mile around beautiful school grounds. One lap for juniors, two for intermediates, three for seniors. I was in grade 9 and still 14 but was forced by the rules to run against all the senior boys, including my older brother Jamie, because I had won the intermediate championship the year before. I had no hope of winning this race, of course, and everyone knew it. I was just a kid tagging along. Nevertheless, I was secretly determined to keep up with the older boys for at least two of the three laps.

The big day came, and it was cold. At the end of two laps my lungs were burning, and that coppery taste from muscles overworking was in my mouth. I was feeling pretty good holding on incognito at the back of the leading pack of six senior boys, who had barely any idea I was there. Then suddenly, for no reason at all, a fellow we had nicknamed "Rubber-Legs" (because he seemed

Against The Tide

double-jointed), but who we all knew had no hope of winning, burst from the pack for no apparent reason and was soon 50 yards ahead. Only smirking followed him.

But at that exact moment a thrilling plan flashed through my mind. I could fake personal insult: "I don't care, I can't let that jerk get ahead of me!" (I was careful to say "me", not "us", to keep it personal). The pack would think that not only was Rubber-Legs making a really stupid move, but so was I, in chasing him. There was a very slim chance they wouldn't give chase. So I sprinted hard and soon caught Rubber-Legs. The moment he turned and saw me he said he felt sick and stopped dead in his tracks. I glanced back: Oh. My. God … They let me go! They fell for it! And there I was. All alone. Fifty yards ahead of the pack and fast approaching a very steep hill.

I cannot describe the excitement with which my heart leapt out of my chest. I decided to keep them the same distance behind me until the bottom of the hill, then fool them by running up like a Killdeer bird that fakes a broken wing to escape a predator, but in fact is just drawing him away from the nest. If, halfway up the hill, I began fake-limping, they would think catching me was going to be easy. But very soon, the cedar trees and the old barn at the top of that hill would hide me from their sight. My chance!

It seemed an eternity. They gained a little on me, but fake limping, I was soon atop the hill and around the barn. "Now go for it! Go for it now!" was all I could think — and there began one of the most thrilling events of my entire running life, better even than my memory of competing in the Olympic Games, which I was to do ten years later. Once hidden from their view by the barn, there were only 200 yards of flat ground ahead of me, just as they started up my limping hill. This was going to be a run to the death. Damn the pain. Foam at the mouth. Who cares? Just don't trip and fall. Sprint as long and hard as you can. And when they see you a hundred yards ahead, they will have a friggin' heart attack. Could this be true? Oh God, I loved it!

Halfway along the upper flats I ran past Mr. Merritt, our history teacher, a wise and gentle man who was marshalling the race. When he saw me, his eyes popped. What? Something is upside-down. What is the youngest boy in the race doing so far ahead of the seniors? We had a special relationship through tragedy, he and I. His two-year-old child had accidently hanged himself by putting his head through his own playground fence the year before. It was devastating for the whole school. I still remember watching Mr. Merritt through our classroom window as he sprinted up the road to his house to receive that terrible news. Our choir sang the *Ave Verum* while staring damp-eyed at the boy's tiny casket, tears running down his dad's cheeks. Mine, too.

We were bonded by grief. And now here he was, cheering me on surreptitiously so as not to be seen picking favourites. But he could see what I was trying to do, for those senior boys were just now rounding the barn, realizing their mistake, and he saw them coming after me as they rose to full panic mode, stepping on the gas. I was 150 yards ahead now, and Mr. Merritt, under his breath, all but shouted: "Go! Go! You can do it!" Secret coaching!

Now the race was really on me in full disbelief, turning now and tearing along a 200-yard downslope where the risk of falling at a greater speed than my numb legs could handle was top of mind, heart thumping out of my chest, spittle flying. "Maybe. Just maybe …" Past the infirmary. Down a really steep hill where my legs almost buckled. Across the last long football field to the last steep uphill. Do I dare look back? What if they're on me? But they were the same distance behind, and joy was mounting in my heart. Approaching that last hill now. This is where they expect you to die. So, this is where you have to discourage them completely, mercilessly. Crush them. I have never run a hill as hard in my life. But at the top, I knew. They couldn't match it. And in the panic trying to get enough air, I felt a smile rising. But watch it. Don't get cocky. Don't sprain an ankle in the bit of forest left, jumping over logs, or along the short stretch of stony beach to come. Get across the last small field. Cross the last wooden bridge over the creek, and on to the finish. Me, alone, in joy, beyond belief, a lot of my teachers huddled in their overcoats with their stopwatches, wondering if maybe they had got the races mixed up? How come the youngest runner is here, ahead of the senior boys?

I have relived that race a thousand times since, and it always brings a smile, because I didn't win it with my legs. I won it with my imagination, and that made it a special victory.

Then came the awkwardness. To repeat: my own father was the first and only Appleby boy in the 50-year history of the school to win the senior cross-country trophy twice in a row, in grades 12 and 13. I had just won it for the first of three times, in grade 9. I didn't know what to make of it the moment I crossed the line, and neither did anyone else; certainly not my brother, older than me by two years, who had to be feeling this was Cain and Abel all over again. So I was amazed and thrilled, but not quite certain how I had got away with it. But that race began a sometimes-dominant taste for chasing renown that has never left (even now, I am embarrassed to say). Perhaps it also planted some of the less admirable qualities one spends a life trying to quell, like a barely disguised egotism, a need to climb above others, to excel by whatever means acceptable? But to go deeper: Whence came this fire in the belly?

Against The Tide

On reflection, as I said, my childhood sickness was a blessing. Crossing that finish line a winner by a combination of physical and mental abilities felt like my entry into a vigorous new life. But had I cheated them a little by tricking them? Surely not. No. This was a dramatic moment in one boy's life that definitively signalled an escape route from physical frailty, a gift I would not let slip from my hands for the rest of my life.

## MY DAD IN WHITE UNDIES

The following spring of 1956, now 15, I competed in senior track and field events for the first time. There were about ten events spread over a week, and again a lot of senior boys much older than me competing for the *Victor Ludorum*. The finals were held on a glorious sunny Saturday before the whole school. A crowd of parents and guests from Oakville were invited, including a lot of those very pretty girls in spring finery. I don't think that first year I won anything or was expected to win anything. So my parents didn't come. I was once again under the radar. But I came second in almost every event, amassing the most points, and ended up beating 19-year-old Stuart Soanes, the favoured grade 13 boy — whose father Dr. Soanes had delivered me at birth — by just one point. And the fabled trophy was mine. This was such an unexpected achievement that I again almost felt I must have cheated.

Back home, with a lot of nice silver, I could only sit on my bed and stare at it for a while in disbelief. Then I heard Dad come in the front door, and Mom telling him what I had done. Suddenly, I feared his reaction. He had not won this championship until 18, in grade 12, and winning it twice in a row had made him a school legend. What was he going to say? Maybe he would just figure that kids in my generation weren't as tough as him and his friends? I mean, maybe we weren't. After all, he was a Spitfire pilot in the war. So this didn't feel quite right. Somehow, I had gotten away with winning *his* trophy at a really young age.

I heard him coming upstairs and was a little afraid. About 15 minutes later he suddenly appeared, framed in the white casement of my doorway, naked, except for his white jockey underwear. He was 37, and as I said, except for his emaciated lower right leg, he had a beautiful, very manly body, my Tarzan. He looked at me, quite blank. I looked at him — a little sheepish. But I could feel what was going through his mind. I had undermined his long-standing high school reputation. He managed to say, "Nice going." But that was it. Two words. He left as suddenly as he had appeared, and we never spoke of it again.

## GO WEST, YOUNG MAN, GO WEST!

I didn't have much time to think about what all this meant. Jamie and I were barely in the front door for summer holidays when we got the word: "Your mom and I have been thinking about what two young men your age ought to be doing to stay out of trouble for the summer and earn a little money." Dad had a serious look, so we figured Mom had put him on the spot "What am I going to do with two growing boys at home for the whole summer, while you're off at work? Do something. Please!" So he did.

"Uncle Jack and Aunt Jane live in Vancouver. I'm going to give you both enough money for a one-way train ticket, day coach, and you can pay me back when you get home. Uncle Jack says he'd be glad to put you up for a couple of days until you find work. But no more." Uncle Jack had decamped from Oakville years before to run the Vancouver office of Gairdner & Company.

The next day we boarded a train for Vancouver. Three days and four nights sitting up, or curling up in our narrow seats to sleep, a small knapsack each of clothes and some crackers and tinned meat, cheese, dried fruit, candy bars, soft drinks, and a little cash. "See you when you get back ..."

That was quick. We had been looking forward to a little time at home. We never saw our parents much during school years except for half-term breaks for a few days, and over Christmas and Easter holidays. At one point, all four of us kids were in boarding school. And we still have no idea what our parents were doing all that time without their children. We imagined them huddling, perhaps in some panic — or maybe scheming is the more accurate word — to send us away again.

So, Jamie and I headed west into the great unknown for an adventure we could not have anticipated while our friends were thinking about cutting their neighbours' grass for the summer, or not working at all, or spending time at the family cottage. We were about to walk straight into a rough-and-tumble men's world we would never forget, for which we were thankful the rest of our lives because it matured us at warp speed in a do-or-die sort of way. We looked forward to it. We wanted to be tough, like Dad.

At 18, he and his buddy Jim Baillie had spent a summer taking 100 horses 500 miles over the Rocky Mountains from Calgary to Vancouver, for shipment to Asia. They looked after three hardy women on that on that roughneck trip with wild rivers and deep canyons, guided by two Indians, as they were then called. "We only lost three horses," Dad said. "One yearling to a grizzly, and two colts that got swept away in icy rocky-mountain rapids." We knew how tough he was. So we weren't about to complain. About anything. He isn't in this picture because he took it.

Against The Tide

He had taken us both on a canoe trip up and down the French River two years prior and exhausted us with paddling and portaging. Jamie and I would paddle in the bow and switch off to get some rest. But he just kept on paddling, eight hours or more at a stretch without showing any fatigue. He was our Indian.

And now, scrolling across Canada from the window of a speeding train: dismal Toronto backyards; then forests, marshes, and rippled lakes; occasional stray dogs. Here and there a deer bounding effortlessly in lambent air. Forbidding granite cliffs framing dark, spruce-dripping valleys north of the great lakes, nights curled up on our stale-smelling train chairs, or asleep on the floor between them. Clickety-clack, clickety-clack, all night. Then flat, endless plains. More endless plains to infinity under a blue metallic sky. Then came the end of endless plains. Then engine trouble. Stopped dead. Indians in blankets climbing aboard. Speaking strangely. Oh, oh … what's this?

But in a half a day we were underway. Indians got off at Edmonton, shawls and braided hair flapping in the wind. Strange to see and hear these swarthy-skinned incarnations of our imagination: the fabled Cree, the Sioux, the Blackfoot — semi-nomadic tribes that adopted the horse after 1665 and had the run of an immense country, fought encroachment of the white man, slaughtered the buffalo — and one another. We knew nothing of them except what we saw in western movies like *Broken Arrow, Shane, and The Lone Ranger*. Tonto seemed like a good guy.

At Jasper, we fogged up the windows staring at snow-laced, grey-toothed mountains towering in the mist. Night again. More switch-sleeping from seat to floor, and back. Clickety-clack. A day of mountains and careening valleys and frothy, seething rivers. Then, we pulled into rainy Vancouver. Uncle Jack picked us up. We saw the Pacific Ocean for the first time and the biggest trees ever in Stanley Park.

The next day, we went walking all over Vancouver, looking for work. Any work. With no idea how to find it. We wore our feet out and had just about lost hope of finding anything when we saw a handwritten sign pinned to the shabby door of a nondescript building:

"Mahatta River Pulp and Paper Project. Now Hiring."

We stopped and stared. Where's Mahatta River? What kind of work? Turning pulp into toilet paper? Newspaper? With a resigned shrug we walked in. And my heart sank. I was 15 and a half, and Jamie 17 and a half, and before us was a big, grumpy-looking bearded fellow in a checkered work shirt behind a counter with a sign that said: "Now Hiring. *Minimum Age 18.*"

We didn't have time to discuss whether we should turn and walk out. Lie to the guy? Sure.

He stared over his grubby glasses at Jamie: "You eighteen?"

"Yes, sir."

Holy, now I was on the spot …

"You eighteen?"

"Yes, sir."

"Hired."

The pay was $14.85 per day. More money than we had ever seen.

He handed us both something to sign, and a stuffed envelope.

"Get down to the outfitters — chits 'er in the envelope — get yr'selves outfitted. Be at the pier by ten tonight, and don't be late."

Outfitters? Mahatta River? Be at the pier?

Hustling out the door, we saw a big map of British Columbia on the wall, with some red pins stuck on it.

Mahatta River was more than 350 miles away at the very northwestern end of Vancouver island. Without really knowing what we were doing, we had just signed on for work at a real lumber camp and would be shipping out for an overnight trip to Port Hardy, then, overland by truck to Coal Harbour, then by small outboard boat to the Mahatta River lumber camp to join 50 lumberjacks. We were both a decent size. Big young men. But I wasn't shaving yet. So we couldn't believe the guy hired us. He just needed workers.

At the outfitters we surrendered our chits for checkered lumbermen's jackets, aluminum hard hats, and calk boots — steel-toed leather work boots with a few dozen serious steel pins in the sole for gripping trees. Our outfitter was chewing tobacco, and between spits into a bowl, said, "Some lumberjacks get to fightin' a lot, and the pins will make a mess o' your face if you end up on the bottom." But we imagined ourselves climbing massive trees with them.

Here we are in Uncle Jack's yard, me on the right. Still boys.

We didn't know anything. In our calk boots, with our hard hats on backwards! But that aluminum shell saved my life weeks later when a two-inch steel cable came down from the sky and stopped just after denting the hat.

We left that night, but not before we bought some chewing tobacco and spent our last money on a couple of hot dogs and a Coke each. From a darkened saltwater and kelp smelling pier we shipped out on a small passenger-freighter for very hard work with grown men, not a penny in our pockets.

We arrived tired and hungry the next day with no breakfast and too late for lunch, and had

to wait until dinner time for food, a delay that felt like a death sentence, or at least a gastric crisis for a couple of spoiled kids. I don't think I was ever quite as hungry, except at boarding school, where the post-war food was very low-end. It was soggy beans, watery potatoes overboiled 'til they fell apart, smelly margarine on limp toast, fried eggs that would bounce if you happened to drop one onto your plate, our grossly overweight "dietician" — we called her "Ma" — rolling side to side between our long tables, her huge white uniform flapping like an unmoored sailboat between long tables of starving boys. "What's for dessert, Ma?" to which she would always bark: "Jam!" That always drew a cynical laugh, and still does when old boys meet.

The lumber camp at the five o'clock whistle was a swirl of dust as a half-dozen eight-man vans called "crummies" rolled into camp from the deeply forested hills surrounding the camp, spilling a gaggle of tired, sweaty lumber-jacks — our workmates for the next ten weeks. They were an endlessly cursing effulgence of dust and sweat; grizzled faces, straggly beards, grimy hard hats glinting in the late sun, checkered shirts half-open, spit-gobs of chewing tobacco splattering in the sand, lunch pails swinging, calk boots crunching on the gravel, a punch in the arm here and there on the way to the showers, amid a hail of swearing and combinations of words the likes of which we had never heard before. Shower up! Dinner at six o'clock! was the call.

I remember the weird feeling of walking into the mess hall with a painful knot in my stomach, stunned to see a 50-foot table that was a cornucopia from Heaven: a mountain of food, platters heaped with hot steaks, lamb chops, salmon, potatoes, carrots, beans, peas, spaghetti and meatballs, and freshly baked bread galore. And a couple of dozen different fruit pies for dessert. Overcome by the choices at hand, I simply couldn't eat for a couple of minutes. But I got over it.

After dinner I was shown my room — and my roommate. Barry Graham was a tall, well-spoken, 24-year old Englishman with a neat black beard who seemed a little out of place in this camp of tough guys. Not a few of them were gritty ne'er-do-wells who lived only to work and to play (for tomorrow, we die). Work hard they did. And each weekend a dozen of them would hire a small Cessna float plane or two and fly to Vancouver for boozing and whoring, coming back late Sunday night to rest up for another week of work. Work, drink, whoring was their gospel.

Barry was different. He seemed really old and eerily quiet. Didn't trust me, at first. Then, after a week when we got to know each other, laughing a little. One night from his bed in the dark he opened up, the end of his cigarette glowing red, jiggling as he spoke.

"Barry. How come you're working in a place like this?"

A long silence.

"Hah. You better shut up if I say."

"Promise."

A little laugh. Then out came his story, in a stream.

"It's a hot evening in May and I'm at the bar in Vancouver minding my own business and I'm getting a little drunk like everybody else and this hot girl — like an older woman, maybe 40 — comes and sits beside me, and is right friendly, like with, you know the come-ons and makeup, and she squeezes against me and begins chattin' me up and winkin' and wigglin' all sexy and actually kind of funny and cute, and before I know it she's buying me whiskies and kissin' my cheeks and whisperin' about how her husband's away for the week … So next thing I know we're in a taxi and in her living room, and I'm doing the old knee-trembler [I interrupted to ask what that meant, and he explained] and suddenly there's this gawd-awful clatter of the front door opening, and its her husband home by surprise. Well, by gawd, she starts yellin': 'Rape! Rape!' and screamin' her fool head off, and you never saw a Limey run fast as this here bloke out the back door and across her yard in three strides and over the friggin' fence and I don't think I stopped 'til the next morning listening for sirens the whole time, cuz, you know, rape is a *looooonnnggg* time in jail and they always believe the woman. So, I signed up for this here place as soon as I saw it and so now … you're tellin' nobody about

Against The Tide

this okay? Or else. Or else … I'll put this 'ere red hot smoke right in yer eye." I was a little shocked and amazed. This here tame boarding school boy had just met his first larger-than-life pop-up character of the Wild West. It was my secret now, dead secret.

## THE BULL GANG

Jamie and I were assigned to the Bull Gang crew for our first week and a half of work. The Bull Gang, eh? Sounded pretty manly. Whatever it was, we heard it was one of the hardest jobs in the camp, and it came to a crashing end not long after we got started.

The Bull Gang drove in one crummy to the site over a pot-holed dirt road, dust spraying through loose wooden floorboards. Through dirty windows we saw daunting high hills, either already logged and starkly naked of standing trees — a scarred, ugly, tormented scenery — or covered with trees too scrawny for logging, but that we would have considered huge back home.

In our half-hour ride we learned a lot. The Bull Gang is the crew that sets up the entire site for pulling thousands of enormous felled trees out of the bush and loading them onto logging trucks for transport to the ocean, where they are dumped into log booms for more reloading onto barges for transport to Vancouver. We stopped in the middle of a dirt road that cut through a cleared circular area more than a half-mile in diameter that ran up the slopes on both sides. As far as the eye could see up those steep hills was a chaotic jumble of giant felled trees, crisscrossed and splayed upon each other in a hopeless tangle, more or less felled to point to the centre of the circle where we were now. So, how do you get a few thousand trees each weighing a few tons — many of them 100 or more feet long and three, four, or even five feet in diameter — out of the bush and into the centre of that circle for loading onto big logging trucks?

The system back then was called "high-lead yarding" or "overhead" logging. Meaning that instead of pulling a log from the bush to the mill along the ground by oxen or with tractors, as in the old days, you set up high cables that stretch into the bush, hook them to the logs lying below with a set of dangling steel "choker" cables, and drag them from the high slopes with diesel-powered machine fury in a chaos of noise and dust, the crackling and snapping of entire 50-foot trees too small to harvest that get smashed along the way to the centre of that circle.

Basically, to do that, you have to do erect a huge spar tree that can be up to 180 feet tall and steady it like the mast of a ship with thick steel guylines that spread far into the bush and are anchored around big tree stumps. Our first job was to head out and cut notches in those stumps with double-headed axes, then wrap the steel cables around them with driven railroad spikes. If there was ever a halt in the work, we would compete to see who could best throw a double-headed axe overhand into a tree 30 feet away and make it stick. That came in handy a few years later, when I got to throw a javelin for the first time ever.

Anyhow, a spar tree has a set of block pulleys at the top (a "high-lead block") weighing hundreds of pounds through which a heavy steel cable runs a half mile or more up the hill to the edge of the circle of felled trees where we were working. It is linked to a thinner cable that runs along the circumference through a set of two more haul-back blocks attached to stumps, then back to the spar tree, completing a dangerous triangle called "the bight."

"Don't get caught in the bight!" People have died in the bight. We got the story about a chokerman named Henry who was was finished setting chokers and was actually standing, pretty satisfied, on a big stump well outside the bight, assuming he was safe. But not watching too carefully. When the cable pulling got underway the neck of one of the logs came up against a big stump, which meant the rest of its considerable 100-foot length got torqued and airborne and swung at a hell of a speed but real quiet through the air, and when it met Henry's back it threw him about a hundred yards and he landed on his neck — and it broke.

We took the point.

The pulling power is supplied by a "donkey engine" — a large diesel engine on a log skid at the bottom of the spar tree that reels the main cable, with four 24-foot steel "chokers" hanging from it, going back and forth along that side of the bight. Each choker cable in turn has a ten-pound steel "bell" hanging from a knob at the end that each chokerman is meant to slide back from the end so as to wrap the cable around the neck of a log until it is "choked" — the knob fitted back into the bell. Then the "whistle punk" guy squeezes his whistle, and the chokermen — us! — clear the hell out of the bight or risk getting killed, like Henry. We got used to leaping and scrambling, often frantically, from one log to another to get out of there. Jamie and I would be chokermen for most of our ten weeks in the camp, except for that first job on the Bull Gang which, as I say, came to a sudden end after ten days. Here's why. When we arrived on the site there was an enormous spar tree on the ground, a confusing tangle of guyline cables spreading in all directions from the head like the snakes of Medusa. Our Bull Gang was led by two grisly, foul-mouthed fellows, one named the Hooker, and his second-in-command, the

Against The Tide

Riggin' Slinger. The competition seemed to be which of them could curse the longest in a single breath between spits of chewing tobacco.

Now, I forgot to tell how the spar tree with its steel snakes gets erected in the first place. That is done with a smaller spar tree called a "gin pole" that is raised that is raised first by a crane and then, when anchored well with steel cables, is used to pull the main spar tree vertical. Cables run from the donkey engine up through the top of the gin pole and down to the top of the main spar tree lying on the ground.

If you look closely at this photo of the spar tree we eventually got up, you will see how small the men are at the base, and how large the donkey engine is. The second photo is of Jamie and me at the point where the logs are dropped then picked up and put on a logging truck for transport to an oceanside boom.

This was heavy, dangerous work. Lots of widowmakers around, like falling limbs, moving trees, high-rigging cables whipping down from the sky, and so on. But slowly, we saw the plan taking shape, had all our trunks cut and all our cables wrapped and spiked, and the big day came to start pulling the spar tree vertical. It was going to be exciting to see all our work come to fruition.

Well, stand back, boys. We cleared away and stood high on a hill to watch the big moment. The donkey engine roared, choked, and roared again. The cables all got singing taut. The gin pole trembled taut and the spar tree groaned as it began to rise from the ground, dropping strips of flailing bark, dust flying everywhere. But it continued upward. Then, at about a 45-degree angle, just when you could see all the guylines we had laid out and fastened to those stumps getting tighter, the gin pole began to wobble. Just a little. Like a hula dancer. Oh, no. Then it wobbled more. We could hardly believe what was about to happen. The wobbles turned to crazy gyrations at the waist of the gin pole, and suddenly, with a resounding crack, it shattered completely like a dry stick, and with a crush of cracking and splitting, the spar tree fell all its cables whipping in the air, heavy blocks crashing onto the ground, the ground shaking, guylines snapping and snaking dangerously overhead, writhing steel patterns in the blue. Then a deafening silence. Dust settling slowly.

Jaws dropped all around. When the shock was over, the Hooker walked up to the Riggin' Slinger, spat a gob of tobacco into the dirt, poked him in the chest, and said: "You're fuckin' fired!"

The Riggin' Slinger, spitting in turn, poked the Hooker in the same way, and said: "And you're fuckin' fired!"

And they walked side by side along that dusty road all the way back to camp.

That was the end of our time on the Bull Gang.

We never saw those two again. The next day we started at a new location as chokermen, running up and down big logs with our calk boots, burrowing and pushing our way under piles of tangled, bark-scarred, sap-sweet trees, any one of which could slip a notch and crush you, to grab the bell, choke the logs, and get the hell out of the bight before the whistle.

On short breaks for lunch, we wandered into the lofty uncut parts of the forest; listening for and following the sound of trickling water to a miniature waterfall of clear freezing mountain water tumbling over shiny, moss-slick rocks; splashed our faces; filled our metal hardhats; watched them turn instantly frosty; drank our fill like young gods of the forest; happy, doing men's work.

The last ten days we worked down by the ocean on the boom. We were boom-cats. Jumping and rolling from one huge log to another with pike-poles, running forward, then, oops!, backward, on bobbing, rolling logs, poling them across the water to where a crane high on a barge would pick 'em up. I only fell into that black and bottomless chilly water once, to great laughter from the others.

The only trouble I got into was from teasing Otto, a very big muscular German fellow who had a beard like Paul Bunyan. We were all bored silly one weekend and I was chirping him over something, like his German sausage accent. It was all kind of friendly, but then it turned sour. He had had enough and got suddenly angry. I was faster than him, but he cornered me and picked me up like I was a pillow. For sure he was going to throw me through the awning window in his room. He would have, too. But as he marched me to the window, I grabbed his big black beard with both hands and yanked so hard

Against The Tide

he yelled like a wounded bear and dropped me on the floor. I didn't miss the chance to flee, and never went close to him again.

Weekends were a bore, with nowhere to to go except deeper into the woods. If you ever felt like worshipping nature, this was it. Every weekend I wandered away from camp up the nearby Monkey Creek, a small stream that splashed out of the dark forest and ran into the ocean. Once inside the canopy of giant trees, there was instant soul-humbling. Unlike the forests farther south, which are an impassible tangle of trees, ancient deadfall, and rocks, a half-mile up Monkey Creek I found primordial paradise. Trees easily five feet thick at the base and 200 hundred feet high reaching to the blue sky in a cathedral formation, streaks of hot sunlight streaming luminous beams to a clean forest floor. It made me feel just as when singing solos in those English cathedrals. I tried singing there, all alone, too, in those woods. But it fell flat.

Monkey Creek got quite a bit narrower, and at my favourite spot ran into a bathtub-sized hole between slick, mossy rocks, and I couldn't help myself. It was like the first day of creation, a baptism of nature, alternately shaded, sunlit, and silent. So, I took off my clothes and, after a deep breath, sank into that little dark pond of freezing water for as long as I could take it, staring up through a tiny blue opening amid towering treetops. Like I said, the first day of creation. Clearly, God lived here, too. I was never made aware of the likelihood that hungry cougars might be roaming around those high woods. I was just happy there were no mosquitoes.

Summer over, and work over, we took the train back home again. The lumber camp had been a kind of initiation rite, and we got through it proudly, in one piece. Feeling quite wealthy, we rented bunks on the train for a couple of nights, and I remember the feeling of extreme envy when Jamie somehow managed to lure a girl he met on the train into his upper bunk. I peeked down the way from my lower bunk and watched her soft-skinned legs disappear into his dark place, her small pale fingers reaching back to close the curtain. I never asked him what happened up there. But I was so green with envy I couldn't sleep. It was hard for me to believe that he was, you know, going at it with a strange girl when he didn't know anything about sex. Or maybe he did? I wondered, was he going to repeat family history and end up in a shotgun wedding? He never spoke of it afterward. He just grinned a lot.

When we got home, the first thing we did was repay Dad our train fare. Then we exposed our parents to about five minutes of creative cursing without ever repeating the same word twice. Well, maybe a few times. The F-word, like a lot of other very old Anglo-Saxon curse words, potentiates with repetition. When we got back to school, everything had changed. Our classmates were still boys, but we were men. Dad had given us a gift of maturity that stuck.

# GO NORTH, YOUNG MAN, GO NORTH!

The very next spring, another school year past, and he did it again. We were barely home a week when he opened The Toronto Telegram (now defunct) on the dining room table and pointed to a photo of a derelict 10,000 ton tramp steamer named the S.S. *Kingsbridge* berthed at Montreal, with an article about how it would soon be leaving for the High Arctic to deliver machinery and supplies to men stationed at Resolute Bay, just 1,000 miles from the North Pole.

Resolute Bay? We ran for our National Geographic maps. And there it was: the farthest northern settlement of Canadian Eskimos, or, as I discovered only recently — a government-enforced re-settlement of Eskimos in 1954 from where they had once lived, to Resolute Bay, as a Cold War ploy to assure hostile powers this previously empty land was a bona fide Canadian territory. For good measure, a couple of dozen scientists were also settled there to maintain radar and weather machinery, along with military personnel at a Royal Canadian Air Force outpost, because there was public alarm about Soviet missiles flying right over the North Pole and blowing up Toronto or Montreal. But for us there was just the thrilling romance of sailing into the High Arctic.

A half-day bus trip dropped us in Montreal, whence we wandered around until we found the Seaman's Mission, booked beds for a night, and took a plain macaroni dinner, which we had barely tucked into when a burly, big-jawed officer in the classic Royal Canadian Mounted Police Stetson and packing a revolver, suddenly burst through swinging doors with two young Brits about our age, in handcuffs. What's this? The place was half empty, but they plunked down at the table right beside us like they wanted company.

What was going on? The Mountie was not shy. He chuckled and raised an eyebrow, or maybe it was a bit of a smirk. "Two ship-jumpers," and the story came out, non-stop.

Instead of doing their two-year military service for the UK as required by law, they had taken the option of signing on for the British Merchant Marine at military pay of $1.65 a day. They had made one three-week voyage, and then this trip to Montreal, where they decided to jump ship, because (in a heavy Scottish brogue): "We canna' take it anymore."

We got an unpunctuated version of their experience on a ship so dirty, food so bad, work so unpleasant, treatment of them so tough — a crazy Polish cook chased one of them across the decks with a raised meat cleaver — dirty Arabs in the engine room "as likely to shove you overboard, or knife you, as look at

Against The Tide

you." So, they decided they'd rather quit. Once in the Port of Montreal, they jumped ship and became illegal immigrants — a criminal offence back then (if not now). So, the RCMP picked them up. They were easy to find, drinking away their meagre paycheques in a nearby bar.

"What ship?"

"The *S.S. Kingsbridge*."

Jamie and I caught each other's eye with the exact same thought and secret pride: WE had worked as tough lumberjacks. *These were just two English sucks.*

Couldn't believe our good luck.

The next morning we found the shipping office, applied for their jobs, and within the hour boarded the *S.S. Kingsbridge*, a scruffy 10,000 ton tramp steamer flagged in Portsmouth that was in such bad shape the Second Steward, a sly and smarmy Brit whom we soon discovered could chug a quart of beer in one go without taking a breath, said, "She'd be effing shot out of the water if y'ever took 'erback t' England."

But she would be our floating home for the next ten weeks, and we didn't mind earning only British Military pay of $1.65 a day.

## AN ENCOUNTER WITH HOMOSEXUALS

June 24th, the day before shipping out, Jamie and I went for a walk in Montreal to see the St. Jean Baptiste parade, a cultural and religious event three centuries old that traditionally celebrates the beginning of summer, but which got commandeered during the Quiet Revolution by Quebec Separatists and is today called the *Fête Nationale* of the pretended "Nation" of Quebec. We were both minding our own business standing on a low stone wall the better to see the parade, when I felt a nudge on the back of my leg. It was a fellow — two fellows, actually — who wanted something. "You 'ave a light?" was the question, as one of them waved his unlit roll-your-own cigarette at me. Very friendly, both of them. They were actors busy filming a CBC Voyageur series of TV shows that summer about the 17th century French Explorers Radisson and Groseilliers[3] — a dumbed-down Canadian version of Davy Crockett. On a break from writing this, I went to YouTube to see if there was any trace of them, and sure enough, you can see these same two dudes from more than a half-century ago parading around in their phony buckskin clothing, paddling canoes with Italian extras painted to look like savages, clubbing, and shooting Iroquois, and so on. It was quite weird to see them again on YouTube.

But they had zeroed on their quarry and were overly friendly. Soon we were walking up dark stairs to their apartment. Beer for boys was like bait for birds. We settled in, drinking around a low table. Soon, Jamie had left the room with Groseilliers, and Radisson began showing me their collection of LP records, and I got a weird, sweaty feeling. What? Where's my brother?

Radisson made like everything was just fine. They'll be back in a moment. But I'm gonna find him. Something is wrong … so down a narrow hallway, Radisson asking me to stop. Straight to a closed door, and I pushed it open.

There, basking in studio lighting, leaning against a low wall, arms and legs spread out, stark naked except for a pair of black bikini underwear, was wet-lipped Groseilliers, rapt, happy, as if preparing for some sado-masochistic immolation. I was stunned. Jamie glanced at me sheepishly, still clicking photos of the guy.

"C'mon. We're getting the hell out of here."

We bolted for the door, but with sweaty palms I couldn't turn the knob.

Shouting "Open the goddamn door!" we, almost fell down the stairs united in panic and didn't stop running until we felt free of disgust.


## ALL ABOARD!

Jock, with a Scottish brogue so thick we needed an interpreter, and Johnny, from somewhere south of London, were our cabin mates — four boys stacked in two bunk beds in a 12 feet x 12 feet cabin, a grimy naked bulb and a single porthole for light. Okay. Up on my bunk. Settle my stuff. I lift the corner of

Against The Tide

my dirty stained mattress and slam it back in place to hide the swarm of cock-roaches running around madly underneath. The "Second" as we nick-named the Second Steward, cackled with sadistic pleasure whenever, bored at sea, he would catch one in his own cabin, and push it through a small hole in the bulkhead, into ours. We plugged the hole.

The first two weeks were spent on two round trips to Sydney, Nova Scotia, to pick up a load of coal and back to Montreal for loading onto rail cars. We glided to the great sea down the beautiful, wide St. Lawrence past a green and gold patchwork of fields that rose from the shore on each side, floating through an agricultural amphitheater, redolent of French-Canadian history and the *habitant* way of life, land ever-more sub-divided, from father to eldest son, in long narrow strips, the blood-red evening sky punctuated every few miles by a tiny Catholic cross against a failing sunset on a green hill.

At Sydney, enormous steel tubes fired a steady stream of black coal chunks into our hull, black dust swirling. Coal dust took over everything. Hair, ears, nostrils, eyes, every crease of one's body, filled with blackness. Our "shower" was a single metal pipe from which cold water ran in a solid stream. At sea you had to sway from side to side with the ship to stay under the stream. Clean for a half hour. Then blackened again. Once back at Montreal for unloading, the ship shuddered as giant scoop-shovels dropped from the sky with huge open jaws and shiny steel teeth into the black bowels of our ship from some mechanical architecture far above our heads. Wham. Wham. Wham. Then, straining, groaning under the load, they would rise from the depths, big black chunks falling, bouncing off the steel deck, dark dust swirling, a devil's tail in the wind, 'round the clock.

The day our second coal run ended, when the last shovel of black gold disappeared over our heads, all fell eerily quiet. Giant crane engines choked and coughed, hovering, silent mastodons peering down at us. The harbour was glassy now, oil-slicked, flat black water in late afternoon sun. I was standing high on the bridge, lost in thought. When, suddenly, from somewhere at the bow, came the deeply rendered sounds of *O Sole Mio*, the very song I loved and had played countless times. Always amazed that anyone could sing so powerfully, this was some kind of contextual shock. *O Sole Mio*? Booming over these harbour waters in such a lusty voice? From where? How so?

And there, perched on the bow, long work pants, naked and sweaty from the waist up, with grimy red suspenders was a burly, hairy-chested, coal-blackened Italian stevedore, white teeth glinting in the shadows, holding a happy fistful of money high in the air, singing *O Sole Mio* for all the world to hear. What a moment.

## OFF TO THE HIGH ARCTIC

Goodbye and good riddance to black coal.

Excitement mounted as we laboured to prepare our grimy ship for the High Arctic. 75 degrees north! A hair over 1,000 miles from the North Pole! *That* was exciting, and everyone felt it was going to be the trip of a lifetime. Hoses were spraying everywhere, washing down bulkheads and decks, paint brushes attacking every surface at a fevered pitch; then, cranes went to work lifting thousands of tons of supplies, food, fuel, and machinery for the personnel wintering at Resolute Bay in –50°C winter weather.

After a week, the *S.S. Kingsbridge* looked about to sink. Thousands of barrels of highly flammable airplane fuel were now in the hold (making us a little anxious). Wooden containers as big as a house, full of canned food and dry goods. More containers as big as another house filled with cases of beer, all disappearing into our dark hold, or strapped down onto the deck, where every other available space was taken up by heavy equipment: a large crane, two dump trucks, big, tank-treaded snow machines. Cartons of rifle ammunition and construction dynamite, and more. We began to wonder how our ship would fare in a rough sea; the thought of explosive gasoline, ammunition, dynamite, and hitting an iceberg, was unnerving.

But we finally set off down the mighty St. Lawrence to the Atlantic Ocean, past those beautiful patchwork farmlands and quiet steeples for the last time, then northeast through the Strait of Belle Isle between Newfoundland and rugged, bleak, godforsaken Baffin Land, hard by the coast of Greenland and Disko island (a place first visited by the Norseman, Erik the Red, and today, an Inuit settlement). Then ever farther north into Davis Strait. Off the coast of Greenland we saw giant icebergs calving from glaciers, crashing into the sea, skyscraping plumes of foamy seawater jetting hundreds of feet upwards against a far distant ice-walled shore and blue sky.

Why, I was a real sailor now, loving the cold wind in my hair on the rolling, pitching bridge from where I could see white dolphins diving and leaping, playing quick and sleek ahead of us, feeling the salty ocean, heaved, and split by our charging prow spraying my face as we sailed northward. Oh, to feel such adventure in the heart, to lick cold salt spray from the lip and love the taste. And there, now, suddenly, far to the port side, an enormous ghostly iceberg looming, lofty and chill-white, majestically artful wave-carved curves appearing from a low-lying mist, a crisp moon hanging above in broad daylight. For the days were lengthening as we headed northward in the wake of Frobisher, Baffin, Davis, and the sorry Henry Hudson, a victim of mutiny by

*Against The Tide*

his crew, set afloat with his son in a rowboat with no food or fresh water in the vast bay named after him, disappearing. Forever. But at least not from history.

Nor could I have known then — how can any of us know our future? — those 60 years hence, in my 75th year I would translate an 18th-century French book called *Le Voyageur Français* into English — an account of voyageur adventure, and Eskimo and Indian life right here, in this very part of the world. These moments, and this adventure were what attracted me so many years later, to that book, bringing me back here.

Soon, we entered vast fields of crackling ice. A misty myriad of ghostly blue and white floes lying scattered randomly on a glassy sea. Countless snow-topped "growlers" — so named for the noise they make pounding into and sliding along our old iron ship's hull — a haunting, chilling noise in the darkness of night that jars us from sleep when the whole ship shakes, lurching, growling. Each growler was about six feet thick, opalescent ice glinting under white snowy cowlings like sleeping monks, some impossible to pass, being half a football field in size. Years later we learned the bow got damaged by that ice when the *S.S. Kingsbridge* went into dry-dock for repairs.

The reason for this was our captain, a gruff, seeming cruel Scotsman, got to drinking heavily all the way north, locked himself in his cabin, and was seldom seen. I would climb up to his quarters balancing a tray of food, leave it on his step, and pick it up empty later. We hit so many growlers because command was weak and so we edged them out of the way when we should have waited for the *D'Iberville* — the sturdy icebreaker sent to lead us the rest of the risky route to Resolute Bay.

But the first mate who took over didn't speak much French, and couldn't communicate with the captain of the *D'Iberville*, who didn't speak much English. So, our icebreaker snaked its way ahead through a mess of irregular floes. Here is that icebreaker pushing ahead of us through heavy pack ice.

We were too far ahead. We did some serious bumping as the days lengthened, the sun stopped going down altogether, and nightfall was no more. The sun travelled a weak glowing yellow arc around the whole empty blue sky all day in a saddle-shaped circle, pausing on the horizon at midnight, then starting around again on another circuit.

Days passed. More pack ice and gigantic icebergs looming. Our immediate boss was the ship's cook, a grimy, crazy Pole with a bad temper whom we once saw, meat cleaver in hand, shouting Polish profanities while chasing one of the Arab firemen around the deck. No one wanted to mess with him (or complain about the awful food). Our Second Steward started each day guzzling an entire quart of beer without a breath from a private supply he had smuggled aboard and was not about to share. Then he would burp loudly, a wicked leer twisting around very bad teeth. About the cook? "Careful at sea, my lads." He let us know in direct terms that on a ship like this with low railings, "It's just a bump from the shadows, and 'Man overboard'." He wouldn't say how often he knew of it happening. But from then on we walked hugging bulkheads.

Meanwhile, the ship's Bo'sun — the officer in charge of the whole crew — a crusty Yorkshire man with bristling red eyebrows who disappeared half of every day, let on that he had three wives in different ports of the world, and he liked it that way ("long as nun'of 'em knew about t'others"). He laughed merrily about cheating them all, but confessed while wiping one leaky eye he was a little worried about his failing memory. I bet.

Every day, out of bed, peel crinkled potatoes and carrots, prepare meals for a crew of 25, wash all the dishes three times a day — sometimes in the same water — and stack 'em in special slotted shelves that prevented them from flying across the galley when the ship rolled. Which she did aplenty when we hit rough weather. There was a pie-shaped indicator on a wall (which I learned is called a *clinometer*) marked with "degrees of roll." It had a brass pointer hanging from its apex. I asked a passing deckhand: "Why does the angle on either side of the pie-shape only go to 45 degrees?" He looked at me as if I were clueless (which I was), drew his finger across his sweat-wrinkled neck, and said "after 45 degrees, it's tits up, mate."

One day, a little bored after chores, I descended through a steel door into the engine room of the ship, far below top deck. Down shaky steel ladder steps, into a noisy, dark, and greasy world. Steam and soot welled up, stinging my eyes. Down, and down again, into the clanging and yawning of coal fires, steam pistons, and spinning turbines that drove the props, as we pushed our way forward in a tossing sea over thousands of feet of cold black water. At the very bottom of our ship I had to stop thinking I was below the surface of the sea now, slipping suspended over chilly deadly darkness.

*Against The Tide*

My feet once on the bottom, there were two Arab men I'd never seen before squatting in their grimy clothes and rag headgear, smiling white teeth the setting for a few gold ones, yellowed eyes ringed with coal dust, alternately smoking roll-your-own cigarettes and eating with their fingers, dipping bread in plates of curried meat and potatoes — potatoes I had peeled. Another was shoveling coal from a large black pile into steam-generating furnaces that gave off intense heat; coal slewed from his shovel into a molten red maw. Iron door slammed shut.

"Come. Have some."

So, I did. I squatted for a while and ate some curry and didn't much like it. And I had a cigarette with them in their mini-Arabia. Curry, cigarettes and coffee, in the devil's doorway.

The next day, we were in Resolute Bay.

## 75 DEGREES NORTH – "THE PLACE WITH NO DAWN"

Excitement was high for the last 100 miles, which were easy going. We glided on silver-surfaced calm open water, past barren, forbidding, pebble-strewn low mountain slopes. And except for occasional growlers or small wave-sculpted icebergs, the ocean was ice-free.

We arrived in a light snowstorm on August 18, 1957, and dropped anchor about a half-mile offshore a couple of hundred yards away from the *C.D. Howe*, an ice-strengthened supply and marine-studies ship we would very soon get to know rather well. On shore was a gigantic array of empty high-octane fuel barrels piled on their sides about six feet high and ten feet wide stretching a quarter mile up and over a ridge, beyond which we heard here was a military airfield, some air force planes, a weather station, early-warning equipment to detect any incoming Soviet missiles, and some Canadian government personnel. Here is that field of empty aviation fuel barrels, with the bow of our resupply ship the *S.S. Kingsbridge* in the left background.

Scattered over the rest of the area was a disorganized tangle of beat-up heavy equipment, and what looked like abandoned metal, wood, and other detritus of a hasty human settlement that had no place to put serious junk. Southward somewhere, over there, over another distant ridge, was said to be an Eskimo settlement — news that intrigued us and set our imaginations afire. *That's* what we came for!

But we got right to work as soon as the anchor hit bottom, unloading those thousands of fuel barrels, machinery, and goods. From out of somewhere a few PT-style landing craft arrived alongside. Ship's cranes got back into action lifting everything we had off the deck and into the landing craft, where we were now deployed. Off to the shore with our first load, where we ran straight onto the pebbled shore, bow ramps dropping with a heavy clang on Neolithic stony ground. Roll out machinery. Roll out barrels. Push them up the shore for transport onto trucks to the airfield. Or load them in piles, thousands of them, for later pick up. All day. Back and forth. Nothing but barrels. And at the end of the day, back to bed, worn out.

Here are the photos of where we arrived and our work site as seen from shore, with the *D'Iberville* at anchor in the background.

We were late getting into Resolute, so there was concern about cold and ice locking us in, and somewhat of a panic among the officers. Visions of a starving and frozen Franklin expedition sprang to mind. Soon there was news we would not get back to Montreal until the middle of September, long after school started. What?

So after a week Jamie found the Bo'sun of the *C.D. Howe* from across the bay, who said he needed more crew, and if Jamie and I would jump ship — leave the *S.S. Kingsbridge* illegally — he would arrange a small boat pick up that evening and hire us without any pay for our last ten days at Resolute, for unloading the *S.S. Kingsbridge*! Then we could fly back free to Montreal early September on a regular military cargo flight out of Resolute. A deal!

That night, about 10 o'clock in a summer twilight that never ends we shared a last smoke with Jock and Johnny, said goodbye matey, moved swiftly to the ship's ladder, climbed down into a waiting skiff and went over to the *C.D. Howe*. Our captain was still drunk in his cabin. No pay for eight weeks of work. So what? This was a real adventure, our own mutiny on the Bounty! And work we did — 'round-the-clock shift work. Three assigned to each bunk, eight hours sleep in rotation. Shake the shoulder of the next guy up, and flop into a pre-warmed bed until the next shakes your shoulder, and out you go into the cold.

Three days before the end we heard that the Eskimo settlement over the south-western ridge was out of bounds to unauthorized people. And we hadn't a clue that one of the main reasons was worry about white-man's diseases like tuberculosis and measles, which white people tolerate reasonably well, but Eskimos and Indians don't. But we were keen for adventure, and in retrospect, thoughtless. I didn't learn until the research for my *The French Traveler* book that white man's diseases had wiped out massive numbers of Indians and Eskimos in the New World over a couple of centuries of early settlement.

We also didn't know that the *C.D. Howe*, in addition to supplies, was a hospital ship. One day while off duty and exploring below decks, I wandered into an area of dimly lit narrow passageways. Murmuring, guttural sounds through the thin walls. An occasional child's laugh. What's this? A door opened briefly. And there, as if a yellowed, medieval painting, a fresco of Hades, was a tangle of dark Eskimo limbs, and darting, apprehensive eyes, set in weather-lined faces of a few dozen men and women. A lot of agitated children, too, in grubby underclothing were squirming between mother's legs, or at the breast. Lots of not very clean looking bandages on hands, legs. A patch over an eye, or half a face here, or there. A splinted forearm. Fur-lined parkas piled high on a jumble of beds. This was the ship's sick bay. White man's medicine, much of it likely for white man's diseases.

An unsettling sight. The door quickly clanging shut.

A worker at Resolute told me the next day that the ship sometimes took sick Eskimos away from their families to the south for cures not available in the far north, some of whom never returned. Here is such a tubercular Eskimo family on the deck of the *C.D. Howe*.

After that medical program started, a lone hunter in a kayak far from shore, who happened to see the rescue ship cresting the horizon across far away ice floes, would as often paddle furiously back to camp to warn everyone to flee before they got seized by the white man and shipped south. Good intentions gone awry. *

At 10 pm one night, or rather day-night, we snuck away, taking whatever we thought we could trade — a steel hunting knife, a small hatchet I packed for this trip, a compass, a few candies — caught a ride on a small boat to shore, and set out on foot for the Eskimo camp, with no idea what to expect. Would we be welcome? Safe? Endangered? Scare them off?

The High Arctic is a remote and forbidding place. There are no trees, or other landmarks by which to judge distance. So what we thought would be a 20-minute walk to the far ridge took an hour and a half of trudging over pebbly ground. Here and there a short-lived yellow arctic poppy huddling in a crack of rock.

Cresting the ridge, we first saw lazy spirals of smoke twirling skyward. Then we heard barking dogs. Across open water, distant low mountains came into view. And then, a few hundred feet far below us appeared a semi-circular pebbled shore, a blue-water panorama of sinuously wave-carved,

Against The Tide

turquoise-tinted icebergs floating grandly in a calm wind-swept bay. A school-boy's fairy-tale. An entire Eskimo encampment unfolded as we came fully over the crest: a dozen flimsy-looking structures of skin, wood scrap and metal sheets, and a large whale-rib or two, smoke skirling skyward, racks of drying fish, husky dogs upset at us intruders ... Oops. We never counted on burly husky dogs. They looked very hungry. Are we the meal? A little close, five or six little kids, shiny squinty eyes set glinting in fur-hooded, weather-tanned faces, half delighted, half wary, very curious about white intruders. Dogs pretty close now, foaming a little, fangs out, barking louder. Oh jeez, what have we done?

A little anxious, I held out a paper-wrapped candy to one of the kids. He giggled a little. Approached me. Backed away. I stepped forward. He stepped back again. Then, suddenly, he leaped forward, grabbed the candy, and scurried off giggling into one of the tent-homes.

We were soaking up this plunge into real Canadian history, our personal time-warp access to Paleolithic reality (mentally subtracting the pieces of metal, a few metal gas cans lying around, and a fur-hooded man in the distance with a rifle over his shoulder). This was a time before the invention of the personal snowmobile, and travel was still by dogsled in winter at some-times −50°C, and by kayak whenever possible. What a thrill. No schoolbook could ever render such an experience.

And then suddenly, all hell broke loose.

First, a distant siren. Then, rumbling over the same crest from which we had descended, we saw the silhouette of a big pick-up truck, red roof-light flashing against pale blue midnight sky, soon about to run us over, screeching to a halt about ten feet away, an angry trail of dust rolling over us — and over our panic.

Words can hardly convey how scared young boys can be when a very angry, red-faced RCMP officer packing a big pistol on his hip jumps out of a truck before it has fully stopped and shakes his pumping fist.

"Son of a bitch! What the hell are you kids doin' here? How did you? Hey! This is strictly off-limits! Get the fuck outa here. *Now*! Or ... it's ... it's six months in jail!"

"*Jail*!" How were we going to explain *this* to our parents? Run. Just run.

As long as he didn't pull his gun, we figured tubby couldn't catch us if we ran fast enough back up that long slope. There are a few benefits of being young, and running away from a man with a big belly is one of them. At the top, out of range, we took one last breathless look at that unforgettable sight — and the timeless, bucolic peace we had disturbed.

On the way back to our ship we stumbled across a circular depression in the ground, 20 feet across, that must have been some kind of ancient Eskimo encampment, because there were a few weathered whale-ribs arching about six feet high from the edges that likely supported skins to cover a tent of some kind. A few huge whale vertebrae that looked like three-bladed propellers were lying around, too. We examined them curiously. Could we get one home? Too big. Then I heard "catch" — one of the guys threw one twirling my way. Years later I felt badly about disturbing all that.

And back we trekked to our ship, empty-handed.

The next day we met a helicopter pilot who was flying supplies to that camp and asked him to take my knife and hatchet to trade for genuine Eskimo things. Anything.

We were delighted and amazed at what he brought back: a baby polar bear pelt, a seal-pelt, and a beautiful soapstone carving of an Arctic goose, which I still have. This was carved long before the rage for Inuit art became popular in Canada, and even now, every time I look at it, I think of that amazing trip.

Two or three brief sequelae.

For the flight from Resolute to Montreal we sat on canvas strap seats in an uninsulated military cargo plane. Not much heat. No sound-insulation. The ear-blasting roar of propeller engines for eight hours. Stuffy, overheated from the waist up; frozen from the waist down; almost choking on cigarette smoke and the smell of vomit from a young man who had refused to share his food, ate it alone, then threw up, splashing it all over the steel deck. Let me out of here!

When we landed at Dorval airport in Montreal and the door opened, the sweet smell of ripe hayfields, apples, and wildflowers hit us like ambrosia from

Against The Tide

Heaven. We hadn't realized that High Arctic air has no smell because there's almost no vegetation, just rocks, water, and ice.

Back at Appleby, Jamie and I felt like strangers among schoolboys once again returned from a secret mission of manhood. About three months later when the mail came around, we both received a letter from that Montreal shipping office with $65 in British military pay for ten weeks of work. Our friends laughed at the money. But we didn't.

I left Appleby after Grade 12 to go to McGill University for a year. But some of us were doing advanced work in Grade 12 and so in my final spring at Appleby I had to write a Grade 13 exam in English Composition. I also had to write Grade 13 Algebra, which in view of going to McGill, I had abandoned studying. I stared at the English exam in a kind of disbelief, for where it asked us to write a "descriptive essay", I saw a list of the most boring topics imaginable. One was "The View From a Bridge." My heart sank at this dispiriting, depressing suggestion. So, I just fiddled with my pen for a while. And then, suddenly, an idea popped up. I could write about the view from "the Bridge" of the *S.S. Kingsbridge*, charging northward into the High Arctic. Yes! Of splashing salt-waves, rollicking white dolphins, monstrous looming icebergs, and Eskimos. The reader would be just as enraptured as I had been but would have no idea I was talking about the view from the Bridge of a ship … until the very last moment. Oh, I loved it. I could deceive and delight at the same time, as my pen moved itself across the page!

Twenty five years later at a dinner party in Toronto, David Scarlett, an Appleby classmate who had stayed on to finish Grade 13, surprised me with a little story. He said the year after I left Appleby the Ministry of Education sent my essay on "A View From A Bridge" to every school in the province as an example of a good descriptive essay. I have tried to locate it, but the mysteries of the Ministry and its digital filing system have eluded me. I felt proud of that essay. Not so proud that I got nine per cent in Grade 13 Algebra — the lowest Algebra grade in the history of Ontario.

## MY TRACK LIFE BEGINS

*"I am a controversialist. People either swear by me, or swear at me."*
~ *Lloyd Percival*

At 17 and in grade 11, I became the first boy in the history of Appleby to win the coveted *Victor Ludorum* for the third time in a row — before Dad had won it once. Ouch. Besides throwing him into an emotional-confusion conundrum, was what I did an insult to the history of the honour? Here is a photo of that day, me in the middle, holding the legendary trophy. The Junior and Intermediate winners flanking me. It was a day that turned my life in unforeseeable ways. Dr. Bell saw the opportunity to take me down a peg or two as I left this photo set-up. He came over to walk beside me for a bit, and said, "You're a pretty good athlete. But not as good as your dad." I thought that was probably true.

That summer there were no manly trips. No lumber camps. No Arctic adventure. No job. Summer was just a blank. And so, Mom panicked once again at the idea of a teenaged son on the loose and sprang into action. She was a good potter, instrumental in forming the Canadian Guild of Potters, and had a friend connected to the Toronto world of ceramics named Alex Stermac. He was a Croatian immigrant and Olympic Water Polo star who became a top swim coach after he arrived in Canada, started the Etobicoke Swim Club, and sent many Canadian swimmers to the Olympic Games. Alex liked my mother. Maybe a little too much. And she had a son who seemed to have some talent as a runner. Did Alex know of any good track and field coaches? He did, and her question changed my life.

The next morning, she was on the phone to a man named Lloyd Percival, about whom none of us had ever heard, but were eventually to hear a lot. And 15 years later, too much! A memoir creates factual and emotional circles in a

Against The Tide

life that emerge from past events to form patterns you can't see when they're forming. In an artsy film called *The Incredible Lightness of Being*, one of the characters says, "The trouble with life is, you don't get to practice." I now think that is a good thing. Practice would paralyze us.

That Saturday morning, I was on a bus to the York Mills Collegiate track in Toronto to meet my first and only track and field coach. There I was, a dozen little kids running around on a loose black cinder track, jumping in sandpits, and me. A sharp whistle-sound came across the track from a short man in a green jacket and red cap, a stopwatch around his neck. It was "Coach" or "the little man", as my future teammates and I came to call him, privately but very fondly.

There was a brief "Hi kid," and a handshake, and he got right to it. Do so many sit-ups. Push ups. Painful stretching exercises I had never seen before. Hold that position. Ouch. Body angles measured with a tape. Jumping tests. Reaction-time tests. Oh my! He was trying to figure out if I was worth coaching, and I felt like a reject already. At the end of a half-hour field-test of my fitness, at a time when the word "fitness" had not yet entered the public lexicon — came the final order. "Now, I want you to run a quarter mile as fast as you can." Yikes! I would never have tried to run that far "as fast as you can." Like, right out of the gate. But an order was an order, and I was plenty scared of disappointing him.

I heard the click of his stopwatch when he said "GO!" and before the halfway mark I was ambushed by searing leg pain and burning lungs. Panic set in. It was a trick. He didn't really care how fast I ran. He knew, and so did I, that no one can run "as fast as you can" that far. But I got sucked-in wanting to please him, and now I couldn't stop. To give up would be cowardly. Not an option. He wanted to see if this kid had any guts. So, I switched to unconscious mode and just about passed out at the finish. With a dizzy grin, swallowing my pounding heart. But I was not going to show him how much it hurt.

While he was alive, Lloyd Percival changed my life, and my family's life, as a coach and otherwise. And when he died unexpectedly 15 years later, he changed my life again.

But he never told me how fast I ran that quarter-mile.

And I would still like to know.

The rest of that summer was a combination of pleasure, pain, confusion, disappointment, and the beginning of what I now think was a fanatical runner's life that lasted almost 20 years. At Appleby — an athletically insular environment — I was a big frog in a small pond. But once outside the pond, I went into a kind of insignificance-trauma that was hard to take. I was being told to forget my mongrel-style of running and learn how to run properly. Coach made it clear: "no one is born a great runner. Great technique in anything is beautiful. You have to *learn* how to run." This was tough, run 'til you drop training, thinking about every stride. Lloyd was famous for turning his athletes into multi-eventers. "You are going to learn the precise biomechanics of running, jumping, hurdling, and throwing — the classic four." Classic, because he idealized the Greeks and their Olympic ideal. For him it wasn't just winning that mattered. It was *how* you win. You win like a man, no matter what. You win with modesty (always shake hands with your competitors), and you lose graciously. There was endless painful stretching, and "interval" training, which was a new system at the time, used famously by the great Czech runner Emil Zatopek, the only man ever to win the Olympic 5,000 metres 10,000 metres and Marathon in the same Olympics (1952). Lloyd got misty-eyed when telling us on multiple occasions that Zatopek trained so hard he would lose feeling in his thighs and had to pinch his legs to bruising as he ran, just to be sure they were still there. We all said, "Wow." And then, how he would run alongside his foreign competitors, and at the half-way mark, already having set a gruelling pace, he would say, in their own language — Russian, Norwegian, English, whatever was required — "Don't you think the pace is a little slow?" And then, just as they felt the shock of his words, he would take off and drop them.

I achieved a fitness level that I never thought possible. It was ten weeks of gut work, very sore legs, banged up and swollen kneecaps from hitting so many hurdles, lots of blister-blood and black cinders in my track shoes. Wondering why I had decided to put myself through all this? And all the while, Coach's ability to read an athlete's mind was surprising. At my wits end one day, head down in the starting blocks waiting for the word "Set," I heard his quiet voice: "Just about now, you are wondering what the hell this is all about, right?" It was like I got shot in the heart. I stood bolt upright. "You bet!" But I felt an instant wash of relief. He was not all tough guy. He understood what I was feeling. That just made me want to try harder.

After our first six weeks, Coach drove me to Hamilton for my first open track meet, and Dad came to watch. Unlike Appleby, where I knew the competition in advance and what my chances were, now I would up be against strangers. And I didn't like them. They all looked mean and unfriendly. What was the point of trying to beat people you don't know? I was entered in five events, and this was long before Pierre Trudeau foolishly took Canada Metric: the 100 yards, 220 yards, a 120 yards hurdle race, long jump, and triple jump. And I came about dead last in all of them, to considerable personal embarrassment.

Against The Tide

I hadn't yet learned the right way to run, jump, or hurdle. Thinking about it too much. So, my legs just didn't know what to do. There is a right way that can be learned. Even a few inches added to a runner's stride will mean a great many yards by the end of a race. Awkward, crushed, and feeling like a loser, this was confusing and hurt my pride a lot. For one thing, my Appleby stardom felt like a fraud. A cruel trick played on a spoiled boy. I couldn't wait for the last miserable event to end, and when it did, I just hung my head and walked over to where Lloyd and my dad were sitting. I could hardly look at Dad and Coach said (this was him, through and through):

"Well kid, there's no place to start like the bottom. You can only go up!"

It was bitter consolation, but I smiled at his confidence. It was confidence in himself. It was pure Lloyd Percival. He always saw the positive in his athletes. So, who was this man?

The more I learned about him, the more I was certain I was in the right hands. For a man only five foot six, he had been a remarkable athlete. When his British parents emigrated to Toronto, they signed him up at a local cricket club at age 13, just to keep him off the streets. He eventually became the team's star batsman and a fine bowler, and at age 22 played the prestigious "first wicket" position when representing Canada on a cricket tour of England, scoring an unprecedented victory over the British Marylebone team at "Lords" hallowed cricket ground in London. That was the same place we choirboys had gone to watch the same club play during our Coronation Choir Tour in 1953.

Along the way, he tried many other sports and excelled at them all. He reached the finals of the Canadian Junior Tennis Championship, losing only to the American champion Frankie Parker in the final. A few years later, he and his brother Alan played in the Canadian doubles tennis final. As if that weren't enough, Lloyd was also a fighting man with a lifelong love of boxing. He had 28 amateur fights as a bantam weight and lost only one — to Vince Gionna at the 1928 Canadian Olympic Trials (Vince came fifth at the Amsterdam Olympics that year). Then Lloyd won a regional Golden Gloves title, in 1930. I had won a lot of boxing matches in high school myself. But the Golden Gloves! Lloyd would have killed me. I was awed.

At a young age, he had seen that sporting success is only partly about talent. Lots of people have talent. It's cheap. But what truly great athletes had, besides amazing perseverance, was great coaching. So, he decided to become a coach. And great he became.

He also became one of the world's first international fitness experts. Through his many sport, fitness, and diet publications, and his CBC "Sports College" radio broadcasts, he was busy changing lives. He certainly changed mine! And that, at a time when it was embarrassing just to be seen wearing a sweat suit in public or doing some training on a road. People would stare as they drove by. If a woman was seen jogging they would sometimes stop and ask what was wrong? One time, out doing some hill running on an early winter's day, some teenagers driving by threw beer bottles at me — "Get offa the street, weirdo!" "Fitness" was considered weird.

But at its peak, Sports College had a million listeners per broadcast, and 22,000 paying "members" who joined by tearing off a Nabisco Shredded Wheat cereal label and mailing it in with 50 cents to Sports College — a shoe-string operation run from his family home on 12 Glen Road in Rosedale, where coaching tips for all sorts of sports were mailed out to kids across Canada. That first summer I spent many an hour helping him and Doug MacLennan, his muscular assistant, stuff envelopes and lick stamps. Doug was a quiet, light-hearted man devoted to Lloyd, with a dry sense of humour and a body like, well, like Tarzan. I figured that's what hanging around Lloyd would do for me.

By the too-early end of his life — a trauma that hit me dreadfully hard, which I will relate later in this memoir — Lloyd had exerted his considerable personal influence on a wide range of notable Canadians, such as highly-reputed culture-critic Robert Fulford (who compared Lloyd's approach to sporting excellence to Marshall McLuhan's approach to communication science), and had coached dozens of different sports, and many hundreds of top athletes in almost every sport worth the name.

Too many to count. So, I'll just comment on a few of the lives he touched. In 1951 Lloyd published *The Hockey Handbook*, an influential analysis of the basic skills of hockey, and still available on Amazon. It was purchased by the Russian hockey federation in the late 1960's and sparked the development of Russian hockey. So much so, that Russian head coach Anatoli Tarasov wrote to Lloyd: "Your wonderful book, which introduced us to the mysteries of Canadian hockey, I have read like a schoolboy."

By 1972, "The Russians" came to Canada, skated circles around our team, and almost whipped us. They had been doing Lloyd's hockey fitness program, while our NHL guys, skilled though they were, had a history of spending every summer at the lake drinking beer and, some of them, smoking. That game came down to the last minute, when Henderson scored an amazing shinny-style goal, to win, and Canada erupted in pride. But it was a narrow escape from a big embarrassment, and the fitness lesson was learned in a way that changed professional and international hockey forevermore.

The day after the game, the Russian head coach came to see Lloyd at The Fitness Institute, in North York, with a translator. My Dad, Doug, and I were

*Against The Tide*

sitting in the room. After some small talk, there was a pregnant silence. Then Lloyd asked the Russian: "What about paying royalties for translating and selling my book in the Soviet Union?"

The Russian coach looked beady-eyed at Lloyd, smiled wryly, and ended the conversation with, "Vee are communist. Vee don't pay royalties," to a little guarded laughter, all 'round.

By the end of his life, Lloyd had touched a great many lives, and mine in ways I only now realize. No one knows exactly how many famous athletes or teams he helped, advised, or coached directly, or indirectly. But there were a lot. Lloyd "Ace" Percival was part of the Muhammad Ali/George Chuvalo fight, too. George came to him to get fit. Lloyd got him off the dreary slow road-running boxers' gig and put him on an interval-training program. A much fitter post-Percival Chuvalo became the only fighter to take Ali to a 15-round decision. He also designed fitness programmes for many of the "Crazy Canuck" downhill skiers, including Steve Podborski, 'Jungle Jim' Hunter, and Nancy Greene, whom I used to watch train at the Fitness Institute. Lloyd made some sports-journalist enemies when he held a leg-strength competition at The Fitness Institute where Nancy leg-pressed more weight than any of the NHL hockey players.

He also trained a great many national calibre track athletes, including Rich Ferguson, one of Canada's greatest milers, who competed in the May 6, 1954 "Miracle Mile" in Vancouver at the British Empire and Commonwealth Games. That was a challenge match between John Landy of Australia, and Roger Bannister of England, both of whom had earlier broken the legendary "four-minute mile" barrier, but never running against each other. Ferguson, a young Olympian himself, was the youngest in the miracle mile. Both men broke the four-minute barrier, with Bannister outkicking Landy in the last half lap to win in 3'58.8". But in an amazing effort, young Rich Ferguson finished third, in 4'04.6" — a personal best for him, and a new Canadian native record. His fine time was overshadowed and unremarked in the fuss over the four-minute barrier and has been forgotten by all but track aficionados since.

A few more of the Canadian greats whose lives he touched were Roger Jackson, gold medallist in rowing at the Tokyo Olympics; and John Wood, Olympic silver in Canoe in 1976 where he lost gold to a Russian by 34/100s of a second. And here, a digression is in order. Just before the race began it was clear the Russian was in trouble. He had held onto one of the judge's boats just prior to the start and got some sticky caulking on his hands. He was in a panic trying to get it off his fingers just before the race, when John Wood handed him his own towel. The Russian was a little stunned, but gratefully wiped his hands clean, and then barely beat John to win gold.

In the two years prior to John's Olympic Games, he worked for me as a gym instructor at The Fitness Institute in Mississauga. I remember how he was usually so tired from intensive training he seemed asleep standing up. After his athletic life was over he became an investment whiz in his own company, 20/20 Financial, and then, after many years struggling with depression, committed suicide in January of 2013. What a loss. He was a handsome and warm human being with unrelenting drive, and his shocking death was a great loss to all who knew him.

I can't resist mentioning a few more of the greats whom I saw going in and out of The Fitness Institute to train or just to see Lloyd for advice and a pep-talk. That was Lloyd. No one knew why. But if you went to him for advice and he said you could fly, you would ask him where the nearest window was. Athletes came in a steady stream. Hockey greats like Gordie Howe and Frank Mahovlich, and most of the Detroit Red Wings players. And the great track cyclist Jocelyn Lovell, who won three gold medals in the Edmonton Commonwealth Games in 1978.

He also helped Olympic divers like Beverly Boys, the water-ski legend George Athans Jr. and his brother Jamie and other golfing greats like George Knudson and Al Balding, whom he introduced to the then very unfashionable notion that better fitness made better golf. Which it did.

Lloyd's biographer Gary Mossman (son of the great Canadian rowing coach Jim Mossman) wrote a fine description of our Coach in *Lloyd Percival, Coach and Visionary* (2013). Many of the moments of which I write were supplied by that book: "He spent his entire life swimming against the current and challenging complacency wherever he found it. He was opinionated, arrogant, vociferous, confident, demanding, unyielding, and destined to become embroiled in controversy. He had an almost pathological need for self-promotion, an unwavering belief he was right, a complete lack of patience with those who didn't share his beliefs, and he repeatedly became engaged in private skirmishes as well as in some that became all too public." And then came the part of him I knew best — in the early years: "Percival was also kind, generous, loyal and self-effacing; he inspired life-long loyalty from all who got to know him, and he was loved and deeply respected by all the athletes he coached."

Lloyd was like a second father, and for four summers interspaced by studies at various universities, where I was left to coach myself, was the only coach I ever had. Athletes dependent on their coaches for success become something like their children. My life got intertwined with his immediately that first summer, and then again, many years later, in ways I never expected. At the end I committed what felt like a parricide.

Against The Tide

# ONWARD ... INTO NO MAN'S LAND

I loved Appleby as a young boy, but as manhood loomed and nature made herself ever more present, a certain biological discomfort grew, and so by Grade 12 I hankered for a more normal world. I had never had a true female friend, and still haven't (except for my dear wife). The mere notion of a warm and sincere friendship with a girl, absent some powerful sexual attraction, seemed so unthinkable — weirdly irrational, actually — that I now believe growing up in a boys-only school, notwithstanding all the things of high masculine value imbued by such an experience, left a residue of unnatural and still unresolved wariness in me — perhaps mixed with a little latent confusion — with respect to female friendship.

Be that as it may, by Grade 12 I had enough of Appleby, and badly wanted out. The mere thought of having to go back for grade 13 was depressing. I had contested just about every sport Appleby offered and had the good fortune to do well in most of them. But the school boxing championships were coming up soon, and I learned too late that Dr. Bell — once again — wanted to take me down a peg or two. Those were the days when too much self-regard was frowned upon as a mortal danger to one's development. So, he exercised some kind of back-room influence over the choice of which boys would fight, and I ended up in the heavy-weight boxing championship of the school in the winter of Grade 12.

But at a mere 170 pounds I was no heavyweight. So, when this was announced I shrank a little. It would be fought in front of the whole school, and a lot of parents. I was being put up against a 220 pound, six-foot-two student named (wait for it!) George Musselman. Musselman! Brother, Jamie was a very hard-hitting boxer, and had beat George the year before, I had been Jamie's second in his corner, offering him coaching points ("get under his gloves, use your uppercut," etc.), and gave him water and smelling salts between rounds. Jamie's punches came all the way up from his toes to George's nose, so George's face looked splotchy-red and puffy by the end of the standard three rounds, which Jamie won easily. After Jamie left Appleby, he won the University of British Columbia boxing title as a freshman — no mean feat. I never went near him in the ring.

So, George was out for revenge on the Gairdners. He was determined to pummel me, and I went to him as a sheep to a slaughterhouse. I had fast hands but was a light hitter. I also had a lot of facial tics, among which were some pretty compulsive blinking fits when I got anxious. Like, eyes squeezing shut in a spasm that wouldn't quit.

But the first-round bell rang. Just try to imagine me in the ring, dancing around and blinking at the wrong moments, with big bulbous George flashing like a snapshot here, then there. Then there. Then here. Then … WHAM! Right off the bat, George uncorked a haymaker punch that seemed to arrive all by itself from the sky. But I was blinking and didn't see it coming. He connected so hard with my right ear I can still hear the ringing. I almost fell over and threw up. I figured the fight just ended with the first punch.

But I was ticked. My only strength was my punching speed, and feinting and ducking a lot. Try to fool the dumb SOB. George's haymakers kept flying over my head like I was ducking under a helicopter, punching away at his size-able gut. Get in, get out, go back in quickly. Sting like a bee.

George connected a few more times, but I was still standing, so I just kept up the lightning jabs to his reddening nose, belly, cheeks, anywhere there was an opening. Points were given just for landing a punch on the enemy, not for how hard you hit. So, rat-a-tat-tat, and pray for the three rounds to end soon. "Ding!" went the final bell. Phew. it's over. I never want to do this horrible sport again!

Then forward came Colonel Joyce, the referee. He was a school legend. The fairest and sternest of men who let an occasional twinkle escape his eye even when scolding us. I got strapped once at Appleby by all the prefects after friend Roger and I got caught smoking in the woods. But the Colonel was the last teacher who ever strapped me, for I can't remember what offence. He had a long black strap cut from thick linoleum of the kind they put over the cement floor in hockey arenas so players can walk to the ice on their skates. To look at it was to tremble a little. Six on the butt, and six on each hand. And you never let on it hurt (which it did, a lot), or the rest of the boys would cry coward. Survive that ordeal without showing any fear or pain and your male-ness stock would rise significantly.

We all respected Joyce. He had a badly scarred abdomen he rarely let us see, from when, in a deep ditch during WWII an enemy grenade plopped in the midst of his unwary men. He grabbed his helmet, held it outward on his belly, and jumped on the grenade. "Really, Sir? Wow!," and it blew him so high in the air he almost died. That story and the sight of those manly scars stuck with us. It was okay to get strapped by a real man.

Now, Colonel Joyce strode into the ring to deliver me from torment. I was bathed in relief the fight was finally over, not caring at all which of us might be declared the winner. With glazed eyes, a brief jolt of ammonia smelling salts drifting in my nostrils, I saw George's big sweaty, tired legs sticking out of his corner, and felt the happiness of a man escaping a death penalty. Head down, the Colonel stopped in the middle of the ring, pulled a score card from

Against The Tide

his pocket, and put me into shock, "Ladies and Gentlemen, it's a tie. *There will be one more round.*"

OMG. What horrible words. My heart fell onto the canvas. I was happy to give the bout to George. Anything but more blind flailing at his lumbering body. But I got up and somehow kept punching, until the longest three-minute round in history — long enough for me to become a permanent convert to the idea that time is relative — was finally over. The bell of salvation rang at last.

The grim Colonel strode into the middle of the ring once again. Fiddled with his score card. And for some reason I will never figure out, declared me the winner.

Dr. Bell's ambitious plan for the reformation of my character was foiled. This time.

I never boxed again after that, except once for a few minutes many years later at Stanford University when my then very new, but only true friend at Stanford, Lowell Cohn, with whom in my eighties I am still close friends, and who knew a lot more about the history of boxing than I did, walked with me past a boxing ring at the gym, and made the mistake of challenging me to a little fight. Lowell was not George, but he talked a pretty good fight, and I was wondering if this dude from Brooklyn had maybe learned some good moves in the streets. So, we got into it.

Sting like a bee. Lowell's nose got red fast, and he started laughing, and talking like a drunk boxer, "Hey. You Cheatin'. You boxed before? You never friggin' told me! No fair! No fair!"

We chuckled, arm in arm all the way out of the gym into the bright California sun.

At any rate, back at Appleby, spring came, and I asked to see Dr. Bell to tell him I would decline to contest the *Victor Ludorum* again because I had received special track coaching the summer before. So, I had an unfair advantage. And anyway, if I tried again and managed to win ("Sir, I don't mean to say that I *expect* to win …"), I did think it might be a little greedy. Let others win now, seemed like the right thing to say. At one stroke I could appear generous and avoid the chance of losing.

The fall prior I had been so disappointed that first summer of real training with Coach Percival that when I got back to school, I was determined never to train like that again. Way too hard. So, nuts to track and field. However, at the end of that summer, after a succession of very disappointing performances, I had finished very well in a 100-yard dash and won a silver medal in an event I had never tried before — the juvenile boys triple-jump — almost 44 feet (13.36m) in the Ontario Championships. I was surprised by this, and in a way disappointed, because although I never told the coach, I was planning to just hang on until summer was over, and then quit. But did it make sense to quit after doing so well? Was it just possible I had some talent I didn't know about that was beginning to show?

Moments after being excused from once more competing against my classmates, I was halfway down the hall, when I got flooded by a very new feeling. Struck by the possibility of independence. What about training alone? A kind of joy of self was born. I spun around and went right back to his office. Could I be excused from *all* school sports, and train alone for track and field? Dr. Bell peered at me over his tawny-framed glasses, sized the question up, waited an eternity, and said Yes. You go train. And good luck.

He had no idea, of course, and neither did I, that four years later, the kid he was staring at, sizing up, weighing that decision, would win a silver medal in the Decathlon at the Pan American Games in Brazil, setting a new Canadian and Commonwealth record, and in the fifth year from now would be the first Appleby boy ever to compete in the Olympic Games in Track and Field, once again setting a new Canadian and Commonwealth record while doing so. As for me, I had no idea that my sudden spin-around in the hallway was the beginning of what would turn out to be almost 15 years of what any normal person might have considered fanatical running. After what? For what? And why? I am still working on the answer.

He wasn't so surprised at my request. But the work of character-formation for one of his many prized boys wasn't done. He was the shepherd and had very precise and particular ideas for his sheep. As was the tendency in those days, "pride" found in a schoolboy — a "swelled head" — was considered among the chief of vices; a handicap that could warp and ruin the rest of a young life. "Self-esteem" — all the rage today — was considered deforming. Estimable actions were the thing, and esteem from others would naturally follow. You shouldn't esteem yourself. And so, a Master at Appleby, in addition to teaching, felt the duty of attitude-correction deeply. With the exception of subjects like math where a very rare perfect grade may be achieved, anything over 75% was hardly ever granted an Appleby boy, no matter how good the work, for that could mean self-ruin. For what good was a high grade, but a preening, flawed character? Dr. Bell wasn't finished. Years later, on The Queen Elizabeth II crossing the Atlantic Ocean from New York to Le Havre, France, I saw a movie, *The Prime of Miss Jean Brodie*, and I remember vividly the instructive moment when Miss Brodie was asked what she was doing with her teaching life? To which she replied: "I am in the business, of putting old heads on young shoulders." Those words made me think at once of Dr. Bell. That was his job.

That final year we had a weekly public speaking class meant to polish us

Against The Tide

up a little for life after Appleby. For "thinking on your feet." We took turns preparing and giving short speeches, and the culmination of the year came with the Public Speaking Contest. Dr. Bell alone would choose five finalists. This was a public event held before the whole upper school, all teachers, and a few hundred parents and guests from the Town of Oakville. Appleby would be on public display.

With my twitching and spasmodic blinking, I didn't like public speaking, or the thought of embarrassing myself in front of a large crowd. I still recall the awkwardness of sometimes having to prop my eyelids open with my thumbs to study a page, lids pulling unpredictably on my thumbs. But I also had a stutter as boy, which panicked me deeply. Was I to grow up sounding like a blinking fool who couldn't get his own words out sensibly? Getting rid of my stutter was an act of intuitive self-salvation that almost made me bow to God in thanks. I retreated into a frightened dark night of the soul and told myself I had better figure out how to stop it. And soon, or face doom and ridi-cule for life. During that night, a possible solution descended. I had noticed that as a soloist in the choir — surely one of the reasons I loved it — I never stuttered while singing. And why? The reason fell like manna from Heaven and lit me up: you don't stutter when you sing, because it is impossible to sing without taking a very deep breath. But when just speaking you don't have a deep breath. So, you stutter. So, try taking a deep breath before every sentence you speak. Yes! I practiced lying there on my bed in the dark. A deep breath. A complete sentence. Then again. It worked. The words flowed. Hard to believe. Really? Deep breath. A longer sentence … and it worked again. OMG. An inner peace descended, could this be true? The chains of this infirmity so easily shaken off?

But I still did too much spasmodic blinking when I got nervous. Deep breathing doesn't stop blinking much. So at all costs, throughout that last year, I was determined to sabotage the possibility of being chosen to speak in front of a public audience. I had no idea then, couldn't imagine, how much public speaking I would end up doing in my adult life.

In that last speaking class of the term, my own self-sabotaging efforts at an end, I was busy looking out the window at sprouting spring grass, hearing the sweet sound of happy birds echo in my drifting mind, soul-singing, lilting with them, dreaming of a final escape from the prison of class, while the ones who were trying to win a place in the speaking competition babbled on about one or another sleepy topic. Soon I would be free, free at last and out of school, forever! I deeply felt that no one must ever have felt such keen longing for escape from that overly ordered world.

Dr. Bell began reading out the names of the five finalists. We all knew who they were going to be, so nobody paid much attention. I was sitting near the back of the class, physically present, but mentally quite absent, when suddenly, after the first four names, out of the blue came a clean right hook to my face in Dr. Bell's commanding voice that decked me completely: "and … Bill Gairdner." I felt utter, reverberating shock.

While saying my name, without looking up, without looking at me, he gathered his papers and left the classroom, his black robe floating behind, sucked along by the vacuum of his firm striding exit. Voices stirred. Chair-legs scraped the floor. A pandemonium of boys eager for afternoon sports slipped away from me. Alone, with just the sweet smell of spring-earth melting.

So much blood had rushed to my head that in a kind of panic premonition of impending embarrassment and doom, my ears began to ring. A terrible, terrible mistake had been made. A miscalculation? Had he not paid attention to my inadequate speeches all term? Did I hear rightly? Roger was leaving up at the front but turned his head back just enough to roll his eyes at me, tossing off his words as to a pitiable burnt offering. "You're screwed, my friend."

I was alone on the cold red tiles of the hallway proceeding westward to the sanctum sanatorium of Dr. Bell's office. Only fools enter, where angels fear to tread. He was a man who knew what he thought, and why he thought it, and said so unerringly and impressively. A grounded man, rich in bias and prejudice, not in the narrow modern sense that he sought to offend, but in the traditional sense that he knew what he stood for. A man, he felt, ought to be biased in favour of what is good, and against what is bad. And a man without prejudice, in the sense of knowing what he thinks about things most serious, and able vigorously to defend them, is rudderless, without thoughts at all. A weakling.

And he knew, too, in contrast to the modern gospel, that a man's personal preferences, or "rights", were utterly secondary to the lifelong job of grasping the truth. In other words, and paradoxically, he gave the sense of being planted deeply in the soil of a rich personal life, precisely because he made personal preferences secondary. On his office wall was a small framed ceramic tile, with Latin wording. Translated, from memory:

*He who does, cannot*

*He who can, does not*

*He who will, knows not*

*He who knows, will not*

*And thus, the world runs badly.*

*Against The Tide*

I had seen this bit of ancient truth two years prior during a Headmaster scolding, and it sank in deeply. You don't mess with a man who has that sort of thing on his wall, in Latin.

Nevertheless, I found myself proceeding, in a kind of sleepwalking, metronomic way, westward. No secretary present today. Knocking robotically on his heavy office door.

"Come in." I searched that tone for anything that might indicate the tiger had no teeth today. But he showed no surprise. He knew why I came, and just stared right through me (like: C'mon, young man. Give it your best shot). So, I figured I would stop him by exposing his own lie.

"Sir. *I* know. And *you* know. I was *not* one of the best speakers in that class." And he did know. But the eloquence of Cicero could not have moved him. I wasn't seeing Dr. Bell. Before me was raw power.

Without missing a beat came his final answer.

"So, now's your chance."

I left very angry, still looking for a way out. I could get sick? Lots of boys faked illness to get a day or two off, especially the sucky ones who hated sports. Take a holiday resting up in the school infirmary. Fake a terrible headache. Moan a lot. Look incredibly sleepy. Vomit. And after the nurse leaves, having stuck the thermometer in your mouth, hold it to the hot radiator for a while, just enough so the temperature goes into pneumonia zone. This was a kind of secret that always worked until one day a really stupid boy got a little too aggressive. The thermometer went to 110F and shattered. Oops!

But I didn't want to fake sick. I wanted to punish Dr. Bell for fibbing to the whole class. It was a dirty trick; the employ of raw power he was certain I could not escape. Using his authority to crush my prideful self and embarrass me publicly, to boot. Take me down a peg. Why did I deserve this? I went to bed thinking about what he said: "Now's your chance."

So would it be a victory of sorts to somehow make him eat his words? Slowly, the thrill of the notion of trying to win, brought a smile to my lips in the dark of night, and it tickled me through and through. Yes. Screw him. Turn despair into victory. But what could I possibly speak about? What would interest the audience? A dreadful blank. How was I supposed to read 300 minds in advance? The question made me feel hollow. So what about changing the question? What would it interest *me* to speak about?

I already knew that the best speaker in the class had chosen to talk about (wait for it): cotton farming in colonial America. Really? That put me to sleep just wondering how I was going to sit through such a speech. When suddenly, my mind turned to Coach for salvation and the right topic popped into my head. I would talk about how every single person in the audience, if they wanted, could change their own lives for the better with something they had certainly never heard of before that Coach called "fitness."

Sleep came with a smile, and that Saturday morning I asked permission to take a bus to Toronto to pick up a bunch of booklets Lloyd had written with titles like *Fitness for the Family*, *Relaxation Is Easy*, and *Fitness for Children*. Even though trained by him, I had only a vague idea what "fitness" was, myself. This was spring of 1959, and except for the subject of biology, no one had ever heard that word as applied to human beings in daily life. To be "healthy" meant to be free of disease. But fitness? I knew it had a lot to do with how to get stronger, more energetic, at least as compared to your old self. But frankly (and I think this strong feeling arose in me because I had escaped from a sickly childhood, and never, ever wanted to go back), I saw it also a way to become … *better* than other sluggish, fat, lazy, or just plain out of shape people. I liked that promise, that secret-weapon possibility, though it was not something to speak about in public. Canadians don't much like someone being better than them in anything, and if they see it, they react by shutting up. So … it would be my job to tell people what "fitness" could mean for them; how they could shed their old selves and change for the better (and like themselves better). Powerful stuff.

Coach was already becoming well-known in a post-war society of plenty, where there was growing obesity, heart disease, and an emerging awareness of, well, unfitness; of what came to be called "lifestyle diseases." A few years after this day, Coach caused a national ruckus in Canada by publishing an article in *The Toronto Star* making a claim that became almost too public:

"*A 60-year-old Swede is fitter than a 30-year-old Canadian.*" That seemed almost an unpatriotic, anti-Canadian thing for him to say. But was it true? He had a knack for attracting publicity, but he also had a 60-year-old Swedish neighbour. So, he called all the national newspapers and told them he was going to fitness-test the Swede and compare the result to the fitness of 30-year-old Canadians. Sure enough, the Swede was a lot fitter, and a kind of national shame ensued. At any rate, he was the right man for this speech.

Pumped with the fitness idea, I told our English teacher "Skin" Dewar, who knew about Lloyd, of my plan, and he let me go to Toronto on the bus. He was the teacher who started my love of literature, and I felt grateful. There is a little poem I wrote at 11 years of age that he put in the school yearbook — without asking me. It made me feel a bit girly, and I got teased a lot.

A little older, when he introduced us to the evocative moods of the lonely and windy moors of Egdon Heath in Thomas Hardy's novel *The Return of the Native*, the first scene made me swoon: Clym Yeobright, leading his wife and children in a mule-cart over the dark moor along a muddy trail under a forbidding sky. I think now this is one of the very great set-pieces of descriptive prose in the English language, and I was amazed by it. Hardy had made his characters seems like a natural growth of the land itself, not just in it, but of it, and the realization that words alone, black marks on a white page, could so move the heart? I wanted to do that someday. To be a writer. Soon I was writing bits of poetry that I showed to no one — well, later on, maybe to a girl or two, if we ever encountered girls — for fear of being teased, at a time when my classmates were getting excited about noisy car-mufflers and horsepower.

Mr. Dewar knew Percival's "Hockey Handbook," and that he was now my track coach. So, he went to bat for me. I think he wanted to meet Lloyd himself. He had played amateur hockey for Canada on a European Tour in what we thought was the Dark Ages. But he notched up very high in our hero-hungry imaginations when he told us that during the second period of a game against Germany — long before anyone was wearing helmets (we didn't wear them either) — he got a deep skate-slash across his face and was taken off the ice. But after they closed him up with 27 stitches he insisted on going back to finish the game and scored the winning goal for Canada. He was a lot more than a teacher to us. It always struck me as odd to watch his big meaty fingers lovingly turn the pages of the novels and poems he felt so deeply about.

At Glen Road, after telling him why I came, Coach showed me a ring he had designed as an award for his very best athletes. "Someday," he said, in a challenging way, "you might earn one of these. You just have to really believe what it says."

It said, "*By Courage To The Utmost.*"

Back at Appleby, I hid the booklets, only bringing them out to study and make speech notes when alone in my room. Skin Dewar would knock on my door some nights to ask with the grin of the complicit, "How is it going?" But I wasn't telling anyone else. No sir. I was still too nervous to speak off-the-cuff from just a few notes, so I wrote, and rewrote my entire speech. We were allowed notes, but were not allowed to read our speeches, so I was going to have to memorize the whole darn thing well enough it would seem spontaneous. But how? On whom, and where could I practice out loud? There was no one to practice on if it were to be kept a secret.

Then came another unexpected event.

Every spring morning before breakfast we had an hour of Cadet drilling, marching, rifle practice, and other such man-making drills. Sometimes, on Battle-Drill days we got to fire a lot of dummy, but very loud, bullets from our army-issue .303 rifles, and from real, tripod-mounted Bren Mark II Machine Guns, at a wave of fellow student "enemies" screaming battle cries as they charged at us across a football field set up with fake barbed wire, hay bales, and other such devices meant to make us feel this was the Battle of the Bulge.

When the human wave reached us, we had to rise up and engage in hand-to-hand, ju-jitsu style fake combat, flip each other around, and make a lot of terrifying cries and stabbing noises to indicate the pleasure of killing — or the agony of dying. It wasn't too difficult to imagine, because most of our fathers lucky enough to survive the recent War had actually done that sort of thing. All taken very seriously.

The Commanding 13 (CO) of our Cadet Corps was by tradition chosen from the Grade Thirteen class by a wonderfully gruff Irish gym (and boxing) teacher named Sargent Major Baillie, or "Sarge" as we affectionately but very respectfully knew him. At a gnarly 5 foot 6, always gruff, but always with a

*Against The Tide*

twinkle, he seemed like some antediluvian crustacean with steel-wool hair, that had just come out of the ground, a presence like no other.

Early that spring, just after the snow melted, Sarge ordered — he didn't know the word "ask" — a handful of us to show up one morning outside the chapel overlooking a large grassy space where we used to run around, wrestle, and walk on our hands at recess. If you couldn't walk on your hands by a certain age, you were a suck. He walked smartly more than halfway to the far end of the field, silver tip of his military baton bobbing under his arm, then he spun around, clicked his heels, and ordered us, one after the other, to issue a military command, as if to a whole company of soldiers, in the loudest voice we could manage. Stand up straight. Shoulders back. Take a very deep breath in anticipation of a very long-drawn-out command. And just do it:

COMPANY! ... PRESENT! ... ARMS!

Maybe it was years in the choir that did it. I don't know. I will never know. But I ended up giving the loudest, most "projected" command of all. That's what he wanted. When men need command, they need a commanding voice. Why, I swear I could feel the windows of the building behind him rattling as I let out my cry. The loudness surprised me. My troops trembled; leaves fell in awe from the trees. Veins popped on my neck with the force, and legs shook a little. But that was it.

Sarge was about to break a very long school tradition. He dismissed the other four boys and told me I would now serve as (not *be*, but *serve* as) Commanding Officer of the Appleby College Cadet Corps. Really? He was putting me in command of our four platoons of Cadets, and of Platoon officers older than me, which included all the prefects of the school. So, I felt very honoured, but a little strange. And they felt more than strange taking orders from their junior. But I didn't fight it. And they didn't fight it. And I liked it. A lot. On Parade day, with a General from Ottawa who had come as our Inspecting Officer, I got to march beside a real General holding my ceremonial gleaming silver sword, as we inspected the troops, to bark commands, and watch them all obey.

At any rate, this digression was to say that our battlefield had an embankment on one side for spectators to watch football games and other sports. And that is where I would go every morning before drilling to practice my speech, a place where all alone I could imagine a throng of imaginary citizens, or soldiers, gathered to hear my every word, make a speech to them as if they were real people, and wait for their applause (unless I stammered or stuttered a little, or forgot a line, and had to look at my notes). I hated interrupting imagined applause.

Public Speaking night came, and we five contestants sat on the raised stage in a semi-circle behind the podium while Dr. Bell welcomed the audience. Rustling and chatter. Then dead silence. Lights lowered. I was the last to speak, which I didn't mind. Though that speech about cotton got me very worried I was going to have to wake the audience up before addressing them.

There was a lot of sweating and moist hands before my turn came. By courage to the utmost. I walked straight to the podium and just stared at the audience for a full minute. Then I told them what I was about to say was going to change their lives. Pretty audacious. But it got their attention. What could it be? Change me? Their rapt attention relaxed me immediately. I was in charge of that room. With breath control all fear of stuttering was gone and never returned to plague me again. To make a long story short, I told them that physical fitness meant much more than freedom from disease. It's about physical flourishing. About creating personal well-being, bodily strength, and endurance that would make ordinary life far more enjoyable.

They were especially persuaded to change their own lives by "The London Bus Study," which examined the health and fitness of 31,000 drivers and conductors in the London England public transport system who worked on double-decker buses all day long. Researchers found that the drivers, who sat all day ended up with all sorts of health problems and heart attacks as compared to the conductors, who climbed up and down the stairs all day, and

*Against The Tide*

so were very "fit." The two groups of men had entirely opposite health and fitness profiles, and even when the conductors did have, say, a heart attack, they tended to survive it well instead of dying, as had so many of the drivers.

The panel voted, and I think Dr. Bell got a little drowned out when he declared to the audience that I was the winner of the Appleby College Public Speaking Contest. I barely heard him, because so many got right to their feet and came forward to ask questions: Where did you get this information? Where can I get those booklets? Do I need to buy some weights? They really did want to change their lives. And I made them want that. Lloyd made them want that. This would the beginning of a circle of my life that I could not have known would close around me more than ten years later. Dr. Bell never spoke to me about this victory. Maybe he wanted me to fail, to learn humility. Who knows? He'd tried that before, but I do think he was quietly proud of the fact he had just put an old head on young shoulders.

When I turned 50, my new life as an author and public figure — or should I say public target? — began. It was a life I never imagined, and I ended up on hundreds of talk shows, had countless interviews, and spoke to many sizeable audiences. But after leaving Appleby — escaping is a better word — I never saw Dr. Bell again, but 35 years later I wrote a short essay in tribute to him and published it in *The Edmonton Journal*. Long before that, I heard he was dying.

He was confined to a bed in Oakville-Trafalgar Hospital. I was unaware at the time that it was Big Jim who began the fundraising to build that hospital, and basically drove it to completion. They were the best of friends. So the news he was in there made it seem like the Gairdners were looking after him. One day, near the end, a nurse came to Rusty's room to check on him. But he wasn't there. Just his twisted, still-warm bedsheets, and a mess of cables, tubes, and intravenous bags hanging forlorn over his absence. He had got disgusted and called his wife to take him home to die.

It was the end of an era.

## THE USSR VS. USA TRACK MEET, PHILADELPHIA, 1959

The summer of 1959, mandatory high schooling honourably left behind, I could hold my head up, with a sense of relief at a sentence well served. But I had no plans to continue formal learning. Most of my friends' parents did not go to university unless they felt called to a profession such as medicine or engineering. So, there was no huge social pressure to go to university. Mr. Fell, one of our teachers, left Appleby to "get his Ph.D." That sounded like getting a disease, and we felt immediately sorry for him as we figured he was entering a monastery and would have no sex life. For many of that generation, the war, or marriage (or their love children, as in the case of my Mom and Dad) took sudden command of their lives.

But I had no idea what would be next. Nothing was taking sudden command of me. Part of the problem was I had a bewildering freedom of choice. But I needed pocket money, so I worked at the local Thornhill Ladies Golf Club by day, swishing heavy dew off the greens at sunrise with a long thin bamboo pole, then raking what seemed like an endless succession of sand bunkers. In the evening, my sister Cassie and I trained for track at Don Mills Collegiate, in North York. Often, we would train into the darkness and Coach would pull his car closer, headlights shining on the hurdles. Our club was called "Don Mills Red Devils."

In 2018 I saw a BBC TV special in which various world class athletes — a cyclist, an Olympic sprinter, and so on — were asked to perform their specialty events in the conditions of yesteryear. The cyclist had to ride on a heavy multi-spoked steel-frame bike. No carbon fiber in sight. The sprinter was Andre de Grasse, a fabulous young talent who took home three medals from his first Olympics in 2016, running on a modern synthetic surface by Mondo, on which are poured millions of microscopic rubber beads that act like mini trampolines. But now, they made Andre run 100 metres in old shoes on a loose dirt track. I swear they filmed this at Don Mills Collegiate, my old track, because you could see a few weeds popping up not far from his fingers when he got into his starting block. Hello, old weeds. Long and short of this test was that he tried very hard, but ran way slower than his usual, and was a little shocked at how tough it was. After seeing this, I drove to the school and walked around that old track, where nothing has changed. Feet crunching slowly in the silence of time past.

One evening we learned a Russian-American Track Meet was going to be held in July, in Philadelphia. This was very big, international-brotherhood news. A lot of excitement was in the air over how the main players in the Cold War between Communism and the Free World were going to duke it out on the track instead of shooting each other. It would be war by proxy. This meet was going to show which system — capitalism or communism — was producing the best kind of people. Everyone suspected "the Commies" had been going into grade schools to drag out potential future Olympians and training them in special government camps. "The Ruskies" were jocks and jockettes trained at huge government expense, while athletes of the free world were all amateurs training mostly in citizen-run clubs like mine.

Come July, Cassie and I were on an overnight train with Lloyd to Philadelphia, city of brotherly love, to watch the biggest track meet of the year.

Against The Tide

Tension was high at Franklin Field, 54,000 spectators checking the scoreboard anxiously after every event. Who was ahead now? Americans had very few women in Track and Field at the time. There were a lot of opinions that girls were too delicate for certain events such as the triple jump. All that pounding would surely injure their baby-making organs. But the Soviets trained girls like men and had lots of them. Surprisingly pretty ones, too. No Babushkas, or farm girls. The Americans wanted to score only the men's events, but the Russians insisted on counting the women's events, too. So, all agreed the competition would be scored as two competitions, instead of one. Betting was the American men would win, and the Russian women would win in the women's competition. But which country would win overall?

Each country was allowed only two athletes per event, and unexpectedly, the men's 10,000-metre race (6.2 miles) which is usually the most boring of all, became the most dramatic race. It was run on a 90°F day with humidity so high it was hard to sit in the stands just to watch, let alone run. At about three laps from the finish of this 24-lap race, some of the runners were succumbing to heatstroke. The two Russians had been ahead most of the race, and Russian #1 won easily. But no sooner had the American Bob Soth overtaken Russian #2, than he started to wander from lane to lane. What's this?

Here is a one and a half minute, heart-rending clip from a Soviet film of Soth staggering and falling on the track: at the 1959 USA-USSR track & field meet.[4]

And here is an as-it-happened description of that moment by a writer from Sports Illustrated:

"Going into the 23rd lap, the American Bob Soth was running with the awful, slow movements of a man in a nightmare. He hit the turn with his feet splaying out helplessly and his body at a dangerous angle, and, for a few torturous moments, he ran in one spot, his legs moving jerkily and his arms threshing with the artificial movement of a marionette. Finally, some vagaries let him lurch forward, and he went on around the track in a slow, mechanical-doll stride. His face and body were dead white, and his eyes were staring, but the legs and arms kept moving until he reached the next turn, where he stepped on the curb, staggered crazily in a tight circle and fell. He climbed precariously to his feet and fell again, his head narrowly missing the cement curb."

All 54,000 people gasped in unison, and great pity arose in every heart as America's hopes collapsed. But then, Russian #2 suddenly started doing the same thing as Soth. Now it was a disconcerting, drunken Charlie Chaplin sort of race. Weaving, high-stepping, arms waving wildly, leaning back weirdly for half a lap. Suddenly, the Russian, face twisted, foaming at the mouth, fell just a yard short of the finish line.

So now there arose a strange combination of excitement at this new opportunity for America, mixed with pity for the fallen Russian, who seemed to be out cold. Would he get up? *Could* he get up? A concerned official walked over to help, but a stern voice from the loudspeaker filled the stadium: "Don't touch him. He'll get disqualified!" *At which all eyes went to* American #2, the diminutive Max Truex, who saw his opportunity and sprang to life, gaining quickly on the fallen Russian, who only had to get up and fall over the line. But could Max pass him before he did so? I remember vividly a very stout woman who jumped to her feet beside me and began yelling at the officials, veins popping from her neck, apoplectic over the fallen Russian: "Pick him up! Pick him up, ya bums! Help him, fer Gawd's sake!"

She got drowned out as Truex overtook the fallen Russian and crossed the line for second place to great cheers. But suddenly an official ran over and told Max: "*You miscounted the laps. You will have to run another.*" What? The crowd's mood fell like a stone again, as poor exhausted Max got back on the track to run his extra lap for third place. Then, just as he began that extra lap, Russian #2 got up and fell over the finish line for second place. In a flurry of protests, it turned out the miscount of laps was itself a miscount. So, Max should have got second place. But the Russians never agreed to the recalculation — there was a mini-Cold War right there at the track — so it was settled diplomatically by the Americans relenting, because they were already winning the men's points competition.

At the end of the day, the American men won 127-108, but the Russian women won 67-40. So the Ruskies won overall, 175-167, and went home feeling like proud products of a superior political system. On combined points, over the next 20 years, they won 16 of the total of 20 outdoor meets held between these two track powers before the USSR and its "perfect system" collapsed utterly, in 1989. The American men won 13 times, and the women just once. Since that time, every country in the free world except America has adopted a system of significant government support for Olympic sport, which is now an armature of the state.

The man who won the decathlon in this meet was the world record-holder Vasily Kusnetzov, one of my boyhood heroes. If anyone had told young Billy sitting in the stands watching him now, that he would be meeting Vasily personally on the track at the Tokyo Olympics five years later, running against him in the 400 metres at the end of the first day of the Olympic Decathlon … I would have said that was plainly a joke and ridiculous.

There were two more memorable events in Philadelphia. One was having

Against The Tide

breakfast with a grisly Russian war vet, and another was my brief encounter with a gorgeous hooker. Sitting in a diner booth the next morning with Lloyd and Cassie over our bacon and eggs, a hawk-eyed, eagle-nosed Russian official sat down across from us, two small, cheap-looking military medals jingling over his jacket pocket. He spoke no English, so we spoke with our eyes. He ate hash browns and toast quickly, leaving his two eggs until last. Then, rubbing his hands together as if preparing for some public performance he picked up his knife and cut very close circles around each yellow yolk with surgical precision. Pulling the whites carefully away with his fork, he ate them first. Then, pausing in a kind of reverent silence he leaned over as if examining radioactive material, slipped his fork gingerly under one of the yokes, and popped it whole carefully into his mouth. He repeated that manoeuvre just as carefully with the second yolk, finishing with just a hint of a smile. Then, he sat bolt upright. Reporting for duty. Fixed us momentarily in a satisfied stare that was prolonged beyond any significance we could see in what he had just done and walked away.

There were traces of yellow yolk on my own plate that I had tried to scrape up completely with an edge of toast, but tiny streaks of yellow could still be seen, and when he left, I felt a tinge of scorn. A war friend of my dad's had told us stories of how starving Soviet survivors of the siege of Stalingrad had to eat rotting dead horses, dogs, and cats to survive. The yolk moment was a harbinger of what any life might be, and I have felt a little shot of pain ever since whenever throwing food away.

That afternoon was sunny and beautiful. I was lounging on a couch beside Lloyd in the lobby of the Warwick Hotel where we and the Russian and American teams and coaches were staying. Lloyd was in his element chatting up another coach, when a hooker came in who was likely cruising for super-jock customers. Planning to drop her thunderbolt sex appeal on an American track star, perhaps? Or maybe on a Russian Prince who might carry her off for a life of exotic delights? Who knows? But she had an impact on me, that's for sure. In all modesty, I had a very trim and muscular young body, ripe for plucking in my tight T-shirt, mellow in my manly mood, daydreaming away in the sunny bustle of that lovely afternoon ….

She appeared suddenly as a dark silhouette in the brightness of the hotel doorway. Well, well. That got everyone's attention. She sported a very sculpted body with a teasing insouciance, dressed in just enough to prevent arrest for indecency. And I got immediately alarmed because she was staring at me and made a beeline for our couch, materializing, so to speak, from her own silhouette with all the warm, voluptuous contours inexperienced young men imagine, but hardly ever see up close. Advancing with purpose, as if about to run me down, she stopped abruptly at my knees, placed her hands a bit too high on my thighs, and leaned in as if to kiss me, or to whisper something deliciously secret, at which I recoiled a little, for she announced loud enough for Lloyd and his new Russian friend to hear — actually, loud enough, it seemed to this very embarrassed young man, for the whole world to hear:

"You're beautiful. I want to take you home!"

Her fingernails were gripping my thighs very tightly, a private signal, perhaps, waiting for my response.

Twisted in confusion, I felt immediate heat on my face. She had already got everyone's attention, and the whole lobby was staring, waiting to see what this young man would do. She certainly got their attention, and now, I had to act. I just knew I was going to look like such a kid. It was no use.

I looked at Lloyd. And asked my stupid question.

"What am I supposed to do?" My virgin naivete was exposed with every pounding beat of my heart.

And the uncertainty ("Beautiful"? Men are not beautiful. What did she mean?). The lost opportunity for someone — certainly not me — flashed through my mind. It ended as quickly as it began. She looked at Lloyd, as if for permission to take me away; he looked at her as if he wished it were him, instead. When she saw that, she slipped away. A silhouette in some other doorway.

I survived, but never forgot this unsolicited encounter with the essence of femaleness on the make. The whole armory of seductive artifice by way of careful make-up, perfume, the glinting, lightly clanging jewellery swinging against my nose; her breath a mix of alcohol and Spearmint chewing gum. My first glimpse deep into an adult sexual underworld stripped of camouflage and pretense of coyness.

## RUNNING TO NOWHERE

I don't think I could have imagined a more purposeless, goal-less, visionless escape from high school into manhood than myself as I was about to head off for a year at McGill University — one of the only two universities in Canada at the time you could enter from Grade 12. Visionless was not passionless, however. In fact a high degree of aimless passion made my lack of vision all the more troubling. Students at Appleby like Tony Little (well-named, as he was in fact very short) annoyed and confused me. He had an age-inappropriate confidence in his own intelligence and future. "I'm going to be a lawyer," he announced one day, age 15, with a self-congratulatory smirk. His confidence struck me as having marinated too long in a poverty of imagination. One day

Against The Tide

he trotted out a famous phrase from Descartes — "*cogito ergo sum*" — and smirked that he knew what it meant, but we obviously didn't. He was right. But a lawyer? Wasn't he a little crazy to know as little about life as any of us, yet write off all other possibilities, condemning himself years in advance to reading turgid, soul-destroying legal language, day after day? That would not be like reading Shakespeare — or Descartes — but I think that's exactly what he ended up doing … for more than 50 years.

I left Appleby in a hurry one day in the spring of 1959, ungraciously failing to thank any of my teachers, or to say goodbye to classmates who would be returning for Grade 13 that fall, when I would be at university. When I got home, I immediately burned all my books except *Ancient History*, by Professor Charles Robinson Jr., of Brown University. It was our only scholarly book, and a favourite I still read, taught by Mr. Merritt, whose young child, as mentioned, had accidentally hanged himself when climbing that playpen fence. To sing Mozart's *Ave Verum* at that little child's funeral, while barely holding back tears through which I could see a watery image of that tiny coffin, was one of the saddest things I have ever done in my life, and it bonded me to Mr. Merritt. And that's what he was letting me know that afternoon with his secret coaching when I tore past him, my soul on fire, during that life-changing cross-country race at Appleby.

That history book is on my lap now, and I leaf through it to see once again what Robinson said about Julius Caesar, the man a recent biographer called the "Colossus of History." Julius Caesar was my favorite Shakespearian play in high school, too. I loved the amazing speeches of Brutus and Antony, and how they each worked the crowd to support their version of justice. My Mom took me to see Marlon Brando playing Antony when I was about 13, and I have never forgotten watching him, another hero, as he stood over Caesar's crumpled body, then cried out, in such amazing lines, *"Oh pardon me, thou bleeding piece of earth, that I am meek and gentle with these butchers!"*

Brando's voice, so passionately underplayed it felt like a shout, almost violently projected the word "butchers", so that you just knew the assassins were doomed. Carrying Caesar's limp, toga-draped form outside to the Senate steps for the crowd to see, and then working up their emotions, was masterful. It was a thrilling lesson in how just the right words, words alone, at the right time, in the right way, serve the speaker as a kind of net to cast over the crowd and capture them. Just so, Caesar/Brando became my hero. And just so, what Shakespeare did with that scene was in part why I wanted to be a writer someday. To own the power of words.

Caesar is too often portrayed by weakling historians as a cruel dictator. But I have read lots about him since, and by him, including his *Commentarii de Bello Gallico*, on the long war against Gaul (yes, in Latin, twice, with the help of an interlinear translation) — the war that made France — and most of Europe in fact — what it is today. Having explained the chaos, robbery, and depression into which Rome sank after this murder, Robinson wrote: "It would be idle to charge Caesar ... whose capacity was boundless and whose personality so warm that it won the passionate devotion of his followers, with having destroyed the freedom of the ancient Republic."

As High School evaporated behind me, and training began once again with Coach, I examined my own life-ambition, and came up with ... nothing. Again. Nothing whatsoever. Very not Caesar. Young men got lots of pressure in those days, envisioned as we were either as good future providers — or complete failures. But I was born with a silver spoon of sorts in my mouth, in a family that had a powerful and impressive, self-made millionaire grandfather-patriarch, whose business shadow extended across Canada with Gairdner & Company, and whose implicit expectations for success in life hovered over us all. In Big Jim, it was the "Big" that daunted, sometimes as direct bullying. A few years along from the rut I was now in, almost finished my undergraduate university term and seated with the entire clan at a Christmas Dinner at his home in Oakville, he suddenly started to shout in a booming voice, and the room fell silent. He was a few tables away, but I could see his ruddy, Dewar's Scotch-primed cheeks, and flashing eyes, party-glazed by whatever was drifting through his mind. It was me he picked for his target that night.

"What the hell are you doing wasting your time at university? I never met a successful man who went to university!"

A deep, tangible silence fell upon the room.

All eyes on me. Waiting. How was 21-year-old Bill going to respond? But I didn't. I just stared right back at him, emotionless, to let him know I wasn't afraid (he was one of those people of natural command who could easily terrify). Why me? On this otherwise happy night? Silence came over me as naturally as did the assault to him. I had to rise above, and the silence of that room was the best reply. It was a full and fair answer, too. Because he stopped staring and retreated a little embarrassed into his drinking and table conversation as two of my aunts calmed him.

To be fair, he had missed his dream of medical school and university altogether, along with his Olympic dream, when he went off to kill Germans from the filthy, germ-infested, muddy trenches of Belgium. And then he came home to a victorious, but broke and broken country and became a self-made millionaire (according to *Who's Who*, he once made the top 20 in Canada). And I had great respect for that, and it was true that he was a more of "a man" than a lot of the profs I had, who seemed always to have immature faces, no

Against The Tide

matter how old they were. By "successful," he was comparing his risk-taking entrepreneur friends with professors and other government employees who as far as he was concerned were hiding from the real fight and sucking the public teat. There wasn't much of a counter argument to that point, though two years later I got a surprise letter from him while living in Tokyo, and I wrote back to give him my full reply to the remark he made that evening.

But at this time, on long lonely walks in the forest, in expectation the answer to my future worries would fall naturally from the sky if I could only beseech the gods with sufficient sincerity and ardour ... I still heard only silence. So, in some frustration, I decided that if anyone asked (and plenty of adults did): "What are you going to do with your life?" (now, the heart rate would shoot up to max), I would no longer say "I have no idea," which was pretty lame. And I was getting too old for such an embarrassing reply.

But I really didn't want to seem empty-headed with respect to my future (which I was). So, after far too much self-torment and soul-searching, I plagiarized the YMCA motto about Mind, Body, and Spirit. It seemed a pretty good stop-gap position. Leaning rather lightly on the word "Spirit," I could now reply with a tone of some confidence: "I want to prepare my mind, body, and spirit as well as I can for now. And when the best course for me becomes apparent, I will be more than ready for the challenge." At least that stopped them asking twice.

Secretly, however (especially for someone who began training so late in his youth), I was thinking mostly about what would have struck anyone as an inflated — or, given my very ordinary talent, even foolish — ambition: a future Olympic Games. Trying to get a little smarter while waiting for the doors of opportunity to open seemed like good insurance. As for the spirit? Well ... I spent eight years super-saturated with Christianity, especially when singing a lot of its gorgeous, and still unforgettable music. But for some reason I still can't explain, the religion itself never took with me. We didn't have any Wise Men dressed in Oriental finery riding camels where I lived. And the idea that God had a human son in a pile of hay with a woman he never touched, just didn't compute. He missed the good part (something I could think, but not ever say out loud).

Like everyone else I lived more or less, imperfectly, by the Ten Commandments. But the business of drinking the blood and eating the flesh of God — even if that was "just a symbol" as we Protestants were told (unlike those rabid Catholics who, to my mind, were closer than Anglicans to actual cannibalism) — it all made me shiver. With one exception. It was *really* wine we got to sip at Communion. And if you could forget the blood thing and just swallow it, that part was okay. An illegal taste of alcohol before the age of consent under the guise of sincere worship felt like we were doing something dangerous under the guise of humility. I was no atheist, however. That came a bit later. In fact, there were transcendent moments in chapel, usually when singing a moving solo, that I asked myself what it would be like to be a Minister? Father William had an okay ring.

Summer over, very fit and improving but with still-mediocre performances under my belt in the big pond of athletic reality — where I was a very small frog — I packed a suitcase and got on the bus for an academic year at McGill University. It was a very rainy September day. I felt like I was running away from something or other — and I was. From the penury and boredom of another year of high school. But it got off to a really bad start. Stuffed into a Montreal taxi in pouring rain with three other students, the driver failed to secure my bag properly on the roof and at about 60 miles an hour it came loose in the rain. You could hear it sliding off the roof and splattering all over the road behind us. Shouts! Brakes! In the rear window we saw him scooping soaked clothing into my broken suitcase and roping the whole mess back onto the roof.

Once settled on the third floor of a rooming house at 3431 Drummond Street, I showed up for the inaugural President's Speech to about 500 First-Year hopefuls. I say hopefuls, because in those days almost anyone with half-decent grades could get into a good university. But only a third ever graduated. I was anxious immediately, because … imagine not passing the year? Well, quiet descended upon the auditorium when the President spoke:

"Look at the man on your left." We did.

"Look at the man on your right." We did.

"Two of you won't be here next year." Words delivered with a hangman's smile.

It was not exactly a cheering pep talk about how we would be going forth to change the world for the better. The university was plainly intent on dumping a lot of us.

Suitably anxious, we trudged to the gymnasium to register for what the university had decided we needed to study. You couldn't graduate from McGill back then without two years of mandatory French and Latin. By a fortuitous mistake on the part of my upper-class advisor I got registered for a one-year condensed course in both. Despite having endured five years of Latin at Appleby, struggling with the Ablative Absolute, and the Passive Periphrastic (don't ask), I went into shock at McGill when, on the first day of class two students shot their hands up and proceeded to converse easily, in fluent Latin, with the professor, while I hung my head.

Against The Tide

The professor was a kind man and a former college wrestler with cauli-flower ears, who had a pleasant, but very beat-up face that made him look like a survivor of the Spartacus slave revolt. But I ended up being very grateful to him. He learned I was an aspiring Olympian, lit right up just to talk with another athlete, and went soft on me for grades because I asked him a lot of questions about wrestling.

My other required courses were English Literature, and Finite Mathematics, and my one elective was Geomorphology and Climatology, the latter subject taught by the renowned climatologist F.K. Hare. Somewhere along the way we had to learn a little neuroscience, too. Not sure why. But I remember becoming engrossed in a famous textbook about neurons, axons, dendrites, synapses, and all that, by Donald O. Hebb, a renowned McGill University Professor. He worked with Wilder Penfield, whom I learned much later was famous for theories of "mind," and for audaciously asking whether or not there is a scientific basis for the concept of "the soul"? Such questions fasci-nated me then, and still do, though I had no experience at the time of what is today called "philosophy of mind," or (remembering Tony Little's braggadocio quote), the real significance (or perhaps insignificance) of what Descartes had done in splitting up all reality into mind and matter, which he failed — as has everyone else who has ever tried — to reunite.

My classes settled, I spent the academic year struggling with Latin; got through French; and (surprising to me) sailed through finite mathematics; loved the earth sciences and ended up with a high grade in Geomorphology. Our English teacher was a frustrated Oxford Brit impatient with dumb responses from Canadian students untuned, as he let us know he uniquely was, to the subtleties of English literature. Every time a student answered a question he would sigh deeply.

But his gift, to me at least, was assigning T.S., Eliot's bewildering but, for the unlearned, intoxicating poem "The Waste Land" — a plain-speaking, symbolic send-up of modern times in mobilizing free verse, backed up by esoteric endnotes I spent hours, with books all over my bed, trying to decipher. This, I had never done of my free will in all high school. I was getting excited and a little invested in real learning. Something I wanted, not something I had to do.

It began:

> *April is the cruellest month, breeding,*
> *Lilacs out of the dead land, mixing*
> *Memory and desire, stirring,*
> *Dull roots with spring rain.*

Eliot was contrasting his dark vision of a spent modernity with the full and flush celebration of a bountiful and lovely springtime in Chaucer's *Canterbury Tales*, which we had been made to read first, and which (in a circumstance wholly unimaginable to me then) I would one day study very closely at Stanford University under Professor Dell Kolve, one of the world's great Chaucer Scholars. What an oft so happenstance adventure any life is going to be. Each of us lives out his own Canterbury Tale.

Once getting what Eliot was doing, we were instructed to think deeply about the contrast of visions. Well, there was really no deep thinking in me then. I didn't know enough. But lots of deep feeling and wondering what deep thinking would feel like when it came, if ever.

So, I read "The Waste Land" over and over, trying to "Get it." Eliot was a devout Catholic, and closed his challenging hatchet-job on post-Christian "civilization" with three Sanskrit words from Hindu religion that I haven't seen since, but still remember: *Datta, Dhayadvam, Damyata.*

It was a healing nostrum for the West. "Give. Be Compassionate. Control Thyself."

I thought I should memorize that. Maybe even try following it? Maybe I could tuck it under my casual commitment to "Spirit"?

But what about my body?

Not fast enough to be a top sprinter. Not big enough to be a good thrower. Not tall enough for the high jump, or high hurdles. Not enough endurance to be a top distance runner. Hmmm. Such realizations made me think often of just quitting. And why not? But Lloyd had said I was best suited for the decathlon ("Jack of all trades, master of none"). So, I went looking for the McGill track coach.

"What's your event, kid?"

He was an unathletic, disinterested, seemingly troubled and fidgety man with a small belly that popped out when he sat to talk. He couldn't look me in the eye when asking that question.

"Decathlon. I want to be a decathlon man."

"Ah, shit, boy. You're too goddamn small for that."

That was the first and last time I ever saw the McGill track coach.

It didn't matter much. McGill had only a mediocre sort of intramural track team anyway, and the track season halted end of October when they quit training entirely. But this was me, and I was serious. And clearly, I was on my own now, at a university which had no indoor track; a weight-room closed to all but the football team; no indoor jumps or hurdling set-up. No throwing cage. And … a bitter winter around the corner. It was a little daunting.

So, I bought a cheap set of used weights, left them in the hallway outside the

Against The Tide

room I shared with an engineering student, and lifted them to failure three or four times a week. Drummond street terminated with 100 steps that begin the climb toward Mount Royal and a street leading to the football stadium. I would grab my 16-pound shot and charge up those steps, as if defying the penalty of extra weight, and head for the stadium where I could practice putting the shot on some asphalt under the overhang. I had to arrange jumping and hurdling by myself, alone in the gym. For eight months. I was off to a poor start.

When the snow came, it really came. One of the only safe, relatively snow-less surfaces to run on was a plowed, less-busy street about ten at night, always being sure to wait for an interval between cars — then okay, now! go! — a few hundred yards until the next headlights loomed, shining from behind, then jump back over snowdrifts onto the snow-packed sidewalk for safety. Another option was to do repeat sprints on the long, snow-free asphalt strip under the overhang of the stadium.

All winter, several times a week I ran 15 x 100 metres under that concrete overhang, at my top speed, with minimal rest between. With no coach to push me, it was all a test of will: today, will it be resolve, self-deception, capitulation? I'm really tired. Enough for today. Why not stop at 13? Nope. Better do what you set out to do, or don't say you're gonna do it. At the end of each 100-metre run eastward, I would turn around to the line and sprint right back westward to where I had started, testing to see how little I could rest between each sprint, and still keep the speed up.

There was — still is — a huge, very old Christian cross dedicated to St. Jean Baptiste atop Mount Royal. First installed in 1643, this is the same Saint for whom the annual parade was held, and under the eye of which those two queer men had tried to pick my brother and I up in our Arctic summer. That's what likely ignited my lifelong queasiness around homosexual men. St. Jean was asleep and hadn't done much to stop them from trying to bugger two young boys. And to judge by the normalization of homosexuality in the West since, it's too late to wake him up. At any rate, that cross shone down upon me as an impassive lie-detector. It was the beacon and only witness of my determination — or failure of same — for that whole year, for I had only myself to cheat.

Socially, my year at university was a dead zero. I no sooner got to McGill than I broke up with Susie, my high-school sweetheart. Young, first love is indelibly sweet. But I discovered by fluke from a fellow student who had met her at French-immersion school that past summer, that she had betrayed my deepest affections. I wasn't going to get close to *that* sort of situation again. Mind you, after I posted her my perhaps overly vindictive letter full of the deepest moral rebuke I could muster, and walked back to my room, I wondered, notwithstanding the deep genuine love I had felt, if just as deep down I wanted to be free of attachments. That possibility made me feel a little guilty. To be free, would I have as easily betrayed her, had the opportunity presented itself? I don't know. It didn't.

The sixties sexual revolution and the age of the Pill had yet to arrive. So, there I was, in a sexual no-man's land. Except for meeting a rare cheap girl I didn't want to touch. If you are cooped up in a boys' boarding school too long, almost any friendly girl will seem gorgeous. But I didn't want my life to be trapped by love. So, I trapped myself, and kept my distance. What was the point of striving to meet a girl so far from home that with my still-germinating ambitions, I would have to leave?

McGill had a tough rule. If you failed any of your first-year courses, you had to repeat your entire year. I was heading for a failure in advanced Latin, but the teacher with the cauliflower ears took pity on me and my efforts. So he gave me a passing grade, and I was promoted to Second year. I was free now, and out of high school, so to speak. Paid my minimum dues to educational respectability. But I was adrift again. McGill had served its purpose, but there is no way I wanted to go back to *that*, and I had nowhere to go forward. Yet. Nowhere I could chip away at the propositions of that YMCA logo, until the light came.

After another summer of training with Lloyd, with mixed results but clearly improving (*citius/altius/fortius*), I asked Coach if he thought an American university with a good track program was a possibility? He had sent lots of athletes far better than me to the USA on track and field scholarships. Those arrangements usually meant you could get tuition free but would have to pay your own room and board. Dad was paying for those things anyway, so he would likely be fine with my going to the USA, right? What difference would it make to him where I was?

Lloyd sent me to chat with a Mr. Gord Eddols, a hockey athlete who had attended the University of Colorado (CU) in Boulder, Colorado. At the time, Canadians believed that American high schools, at least, were well below par. I didn't want to go somewhere to end up with a tainted university degree. I had no idea that America rightfully boasts some of the best universities in the world. But he said something that stuck: "If the university you attend has a good library, you have no excuse for not getting a good education."

That did it. I wrote to the CU track and field coach Mr. Frank Potts, listing my best performances in about six events (only "tweaking" a couple of them), and waited. Anxiously. I didn't feel too bad about the tweaking — well, it was fibbing, actually. But barely. I told myself it was a semantical thing between have done and will do. But I knew I was training my butt off in terrible wintery conditions and was stronger than ever. So, in all honesty (that phrase!), I knew

Against The Tide

with 100% certainty that the first moment I set foot on a decent track instead of slogging it out on the next-door golf course in a foot and a half of snow, with Aron, our dog, chasing rabbits behind me, I would do everything I told him I had already done. If not, I would die trying (so it wouldn't be an issue). At any rate, I generated a little private dishonesty-tension that only I would be able to dispel, because only I knew about it. My first race for Coach Potts was going to be about a lot more than running.

## WHERE GOD LIVES

Someone — perhaps more than one — has said: "to part, is to die a little," with respect to places or persons we deeply love. To die because some part of ourselves is cleaved and stays forever with what we leave behind.

Georgian Bay, the "30,000 Islands" — once called "the Sixth Great Lake," by daring Voyageurs — is a 120 x 50 mile bay on the East side of Lake Huron, peppered with whaleback granite rock formations billions of years old that rear from crystal-clear fresh waters, dive under, and reappear somewhere else. Most of them are topped by wind-bent, tortured pine trees with splayed, beseeching branches that moan in the wind. I first saw this beautiful, forlorn region at age eight, and it parked in my heart forever. There, we see such a contrast between that forlorn and violent raw nature and the delicacy of innumerable wind-bent pines struggling upward in branching plying for light and air, the smallest of them bonsai-like sproutings from tiny granite cracks.

Everyone has some place in their world they love most of all, and that's where God lives. For me, it's Georgian Bay. I am not fooled. I know this love is also deeply artificial. But it's deep, nonetheless. Artificial, because in temporary escape from the pressures and problems of modernity we thrill to imagine ourselves primitive, unencumbered — as we must have been in the first dawn of nature before civilization. I have always been aware that walking on those islands you can deliberately step where in billions of years no man has stepped before, a primal, unique human contact with the beginnings of this earth.

But it's very unlikely I could survive for long at Georgian Bay without civilization as my backup for food, cabin, and boat (and yes, a little beer and wine). To be stranded at a remote cottage by waves and wind so high you would be a fool to venture out, and not another soul in sight, is thrilling when all is well. But it's pure chill and panic if it's not. A child's broken leg? A rattlesnake bite? A dangerous fever in the night with no hope of getting help? You take your chances with the luxury of voluntarily primitivizing an otherwise very secure existence. But then ... danger illuminates beauty, as absence illuminates love.

This is also the place where I got my first shock of insight into the terrible power of alcoholism to grip the soul. At the age of 18 in the week before taking my dad to the Bell Clinic, a well-know addiction rehab clinic, for the first time, my brother and I and a helper were rebuilding the cottage we had bought from the estate of the artist and co-discoverer of Insulin, Dr. Frederick Banting. Dad, an excellent carpenter, and all-round fixer stayed at the Weis's cottage — owned by the family of his best friend, and my namesake, nearby where we were staying, to drink all by himself. Within five days he went through a bottle of gin a day and sang us raunchy Air Force songs at night. We badly wanted to wrestle him into the boat and take him home for treatment. But we knew he had to surrender first and ask for help. On the sixth day I went back to take him some lunch. He was sitting on the edge of his bed, half-naked and broken, head hanging in despair.

"Take me down."

"Okay Dad. We'll look after you."

But he had only one bottle of gin left, and we knew enough that we had to keep him drunk for four more hours or he would have an attack of *Delirium Tremens* in the car and try to crawl out the window. He could hardly walk, so I cradled the bottle carefully in my sweater under one arm and led him along the steep rocks down to the boat. The journey was starting. Maybe this was the beginning of healing? But suddenly I slipped on some damp lichen, and the bottle shot out from my arm, crashing on the rock, spraying gin, and glass all over the place. I cannot describe the feeling of doom that descended, and the hurt when my own Father looked at me with such anger in his eyes, and said,

"You son-of-a-bitch!" My father called me that. I was stunned.

"Dad. I'm sorry. I didn't mean to drop it.

I sat him on the rock, rushed to the main cabin, and broke in to see if the Weis's had any booze hidden away from winter trappers who regularly broke into cabins in those days. I found one bottle of rum, wrote a note of apology, and grabbed it, very tightly. That is the only bitter memory of Georgian Bay I have ever had. All the other memories are about love of the place.

Here is the first of three love poems I have written to Georgian Bay. The first was done in 1978 just after I ended my first marriage and moved out with the clothes on my back, leaving home and two lovely little girls behind, but for visiting them regularly, while trying to fix a badly failing business.

It's about a naked soul lying in a dark and windy star-splashed night, in the Banting cabin that we fixed up. The Banting cabin was fixed up from a state of abandon over the course of a year but was already the stuff of Canadian legend. Banting was co-winner, at 32 years of age, of the Nobel Prize for the

Against The Tide

discovery of Insulin. He used the cottage for duck hunting, fishing, and oil painting, of which he was a master, like some of his Group of Seven friends who enjoyed the place with him. We know for certain that J.E.H. MacDonald made many trips with Banting to this very place, as did A.J. Casson.

At any rate, this first poem was published in *Waves*, a York University poetry magazine, in 1978, in a rare little volume that includes a lot of nice artworks by the Indian artist Norval Morisseau, and so it's a keeper. Life is full of circles. Five pages after my poem is one by Giorgio di Cicco, a legendary Canadian poet whom I first met 15 years after my poem was published, at St. Mary's church — just a chapel, really — outside of Nobleton, Ontario, where he was the presiding Priest. A few years later he was appointed Poet Laureate of Toronto. So, while writing these words I thought to call him because we had not spoken for almost a year. No luck. No reply. Browsing for his name, I was shocked to see his obituary pop up. He collapsed of a stroke in December of 2019.

In addition to many great times together talking about poetry and life and God, my favourite memory is when I took di Cicco to hospital for laser surgery on his eyes. He was terrified. When the nurse came out with a blue hospital cover-up and told him to change right away, he dragged me into a change-cubicle with room for only one person. Like, this was a little too intimate for undressing. But I helped him undress to his undies. Then, he pulled a little silver box out of his jacket, took a communion wafer out, and ordered me: "Open your mouth."

"Me? ... Giorgio. I'm not a Catholic!" I was sensing some immanent damnation for lying, both for me and for him. "Never mind. Stick out your tongue." I did. He placed the wafer on my tongue, while looking at me in a way that suggested he was not convinced there was much chance of saving my soul, said a few words of Latin, then put the hospital gown on.

He was a complex and somewhat tormented man who once when we were debating what makes great art, said: "Great art uplifts the human spirit." That has been my standard for great art ever since (a dangerous thing to say when presenting readers with one of my own poems).

Looking back at the span of 70 years during which I have known and loved Georgian Bay, gives rise to such a flood of memories and attachments. Barefoot scrambling with siblings and childhood friends over hot rocks; diving into a favourite lagoon; or with goggles and flippers becoming pure water-sprites for a whole summer; spearing a really big pickerel; dropping a rock on an occasional rattlesnake, coiled, reared to strike, having already struck the fear of death into us. And on day trips up the red-rocked Pickerel River, or to the French River, or to the beautiful Bustards Islands, where Mom and Dad eventually built a new log-cabin cottage; or, high-cliff jumping from Devil's Doorway into the Bad River.

## Nightlost at Georgian Bay

*One of the darkest*
*whispers I hear,*
*is the restless wind,*
*that shakes us upright,*
*only to stare into our own clear waters,*
*or fall on rocks to shatter.*

*This is a land for pagans,*
*and the rightful ghosts of voyageurs.*
*I heard their paddles sighing,*
*in my sleepless night,*
*saw chanting fires,*
*felt their souls' beckon,*
*in the loon's mad cry —*
*knowing we were nightlost.*

*I cannot count the price of searching,*
*or the peace of finding,*
*so wind will never ask to blow,*
*nor tree to bend.*

*There is a secret company*
*of souls I love,*
*wordless, ancient, water-borne;*
*one of the voices of care,*
*that cannot be found*
*unless already there.*

Or swimming in Voyageur's Channel, where blue-black water empties from miles north of us, roiling, rushing past, washing over us as we cling to rocks; where we once saw our Dad in an iconic act spring in an arcing dive to save our buddy, 12-year old Rodney Mayor, from drowning. He had let go of his little rock, got caught by the tugging rapids, and swept away from us; then, pressed by the pressure of the flow against an inverse rock wall, the top of his blonde head began to sink slowly — a floating straw wig.

Against The Tide

Jamie and I froze: "Dad!"

The sun was blotted momentarily as his lithe body arched over our heads; an image suspended in memory still. Knifing into the fast black deadly flow, he was on that blonde wig in three powerful strokes just before it went under, grabbed it, pulling sputtering Rodney back up to life and at the same time he was pushing himself and our friend away from the suction of the wall, Rodney gulping sweet warm air with pale blue lips.

And in quieter moments. No one. Not for miles around. Hot from the sun and swimming naked in that cold, delicious forever water. To shiver a little, then to lie on the hot granite and feel the warmth of rock penetrate through and through. A special feeling of connection with some ultimate timeless reality that could not be simpler. Ever. Simple, still, mysterious, lying to warm ourselves in a hot curved groove of granite rock we kids called "God's Sofa."

At a very young age I had my first philosophical experience standing naked on one of those whaleback rocks staring down through five feet of clear water at a sandy white bottom, a quiet in my soul as the first day of creation. A feeling arose that day which has always returned whenever I think of it and that I still cannot explain. I was idly examining the sandy bottom, when suddenly, the water simply collapsed and disappeared. I mean, the surface upon which my eyes had first come to rest, which gave the sense of a very clear substance I was seeing *through* to the detailed ripples of sand on the bottom, was suddenly gone. There was no surface. No *through* any longer. Just contact between my eyes and the sandy bottom.

And so the question arose. If water can be so clear it disappears. If it's not there to the senses, then … what keeps it from collapsing? I could not grasp how a substance I knew logically must still be there, could be suddenly gone, how when it was "there" it was somehow "up," rather than collapsed into itself, and perhaps lying on the bottom? Which something invisible and without substance would do, wouldn't it? What is it that keeps water up? How can something which looks like nothing, be wet, heavy, take up space, and be invisible? Here is the scene of that transfixed little boy.

Much later in life I learned that perfectly clear water is one of the three principle *diaphanous* substances, the others being air, and light. All three in their pure form, are invisible. Yes, light is invisible too. We can't see light. We only see the bits of light that are reflected from something material, and then we see colour. We don't see pure air, either. Yet all three of these invisible substances are required for life. As it turns out, water is weirdly mysterious, a substance that behaves like no other on earth, the only one that when frozen will float as ice in itself when liquid. If that were not the case, all ice would sink to the bottom of every "lake" in temperate and polar regions and pile up each year. Lakes would be water-starved most of the year. Only the top few feet would melt in summer, motorboats buzzing around over barely a couple of feet of water covering enormous ice-lakes hundreds of feet thick.

Anyway, staring at invisible water was my first philosophical experience. Since, I have learned a little about the material world, about atoms, molecules, quanta, the four main physical forces of nature, and so on. And I have seen a chemist make water — $H_2O$ — by squirting exactly twice the amount of Hydrogen as Oxygen into a closed jar. Poof! Suddenly, a couple of inches of water appeared instantaneously where there had been only two invisible gasses a millisecond before. But my experience on the rock was not about the physics or chemistry of water or about *what* water is. It was about the mystery of direct contact with *how* water is. There. I can say no more, except that these are experiences that open us to the mystery of how.

Almost 83 now. So, the runway of my life is scarily shorter. And that has

Against The Tide

necessitated a facing up to reality I am finding hard to manage. The immaturity of clinging to the illusion it's going to last as it is now, is far more comforting. The Stoic philosophers would have it that a man who does not know how to die, does not know how to live. I get this advice. And I think I know how to live and have lived well. I mean properly. Fully. But are they saying you have to keep your own death always in mind? That seems very sad. Or just to keep the realization of your own death sitting like a bald fact on the back burner, always staring at you, so to speak, will make you attentive to what's most important in the moment? In the past, world-wise people kept a human skull in the library as a reminder of the future. But without the fallback of a God and the promise of a pleasant afterlife as a final destiny, an extreme death-awareness leads to absurdity and immobility, doesn't it? While the extreme of ignoring death awareness (which I have never been able to do for long) is like psychological immaturity in a wasteland of meaninglessness. I have spent a lot of my life, especially as a young and vital man, and long before any resigned acceptance emerged, walking in lonely places late at night, railing at the heavens. Looking up at the night sky, thinking about the unthinkable absurdity of infinity, or Absolute Zero, or the idea of a total vacuum. Or the question: how can we speak of "the universe" as an object, if we think it is infinite. And then, if it is not infinite, if it's a bounded thing — then what is "outside" it? At such questions, the soul-piercing observation of the French thinker Blaise Pascal strikes hard:

*Le silence éternel de ces espaces infinies m'effraie.*

"The eternal silence of these infinite spaces terrifies me."

It was the silence that spooked him, not the infinity. We can't conceive of infinity. But we all know what silence is. Like, maybe there's nobody there. It spooked me, too, and still does when you actually think about it. When I was 50 and we had a cottage on Lake Joseph in Muskoka — another gorgeous part of this sweet earth — I bought a Celestron 14-inch backyard telescope so I could look for God (well, I didn't tell anyone *that*). It was so big you needed a ladder to climb up to the eyepiece. Maybe getting closer to the heavens I would hear something? Well, I did. My amateur acquaintance with astronomy, looking at galaxies, globular clusters, and other amazing objects so far away, turned me off my casual, poorly thought-out atheism. Like most young people, my first and most passionate and defiant assault on religion was rooted in what seemed so plainly to be the absence of justice on earth. How could there be a good and omnipotent God (who could make this world to be anything He wanted) in a world so obviously bad? I had not yet considered Augustine's point that there is no such thing as Bad. There is just absence of the Good. I began to see that just as belief in God is an indemonstrable faith, so is belief in no God. My sister Cassie's husband David Steen — then a dear, curious, but very skeptical friend (for more than 30 years now, gone into a post-divorce reality-warp on a hippie island in BC), pushed back: "What do you mean atheism is "a faith"?

My reply: "Those who believe God exists, can't prove it. So, they have a faith. And those who believe God does not exist, can't prove that, either. So, they have a faith, too." So, on what basis do you choose no God over God?

This subject will rear its head again because it is the only and deepest permanent question of all existence and can't be disappeared. But for now, I share another poem about my beloved Georgian Bay, prefaced by a brief explanatory note to set the primitive and eternal mood I always find there, and only there. Sister Norma, who has loved Georgian Bay all her life, said it best: "My heart is at rest here."

## *Seafarer II* ... *Out of Key River, to the Bustard Islands*

*Wind rises too restless, as wide river wanders,*
*while friendless Weird watches, this soul-seeker wend,*
*to great water gathering.*

*Slick-shadowed gull-gliders, scatter to hear me;*
*frost-feathered visitors; veering in wind-scoops.*

*Secret they skim; lonely they screech,*
*to pester my boat-slap.*

*So fierce-cold my fingers, no mother to warn me,*
*waiting for world-candle, wide mere to warm.*

*I run the rock-gauntlet, glacier-cuts winding,*
*past grey-granite rock-ribbons, wrestling in time.*

*Where moss-weeping, wet-seeping, rain drips to river,*
*no father to mourn me, beard covered in rime.*

*Soon I rise on each foam-furl, fall deep-panic down,*
*as merciless whale-rocks, (gaunt grim-ghosted perils),*
*make memory my mentor, make hope my best course.*

*Fear-freighted, I tire.*

*Though misty the buoys, though false-friend this water,*
*man drives to his life-end consumed by his fire.*

The original *Seafarer* is a haunting Anglo-Saxon poem composed by an anonymous poet of the period 950 to 1100 AD Old English poems are robust, highly alliterative, and were most likely sung or chanted to the accompaniment of a harp or lyre. They have a lilting, hypnotic rhythm, rather like modern rap music. They also make use of an intriguing device called a *kenning*, which is a metaphorical compound word or phrase. "World-candle," for example, refers to the sun. Two other Anglo-Saxon terms are used in this poem. "Weird" means fate, or unknowable destiny. "Mere" refers to a seemingly boundless lake or sea.

## GO WEST YOUNG MAN, AGAIN …

In January 1961, I was on a train to Denver, Colorado. The short bus trip from Denver to Colorado University in Boulder is over a high, dry plain at 6,000 ft. altitude, then suddenly, the town of Boulder appears in a nestled valley set against huge flatiron slab rock formations, wrenched, and tilted by some ancient geological torment of this earth, all set against distant white-capped Rocky Mountain peaks, under pure blue skies. The clarity of light at high altitude makes everything clean and clear as if pasted to your eyes. Green grass on campus in January? My private dream was about to restart.

Coach Potts, a grandfatherly, tousle-haired man in a beat-up coach's cap, picked me up at the bus station in his dusty old Chevy. There was a kindly twinkle in his eyes, a small wad of white cotton in each ear, and he was smiling with curiosity to meet his first "Can-eh-jan." He spoke with a slow Oklahoma drawl, hesitating a little between each word, or phrase, whatever he was saying punctuated with the same twinkle.

"We've never had a … uh, a … uh, Can-eh-jan, before. Pretty uh … cold up there?"

"Yessir." I liked him immediately. And I soon learned most Americans see only a wall of ice at the Can-eh-jan border. To enter the Boulderado Hotel where he was putting me up for my first night was to step into a mothballed black and white Western movie. A ceiling fan turned slowly over the front desk, and over a clerk who wore a green forehead visor, just like in the movies, and held a carpenter's pencil ready to mark his guest book. Coach left. He would pick me up and show me the indoor track and my rooming house in the morning. My heart sank. You really did it, Bill. A long way from home, and all you have to prove it was a good move and make you honest, is your legs.

The place was tombstone quiet. Thin walls, flimsy door latches. The slow click and rattle of cowboy boots, spurs clacking on creaky boards along the hallway. A few ornery looking, don't mess with me fellows wearing oversized Stetsons were hanging around the bar, with real six-guns, live bullets stuck in their gun-belts. Really. I know live bullets when I see them.

The next morning, I inhaled the heart-filling sweet smell of green grass in January on the way to see the indoor track, and the boarding house where I signed up to room with four other track athletes in the same room. The indoor track was the most amazing training place I had ever seen. A gritty, dirt-surfaced, 220-yard track with four right-angled banked corners that you would have to be moving very fast and leaning at about a 45-degree angle to get around cleanly. My job every midday would be to spend an hour and a half watering it with a firehose so it wouldn't be like concrete for afternoon training.

My four-man room was like being at Appleby again. No problem. It was cheap. One of my roommates was a slight, thin-bodied fellow with a ready wit, a good 440 runner to whom I would be passing the mile-relay baton more than once that year. He eventually left for medical school. Six months after that I came home one night to find a note on my study desk.

"A present for you in your top drawer."

It was a slightly greasy brown paper bag.

I figured maybe he had left me a cold cheeseburger.

But no. Inside the bag was a leathery, oily breast cut from a woman's body. It looked like a piece of cold, fatty pork rind, except the nipple had turned black, and a couple of tiny hairs were sticking out of it. This was post-mortem contact with an intimacy to which I should not have been party. It seemed a violation of that woman to be seeing those little hairs.

Somebody's mother. Somebody's daughter. I turned her hardened breast over in my hand — fatty side/nipple side — shocked at what he had done. Quick, uncaring knife strokes. Like meat. Not careful, like that Russian with his egg-yolk. That little shock has never changed. Perhaps our lives have a reservoir for little shocks somewhere deep down, where they sleep until awakened again, as now, while writing this. I put her breast back in the paper bag — the paper so naturally oiled by her skin — and called him, wondering how I was going to get rid of it.

"You shouldn't have done that."

"Aw, c'mon. It was a dissection class. You need a little levity to escape the gruesome stuff they make you do. A lot worse than a damn breast. Sometimes we prop the dead bodies up in the corner and throw knives at them, just for fun." I resolved then and there never to donate my body to science.

When I was a young man and asked my dad what it was like to see a dead body, he said "It's like a house with nobody home." But this woman could never have known when she donated her body that a student was going to

*Against The Tide*

slice off her breast to shock a friend. This was not so much a violation of her. How can you violate a self that's not there? It was a violation of how she imagined herself being treated after her death, and I figured she had ownership of that thought.

## ALONE IN PARADISE

From an aspiring runner's perspective, leaving the frozen snowy cold of Canada to arrive at the University of Colorado (CU) was to arrive in Heaven: stylish pale-pink Colorado sandstone buildings with red-tiled roofs and black railings set in a garden of green grass, towering elm trees, and winter flowers.

However, the first week there my heart sank when an ominous darkness suddenly loomed over the flatiron peaks abutting Boulder, and it snowed a foot and a half! Crikey. Winter followed me? But four days later it had evaporated, melting upward, so to speak, and there was that warm spring-smelling grass again. I was safe.

As for the work of the mind? I was free at last. CU accepted a lot of credits for my work at McGill and was far freer in terms of elective subjects. I wanted to major in English Literature because I secretly harboured the notion of someday writing like Hardy. I didn't know I was setting myself up for a really major career disappointment ten years later.

CU was footing the bill for my tuition, so I had earned that; and Dad, who was expecting me to make something of my life, was sending money for room and board. So he had a kind of unspoken authority over my education. When he asked me what I was going to major in, I did, rather tentatively, say "literature."

A long pause. Then, the man who could quote long poems by Tennyson or Shakespeare by heart, never having looked at them since high school, and who was a lovely letter-writer himself, crushed my nascent dream.

"Literature is something people do at night, before bed."

My heart sank. There was even a little edge of mockery of things effeminate in the voice of this man, whom I knew deeply loved his literature. Reciting poetry was about the only time we ever saw him emotional and teary. Then I got the word.

"You better pick a subject that's useful."

Three days later I called back to say I wanted to major in psychology. I figured it was a subject not so distant from literature because great writers were some of the best psychologists, weren't they? Dad listened. Pausing. I was real concerned he would say "forget that" too, and recommend something to choke on, like business. But he was okay with psychology when I said, "It will help in any walk of life, won't it? Even business? Because it helps you understand human character and motivation."

That did it. I was free now, and on my way. Psychology was the back door to writing some day — the dream was still alive!

What I didn't know was that "psychology" at CU was not very concerned about human beings. It was wholly absorbed in controversies and convictions swirling around something called "behavourism," work by the Russian scientist Pavlov with dogs, which he cleverly trained using Stimulus and Response techniques. Well, that did come in useful for me a few years later — who knew? — in conditioning an annoying human being in Tokyo (as I will eventually relate). And of course, there was a lot of talk about rats and Skinner Boxes. A lot of the classes were about how we might be able to train humans with such techniques, and how psychological methods might bring about the perfect society, some day. But we seldom read or thought about real human beings in psychology class at Colorado. Though I did. There was a sad quirky girl sitting beside me in my Abnormal Psychology class who was in the habit of burning little holes in her forearm with a lit cigarette. She was a kind of humanizing relief, actually. I did manage to feel her pain, as they say these days, and I eventually talked her into going to see a psychiatrist at the student health centre. So she went, but never came back, and I have no idea what happened. I worried I had sent her off to a loony bin.

Anyway, the one class I did really well in was Abnormal Psychology. Some people are deeply abnormal — we weren't to call them "crazy" — and I got interested in what makes them tick. I figured I might not be Dostoevsky yet, writing about darkly unpredictable characters like Ivan Karamazov, but maybe someday. "Psych" was a step along the way.

## ON THE RUNWAY NOW

I had been told of tough parents in the past who figured the best way to teach your kid how to swim was to throw him in the water. If he swims, he lives.

My first workout with the track team at the CU fieldhouse was a bit like that. When coach Potts saw me arrive he motioned to a big, mean-looking fellow and said, "uh, well now, let me see, Gairdner. You come along with this fellow here, and uh … let's see you run a little." The little distortions of truth that got me into CU loomed as a spectre about to undo me. Oh, oh. Could I do at least a couple of laps to warm up? I didn't have a chance to warm up thoroughly the way Coach Percival had taught, and when I had done my two

Against The Tide

laps and shook out a little you could see the guy in charge of breaking me was eager to step on the gas, show this here Can-eh-jan newcomer how to run.

Coach Potts said we should do three x 200 metres to start. Well, I had done zero speed work so far that winter, and I expected we would run about 26 seconds each, then rest and maybe do some more. But this fellow just took off without saying a word, and I tailed his afterburner as close as I could as we blasted down the backstretch. I thought the top of my head was going to come off. We did three of those runs in just under 24 seconds apiece, which is pretty fast on a rectangular dirt track in the middle of winter. I wasn't going to let him get away, though, and when we were done, my legs were shaking. I hadn't adjusted to the 6,000 feet altitude at Boulder yet, and could hardly breath after that, nor walk for about a week.

But I soon got used to things. Coach Potts was a kind and gentle, but spectacularly unoriginal man, so the routine was the same every week. All year. No changes.    All year. No change. Sink or swim.

*Mondays: 16 x 200 metres (at 80%)*
*Tuesdays, 3 x 400 metres (at 95%)*
*Wednesdays, 3 x 300 metres (at 100%)*
*Thursdays, 12 x 200 metres (at 80%)*
*Fridays, rest*
*Saturday, a time-trial, or a Meet.*
*Some beer Saturday night we never spoke with him about*
*Rest on Sunday*

That first season we had about 12 weekend meets in a row. The American track and field "system" is no system at all. It's do-or-die. If you love hard work and lots of competition, can take the punishment, and don't get injured, you will do well. American track athletes are not like European or Canadian hothouse flowers trained progressively to "peak" for the one or two most important meets of the season. They are ready for all-out performance almost anytime, and if not, they get dropped and replaced. On the technical side, there was simply no coaching at all. Coach Potts never spoke to me once, not once, about improving technique for any of my 10 decathlon events in the three years I was there. The first race I ran for CU was a 300-metre hurdle race in which I came third. Coach pulled me aside after. I thought, "Oh. Good. This is America, greatest track nation on earth. *Now* I'm going to get some great coaching, right from the top.

"Well, Gairdner. You, uh … if you. If you wanna win. You're gonna have to … have to run faster."

My jaw dropped all by itself, but I suppressed my incredulity out of respect. That was it. In all those three years. "You're gonna have to run faster." So, for the next race, I did run faster, and I did better. But it was clear that US track was mostly a kind of athlete-grinder. You figure out how to run faster yourself or get spit out of the grinder. My American teammates at CU didn't know there was any other way, and at the end of the season when they went back home to rest and play or work for the summer, they couldn't believe that this Can-eh-jan was going back home to train and compete all summer. "Are you crazy?"

I wanted to be a ten event decathlon man. But coach saw I was pretty good at running and hurdles, and didn't want me to do much else, "Cuz you might get hurt, and we need you for the relays." That took care of three running events, and the hurdles. But the decathlon is divided into two days, so I had much more to do:

*Day One: 100 metres, Long Jump, Shot Put, High Jump, 400 metres.*
*Day Two: 110 metre hurdles, Discus, Pole Vault, Javelin, 1,500 metres.*

This meant sneaking over to the fieldhouse a couple of hours before regular team practices, and training by myself for the other six events. It's hard to coach yourself because you can't see yourself in action to self-correct. A video camera — not yet invented — would have helped immensely. Sometimes I practiced the throwing and jumping events with other team members. But mostly, I got used to training alone, just like at McGill. Except conditions at CU were a ton better. This was paradise. I wasn't complaining.

One of the most talented men on the team was Bill Toomey, an incredibly gifted fellow, naturally fast and springy. Monday running workouts always formed into little groups of four or five according to ability, and if Bill was in your group, it was going to be a hot pace. He was always going to finish just a little ahead of everyone else. I have never met such a relentless, naturally-talented athlete.

After the last workout of the week we would walk up to Tulagi's Bar and Dance Hall on the main street of Boulder to drink some so-called 3.2 beer. Tulagi is an island in the South Pacific where the bar-owner's son was killed in WW II. On the wall behind the stage of this large dance hall where hopeful young bands played was a huge mural of Tulagi island, palm trees waving in a fake setting sun, with, you know, fake sunrises and sunsets going on all night. Overcome with grief and pride, the Dad had built Tulagi's so that young people just like his son, like us, could drink, dance, and celebrate just being alive.

The beer was supposed to be only 3.2% alcohol and was legit for teenagers over 18 in Colorado, because supposedly you couldn't get drunk on it short of

*Against The Tide*

drinking half a barrel. I had a business law Prof at CU who got hired by some wealthy parents to prove that their itinerant son could not have gotten drunk on 3.2 beer prior to being charged with drunk driving. So, the Prof bought a six-pack and drank it himself as evidence before fight the case. When he got to the courtroom, he was so drunk he resigned as counsel. Well, after our tough workouts you only needed a few 3.2 beers to feel pretty good, and we were so keen to win meets we didn't go much farther. Ever since those Friday beer days at CU I have always said that hard training makes for an inexpensive social life.

I had no idea my life was going to get entwined with Bill Toomey's in ways I couldn't have anticipated, and in a way, still is. A week before writing these words, almost 60 years after that first year at Colorado, he called me out of the blue from his home in Lake Tahoe. Just to talk. For a half hour. Mostly about himself, and his various exploits after he left CU and became an international track star. Other people's self-absorption (as distinct from one's own) can be very off-putting. But Bill is amusingly boastful while also self-deprecating. His non-stop self-congratulation is intertwined with so much witty self-crit- icism and descriptions of his follies, and those of others, it's like watching a side-show as he speaks. He talks. You listen. And then it's over. He started the conversation telling me more than once:

"You were my first coach. You got me started. I didn't know anything about the friggin' decathlon." Soon I will tell why he said that, and about my brief life with Bill after I left Colorado and headed even farther West, stopping just before I drove into the Pacific Ocean.

## A SPORT LEGEND

Some things stick in memory as encounters with the primal, and serious sport calling for utmost effort, heroics, and drama, is an arena where explo- sive human experiences can often just pop unpredictably into existence. For men, at least, strenuous sport is a kind of substitute for war. With a relay baton in hand, you transcend yourself, going beyond all personal limits for your teammates, an out-of-body experience of dedication to a cause greater than yourself, and when thus engaged you get sympathetic feelings and see in others, and they in you, a kind of primordial bond in common human striving.

Legend at CU had it that Teddy Woods, a tall, powerfully built black man who hardly ever spoke, and who was a freshman running back on the CU football team, wandered over to the track one day in January of 1960 for a little winter jogging in his basketball shoes and baggy grey sweats, just minding his own business, chewing gum, and sizing up the high jump bar which someone had set at six feet.

Footballers at CU were like athletic gods playing for near-hysterical sell-out crowds of 50,000 fans, and they had a high opinion of themselves. We track folks were second fiddle, athletically speaking. In fact the gate from football games paid for all other sports at the university. But we figured most football players were lunkheads taking dumb phys ed classes. Not *real* athletes, like us, who could handle a very tough running workout without puking. Which was true. Not one of them could handle our workouts. And the idea that a 200-pound footballer might try to jump over a six-foot bar was a joke in the making that was about to bring him down a peg or two. Coach Potts happened to see Ted circling, like a lion, eyeing the bar, taking an extra chew on his gum.

Then someone called out, "C'mon, dude. Take a shot!"

Without hesitation, Ted jogged slowly up to the bar and popped over it clean as a whistle, as if it weren't there.

So, Coach Potts made a beeline for Ted as he was climbing out of the pit.

"Ted. Have you … Uh, have you, uh … ever tried track and field?"

"No. A little in high school."

"Well, you should. There's, uh, a track meet right here, this uh, Saturday. What about you, uh, comin' out, and tryin' this sport? We could put you in the sprints."

Ted flashed an affable smile, said thanks, and left.

On Saturday he showed up too late for the sprints because, he said, he was sleeping. Wasn't there some other event? So, Coach Potts entered him in the 440-yard race. Ted had never run that far.

So, when the gun went off, everyone watched to see what they figured would be a Teddy meltdown by the fourth of eight turns and went into optic shock and awe when this thick-muscled, curiously graceful runner took off and set a new CU indoor 440 record of about 48 seconds flat on his first try, obliterating the field. A star was born.

That spring, he won the 440 in a new NCAA record time of 45.7 seconds — on a cinder track — and was named as an alternate on the US team for the 1960 Rome Olympics that summer. Pretty good for guy who just wandered out to the track one day chewing gum.

More legend. Or was this jock-apocrypha? I don't know. But by 1966 I was training with, and running against, Jack Yerman, another talented member on that same Rome relay team, who told me that when Teddy got to Rome, he slept a lot, and hardly ever went to train. He was a natural for the relay, but the American coaches never knew where he was, and got nervous.

Against The Tide

"Ted. You have to come train with the team."

"Why, coach? Training makes me tired. Just give me the baton. I'll do the job."

But they dropped him instead.

I only tell of him because watching him in action was as close as anyone could ever get to primordial athletic experience. In spring of 1962 at the Kansas Relays, after running the first leg, I was standing at the final bend of the track ready to yell for Ted who was running anchor on our 4 x 220-yard relay team. To this day what I saw and heard in the eruptive din of 50,00 rabid fans going crazy, defies words. But I'll try.

All tracks back then were dirt, so not as fast as today's artificial surfaces, especially when chewed up from so many races by the time the relays are run at the end of the day. And certainly no one had ever heard of anyone, ever, breaking 20 seconds for a 220-yard sprint.

Our third man came into the exchange zone in about fourth place, handing-off to Ted, who took off so fast and powerfully the entire stadium swelled in a single roar as he tore around the corner, gaining fast on those ahead. When he got to me what I saw got etched in memory. Whatever else he may have been had vacated his person entirely, leaving only the pure spectacle of a human body in overdrive leaning into the turn on legs thrusting so powerfully he seemed not to touch the ground. It was the perfect form of Man running, frozen in time, or rather timeless, every straining fibre and vein popping, driven by some deep, fierce, strangely lucid, and quite singular concentration in his eyes as he went for gold.

Ted won the race for us, and moments after he crossed the line came the announcements, he had run his 220-yard leg in 19.8 seconds. Another roar of awe from the crowd.

Whenever I think of pure athleticism, Ted always springs to mind. Compared to all that talent and power I was close to an athletic zero, like most of the human race. In the athlete-lottery he was a god. In the longevity lottery, I got a little luckier.

Ted Woods graduated from CU, then played football for the Calgary Stampeders for a few seasons. He prudently saved his money, and in off-season went back to CU for a degree in Business Admin, and then also for a Law degree. Pretty impressive for a guy we thought could hardly talk. For 15 years he was an unfailingly kind and successful man known as "Papa" to the many people he helped along the way. Then, one sunny September day in 1988, aged just forty-seven, while walking to the Denver courthouse and quite unaware his bold heart had become an arrow in his heel, Papa collapsed and died.

My first experience with racism was on the CU track team. I was a young fellow from a country where in the early '60s, black people — for that matter, anyone we would say today is a "visible minority" — were seldom seen. So the feelings surrounding race I sometimes sensed at CU — not many — were new to me. One day a fellow in the weightlifting gym told me he thought black people were inferior, and he didn't like Jews at all. I had never heard this kind of talk before. It's easy to tell who's black, I said. But how does anyone know who's a Jew? He just looked at me like I was from planet naïve. I was. My close and only Jewish friend Lowell, with whom I had that five-minute boxing match, and with whom I ran a lot, drank a lot, and confronted the deepest problems and glories of life, told me the moment he walks into a room full of people he can pick out the Jews. Not me.

Looking way back from the protests, race-rioting, and looting sparked by the death of George Floyd in 2020 I would say I was race unconscious when I first went to Colorado. And truth to tell, the place seemed race-friendly to me. We had three black men on our track team. The phenom Ted Woods, Jim Miller, and Leander Durley, our high jumper. If you had called any of them a "black" back then, I can't imagine the upset. That was the slur of all slurs. Jim became a close friend. Lots of training. Lots of talk, laughs, beer. Even one or two all-black parties he took me to where amidst the loud soul music and a mass of black bodies weaving and clinching in the dark — an occasional query-glance at the white intruder from a pretty girl otherwise buried in sensuous blackness with her man — I definitely felt my marshmallow existence. Jim was my protection. We were teammates but also competitors in the hurdles events. He was a little more gifted athletically than me, but we had some close races. He was faster on the ground, but we were always close at the tape because I got over the hurdles faster. Here is a photo of us winning first and second place in an indoor 50-yard-high hurdles race in the CU Fieldhouse, winter of 1963. You can see I was not happy to lose by a foot.

Now I want to tell of my first direct experience with actual racism.

But before that I should mention I have connected with Jim from time to time over the years. He even came up to stay with me for a while at beautiful Georgian Bay. The last time I saw him was at a reunion of our track team in Boulder in 1993, during the raucous swell of CU's Homecoming football game. Thousands of fans in tailgating parties, munching on juicy turkey drumsticks. Air Force Jets booming overhead. Bill Toomey, me, and a half dozen other Colorado Olympians were asked to walk across centre field to grand applause. Americans really celebrate their champs. It felt good.

Against The Tide

So, after posting this picture, I'm asking where is Jim now? Alive and well? Maybe … gone? It took a little sleuthing, but I found an old cellphone number and in the slightly higher-pitched voice of the elderly, he answered. Well, by golly. I caught him heading out for a game of golf at 78 years of age. His wife had come down with Covid-19 and suffered badly but survived. Home from hospital, she had to go back for surgery and lost a lot of her insides. A close call.

Jim: "I'll send some pictures of you and me." He has spinal stenosis so bad, he says "I can't bend over to tie up my own shoes." Jim can't tie up his own shoes? But he could sure tie up the competition. My racism experience with Jim and Leander was abrupt and shocking. Back then racism was hardly even a word in Canada (though our Indians, as we called them then, might disagree). And Americans on the team were embarrassed but used to it. So, I never thought about it. Our whole team was on a spring break track trip heading for the Four Corners, to go up against the universities of New Mexico and Arizona.

Red buttes, mesas, wind-sculpted rock columns, prickly saguaro cactus in swirling desert sands. Arapaho and Hopi hanging around forlorn stops made of flimsy shops that must be hammered back together after a high wind. Indian leaning asleep in colourful *sarape* against weather-yellowed drywall in hot sun. Thirsty jocks kicking a beat-up old Coke machine. Frosted black bottle clanging in the dark interior of a complicated mechanical tunnel, a tinny bang in the final slot. Phew. Twenty five cents. I would have paid five bucks.

Indians peddling hand-crafted silver jewellery, rings, belt buckles. Getting a lot of mileage from tautology — the phoenix is a bird symbol rising from the ashes, and all that. Smoking, with long sucks on roll-your-own cigarettes; soggy, brown-juiced paper ends sticking to the cracked lips of an open mouth; smoke drifting lazily up and over a tanned cheekbone into a squinting eye — a pale bird's egg resting in a nest of tarry wrinkles.

Arizona was fine and beautiful. Here is a photo of my 220 yd. hurdle race at Arizona State University, in the lead halfway, but I got nipped at the finish.

But Texas was trouble. We got turned away from the student residence at the university gate because ... we had three "coloureds." What's this? Nobody asked before we drove all the way down here, and now we're not welcome? So, we had to sleep in flimsy screened-in bunkies in a public park near the town

Against The Tide

zoo, mosquitoes, moldy mattresses, and all. Next day after the meet — in which our three coloured men had won half our total points, six of us went to a local pub for some cold beer. Parched with thirst, this was gonna be good. Frosted beer mugs, a quart of beer in each. Ready, set, go. First wonderful cool draught and then an obsequious manager frowning under an oily jet-black brush-cut came over and whispered in the ear of Bill Wells, one of our jumpers. Bill turned scarlet, eyes bulging upward as if he had just stuck his finger in an electric socket.

The manager slipped away from tongue-tied Bill.

"What did he say?"

Too ashamed and upset to speak above a whisper, Bill took a deep breath, looked straight at Jim and Leander in a fog of confused sympathy.

"He said they don't serve coloured folks here." None of us had ever used the word "coloured" before, and Bill slid it carefully between his honesty and his shame.

But we all heard it. All cringed as one.

You can't be serious.

I felt a helpless stab of empathetic pain for my friend Jim. Saw his eyes turn blank. Jim and Leander couldn't look at any of us. Didn't see us. Suddenly, we were outsiders. Convicted. They got up as one and made for the door without a word.

Bang. Bang of the door. Banging shut on our silence and shame. Our race history condemned us. They couldn't look their own good friends in the eye.

I don't know who suggested it. But in a swell of team bonding and simple human empathy we each took the hard placemat from under our big frosted beer mugs, put the mat on top of our mugs, turned them upside down on the table, and pulled out the mat so no one could pick up those mugs without beer flowing all over the table. All over the seats. The floor. Then we walked out as one. Without Jim and Leander, who never saw us do it. I wish they had. It wasn't exactly a civil rights revolt. But it felt pretty good.

We didn't see them until later that evening when they showed up at our racialized bunkies in the park.

Where did you go?

"We went to the Zoo and shouted at the animals."

I bet they did.

In retrospect, especially in view of the riots over Black Lives Matter, I see how even though we were all close brothers bonded in track, passing relay batons to each other, devoted to the same unifying goal, the moment that manager stuck his face in Bill's ear and said what he said, the guillotine dropped between black and white. We had no chance to reach out. Sympathize. Recover from racial shock. We were sorrowful for them. But it didn't count. We became the enemy. Historically, we were the problem. I could see it in their eyes.

I have been thinking a lot about racism lately, and I take the thought of the great Russian writer Alexander Solzhenitsyn to heart. *The line between good and evil does not run between human groups. It runs through every human heart.* Racism and other forms of oppression are to be reviled and stamped out wherever possible. But I have no doubt whatsoever that if whites were in the minority in a predominantly black nation, the shoe would be on the other foot. It is quite possible that racism — exerting power to oppress another race — is a hard-wired human defence against external threat to the group, a Darwinian survival mechanism. That doesn't justify or excuse injustice, but it would explain why racism has been, and still is practiced by every race on earth that sees an opportunity to benefit from it.

## WINTER ASCENT OF JAMES PEAK – 13,300 FT.

We had two really tough "Mikes" on our track team. One was rugged Mike Gallagher, who cross-country ski raced for CU in winter (and competed in four Olympic Games in that sport), then ran the mile for our track team in spring. The other was "Red," or mountain-man Mike McCoy, a bean-pole skinny red-headed distance runner who could train everyone into the ground.

I asked Gallagher to explain cross-country skiing and maybe take me into the mountains to show me his sport. I had a romantic vision of hardy men trekking across vast winter landscapes under their own power and was keen to try it. But that never happened. Little did I know then that cross-country skiing would consume all my athletic interest after I retired from Track and Field — a happenstance that changed master's skiing in Canada, and in the world.

Red was tough as nails and a man of few words. You could imagine him coming out of a log cabin high in the mountains in a rabbit-skin cap, packing snowshoes and a serious rifle. One day he was lamenting his poor racing and said he ought to quit and just climb mountains, which he loved more than running.

"You climb mountains?"

That was all I needed. It's a good thing I wasn't born in mountain country, because I would have been dead long ago. "Summit fever" is an irresistible force to those who feel it overtake them when they see a mountain they haven't climbed. Yet.

Careful not to speak of this to teammates or to Coach Potts, we packed our winter gear and set out at 3 a.m. one dark January morning, driving deep into

Against The Tide

the Colorado mountains to the starting point for what was going to be a of James Peak, a well-known mountain of 13,300 feet that is only a tough hike in summer, but is rated "difficult" in mid-winter. This was vigorous hiking and steep climbing with an ice axe handy, but no rock climbing with ropes. Nevertheless, if I had known anything about the possible dangers of winter climbing in unpredictable weather I might never have tried. But Mike was in charge.

We began in snowshoes. After a few hours of trekking upward in the dark, in a very cold wind, we rounded a corner and there was James Peak, still three miles away, parked on the horizon, brooding. The wind was sucking snow off the top in a long white horsetail.

"That's where we're headed," Mike drawled, through lips numb with cold.

My right thigh was cramping badly due to a broken snowshoe harness, so I didn't think we would ever be on that blowing peak.

We saw bad weather coming and decided to camp for the night before we left the treeline behind. I took off my showshoes to avoid more cramping, and so did Mike. We began heading over the last snow-crusted, rounded ridge to get to a sheltering copse of tall trees when my right leg plunged through the crust right up to the hip. Then, to get my right leg out, I had to put my left leg on top of the crust. But that leg broke through, too. Mountaineers called this exhausting business "post-holing."

I was a bit trapped in post holes and couldn't pull either leg out without some purchase for the other. So, I stuck my ice axe into the crust and lay forward to pull out. Way far down to my left, over that shiny rounded crusty crest, I could see only the dark lofty tips of snow-burdened fir trees, about 100 feet below where we were scramble across the crest. Mike was in front, stabbing with his ice axe. Pulling legs out, placing them again. When suddenly, one foot did not get through the crust, and he started to slide downward. I will never forget the high gurgling yelp "ahhhh," as he went over the crest and disappeared. I imagined him impaled on a tree down there, or worse, crushed on a rock pile, dead. The wind was picking up and you could see a snowstorm looming, a roiling white wall moving toward us from a far valley.

"Mike? Mike?"

OMG.

Yelling hard now: "Mike?"

No answer from below.

I am still a little ashamed to admit that my first thought was for myself. How was I going to get to the edge to see if Mike was okay, without falling down there myself, at high speed, and slamming into a tree, like him? Crumpled on rocks? I was no mountaineer. The idea of a puny ice axe holding my weight as I tried to kick in footholds to climb down to help Mike? A vision of the two of us huddling in a snow hole down there, Mike crying in pain, gave me a sinking sick feeling. Would I have the strength to carry him, injured, back up that dome of crusty snow? And even if I could, I had no idea how to find our way back to the car in the windy darkness. In all my life I have never felt as alone and imperilled.

So once again, "Mike? Mike?"

Moments of dreadful emptiness, until finally I heard a faint reply.

Very faint in the wind,

"I'm okay."

No man was ever so glad to hear another. Mike's ruddy face was there, on the crown of snow, his spittled lips parted in a shy smile as he ice-picked his way back to me over that slippery crust.

That was enough terror for one day. Using our snowshoes as shovels, we dug a three-foot deep trench in the snow under the sheltering limbs of a group of fir trees and pitched our tiny tent. With nightfall it would be well below freezing and we both knew that if you get deep enough into snow you get protection from severe cold.

We got into the tent to eat, lay uncomfortably close, and slept for about 12 hours. Morning was as still as the first day of creation, crisp, cold, and blue, and in the distance thousands of feet below us on the plain, we could see the city of Denver. I loved the scale of all this. Mere man scaling mighty nature, one step at a time.

Not far from our little bivouac we got above the treeline and saw the summit of James Peak more than 2,000 ft. above. It wasn't a really steep ascent, so no ropes needed. But it was a steady upward climb, steep enough that if you stood up straight and slipped you would take a long sliding tumble backward. Oxygen deficit was taking its toll, and I had to stop frequently to catch my breath. Eat a little snow to quench thirst. Rest plodding legs. Everything felt slow motion, and there was an obvious delay between deciding to do anything, and actually doing it. The amount of oxygen in sea-level air is 20.9%. At 13,300 feet it is only 12.5% — just over half. The difference is felt immediately on exertion.

But summiting felt great. We played mountaineer with photos at the top (no selfies in those days).

It was a grand thing to stand atop the Continental Divide and peer down at all the world, white peaks receding in the distance on all sides. We touched the deep blue sky; no hurry to leave. What a planet. On the way down, I had plenty of time to ponder how we had escaped certain death.

Against The Tide

## A PANIC MEMORY?

After writing about this, I got curious to check on my memory of that situation, and how Mike remembered it. What really happened to him down there, far below me? How, in fact, did he ever climb back up? In retrospect, would that have been possible? Maybe my memory was off, I searched the web for his email address, and wrote him.

Three days later I was shocked to read how Mike saw his brush with death. Here is his email:

> **Hello Bill,**
> **Great to hear from you.**
> **This event occurred in the winter of 1962.**

At one point on the summit ridge.

I hit a patch of ice and started to slide toward a precipice leading to potential catastrophe. You took it upon yourself to take position and stop my fall. I periodically think about this. If you had not taken the risk to stop that slide, I would have dropped over the edge and the rest would have been carnage.

When I started the slide, I felt the end had come, and I am sure voiced the terror I felt, and one second later you stopped the slide. Not much was said. But I knew at the time you saved my life.

All in all it was a great trip and the views were spectacular stretching from the great plains in eastern Colorado to the mountains in western Colorado. All the Peaks were snow-covered as it was midwinter.

I guess I never thanked you for your heroic act but I will say it now. Thanks Bill. You acted instantaneously or the outcome would have been very different.

It would be great to catch up sometime.

Did you qualify to compete in the Olympic Games for Canada? The track and field days at CU were great days, moments I will never forget.

I hope this information helps.

Keep in touch.

We are getting close to the 80-year mark!!

Mike

Forgive the cliché, but Mike's description of that chilling moment was jaw-dropping. I just could not, still cannot believe or figure out how I got it so wrong. How could I be so sure for a half-century that Mike had gone over the edge, if he actually hadn't? I have no memory whatsoever of reacting reflexively to save Mike's life. But he swears by it.

The only explanation for recalling my (apparently false) version with such clarity and certainty is that as we both agree, he began to slip and cried out. But when I reacted to stop him, in a moment of pure terror, my mind must have been so seized by the sheer panic of what was about to happen that I mentally completed the "what if?" of Mike continuing to slide. Disappearing from sight. And then somehow climbing back up. It was my panic-imagination that continued his fall. His disappearance. His return. Because there he was. The panic-memory of imagined disaster lodged immediately in my mind and displaced all recall of actual events.

Here is a nice photo of James Peak in winter. We climbed up the left flank.

Against The Tide

## QUATROS JOGOS PAN AMERICANOS, BRAZIL, 1963

One evening after our mountain trip there was an official-looking letter for me from the Canadian Olympic Association (COA). What's this? There was a quizzical feeling of anticipation, fingers fumbling to open the envelope, unfold a letter. And there, on COA letterhead:

> **We are pleased to announce you have been selected for the Canadian Team to the Pan-American Games, to be held in São Paulo, Brazil, April 20.**
> — May 5, 1963.

My first, deeply embarrassed reaction, was to quit smoking.

My not very serious social habit as a party smoker, was a hangover from the trepidations of boarding school, a reaction of sorts to the wrap-around prohibitions with which life there was surrounded. To sneak away to the woods or hide in the furnace room with my buddy Roger for an occasional smoke, careful to be so very still and quiet; sweating a little when we saw the shadow of the master's feet under the old wooden door while he paused, wondering where we were. We were daring escapees from Stalag 17. It took a certain nail-biting courage to chance the system; the smokes were mostly the punishable pretext.

But there was no way I was going to represent my country as a national team athlete and be caught with a cigarette in my mouth. Quitting was easy because I had never been hooked. So, letter in hand, and having disposed of that problem, I felt an immediate swell of amazement and pride in my heart, while flooded with curiosity. This news came without warning. Surely it was real. Not a joke. Until that letter fell open I had no idea I was being considered for Canada's Pan Am Team.

The next day I received the following Telegram from Coach Percival, with stirring words to his young protégé — and finally, I received one of his rings!

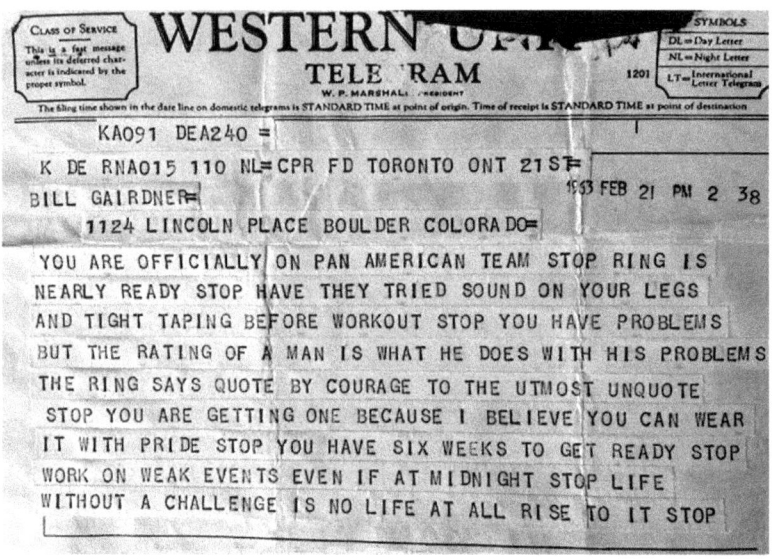

The summer before, I had won the Canadian Decathlon Championship at a charming but barely adequate track and field facility owned by the Estonian Kalev Club in Udora, Ontario. This club still exists, though the track long ago succumbed to weeds and surrounding vegetation. The meet was organized by Finns and Estonians who were members of an athletic club called SISU. Back then, all tracks in Canada were 440 yards. But the international standard was 400 metres. So, to get their meet approved, they spent months building Canada's first-ever 400-metre track. The whole scene was laid-back and very homemade. They used thin pine trees with the bark still on them for pole-vault standards, and the high jump pit was just dug sand. I was charmed. We were going to compete in ancient Sparta.

SISU is an old Finnish word said to have no equivalent in English, meaning "stoic determination, tenacity of purpose, grit, bravery, resilience, and hardiness." Finns believe this concept defines their national character. So do I.

*Against The Tide*

Wholly unbeknownst to me, my future discovery of cross-country skiing was going to be directly and deeply shaped by really tough Finnish athletes.

Winning that decathlon at Udora must have been what won me a spot of Canada's Pan Am team to Brazil. But after the wow feeling, my mind turned to how was I going to do this? I was on an athletic scholarship, and the Games would be happening during a university semester. Could I take a whole month off classes, drop responsibility to my CU team, and fly off to … Brazil? How exotic was that? My mind was spinning. So, I met with Coach Potts.

He could have said no. Full stop. My leaving would not be of any help to him. But he was a warm and sympathetic man, used to putting old heads on young shoulders. He just sat there with his peaked Coach's hat a little angled on grey tousled hair, leaned back in his springy chair with paternal softness in his eyes, and heard me out. I hadn't much hope, but I have always figured you have to go for it, whatever it is. I only won a few races at CU. But I would usually place top three in every event I entered, so I was a steady point-getter for the team. My leaving for almost a month was going to hurt him. My first chance for an international competition was in his hands.

He was a man of few words, which I knew from experience.

One fall day Coach Potts and I were standing talking in the grassy end zone of the football field, about three feet apart when we both got an awful surprise. The Colorado stadium is dug into the side of a hill, and far above, on an embankment is an archery range. Well, right in the middle of one of his slow sentences, a stray arrow flew down from above and slammed right through his padded jacket into his right shoulder. One moment we were talking. The next, Coach is standing there with an arrow sticking out of him. We were both shocked and I guess relieved neither of us had got it in the eye.

What did he do? You had to see this. He turns his head a little, as if to study the arrow, and with not a syllable of complaint says, "Well. By golly. Look at that." And reaching up with his left hand he pulls it clean out. A man of few words.

Sitting before me now sizing me up I figured he must have been pretty proud one of his athletes had made a Pan Am team, because when I was done pleading, he just grabbed his clipboard, like that arrow, to head for practice and said, "Well. Good luck now, son. Hurry back."

The next problem was missing so much schooling. I had a 3.0-point grade average — in fact, I was on the so-called "Dean's List" for those with above a 3.0 point average and got access to the brainers' private reading room. With a month away, it would be tough to keep that up. But I bought lots of carbon paper, found a pretty girl in each class, and asked each of them to slip a sheet of carbon under each page as they took notes. Mostly, they did, though some a lot better than others. I brought each of them back a bracelet of colourful Brazilian gemstones. But my average for that semester fell badly.

Two days after that talk with Coach Potts I was on a flight to Toronto. And from there to São Paulo, Brazil with a very excited Pan Am team, all decked out in special crested jackets and hats for the Opening Ceremony.

São Paulo was an exotic, smoggy, third-world city of almost 5 million people (22 million by 2020!), teeming with endlessly honking, beat-up old American cars threading around an occasional shiny limo, a donkey-wagon, or a stalled bus, busy sidewalks thronged with people of exotic ethnicities streaming past a patchwork of dilapidated storefronts, here and there the recognizable logo of some Parisian fashion line.

We were housed in the Pan Am village, four or five to a room in a collection of very basic government-style ten-storey apartment buildings that were to be leased out after the Games. Village food was very bad. Lots of bananas and rice. But the Brazilian people were charming. We trained at the *Esporte Clube Pinheiros* (The Pines sport Club), a private sport facility with its own cinder track, hurdles, jumping pits, swimming pool, and more. But you were on your own. No organized training or coaching. Make it up.

Two days before my decathlon I asked a tall American fellow if I could tag along on his 300-metre training effort, corner to corner, which is to say, around both turns. I needed to make sure I was ready for the 400 in my upcoming decathlon, and on this day, I didn't want to run alone.

We took off, and I felt like I got a bad start behind a racehorse, bits of earth from flashing hooves flying past my face, Ben Hur in his chariot. He had a huge stride, which I tried to match, but couldn't, and he was so powerful I just surrendered and got sucked along to the finish in 34.0 seconds flat, which was a very good time on a soft cinder track. That set me up wonderfully for what I didn't know was going to be the best 400 of my life. I loved the proximity to raw power. You can watch power in the abstract. From the stands. But running that close to it, you feel it. Thrill to it. And never forget it.

Later I learned that fellow was Earl Young, of American track fame. At the tender age of 19 he had competed in the 1960 Rome Olympics on the American World-record 4 x 400 Gold Medal relay team and had also equalled the world record that year for the 400 metres. Our lives are filled with unexpected intersections. Teddy Woods had been an alternate on that team with Earl, and in the race, Earl handed the baton to Jack Yerman, against whom I was to run an indoor 600-yard race four years later at the Cow Palace in San Francisco. Small world.

Jack was sent on a US State-Department tour of Kenya after the Rome Games where he was required to race 400 metres against all sorts of local

*Against The Tide*

champs, and once, even against a Maasai tribesman at a small village sports field. He showed up in his nice blue and red USA track suit and new Adidas track shoes. But there was no track. Just a broken-down WWII tractor dragging a harrow around a dusty cow-pasture, no opponent in sight. Three tall black officials in Kenyan sport jackets, track and field badges glinting on their lapels, were smiling over some private remark, and told Jack to go warm up. "Your competition will be here in one moment." So, Jack jogged around that harrowed dusty field, tall looming jungle encroaching on his right, perimeter dripping green with leaf and vine, the harsh squawk of a parrot deep in inky shadows. Jack heard — "I swear," he said — a jaguar's throaty gurgle and he sped up a little, but — "I swear" he repeated — "there were non-stop piercing squeals of smaller carnivores in the man-eating deep."

"He'll be here soon" the officials assured him. But Jack figured maybe he was going to get a day off? He was ready to go, but still no Maasai. Then, from the far side of the track a very tall, barefoot black man materialized from the darkness, in a loincloth. Jack said he had to be a seven-footer, and he had large wooden plugs inserted in his earlobes. Jack felt like prey. The fellow approached him with a friendly greeting, white teeth gleaming, looking down at Jack, sizing him up. Then he carefully flipped the two discs out of his ears, tied the earlobes behind his head, smiled, and at the gun, huge pink-bottomed feet flashing high behind him on each long stride, ran Jack into the ground. Then he loped away, smiling, waving, white teeth flashing again, swallowed up in the dark.

As for Earl, he got featured on the cover of *Sports Illustrated* in 1961, where they described him (quite accurately, I'd say) as "huge, for a dash man, standing almost 6 feet 4 inches tall, with broad shoulders and long, beautifully muscled legs, which carry him over the ground at eight feet per stride. He is smooth enough, but the main impression one receives while watching him run is of tremendous power. He looks as though he could run right through a brick wall." True.

I am still grateful Earl so graciously said yes when I asked if I could tag along. The only thing that salvaged my immediate and profound sense of athletic inadequacy while bent over to suck air at the finish, was that Earl could run like the wind, but he couldn't hurdle, or jump, or throw, like me.

## THE PAN AMERICAN GAMES DECATHLON

This competition was up for grabs.

Because of their almost complete world dominance in track and field,

Americans tended to send their second- or third-stringers to the Pan American Games to avoid the perception of being an international sports-bully. J.D. Martin and Russ Hodge were the two American decathlon entries, and Martin was expected to win, mostly on the strength of his pole vaulting, which had already won him a couple of All-American titles. Russ Hodge was a 6'3" 220-pounder with immense talent, who three years after these Games broke the world record in the decathlon. Little did I know I would meet up with him again and train with him occasionally in California, a couple of years later. The South American champ, and a huge crowd favourite, was Hector Thomas Martinez, of Venezuela. Then there was me, an unknown Canadian.

The decathlon, a little-known event then, and far below the radar, as they say, is today touted widely as the toughest all round athletic event. But it's not actually that tough. It's the training for all ten events, year in year out, that's tough. Except for the pressure of doing your best in a meet and not hitting a hurdle or fouling out for zero points in any of the field events, and the fatigue of warming up, competing, and warming down ten times in a row over two 12 hour days, it's actually a very enjoyable event with an unusual degree of camaraderie between decathletes.

Day One began well for me and ended better. The tension in a decathlon comes from the fact that in open competitions in field events like the shot, discus, javelin, and long jump — you get six tries. But in a decathlon, you get only three. So, the pressure is immense not to foul any of your tries. Many a good decathlete gets so anxious they foul the first throw in the shot, then they get even more anxious and try too hard to make up for it in the second, and so foul again. Oh boy … now, with only one try left, they have to do a safe, under-par throw for a lot fewer points, just to stay in the competition. Fouling out of any one event, or hitting a hurdle and falling, or just not finishing a race, will net you zero points in that event. So, you might as well go home. That's publicly embarrassing for the athlete, and for the nation that paid to get him there.

Coach Percival always said: "Take it easy on your first effort. You may have a below par performance, but you will at least get decent points and stay in the competition. Then, you are free to go for broke on your next two tries." That got me through most of the first day, which was long. Only the 400-metre run was left, with night falling quickly. The stadium lights clicked on, green grass glowed warmly, the rich red brick-dust track lay in wait for us to run our guts out in the 400 metres.

Just before this race I was surprised to be in fifth place overall. The 400 should be a point-getter. Not yet finished my warm-up, big Russ Hodge, tall and hugely muscled, eyes darting about erratically as if looking for something

Against The Tide

to land upon, landed on me, and came over to chat. He was a fast sprinter for his size, and so big I wondered if he might tie-up in a 400 race? I had lane four, he was in lane five. My chance for a rabbit.

"How do you run this race?"

"You're a fast runner, Russ. Just go like hell for the first 200m and hold on."

For me, drafting someone was always easier than leading them out.

The "sweats off" whistle blew. We walked to our lanes. For some reason, all the runners had a starting block — except me. Then suddenly, from behind a chain-link fence likely put there to stop rabid soccer fans from killing a ref, came a high-pitched shouting. We were astonished to see an apoplectic man, foaming at the mouth, clawing at the fence like a panicky orangutang at the zoo. It was our flaming red-headed team coach, Lloyd Swindells. He was very upset. With me. Spitting mad. "You bloody well get a goddamn block! You need a block! Get a goddamn block! No way you are racing without a#%$&@#$ block!" He was right. A block might make a tenth of a second difference. Why give up forty points or so?

The whole meet was held up until I got my block.

There is an ultimate silence before a starting gun explodes. And when it does, the mind turns off. Russ was off in the lane outside me, like I told him, a Sherman tank on overdrive. It was like running behind Earl. I have never felt so fast and easy in my life, sucked along in a vacuum, and when Russ began to fade — *mea culpa* — just before the 200m mark I was in a euphoric sweet spot, sweeping around the final bend toward the shouting fans and final straightaway. Far above to my right I saw portly Ken Twigg, one of Canada's team officials standing like a roman godlet on a white pedestal, waving and cheering with all his might, and I managed a wan smile on the way by. I won the 400 event with a time of 48.8 seconds, which was my PB, and suddenly I was in third place in the decathlon, which I maintained until the last event of the second day.

## DAY TWO

On day two I won the first event, the 110 metre hurdles, had no fouls, and was still in third place prior to the last event, the 1,500 metres. This event is justifiably feared by most decathletes. They know if they train very hard for the 1,500 metres, they will lose too much muscle-mass to do well in the throwing events, which garner them far more points than the 1,500. So, most of them just gut it out when the time comes, knowing it's going to hurt. A lot. But I had done okay in cross-country at Appleby, and I knew that if I ran my usual race, the bronze would be mine. Not bad. Hector Thomas of Venezuela who was already in solid for the silver, was a real gentleman, a fine athlete, and the crowd favourite by far. They all knew that on this evening he was gunning to hold onto his silver. It looked like status quo until the end. But then, I was gunning for silver, too.

Hector had not been fast at the 400 the night before, and so I was asking myself if he might be vulnerable? Or had he been saving himself for now? Just then, Coach Swindells showed up at the side of the track with a copy of the decathlon scoring tables.

How much do I have to beat him by, to get the silver?

Athletes were already assembling at the start line.

Coach was flipping pages frantically, pencil in hand.

"The Spic guy has only run just under five minutes. You have to beat him by more than half a minute to win the silver." Half a minute! He gave me a sorry-my-boy, smile. "Not likely but do your best."

I joined the others at the start. Half a minute! Half a mi-nute? The gun went off, me trying to do the math while running. The race is three and three-quarter laps. Thirty seconds at a good pace is 200 metres. To beat Hector, I was going to have to put more than 50 metres between him and me, on every lap. Fifty is a long way. It's half of a 100-metre race to be gained on each lap. That didn't seem very likely.

But coach Percival had taken us aside one day and said something I never forgot.

"A decathlon man may be the best in the world. Winning easily, but if he doesn't acquit himself well in the 1,500. If he just takes it easy. Runs beneath his ability. Or worst of all, falls on the track at the end groaning, he is not a man, and he will ruin the nobility of this event. Don't let me ever catch you dogging it in the 1,500."

After the first lap, which I ran a bit too fast, and felt it, I looked back. Hector was about 40 metres behind me. OMG. I have to push harder! By the second lap he was almost 100 metres behind. Was there a chance? Two more laps went by. But if, when I had just a half a lap to go, he was passing the same halfway mark as me on the other side of the track … would I get enough points to beat him? Close. Was it possible?

The crowd was extremely pro-South America. Pro-Venezuela. And pro-Hector. They were getting riled to a high pitch by the announcer, who was shouting excitedly in Portuguese for the Brazilians, then in Spanish for the Venezuelans, and then, in broken English, "Kanada try to upset Thomas of Venezuela!" And then, "Thomas must keep pace for silver medal," and so on.

As I rounded the second to last turn with just 300 metres to go, I saw that

Against The Tide

I had almost half a lap on Hector, but not quite. Was he going to speed up now? Did he have anything left? I did not want this moment, this possibility snatched away, and the crowd knew what I was trying to do. They had been very quiet, hopeful for Hector. So hopeful, the shouting fans fell eerily quiet each time I passed, watching the drama unfold. I could feel their disapproval, and I almost — no, I did feel, a little guilty trying to beat their favourite.

But now, while sprinting past them on my last lap, a few thousand of them suddenly jumped to their feet and started to cry out, cheer, and clap very hard. Oh God, Hector's sprinting? Gaining on me? They're cheering him on? My heart sank. The gambit is over. But still, run harder. And as I did, they clapped harder. I tried to look behind, but I couldn't see Hector. Where? Is. He?

And there, straight across the track, exactly crossing the half-way mark at the same time as me, was Hector, hurting badly.

My goodness. They weren't clapping for Hector. They were clapping for me! For me? I was so very surprised and moved. They were rising above partisan preference to express admiration for the honest effort of the enemy. I had tears on the run, and couldn't help a smile of sorts, and the harder they clapped, the harder I ran. It was a wonderful moment in my sporting life.

Standing on the podium, the silver medal around my neck, Hector was at my side, a good man, and a friend. I was wholly unaware I would be meeting him again in Tokyo for a rematch in a year and a half at the 1964 Olympic Games.

He is preserved in memory now. Writing about him makes me want to reach out and say hello. But Hector died of cancer at 70 years of age. Here is how I remember him.

# HOW I ARRANGED AN ABORTION
# AND ALMOST FLUNKED OUT OF COLLEGE

On my return from Brazil I had to scramble to make up for missed schoolwork. There were more track meets to run, papers to do, and rushed preparation for exams. Then a mini disaster befell me.

It was very hot afternoon before the final exam for a course I intensely disliked called "Psychological Tests and Measurements." I had a small room on the second floor of a rooming house, and our shot-putter Bob Crumpacker, a huge man, intensely intellectually curious, who eventually became a doctor, had come over to chat. Bob and I, and David Grant, our discus thrower — who not long after graduating became deeply schizoid — were fast friends. David was majoring in quantum physics, and always got the highest marks in the subject, though he never went to class. I think the notion from the famous "two-slit experiment" in quantum physics, which implies that a single photon is aware of the intentions of the experimenter, drove him crazy. He enjoyed telling us that even though all physics is based on the belief that nothing in the universe can travel faster than light, he knew something that could. What? Alright David. Let's hear it. What is it?

"If you close the handles of a pair of scissors with infinitely long blades at the speed of light, the ends of the blades have to travel faster than the speed of light to close." I still can't figure that one out. I think the trick was the ends of the blades would be infinitely far apart and so would have to travel faster than an infinite speed (whatever that might be) to close.

At CU, Bob, David, and I would sit around late at night with pizza and beer after a good foreign film, critiquing it, or trying to figure out if a novel like James Joyce's Ulysses was just a bag of clever tricks — except for Molly's unpunctuated, very sensuous soliloquy, which we loved. On this hot afternoon I needed help, and Bob was up on statistical calculation, which I found difficult and boring. The course in question was required for my psychology major, and it was impossible to graduate if you got less than a C in a required course. I had a B– going in, and how I did that, I am not sure, for I all but hanged myself with the Prof one day when he made the mistake of asking our class: "What do you think of this course?"

I thought it was silly for a highly trained Professor like Dr. Lindsay to be asking naive students what they thought of his course. But I did hate it, and I still can't believe what I said. Back in the day, transparency and honesty of my personal opinion was virtue signalling, and I fell for it. I was insolent and rude.

The course felt dishonest because almost every psychological test used on humans that used word choice amounted to a series of questions designed to

*Against The Tide*

… Well, that was my problem. Designed to what? I was language sensitive. I had already complained aplenty that too many of the questionnaire results we were asked to evaluate depended for their outcome on which nouns, adjectives, or verbs the test designer had chosen to use. It was easy to invalidate an entire experiment by showing that in changing one word of a question you were fishing for the answer you wanted. After a while, I gave up taking such projects seriously. What did we think of the course? There were about 30 of us in the room, most giving suck-up answers. When he got to me, I took a deep breath, and said, "Sir, I think this course should long since have been relegated to the dusty bins of triviality."

The room fell suddenly, deeply silent.

Dr. Lindsay heard, but remained rigid, as if he hadn't. His lips cracked open, a tiny drizzle of saliva connecting them as he stared quizzically at the ceiling, pondering what I had just said, then moved on to another student while I stared in frozen regret at my notes.

Meanwhile, Bob just confused things for me. A lot. While helping me that afternoon we heard a girl's voice calling "Bob?" repeatedly, as she came up the stairs toward my room, and … through the door swept a girl I had never seen, in a flaming, wispy red dress. A fulsome girl with sculpted features, shiny brunette hair, and no makeup, which would only have detracted from her natural beauty. I still think of her as the girl in red who almost got me flunked out of university. She had been calling for Bob, but I sensed she was actually looking for me, which I couldn't figure out — or get details from Bob, because he immediately had to leave, and so there I was. There she was. Sitting on my bed already — a bit forward I thought — whereupon, after a few minutes telling me of her distress, she quietly started to cry, lowering her face gently into cupped hands, tears running damp between her fingers. Jeff, her fiancé, had left her two months before. And … she was pregnant. Her family knew nothing, and she didn't know what to do. But how did she land in my lap? Why come to me?

I melted at once, and after several hours of yes and no to the big What to Do? question, I told her she needed an abortion. That was dangerous talk, for abortion was illegal everywhere at the time. And me? I was like every other young man playing sexual possibilities for advantage, and so an abortion seemed like a logical solution. It was still very early — the fetus (no one used the word "baby") was still "just a teaspoon of cells." I didn't want her to find some cheap doctor. That might implicate me. So, I thought, this is *so* bad, something very bold is needed, and to her immediate shock I told her I was going to drive her to Denver to see her dad. We must tell him the whole story of how Jeff callously abandoned her. Dad would give her lots of money for a good doctor.

It was a long night. Dad was a big-time advertising executive, and he almost fell over when I got through the door of his sky-high office and said, "I'm just a new friend. New tonight, actually, your daughter's fiancé has run off and left her pregnant. So … she needs an abortion. Right away." Dad turned pale, gave me a rather sudden, violent look, like maybe it was me? But no. His pursed lips relaxed, with "It's late. Let's get a bite and think a little." Which we did. But when I went to the loo, the girl in red got the cash from Dad and fled in the dark for her abortion.

Back at my place by 7 a.m., emotionally worn out, there was no use trying to catch a little sleep. I walked into the exam a zombie to face a hundred multiple-choice questions, every one of which seemed aimed like shrapnel at my brain. Each question had four possible answers, and we were to choose the best one. But in my uncertain, now feverish state of mind all the answers could, with sufficient imagination, be true. Couldn't they? Oh dear. What a confusion. I knew at least that if you randomly check a list of multiple-choice questions you have a chance of getting a third of them right. So, I answered the ones I knew, checked off the rest at random, and left the room.

The next afternoon I went to the wall outside Dr. Lindsay's office.

To imagine the worst, then have it actually happen, is no surprise. But it was still a shock. There was my name with a D+. A pass. But I needed at least C– in all my psychology courses to graduate. I had made the Dean's List that year with a B+ average. So, this was embarrassing deep doo-doo, and just the thought of having to re-take such an awful course was unbearable. So, I went straight back to my room, called for an appointment with Dr. Lindsay, and got dressed in a nice white shirt, tie, and jacket.

The knock on his door was a drumbeat in my head. My immediate future was hanging on how I was going to play this. Oh Gawd. What if he decided to get even for what I'd said? Maybe he forgot? Fat chance. Dr. Lindsay, bent over his desk, was frowning through thick glasses at a mess of papers, unlit pipe in hand.

"Yes?"

"Sir, I have come to beg mercy." That got his attention. "But first, to apologize for what I said about your course. Honestly, I didn't like the course at all, and I was no good at the statistics. But I did try. Hard. It was hard. But I did think a lot of the experiments were poorly designed and, well, not credible. That's just my honest view, sir. And you did ask for our views. But I didn't have to be rude about it. I was frustrated. I apologize. And sir. This exam. I … I … it was sure a shock. But I had to take a beautiful girl I never met before to her

*Against The Tide*

dad the night before the exam. To help her get an abortion." At this, he pushed back bolt upright in his chair, peering over his glasses. Abortion was illegal. A crime. He was sizing me up. Asking himself what he might have done?

"I mean, to get the money from her dad. To protect her. I couldn't study. Sir. So I got a D+. And now I'm in a jam. Cuz I'm a Canadian here on a track and field scholarship, and there's no way I can afford to pay tuition myself." Suddenly, he lit up a little.

"You are? I used to run track." Pipe out of his mouth. "Gosh. I'm sorry to hear about the abortion. I mean the story. Maybe it's a good thing. I can't say, of course. But you better shut up. And I hope she's okay." I nodded she was. Would be.

"What events, Sir?"

"I was a half-miler. And not too bad, either." He was beaming up his memory, breaking the tape at the finish. I watched him do it. What luck. Athletics was coming through again, as it had for my Latin professor wrestler with cauliflower ears at McGill.

The Prof/Student gap evaporated right before my eyes, and while not exactly buddies, we were fraternal suddenly, in a way athletes understand. He was remembering, faraway and happy-eyed. If track never gave me anything else, this was pretty good.

"So, Sir. Psychology is my Major. And if I have to take this course over? I mean, I have no money. And without a scholarship, no Visa, either. And I need to get out of school and train for the Canadian Olympic trials — they're in six months."

"Sir, honestly, I panicked, and with that girl? It was tough, and I never slept at all. Those test and measurements got jumbled in my mind. Sir. That's the honest truth. I need a C- in this course to graduate. Really, I've been on the Dean's List for a couple of years. I've been a good student here. For me, a D+ is a shameful grade. But … is it really much different from a C- ?"

Then came was the longest five seconds of my life.

He put his pipe down, got slowly up from his chair, and honestly, he took my arm like a teammate, pulling me close, and walked me outside to the bulletin board where the grades were posted. With his marker-pen he drew an arrow up from my name with the D+, inserting it into the C- column, and leaning his head into me as if sharing some espionage, said:

"Go on. Get the hell out of here," *sotto voce*, in a secret man-to-man way.

And that's how I graduated on schedule from CU.

Meanwhile, the girl in red came back to school in fall and married Jeff, and he and I became wary friends of a sort.

## SHOCK AND DECLINE OF AMERICA

On November 22, 1963, my brother Jamie's birthday, President Kennedy was assassinated, and the world ground to a halt. Everyone remembers what they were doing when they got the news. Kennedy's slumped, bullet-torn, bloodied head. Jackie reaching over the rear of the speeding car for the FBI fellow trying to climb aboard. I was so upset I went running. Do something normal. Something really tough was all I could think of in that atmosphere of international shock and dismay. Mine was a normality protest, a way of not thinking about what such a grisly event really meant. No one knew. They still don't. But I mark the decline of America from that day.

Perhaps that assassination was but another violent expression of the growing "rights fever" in America. Ever since the Declaration of Independence (1776) with its memorable lines about everyone having an equal right to 'Life, Liberty, and the Pursuit of Happiness," about having "Certain Unalienable Rights" and so on, America set itself on the path to hyper-individualism more definitively than any other nation in history. The notion of rights as indwelling qualities of human beings, each determining his or her own moral and political boundaries was a recipe for political and moral absoluteness and extremism, and so for the breakdown of human community because it removed the essential notion of obligation and duty as an obligatory concomitant of rights.

One example will do. The Declaration, a Jeffersonian libertarian sort of document, declared a "right" to an unbounded liberty for every citizen. No mention of boundaries to liberty, or duties to each other. Edmund Burke was a lot wiser, defining true liberty as "an equality of restraint." European nations are very different and consider liberty to be contextual. The German Basic Law, for example, also grants every German citizen a right to individual liberty, but only as "limited by the Constitution and the Moral Law." The consequence in America (and since the Charter of Rights and Freedoms of 1982[5], also in Canada) has been a growing "rights fever" among citizens tending to angry claims about absolute unbounded rights, even against each other.


## CALIFORNIA BOUND!

As compared to the burden of too many material possessions in later life, there is a wonderful animation of soul that springs from the freedom of throwing your few worldly goods in the back of a car and heading out, fancy free into the great unknown.

January 1964 was the end of undergraduate school for me, and with an eye on trying for Canada's 1964 Olympic Team I was stuck for what to do next.

*Against The Tide*

Toronto had no indoor track facility whatsoever in those days, and a daily slog through a foot and half of snow on the golf course at −10°C with the family dog did not quite qualify as high-performance training — except maybe for the Mukluk Games.

As luck would have it, Bill Toomey called. He had graduated six months before me and was living, and training poorly, in Burlingame California, taking a master's degree in education at Stanford University, teaching and training at the local High School. Bill was so very talented he had already won the American Pentathlon title on the strength of his running and bouncy jumping. But he had never really trained for a multi-event like the decathlon and hadn't much of a clue where to start. He was so weak he couldn't bench-press his own bodyweight, which was kind of basic. C'mon Bill. Really? So, on this phone call he pleaded: "Come on out to California. Great weather. Great chicks. We can train together. You can live at my place. No rent. What about it?" That sealed the deal. Ka Chung. My life took a whole new direction; correction — directions, in ways I could never have imagined.

My Nash Rambler and I hit the road West through lofty Colorado mountains, past that chilling, near-death experience on James Peak; rolled into the warmth of Utah and the Salt Flats; leaving behind memories of university track trips to New Mexico, Texas, and Arizona, of ochre-coloured buttes and mesas, of Indians in striped blankets rising out of the ground between giant splayed saguaro cacti, weaving optically against the land, in heat-distorted light. Fancy-free, I was enjoying my comic-book memories of Black Rider, Tonto, Kemo-Sabay, and Cochise; of the Lone Ranger, Shane (that little kid, yelling "Shane!"), all sorts of six-gun fantasies and heroes springing to life; long strips of super-heated empty highway stretching to a needle-thin ribbon dipping over far desert ridges into my unknown future, under clean blue skies, the sands of time closing quickly behind.

Then came a passage of desolation through the hard-packed, parched, and lifeless high desert in Nevada, with its legends of lawless bars and desert whorehouses — "Mustang Ranch," The "Jolly Dolly." For a guy from "Toronto the Good" this was licentious lala land, though I didn't see any whores around. Finally, I got to Lake Tahoe (where Toomey lives today) and drove 7,000 ft. up a steep road to Donner Pass. You could touch a deep blue sky now, with Donner Lake even more blue far below (though for a Canadian used to huge beautiful lakes, it wasn't much). The pass was named after the 1846 Donner Party of more than 80 California-bound settlers who got stranded by snows on the Eastern side of this pass. Snow piles up over 50 feet here most winters. That year it was so deep they couldn't go forward or back and had to over-winter. About 45 survived, a lot of them by cannibalism. Some said that was normal. Others never talked about it, ever.

Then, a steady sweep downward from the Sierra Nevadas into California's interior valley. By nightfall I could see San Francisco in the distance, city of charm, earthquake, and fire, rolling hills, clanging cable cars, and a rep for the full menu of human vices. Over the Bay Bridge, and straight into a forest of flashing bright billboards like a giant pinball machine. Then, southward on highway 280 through beautiful, Tuscan-like winding grassy hills, olive-coloured shade trees, and the smell of eucalyptus, to the town of Burlingame on El Camino Real, my new home for six months.

## EVERY MAN FOR HIMSELF!

El Camino Real is a 600-mile "Royal Road" originally built to connect 24 Catholic Missions from San Diego in the South, to Sonoma, north of San Francisco. Sonoma, silently simmering in golden-grasses, rolling hills draped in the iconic speckled dark-green shade of spreading trees. *Knock Knock* at a modest two-storey white building smack on busy, very noisy El Camino Real, and Toomey opens the door into his one-room apartment. His bed, a cot for me, a kitchenette stove-top, a tiny fridge, and a slide-in shower. Two jocks gambling they could make their dream real. Two lone-ranger athletes. Independent. No money. No coach. Definitely not East German or Russian athletes on the government dole.

Bill was just happy to see someone who shared his fanatical obsession with track and was his usual wry, somewhat shy, somewhat self-obsessed, self-deprecating self. The toughest athlete I ever met. "Great you're here. Let's get something to eat." I was beat, but okay. Hello to you, too, as he turns me around for the car I just got out of after a 24-hour drive. I was hungry but had no idea the latent violence and cheekiness of the American frontier was just around the corner. We were a mile down the road and came to a red light where two sturdy young men were hanging out. When I stopped, one of them pulled open my rear door and they both jumped in.

"Take us to San Francisco."

A car invasion? I'm maybe a little culturally confused because I'm in La La Land now. So, I look at Bill. Like, what do I do? Bill turns his head and sees these two scruffy dudes getting way too comfortable in my back seat.

"I don't know about your country," I say to Bill, "but we don't do this in mine."

That did it. Let the show begin!

Against The Tide

Bill jumps out, spinning on one foot to the rear door. By this time the guy on his side of the car realizes what's about to happen. OMG. So, he grabs the door handle and holds on tight. Very tight. Toomey was always mild-mannered. No one on our track team had ever seen him get mad at anybody, for anything. But Clark Kent was into the phone booth and out as Superman so fast he was already pulling on the door the guy in the back seat was holding shut for all he was worth. Now Bill's foot goes up on the side of the car. I'm watching this show, aghast. The light turns green. We're not moving. Bill yanks harder. Traffic stops on all sides. Hey, it's live entertainment. Bill gets the door open on the third try, but the guy still won't let go, so he gets pulled right out onto the street by the handle, and Bill stomps on him. Flattens him. Chest down on the pavement, squealing. Real worked up now, he lunges back in for the other guy, who is grabbing the opposite door handle. Also, for dear life. Bill has a hold of his legs. Now he is pulling the guy's pants off. "Hey dude. Let me go! Alright!" But Superman ain't stoppin'. He has one leg in the car to pull, the other foot still on the first guy on the ground when number two loses his grip and Bill drags his sorry body over the first guy, all the way onto the side-walk. Now number one, eyes jiggling, tries to stand to take a swing at Bill. Big mistake. Down he goes again. And I'm, like, where am I? It's all of a 30-second show, which Bill ends by dragging the second guy to the front of the car, bangs his face on the hood three times, and drops his sorry ass on the road.

Then, Clark Kent gets back in the car with a laugh. "Let's go eat."

Welcome to California.

## DOWN THE MAYBE OLYMPIC ROAD, AND THE START OF MY WRITING LIFE

My secret dream and hope — one I couldn't share even with my mom or dad — was to be a writer someday. So, you better get started, was my inner mantra. I had no money, no job, and was out of school. Free. A floater. So, I bought some writing paper and got started with a little writing that I didn't know was going to change my life radically. First, a few sea stories about my Arctic trip. Toomey was off to teach every morning. Midafternoon — it must have been a strange sight — we two unsupported, unknown, Olympic hopefuls with no coach(es), and no money, both needing jobs to eat, went out the door to Burlingame High School to train, laden with javelins, discus, shots, and various special well-worn shoes. Word soon got around sleepy Burlingame that two aspiring jocks — one Canadian and one American — were friends and competitors, training together with a common dream of making it to the upcoming Olympics. So, the sleepy Burlingame newspaper came to the track for some pictures, and a story. We felt pretty good. The writer said I was "already assured" of a spot on Canada's team. But not so. I would have to score above the Olympic Standard of 7,000 points, and even then, there was no guarantee of a place on the team. But somehow, this story made our little adventure more real. It was game on!

A few weeks later, we went to Stanford University because Bill had to drop off a late course assignment. It was a fluke visit. Life is a fluke. My first impression driving along that famous palm-lined entryway toward Stanford's iconic low sandstone buildings, red-tiled roofs suspended over the long, shaded walkways of the Stanford Quad, basking in the afternoon sun, somnolent with purpose, was indelible. In this very place, my future was going to unfold in ways utterly unforeseeable.

It seemed odd, but naturally enjoyable to be coaching a fellow so much more talented than me. I was of such ordinary abilities I had to do a lot of thinking about each of the ten events in the decathlon. Technique was my strength, as compared to more naturally gifted athletes like Bill. Running and jumping was mostly what he liked to do. But he had never really trained for skill events. So, I had to show him how to put the shot, throw the discus, lift weights properly. Here, Bill, is the position you need to take for the shot. How

*Against The Tide*

you accelerate yourself, and this 16-pound ball so you can punch it out hard at 45 degrees, reversing feet at the last moment to prevent fouling. He had no idea. He just wanted to try three half-hearted throws, then go run. No, Bill. No. Maybe 30 throws. It's about your technique, which is awful. And then the discus. And then the next event. And *then* we run.

He was quite weak. That very day I took him to the weight-room. With just a few months before the US Olympic Trials, he couldn't bench-press his own 175-pound bodyweight. That was a little shocking. Two years later he found steroids. Or rather, they found him. So, he shot up to 195 pounds and by then was benching 360 pounds. Steroids like Danabol, and other performance enhancing substances and techniques found most talented athletes about 15 years or so before their use was banned. They even found me, on doctor's orders, five years later.

To make a little money for food and such, I found a fateful job working at the Burlingame Golf and Country Club, digging and weeding flower beds, my nose in aromatic heavy pollens all day. Then off to track after work, with tired legs. Burlingame G & C was leisure for the rich, and I distinctly recall being treated like a Mexican worker when rich and famous crooner Bing Crosby and his wife followed the plop of their golf balls onto the green I was working on. Bing was muttering to himself about putting posture, a nice guy in harness to an aging harridan. She didn't like the noise I made picking weeds.

"Now you stop that, young man. It's hard enough to concentrate, without …"

Bing just kept his head down. A sorry multi-millionaire, he gave me a look of sympathy from the silent brotherhood: *this is what I have to put up with.* I sent him back a knowing grin from the brotherhood of Chicano gardeners. I had feelings of class anger. Where does a rich bitch who marries money get off treating me like scum? I could take it if she'd earned the right. Maybe.

After a few weeks of this I got hit by the first arrow in the heel of my Olympic Odyssey. I woke up at daylight trapped in eyelid-ruddy darkness with a massive headache. Both eyes crusted shut. Completely blind. A fever. Aching muscles. "Bill … Bill … help me to the sink."

"I can't see. My eyes are glued shut. Gotta …"

A lot of water washed off a lot of crust to reveal flaming red eyes. What a mess. What the @$%&@ was this?

"Acute sinusitis," said the doc. "Some of us have tiny holes in our roof. But if it never rains, we never know about the holes. Pollen is like rain. If you walk into a pollen storm with holes in your roof, you can expect sinusitis."

Pollen rain eight hours a day. Oh dear …

Two weeks later we drove to Los Angeles for the Mount San Antonio Relays Decathlon. I was a little weak, not in the best form.

But the first day, first event, I ran a PB 100 metres in 10.9 seconds. This was going to be good. The Olympic ideal shone brighter.

But in the second event, the Long Jump, I nearly broke my back. The sand was wet, and the pit had not been dug deeply. Going hard for my best jump my torso collapsed forward over my legs from the impetus and I heard the BANG of a gun going off. But it wasn't a gun. It was an exploding lumbar disc, and the end of Mount SAC. Maybe the end of everything. I walked like an ape for ten days. Five years of training and dreaming, up in smoke. A dead end.

But no quitting. I got walking okay by putting myself in traction, hanging upside down by my knees on a chin-up bar ten times a day. Soon I could jog gingerly. Then do laps. Within a month, running hard was back. That one jump, that one millisecond in time, gave me back pain and trouble for the rest of my life, and emergency back surgery 35 years later. As I write these words I lean back in a La-Z-Boy chair with my laptop because I can't write sitting up straight. And I did this to myself. So, I couldn't ever complain, or demand an answer to the "Why me" question, ask about the unfairness of life; about how offended I was. You're an athlete. Suck it up and shut up.

## MEETING "THE PROF"

One sunny, uneventful day in May (what an understatement "uneventful" would turn out to be!) I drove alone to train at Angell Field on the Stanford campus.

Standing by the finish line was a handsomely dressed mid-forties woman holding a stopwatch, speaking French to her ratty little dog, the dog pulling on his leash in doggy desperation to find a ratty little tree.

Oh, why not. "Bonjour," I say.

"Bonjour," followed by a few elegant French phrases that got me switching to English.

What was she doing here? At the track? With a stopwatch?

She seemed resigned to something she wasn't so keen on. But with a warm "you won't believe this" look, she furrowed her brow, leaning toward me to share a secret,

"I am timing my 'usband. 'E is trying to finish two miles. *And when 'e sees you … 'e will start to sprint."*

How odd. I saw no one who might remotely fit the description "husband" of such an elegant woman. Seeing my bewilderment, she motioned across the

Against The Tide

track. There, 200 yards from the finish, shuffling lamentably, completely bald but for a shock of grey hair wrapped in a damp diadem around his bobbing head, was a bent old man, an aged Quixote doing battle with inner demons, urging himself forward with little grunts, head bucking with every stride.

And again: "When 'e sees you, 'e will start to sprint." She grinned impishly.

Got it. Vaudeville is happening. Character unfolding.

Sure enough, on cue, the moment he rounded the corner in halting first gear and saw me standing beside his wife he shifted into overdrive and began to sprint — in a manner of speaking. Intense. Concentrating. Overtaking the great Emile Zatopek before a wild crowd, eyes fixed on the finish line, spurring himself to victory.

But not a step further.

With all four limbs more or less working together at the finish, he slammed on the brakes, tripping a little over the latency of his feet, just as the elegant lady brought his performance to an end with a click of her stopwatch. A bent-over display of heavy breathing ensued, the wrinkles on his bald head squirming in a variety of wormy patterns. Sweat running off his nose, making dimples in the dirt.

"The Prof" had just run into my life and changed it.

"Alphonse. Meet William. William, Alphonse."

This was a bit odd. She was around 40. He looked 70. But that changed as soon as he caught his breath, lit up a cigarette, and flashed a luminous, rather overly friendly smile that made me a little wary.

But we bonded like Kwik Dry cement as soon as he heard I was training to make the Canadian Team to the Tokyo Olympics. Really? "Yes. Bill Toomey and I are training together. Sometimes here. At Stanford." Bill Toomey? He was all over it. At once, he invited me to his home for a cold beer, and more track talk. Here is a character shot of him prepping for our first track-chat in his back yard.

That weekend, Bill and I returned to Stanford to watch some track races and meet "the Prof," as we were calling him already — a label he wore for life. He showed up wearing what we learned was his signature gentleman's suit, a white kerchief in his jacket pocket and a rose on the lapel. This was his proudly "reactionary" outfit on a campus that was just beginning its fateful turn to the far left, and so, as he put it, was already teeming with "conformist" students decked out in their standard uniform: blue-jeans, a T-shirt with images of various revolutionaries such as Che Guevara and Marcuse, to the latest pro-abortion feminist persuaded that individual "choice" is the only guarantor of the good. That's when I heard one of the Prof's infamous plaints for the first time: "*I am the radical on campus.* The only one in a suit. All these youngsters are the conformists." It was true. That was him, always the first to see the ironies. Here's a warm shot of this wonderful man.

At the time I hadn't a clue what "a reactionary" was, couldn't have cared less, and had no idea I would eventually become one myself. Political thought didn't interest me at all, until some years later when the Prof, who by then had created, and was running The Stanford Conservative Forum, clued me in. That changed my life, too. Big time. He brought famous speakers to campus, among them the (in)famous conservative writer William F. Buckley, who later was to come personally into my life. I hadn't a clue who Buckley was, but I got to know. Twenty five years later, thanks to the Prof's introduction, I chased him by email across much of the world to get his glowing blurb for my first political book.

Suffice it to say that over the next 36 years I became what I became mostly because of the Prof and Stanford, because of the help and direction he gave to my wandering soul. Another surrogate father and a different kind of coach. And in many ways he became what he became — healthier, a non-smoker, and a World Masters track champion, because of me. Ours was a kind of code-pendency. I'll help you run fast if you help me get smart. I bought him his first pipe and he foreswore his three-pack-a-day cigarette habit. He gave me a list of books by conservative authors, most of which were "out of print" at the time. He ran a lot faster. I'm not so sure about the smart part of our deal.

Against The Tide

# WE HAVE TO CHANGE HOW WE TRAIN

Toomey and I were down to the wire now. Is there time? Just three months before the Olympic Trials for both of us. We weren't making progress fast enough. Something had to change. So, I told Toomey, we had been training all wrong. Plain wrong. For three years. Coach Potts at CU had us doing middle-distance running. Sixteen x 220-yard runs at 85%, and so on. We were in the best possible shape … for the half-mile. But we never ran the half mile! So, what were we doing? The decathlon running events — 100m, 400m, 110m — are all-out, dynamic, full-speed events, where every tenth of a second faster means a lot more points. The 1,500m at the end of the last day? That was a gut it out, do-or-die event. I was rethinking all our training.

One afternoon a grad student showed up at Angell Field who wanted to tell us about his Ph.D. dissertation on what he called "High Performance Training." This was going to be interesting. He had researched all the best methods and here were two Olympic hopefuls for an audience. After boasting a little about the incredible comprehensiveness of his research, this bespectacled geek, with an annoyingly self-satisfied demeanour decided to ask us a key question to which he clearly felt only he had ever discovered the answer. He was obviously no athlete himself. I mean, not like us. But he was going to point us in the right direction. Give us the inside secret.

"What do you think is the single most important concept in all athletic training?" Drums rolling …

I had been thinking a lot about what I was going to say to Toomey that very evening. So, it was classic to see this fellow's jaw drop open, and his eyes pop in a kind of disbelief, when I said "*Specificity*. The best training has to be 100% specific to whatever your sport is."

Well, he was crushed. His secret was out. How did an ordinary undergrad athlete standing in the hot sun at Angell Field know the answer?

"Yes. that's it. *Specificity*," he mumbled, and walked away, an uneasy mixture of Ph.D. satisfaction and perplexity, his balloon pricked.

But he had verified our new training regime.

The next day Toomey and I began a final surge for the Games in Tokyo. Very few, but very high-speed efforts, much more rest between each. Simulations of competition for each event. Practice technique a lot. But then, just three tries, that's it. No fouling. Max efforts in the weight room. We had awfully sore legs until we got used to this. And this is still why, whenever Bill, who was to become the greatest decathlete in the world calls me, he's always generous in saying, "You got me started."

Specificity was our secret weapon.

It was all training now, working only part-time (and some secret writing, a little more each day), until late June when I left California, with no mind ever to return. Good luck at your Trials, buddy. It's been a good time. See you in Tokyo! Wow. Really? You think so? Then into my Nash Rambler for a 45-hour drive back to Canada.

## THE CANADIAN DECATHLON TRIALS AND C.K. YANG – WORLD DECATHLON CHAMPION

I'm not sure why or how it happened, and there could hardly have been a more incongruous setting. But for some unexplained reason, one of the highest-scoring decathlon men in the world, an anti-communist Chinese national from the Republic of China (Formosa, now called Taiwan) named C.K. Yang — the very man who had lost a gruelling fight for gold against the American Rafer Johnson in the 1960 Olympic Decathlon in Rome — was coming to Toronto. He had set a stunning world record of 9,121 points in 1963 at California's Mount San Antonio College — the very same place where I badly injured my back just this past spring. And now, this legend shows up in Toronto? At the crappy little track in East York where our Trials were being held? Those were the days before synthetic "Tartan" tracks and jumping surfaces (made of a rubbery material created by 3M) came to Canada. Why was this Prince among athletes here, with a bunch of Paupers?

"C.K.", as he was known, was living and training at UCLA in California, but had friends in Toronto. Our Olympic Trials would be just a training event for him. A few other world-class Americans aiming for the U.S. Olympic team came too. Among them, Willie Davenport, the world-class hurdler I spoke of earlier who was to win Olympic Gold in Mexico in 1968 in the 110m high hurdles. On this track he managed only 14.1." I think of his impressive ebony figure jetting over those hurdles, then of his future sudden death by heart attack at age 59 at O'Hare airport. Lights out. The ephemerality of life strikes me. If only he had known. Maybe better he didn't. Two months later I set a Canadian Native Record of 14.2" in this event at the CNE stadium — on another really bad track. Willie must have been taking it easy. Mel Pender came to this meet, too. Good 'ole, "How's your mom?" Mel. And Al Oerter, too, probably the greatest discus thrower ever, and eventually a four-time Olympic Gold medallist. But I can only imagine what C.K. thought when he saw this track. After a few events the soft inside lane was a mess, so dug up by runners' spikes it looked like preparation for a bad vegetable garden.

The qualifying rule for the Olympic Games is that any national Champion

Against The Tide

is *eligible* to compete at the Games without regard to level of performance. But if a nation wants to send up to three athletes in any event, the second and third have to make the Olympic Standard. In Canada's case, all we knew was that no Canadian, national champ or not, would be considered for the Olympics without making that Olympic Standard. In the USA, if you finish in the top three at the Olympic Trials and make Standard, you are automatically on the US Olympic Team. You could be the world record holder, but if you don't finish in the top three, you're done. But in Canada, where there was less money to send athletes, word got out, sort of, that only 12 track athletes would be picked for Canada's Olympic track team. So even making the Standard was no guarantee. The Selection Committee, tired after long Trials, would sit around a table well-lubricated with scotch whisky and argue until midnight about which 12 Canadians of the 30 or so who had made standard in various events had the best chance to do well at the actual Games in Tokyo. It was a crapshoot.

The 1964 Olympic standard for the decathlon was 7,000 points. I had won my Pan American Games Silver Medal in Brazil in 1963 with 6,812, which at the time set a new Canadian and Commonwealth record. So, I had a shot. But these Trials took place at two levels. There was C.K., who had won silver in the prior Olympics, had a world record under his belt. He was also one of the world's finest pole vaulters, using the new type of fiberglass pole which over-night had changed that event from pole vaulting, to catapulting. I didn't have a fiberglass pole and was still using a rigid steel pole while this Chinese world champ was going into orbit. I was vaulting. He was catapulting — something I never learned to do in time for the games.

The drama of the Trials for me was whether or not I was going to make 7,000 points to qualify for our Olympic Team. After each event some official would get the scoring tables out and speculate over the loudspeaker on "what Gairdner still has to do" to make 7,000 points, how far off I was, and so on. For two days.

As it happened, C.K., a really quiet, sweet man, was the embodiment of the Olympic ideal: Citius, Altius, Fortius. He was Faster, Higher, and Stronger … than me, and everyone else in the world. He proceeded to do his own thing, as the saying goes, and I did mine. Well, maybe not stronger than me. He beat me in 7 events, and I beat him in three, which included the shot, discus, and 1,500 metre events. C.K. won easily.

But whether or not I was going to make the Canadian team came down to the last event, the 1,500 metres. I'm sorry to say, C.K. was embarrassingly gutless in this event. Lloyd would have ripped a strip off him for cowardice. I would have to run tired and alone, under 4'31" to make over 7,000 points, and he would be of no help at all. Ordinarily that time would not have been a problem. I was ready. But the first lane was so chewed up after two days of races I seriously thought I might have to run most of the race in lane two. But that would add about 20 feet to each lap. Not a good idea. I could switch to lane two just on the straightaways, couldn't I? But I would still have to run about 10 feet farther, but maybe enough faster to make up for that? It was a Games/No-Games dilemma.

The gun went off, and my heart took off. The guy on the loudspeaker knew what I had to do, and let everyone know, lap by lap. My Olympic hopes were ticking by, second by second. Try to run smoothly. Fast legs, but not too much push on the footing, cuz it will just give way like sand and wear you out. This was a technical challenge as much as a physical one. I ran alone the whole way and finished, overcome with relief, in 4'28.3". That time beat C.K. by almost a full minute for a point total of 7,030 which exceeded the Olympic Decathlon Standard and set another new Commonwealth and Canadian record. At the finish, I had time to turn around and see this world-beater, king of decathlete's, finish his 1,500 lamentably, phlegmatically, plainly afraid of the effort. Afraid of pain. Coach Percival's words were "be a man, son". Fear nothing. Rodents feel fear. Men feel "reasonable apprehension." The only thing to fear, is fear itself. The Olympic ideal includes manliness. Rage, rage. Face the storm. Go forth boldly. I was amazed at C.K.'s talent, but ashamed of him, too. His weakling effort tainted my admiration.

But it was over. Now I just had to wait to hear from the men sitting around the table all night with their scotch. But there was no word. Just silence. Please

*Against The Tide*

put me out of my misery. But still only silence. Then word leaked that "the Badgers" — our athletes' term for self-important track officials — would announce Canada's Olympic Team in Montreal, after the Open Trials the following weekend. So, now I would have to go to Montreal to compete in the 110m high hurdles. And maybe in the 400m hurdles, too? How many events would I have to compete in to make this team? I was angry now. My Olympic chances seemed much farther away. Now I would have to compete against specialists in individual events.

## THE OLYMPIC TRIALS, MONTREAL

The scene on the track at St. Lambert Stadium in Montreal, was chaotic. Forty-mile-an-hour winds were shaking the CBC's two plastic-shrouded TV towers and collapsing tents set up on the infield for press and officials. Badgers were everywhere, leaning into the wind, or backward, heels in so as not to be pushed too fast as they walked, most of them clutching pieces of paper, some of which would escape their grip and sail off to Montreal without ever touching the ground.

On the Friday evening I was to run the final of the 110m high hurdles. It didn't look good. Cliff Nuttall, a 6'3" man with whom I was always trading wins, was the favourite. The headwind favoured him, because in a sprint-hurdle race, even in calm air, but especially with a tailwind, a long-legged man has to chop each stride, or he will hit hurdles. But in a headwind, he can let 'er rip. An all-out sprint. However, a short 5'11" guy like me has to struggle just to make it over each hurdle even in calm air. High hurdles reached up higher than my bellybutton; so, I loved a tail wind pushing me.

But on this evening, it was a ferocious headwind. Erratic, gusting. With "On your marks," the plastic shroudings on the TV tower were snapping like the dogs of hell. Then the gun, and it was a sprint for all you're worth. Stay low. Cliff and I were thundering, side by side the whole way, hurdle by hurdle, striving, diving, and got off the last hurdle exactly together. But at the tape his lean beat me by a couple of inches. Neither of us had a chance to make Standard into that wind. But I had just won a silver medal in the Canadian High Hurdle Championship. Jeez. A few inches, and … well, that would have to do. I hoped the Selection Committee took note that I not only won the decathlon with a national and Commonwealth record but came down here and just about upset Canada's best high hurdler.

In the morning, I got up with my pride intact and excuses ready. No way I was going to run the 400m hurdles. I shouldn't have to. Enough, already. Jeez.

C'mon. But on the way to breakfast I had to walk past Coach Percival's room, and his is door was wide open. So, I let him know the score.

"Coach. Honestly. I don't think I have to … I mean, I don't really *want* to run the 400m hurdles." Assertive. "I've done enough, coach, right?" He was lounging in a green dressing gown on an easy chair and didn't say much. But the silence was loud. I was bracing myself for a coaching speech. Like, one of his "Kid, if you want to fly, you can fly" speeches, that were so hard to resist.

But he just looked at me impassively. "Your decision, kid." Oh dear. *My decision*? I wasn't quite ready for that. I wanted my not running to be *his* decision. Walking away, I felt pretty good I had taken control. Still, I sensed he was sizing me up.

So, I would overeat my breakfast to eliminate the question, right? No need for discussion. On the way back, after walking past the track, seeing all the 400m hurdles laid out and ready, I told Coach I ate a lot. *A lot.* He knew I was trying to sabotage myself. So, I would see him at the track in a couple of hours and we would watch George Shepherd, Canadian champion in the 400m hurdles try to make the Olympic Team. No one was going to make Standard in this wind. So, it was almost stupid to even try, right? But George was tough and would certainly try. And I wanted him to make it. It felt a little mean-spirited to think I was expected to make it tougher for him. Wouldn't not running be more generous.

So, I lay down to digest, like an Amazonian python had has just swallowed a pig. They can dislocate their jaws. I saw a picture once of a python doing a three-month digestion of a cow, asleep, head and horns sticking out of its mouth. Yuck. True, I really sabotaged myself. Running would be impossible now. It was over. That brought a smile of satisfaction and relief. Maybe I should try to sleep?

But I couldn't. Digestion was running way ahead of schedule. In an hour or so I began to feel too good. Pancake power. And couldn't get the image of those hurdles, standing so neatly, out of my head, calling, calling. Just like summit fever. The silence of those hurdles had me tossing, turning. Oh, Jeez … I was in trouble now; doubt was turning to dare.

Cursing at yourself is ridiculous, but that's what I heard as I jumped out of bed, "Damn. Damn. Damn" [expletives deleted], as I pulled on my running outfit and went straight to Coach's room.

He was waiting, in his eyes a knowing mix of relief and pride. I was one of his Red Devils. One of his kids. It was himself he saw in me.

"Okay. Just the heat, Coach. Just for fun. Just to see what happens."

"Sure kid. You go get 'em. One hurdle at a time." And then, "Hey. 'By Courage to the Utmost.'" Coach had always said you can't take all life's hurdles at once.

Against The Tide

You take 'em one at a time. If you start thinking about the next one while you're on this one, *you're gonna hit it*. BANG. Finished. The 400m hurdles, one of the toughest races on the track, is not about guts. Or self-control. It's about both. The classic challenge of mind over body, of not getting beaten by yourself. Grace under fire. I had run 300m hurdles at Colorado, but this would be my first 400m hurdle race. So, I really had no idea what I could do. One hundred metres farther, with two more hurdles to get over, dead tired. It's a classic test of athletic prowess requiring acute self-knowledge while in numbing pain and fatigue. By the 300-metre mark, you can't feel your legs, and so the risk of smashing into a hurdle is huge. It was precisely this self-mastery challenge I liked.

At the track the same crazy wind was flapping and snapping. Nothing loose had a chance. But it was my wind now. It would blow me down the backstretch for the first half and when I came into the wind on the home stretch, adding a stride between the last two hurdles, it would be perfect.

George wasn't talking. To him I was just a decathlon man. Jack of all trades, master of none. An interloper. So, he ignored me. Top four to qualify for the final, and his heat was first. George took off and won easily, and then walked past me avoiding eye contact. A psych job. I was up next, and oh, the Gods were smiling. I had expected to be leg-tired from two my high hurdle races the night before. But this was one of those surprise days athletes dream of. On fire. Floating over the ground. No fatigue, as I brought it home first into that wind, gearing down, being sure to qualify a little slower than George, so as not to alert him. But it seemed fair to warn him, "Get ready, George. It's gonna be fast!" That would be true. I had nothing to lose, and he, everything. George had made the 1960 Olympic Team in this very event, and badly wanted to make it again. Good heavens, *I* wanted him to make it. If they had already picked me, I could have left this race to George. But no such luck. He was going to have to beat me to get to Tokyo. And I was going to have to beat him to get to Tokyo. One of us would soon be collateral damage. Which would it be? With my "fast" comment, the knife was in. George was annoyed now and just a little worried, so he wandered away, still with no eye contact.

Two hours later, a colder wind was blowing. I had lane four, and George five. I would be able to watch him all the way until the time came to try to pass. All runners were standing in their lanes, except me. I was never a really fast runner, so exact hurdle technique and a super warm-up were crucial to my effort. It's a big mistake to take sweats off too soon in a cold wind. Where could I find refuge from the chilling? After a great warm-up I stole inside an officials' tent set up near the start of the race. They were a little shocked. "*This is for Media only*." But I made like I didn't hear them, lay down quickly, and put my legs up. "Two minutes, gentlemen." I would get the instant leg-heat and refresh I needed before they figured out how to toss me out. Deep breathing. The heat and sweat came on strong. I could see my competitors taking their sweats off too soon, vapour spiralling from their thighs in the cooling wind as they waited for the starter's call.

And for me.

From the loudspeakers: "Lane Four! Where's lane Four?"

I bolted from the tent, stripped off my sweats, and stood ready, with very hot legs.

"On Your Marks!" There is no more tense moment for a hurdler. Miss your stride pattern, hit one hurdle, and it's over. Five years on the line. A moment in time. Why does it matter? Why write about it? Because everyone has moments in time that shape their lives for better or worse. That's why we remember them and write about them. Tokyo. No Tokyo. Tokyo. No Tokyo. That would be my gamble on all ten hurdles.

George and I were off fast, over each hurdle together, and back on the ground running. This wind-aided part of the race was fast and effortless. I got to watch George, a mirror image of myself, except I was on and off each hurdle just a little quicker than him. Closing on him now. But save it. Around the bottom turn there will be major wind-shock against us beginning halfway to the eighth hurdle. Hurdlers have to know such things with precision, prepared to shorten, lengthen, or add a stride as suddenly as conditions change. At the eighth, the hurdles are side by side. And George and I were side by side. As the wind hit us, the real race began. Ninth hurdle, still side by side. Tenth and last, still side by side. The wind, and shouts of the crowd, excited by a close race, were filling our ears.

Our lead-leg touch-down was precisely together off the last hurdle. And then, we began a classic, timeless footrace over 40 metres to the finish. Peripherally, I could see George's arms, his head twisting with effort, and he saw me, each knowing what this meant, as we drove hard as we could, then harder still, with blasted, knotted muscles, searing lungs — in my head, in George's too, I was sure — were fleeting images, a kind of visceral awareness of all the great runners who have done this very thing, just like us; called to win; striving physically of course, but metaphorically taking their place in a kind of brotherhood of striving that echoes down through the ages. This was the reality of all my boyhood imaginings under the covers at Appleby reading about legendary track heroes who achieved the impossible, winning when everything was against them. We were all of them now, time and history collapsing in slow motion, placeholders in that brotherhood of athletic heroes, making our own history in this very moment. And in that moment,

Against The Tide

George slipped slowly behind just before I crossed the finish line. Receding in sight and time. A slow-motion fade. In my first try, I was now Canadian 400m Hurdle Champion. It was a real upset, and everyone knew it. Joy for me. Tragedy for George.

Bent over, barely realizing what had just happened, I almost got disqualified, because there was a well-known rule: "no coaches on the infield." But as I stood upright, I saw Coach Percival climbing over a waist-high fence separating the stands from the track, running toward me. A Badger shouted something about breaking the rules, but Coach didn't care. Impulse had him in its grip. "The little man" ran toward me, grabbed me by the waist and hoisted me in the air, and then, oddly for a man who never swore, cried out [expletive deleted] "You @#$&@ hero!," and ran back into the stands. Classic Coach. Late that evening, I was named to our 12-man Olympic Track and Field Team to Tokyo, for both the Decathlon and the 400m hurdles, and went joyfully, buoyantly, feet not quite touching the ground into Montreal for some celebration.

Close to midnight, after bar-hopping on Rue Sainte Catherine with a teammate, the smell of *pommes-frites* in the air, rock and roll music roiling from darkened doorways, we climbed up to a second-floor bar, and ... the first person we saw in that near-empty, smoke-filled place, sitting behind a row of empty quart-sized bottles of Molson beer, was George.

Hunched shoulders. Both hands gripping a sweating beer bottle, as if trying to squeeze the race he had wanted from the bottle. Tiny specks of perspiration on each cheekbone. No greeting to speak of. He got right to his point, which, it was quite apparent, was one of deep disappointment that (to employ a terrible metaphor) had been blowing around in the windmills of his mind that whole tragic evening but was just about to make an exit. He let go of his bottle, sat bolt upright, finished a deep, sad, weary breath, and said,

"You got lucky."

I was going to push back. That was not luck, George.

But I didn't. He looked too sorrowful, I just couldn't.

"You know George, you're right. I got lucky."

## TO THE LAND OF THE RISING SUN: THE OLYMPIC GAMES, TOKYO, OCT. 10-24, 1964.

The Tokyo Olympics was the largest Games in history — over 5,000 athletes from 93 nations. It was opened by the Olympic torchbearer, Yoshinori Sakai (d. 2014), who ran into the stadium to the roar of the crowd and then very gingerly up hundreds of steps to the top of the stadium to light the Olympic Torch with the eyes of the world on him. He was born August 6, 1945, at the very moment the world's first ever Atomic Bomb exploded over Hiroshima, instantly incinerating over 100,000 citizens asleep in their beds. Sakai and the flame were an international symbol of peace, of homage to the dead, and of Japan's reconstruction from a disastrous war with the West.

Here is a keeper photo of me going over a hurdle that appeared in a *Globe and Mail* article about the Canadian team to Tokyo.

It was also the last Games held on a dirt track, using hand-held stopwatches; the first to allow fiberglass pole vault poles; and as I like to say, it was "the last happy Games" because there were no drugs to cheat with, no money paid turning amateurs into pros, and no politics to disrupt the Olympic Peace, as it is called.

Here is a photo of our Canadian Team standing in the shape of a Maple Leaf on the Tarmac at Vancouver International Airport, ready to board for Tokyo.

Our first moments in Japan were not very Japanese. We got spirited by bus from a darkened airport to our Olympic Village — a collection of Western-style bungalows in a restored US Military complex in the Yoyogi neighbourhood of Tokyo. There was a training field nearby, flags from all nations flapping cheerfully. Western buildings. Western food. Nothing very Japanese yet. But dramatically modern Olympic architecture by Kenzo Tange, as seen below. Tange won the world's highest award for this building, "one of the most beautiful buildings of the 20th century," in 1987.

*Against The Tide*

Our sudden saturation in all things Eastern came upon us delightfully when, on our second evening, a few of us took a modern western subway train to Shinjuku station and climbed the stairs into Japan for the first time. I have been reluctant to write about this for so many years for fear I cannot do it justice. But here goes …

We climbed the stairs from the Subway and were immediately surrounded. Invaded? Engulfed? Swallowed up? Senses filled, captivated by the sight of red and white paper lanterns, delicate black and red swoops and swipes written in this new, strange-sounding calligraphy brushed so artfully on them, bobbing gaily out of sight all along that crowded narrow street, hanging by doorways of tiny shops, their small, paper-paned wooden windows sliding open to entice buyers, then closing again; small eating spots with but a half-dozen seats behind decorative cloth banners luffing in the light breeze, under which you had to duck to get in, swirling smoke, the smell of sizzled *yakitori* chicken, the novel sight of *sushi* — raw fish? They eat raw fish here? — and then, lovely, kimono-clad Japanese girls mincing along side-by-side on wooden clogs — clack-clacking on the street — delicate pale fingers over giggling mouths. And from second-storey windows, raucous, black-tuniced university boys with *sake* reddened cheeks, singing loudly, regaling their friends across the street from their window-perches with such gusto they almost fell out, as fascinated to see us, the *Gaijin* — foreigners, or outsiders — as we were to see them.

"Hallo! Hey! *Konbanwa*," — good evening, we shouted. And when they saw our Maple Leaf, they shouted back, "Hai, Kanada-Jin!" All Japan was caught up in Olympic Joy, and we loved it.

## THE OPENING CEREMONIES

Nothing can quite capture or compare to the feeling of marching with your country's best athletes into a stadium of 80,000 excited people. Here is a photo of that scene, pigeons flying all over the place.

After some searching, I found a British film on YouTube of this moment our Canadian Olympic Team marching into the Olympic Stadium.[6] At minute 13:11 I see myself briefly, near the rear, third file in, with dark glasses.

Unless they are drunk — and in this respect I discovered that like our Indians, they are quite unable to tolerate much alcohol — the Japanese people are emotionally undemonstrative (an under-under-statement), in the Western sense. After living among them awhile, the signs of deep emotion are easy to see migrating microscopically about in subtle glances and tones of voice. But for a Westerner, the silence can be very unnerving in a crowd of 80,000. I did run the 400m hurdles in Tokyo but had not really prepared for it. The Decathlon kept me busy enough. And I had no chance to make the final in the hurdles, anyway. So, I ran the heat just to get rid of the heebie-jeebies. That was a good thing, because it was a little wet when we first walked into that massive crowd in the Olympic Stadium, and if you haven't ever seen 80,000 umbrellas opened over the heads of a people who express their excitement with profound silence, you can see this at minute 52:21 of this film. The presence of absent sounds.

You can also get a glimpse of the Olympic village we lived in at 1:10:42.

And in sadness, you can watch the dramatic end of the Marathon at 1:55:11 when the Japanese favourite, Kokichi Tsuburaya, with whom I spent a little time, gets beaten for the silver medal by the Englishman world record-holder, Basil Heatley, in the last few hundred yards in front of his home crowd, which crushed him.

I sat with him on an airplane on the way to a meet in Osaka after the Games, when he revealed his deep sadness and shame, a shame from which he could not be shaken. He told one of his teammates after the race, "I committed an inexcusable blunder in front of the Japanese people. I have to make amends by running and hoisting the Japanese Flag in the next Olympics, in Mexico."

Even so young he was already a sport cripple, so to speak, in the service of the emperor, whom the Japanese considered a quasi-god. By sport cripple I mean he had already bent his life out of shape for a single ideal at the expense of all others. You can see it in his face on the podium after this race. With considerable shock I learned some years later that he committed suicide by slashing his wrist in January of 1968 at a training camp for the Mexico Olympic Games. He was found in his room, lying on his bed, clutching his bronze medal to his chest. He left a note to his family, in which he spoke of himself in the third person, saluted all his siblings, as customary:

> *My dear Father and my dear Mother,*
> *Kokichi is too tired to run anymore.*
> *I beg you to forgive me.*
> *Your hearts must never have rested worrying and caring for me.*
> *My dear Father and Mother, Kokichi would have liked to live by your side.*

I well up just reading his mournful note.

## MY OLYMPIC DECATHLON

A curveball number one came from team member Bruce Kidd two nights before my decathlon. He was an astonishingly talented distance runner as a teenager, but unfortunately for his career, had the worst running technique imaginable; an engaging style of running very high on the balls of his feet and bobbing and scooping his arms in a way that was hard not to watch, because biomechanically speaking, it was as if he was trying to go backward and forward with every dogged step. Coach Percival had warned Kidd's coach, Fred Foot, that this technique was so bad it was going to cripple Bruce with achilles tendonitis. But Fred didn't listen. So, Kidd kept bobbing along from one impressive race to another. We were watching an athlete destroy his own ability. By the time he got on our Olympic Team he was injured so badly he ran like a straggler, finishing close to last. Sad. But he was also committed to reporting on the Games for the University of Toronto Student newspaper and had decided that late at night when the rest of us were trying to sleep would be a good time to write his little stories in a closet space between the toilet and the bedroom on an old mechanical typewriter, each metallic key slamming like a hammer. OMG. Really?

So, I was out of bed at least three times to ask Bruce. Please. Stop. Oh, he pleads, "I have to make deadline." Yeah, but the rest of us have to sleep. This went on for a long time, and I am not quite sure why I didn't just throw his puny body out on the street. Very late, me losing more sleep, he finally stops, and I finally get some rest. It was unforgivably selfish.

Curve-ball number two was the worst, and a fluke I inflicted on myself. Mom and Dad had come to Japan to watch the Games as the first leg of a planned trip around the world, and the night before my decathlon, invited me to have dinner with them at the Tokyo Hilton. Better food than at the Olympic Village, I thought, and surely safe at such a high-end Western hotel.

*Against The Tide*

It was a bad move that could not have been foreseen.

Back at the Olympic Village by nine o'clock, my Olympic Games began to implode. Or perhaps explode is a better word. At first, minor abdominal cramps. Then bad. Then very bad, with non-stop visits to the washroom. This went on for many painful hours, with useless returns to bed, legs very stiff and sore from so much sitting on a hard toilet seat. Someone called the team coach, who found me groaning and miserable, curled up in bed, so he sent for the team doctor, who was in Tokyo with the Geishas, and didn't show up until three hours later at 4:30 a.m., when he gave me *laudanum*, a kind of opium that stops cramps. Within a half hour, and about five pounds lighter, I slept for two hours, quite exhausted. Meanwhile, my dad was back at the Hilton with the same problem. It turned out we had ingested the *Yersinia* bacterium, and the problem didn't clear up for six months. When I awoke, I could not bear the thought of eating, and considered dropping out of the Games. Should I? Would I? Could I? It was unthinkable. Shameful. But how was I going to compete in a gruelling two-day event in such a weakened state? Then Coach's words came: "You can only get over one hurdle at a time, in sport, or in life." So, I decided to stay the course. The warm-up is the first hurdle. Just get through the warm-up, Bill.

I remember walking into the stadium before the 100 metres, the first decathlon event, my mom and dad high in the stands. I pointed to my stomach and bent over, and so did dad. Oh dear. At least they knew what I was facing, would understand the failure ahead of me. Very stiff and sore legs made my first of ten events a graceless labour for fewer points than I ought to have earned. My best 100 metre time was 10.9" in that Los Angeles meet, but with stiff legs there was no chance of doing that again. Here is a photo of the finish with the bronze medallist Hans Walde of Germany on my left, at 11.0" and Rein Aun of the USSR on my right at 10.9," with me trailing at 11.2."

From then until the last event of the first day ten hours later, the 400 metre run, I was executing a robotic emotionless sequence, warming-up for each event, competing, then drinking more green tea, which was all I could keep down. Evening was falling, the stadium lights came on, and I was still a little shaky, still not fully present. Bitterly upset; no, deeply angry, deeply disappointed, chagrined at this fluke, like, there is no God, or some such ridiculous self-absorbed note of despair. But nothing was owed me. Life is full of curveballs. Not your fault if you get knocked down, but your fault if you don't get up, and all that. I know, I know.

So now I'm standing on the 400 metre track at the Olympic Games in Tokyo, in lane three, with Vasily Kusnetzov of the USSR, in lane four, the veteran eight years older than me, who had competed in the 1956 and 1960 Olympics, and who became a hero when I watched him compete in Philadelphia in the USA vs. USSR meet in 1959, the same year he broke the world decathlon record for the second time. If I was going to salvage something, anything, from this awful first day, make the memory of it something to be proud of, it would have to be personal and private. So, beat a world-record holder in this race? That would feel good.

At the gun I was on automatic pilot, and to hell with sickness and my feelings. Vasily had never in his career broken 50" in a decathlon 400m. But he was moving fast. As we swept down the backstretch I had the pride of my 400m victory in Brazil in mind, was gaining slowly, and overtook him at the 300m mark. Yes! And Yes, again, as he disappeared behind me. Vasily ran 49.5" for the best 400m of his life. And I was deeply gratified to beat him with 49.2." This wasn't exactly making history, but that's what it felt like. I'd saved a little face, with myself, at least.

After a decent sleep and some food, I felt better the next morning, though legs were still not back to normal. The first event on day two is the 110 metre hurdles, normally one of my best events. On September 9th I had equalled the Canadian Native Record at the CNE grounds in 14.2," competing against

Against The Tide

the World Indoor champion, the American Hayes Jones, and the Canadian Champion Cliff Nuttall, who had beaten me at Montreal a month before running into that horrific wind. That record race was at Toronto's Exhibition grounds on a track even worse than the one at East York. Race cars one day, runners the next, that sort of thing, and they pack it down a little in between. Really. Jones was going to win easily but I wanted at least to beat him to the first hurdle. Which I didn't. I tried so hard I hit it, instead, and almost fell flat on my face. But somehow, the shock of hitting that hurdle gained me such a shot of adrenalin I literally bounced back up and ran my fastest race ever, passing Cliff Nuttall on the way to that record. Alas, in Tokyo I had a lamentable race of 15.4" and lost about 100 points that should have been an easy get.

As sick as I felt, I don't know how it happened, but I managed two personal bests in the last two events, the javelin and the 1,500-metre run. The javelin left my hand and disappeared into the sky, soaring in a perfect trajectory, a round shiny silver dollar stuck on a baby-blue sky, landing almost 200 feet away. I was happier now, with at least one PB.

By the time of the 1,500 the crowd was melding into darkness, staring down at what must have seemed to them very small figures in the stadium lights. There were five of us in my heat, and I ran with the pack for some time in a kind of mindless stupor, just glad that each step was getting me closer to the end of a very bad experience. Then, with a lap to go, and still in the middle of the pack, something quite unexpected happened. I was worrying about what I had left in the tank, when suddenly, in that ominously quiet stadium, a familiar voice broke the silence, booming from on high:

**"GET THE LEAD OUT, GAIRDNER!"**

When I heard that voice I sprang ahead as if jabbed by a cattle prod, but grinning from cheek to cheek. It was Bill Toomey! I had no idea he was in Tokyo, as he hadn't made the American team. And as if to connect with our time together, to acknowledge the dream we shared, I was now going to give it my all, for me, and for Bill, and I fairly sprinted the last lap to win by a hundred yards in 4'24.2," the best time of my life.

Overall, I was unavoidably disappointed to have fallen sick, not to have been at my best, but was overcome with a sense of relief the ordeal had ended. On the bright side, even though placing what I felt was a mediocre eleventh of 22 nations, my score and PB of 7,234 points again set a new Canadian, and British Commonwealth Record.

I never saw Bill at the games and had no idea where to find him.

But he sure got the lead out.

# ANOTHER TWIST OF FATE

October 23rd I was packing up for the trip home the following day when the *Chef de Mission* of the Canadian team, definitely on a mission, burst into our cabin without knocking and made a beeline for me. He was concentrating on something that once again was about to change my life.

"Bill. There's a Triangular Track Meet in Osaka this weekend, between the USA, Japan, and the British Commonwealth. The Commonwealth doesn't have a javelin thrower. How would you like to throw the javelin for our side?"

This drew a blank.

"Sure. Great. But we're flying home tomorrow. How do I get home?"

Then he pulled the rabbit out of the hat.

"We give you an open ticket."

"Really?"

"Yup. You come home when you want. Or … not at all." The tack-on words were delivered with a gift-giver grin and the intimation of an older man, thinking, "I wish I were you, and had that option." Holy opportunity.

I went straight to the Tokyo Hilton to tell my parents I was going to stay in Japan for a while. Not sure how long. Couldn't say why. Not sure when I'll be back. They were a little surprised. So was I. And still lost in terms of committing to any sort of serious future in line with Gairdner male history, but I figured I better get on with — with what? I disliked the phrase "I need to find myself," so I didn't try it on them. I just said I thought being immersed in a wholly alien culture and language for a while would help me see things more clearly, without Western ways and presumptions, or family life and Gairdner expectations (Big Jim: "I never knew a successful man who went to university!" And Dad: "Literature is what you do at night before bed"). Oh boy. More stalling. But there was a slim chance I might come out of a sojourn in the East with clearer vision. Something could emerge naturally, Zen-like, unpremeditated, from raw experience, right?

During the Olympics, all Tokyo had been draped with signage in English, French and German. So, Japan didn't yet seem foreign, alien. But the Canadian Team was gone now, and I was on a plane to Osaka, chatting awkwardly with the gentle, fated Tsuburaya, with no idea then he would be stone dead in three years, blood-dripping wrist hanging from his bed.

I threw the javelin for the Commonwealth, then got dropped back in Tokyo, more-or-less on my own. Western languages stripped clean away. This was VERY foreign. But as fortune would have it, Dad was a member of the Young Presidents' Organization (YPO), and had written to a Mr. Okabe, a Japanese YPO member who had kindly sent me a written invitation, beautifully scripted

Against The Tide

by hand on delicate rice paper, and who had asked us to contact him when we got to Japan. So, we did. After Dad and Mom left he sent his aide to help me to find a rental room in Shinjuku. I wanted to live with a lower-middle class Japanese family that spoke no English. We found a ground floor, six-*tatami* room in a home owned by the Kamata family at 118 Tomihisa-cho street — a typical tight Tokyo laneway with a public bath at the end. This picture captures the mood.

Every morning, on a short walk you could easily reach food stall merchants selling all kinds of Japanese food, including familiar items such as *tamango* (eggs), *pan* (bread) and *mikan* (mandarin oranges), which became my daily breakfast. A *tatami* is a rice-reed mat 6' x 3'. My room was less than 100 square feet in size. Enough for me, a futon, a small bedside table, and a sliding-door cupboard to store the futon each morning. Down the hall was a common toilet (*benjo*) and a dark, tight little cubicle with a sink and a small gas-burner for cooking. The rent seemed okay until I learned they wanted the same amount in "key" money. Tokyo law forbade charging rent above a certain amount. So, they didn't. They charged extra for the key.

My world was now intensely Japanese. "Kanji" (Japanese written characters derived from ancient pictographs) seemed everywhere. No English to help navigate. Kanji are borrowed from Chinese, which is a tonal language without inflection. But Japanese is a syllabic, inflected language with case and tense endings, and the like, so they had to invent a set of scripts and tack them on to the Kanji to make themselves understood. What do these often beautifully elegant hand-drawn characters mean? The typical Japanese university student will have to learn over 10,000 *Kanji* before graduation, an arduous process. But with a mere 26 letters, we can write anything a Japanese can write. What happened? They missed the incredible simplicity of our alphabet. We missed the incredible visual esthetic and historical nuance of their complex characters.

Upstairs lived a soft-spoken, shy student named Shigenori Nagao, from the southernmost island of Kyushu, with whom I lost touch after leaving Japan.

I traveled with him and his friends on a crowded train with lots of rice-eating passengers to Hakone to see Mt. Fuji, reflecting on its majesty across serene Lake Ashinoko.

*Against The Tide*

My immersion in a in foreign culture was successful from an isolation point of view. Just me and a couple of books: Alan Watts's *What Is Zen?*, which I figured would introduce me quickly to Oriental thinking; and Hannah Arendt's *The Human Condition*, a title that intrigued me, because I was trying to figure out my own condition. She was interesting, but of no help. At first I got in the Zen mood, but after a while decided there's too much suppression of passionate feeling. I did catch on to the gist of Zen a little, especially, I think (but don't think too much — you'll ruin the experience!) when I read a little story about a Zen Abbot (a *Jushoku*) who died, and the monastery needed a replacement. So, the interim leader told all mourning monks that the first one who could say what the empty jug he placed on the floor at the front of the room is — *without saying what it is!* — would be the next Abbot of the monastery. That got my attention because it seemed illogical (the point of the question). How do you explain what something is without explaining what it is? It was a Zen head-scratcher, and all the monks tried hard for many days.

When they failed, a collective dejection arose, and at the very moment they gave up, the lowly cook of the monastery happened by and asked what was troubling them? They repeated the question. The cook paused briefly, then strode straight to the front of the room and kicked the jug over. Everyone was amazed and enlightened, for without saying a word, the cook fully revealed the purpose of the jug in a flash of insight simply by negating its function. So he became the new Abbot.

As for Hannah Arendt's fine book? Frankly, I wasn't really awake yet to that level of intellectual inquiry, but it was enough to create quite an appetite for high thought, which has never left me. She was a Jewish student, and then lover of Martin Heidegger, a German thinker often hailed as the greatest modern philosopher in the continental (non-analytical) tradition. He was also, I was to learn, a member of the Nazi Party (a membership he never renounced, even post-war), and the intellectual father of a lot of brilliant thinkers whose work I was subsequently to study, such as the works by Karl Löwith (*Meaning in History*), and Hans Jonas (*The Gnostic Religion*).

I may get to these later in this memoir because they reconfigured my notion of Christianity and of Western civilization. The combination was interesting because Heidegger thought with a kind of pre-logical Zen intuition. In his most influential and inscrutable work *Being and Time*, he was flirting with the relationship between "Being" — like, what *is* existence? — and Nothingness, and how they produce each other, so to speak, just as for Zen philosophers, the jug that got kicked over to reveal its meaning, was kicked out of its inert nothingness, into the fullness of its unique purpose and being. Without this sort of insight, you can't understand Heidegger (not that I do). We Westerners sometimes have the same sort of Zen insight such as when we describe dying as "kicking the bucket."

So much for loneliness and the mind. My body was acting up now. The worst of my sickness was over. But I was getting very fidgety from lack of exercise, even getting some of my boyhood tics back. But what I loved had betrayed me, a broken dream, and so for a while at least, the mere idea of running was repugnant. Perhaps in the back of my mind I imagined that when I recovered, I might train for the Mexico Olympics of 1968? Perhaps by then I could approach 8,000 points? But for now, I was losing sleep fidgeting from unspent energy. I was also running out of money and had to find work.

But I got lucky. Not long after the Games ended, I received a letter from my grandfather Big Jim with just the word "congratulations" and three exclamation marks. He had lost his own shot at making an Olympic Team when he went off to fight Germans and dodge bullets and mustard gas in the trenches of Belgium. Included with his brief letter was a cheque for $1,000. In 1964 that was a lot of money. Big Jim never spoke much. But that was quite a speech, and I banked it right away.

Each night, Nagao San and I would walk up our darkened narrow laneway in kimonos to the public bath, a lovely evening ritual. During the day I made decent money as an occasional teacher of English conversation, mostly for

Against The Tide

young girls. I became known in the neighbourhood as "Aran Deron," which, because there is no "L" sound in Japanese, was their way of pronouncing the name of the best-known French actor of the day, Alain Delon. That's also why they called me "Biru-San" for Bill-San, which got them giggling, because the name for beer in Japanese, is "Biru."

As for the baths? For many centuries, the Japanese enjoyed communal, mixed bathing, men, women, children, sometimes a few dozen people or more at once, which must have been quite a sight — unless you were blind. The Japanese first wash their bodies completely at a spot station outside the bath, and then get into a big tub to steep in clean hot water, contrary to Westerners, who clean the dirt off their bodies while in the tub, and then soak in their own dirty water, the mere idea of which makes the Japanese cringe. It is cringeworthy.

This hygiene difference between East and West was underscored one evening when I was invited to enjoy a little TV with the Kamatas, my host family. We were watching a Western movie with Japanese subtitles — Jean-Luc Godard's *Breathless*, I think, with Jean-Paul Belmondo and Jean Seberg. There is a scene in which Belmondo is lying in a bathtub grinning, copious soapy bubbles up to his chin. Having loved and partaken of the Japanese bath every evening for a few months, I remember feeling terribly embarrassed for our western way while watching him, when suddenly Belmondo stood up, bubbles clinging to him in all the essential places. The entire Kamata family immediately cringed — and I with them, flushed with embarrassment. How was I going to explain why we bathe in our own dirty water?

The bath at the end of Tomihisa-cho street was not communal. It was divided into male and female sections by a wall high enough to prevent most men — except some Westerners — from gawking at naked women in vulnerable postures on the other side. Sitting atop the wall was a sleepy woman collecting the ten–*Yen* fee. She was watching both sides and must have gotten very tired of seeing a hundred or so naked men and women every night. At any rate, it was clear the Japanese don't care very much about nudity, nor feel anything close to Western shame to see nakedness or be seen.

Pleasantly lodged in memory is the sight of men and women in evening kimonos shuffling along our damp barely-lit street to or from the baths at evening, happy of a cold winter's night; some shivering along the way; warm vapours rising from the shadow-shapes of those heading home; soft voices escaping the pale fingers of women holding their hands over their mouths as they giggle over a pleasantry; stray dogs scuttling across a watery gleam of yellow lamplight; everyone eager to slide into bed and sleep the night away.

## ME, DOUG ROGERS, AND JUDO –
## AND ANOTHER SET-BACK

Doug Rogers[7] won the only Olympic Medal — a silver — ever taken by a Canadian in the sport of Judo. I searched him out in the Olympic Village the day after I decided to stay in Japan because I heard he had been living there for four years and I figured he would be a good introduction to Japanese life. JU-DO means "gentle way." It's a sport meant to immobilize your opponent, rather than to punch him out — the aim in boxing — or to hurt him in a lot of different ways with kicks, and karate chops. You're supposed to just make it impossible for him to hurt you. Most of the art is very Eastern. Not force against force, as in football. But rather, giving way at the right time to take advantage of your opponent's force, throwing, or tripping him up as you do so, getting him to fall from his own momentum so you can pin him on the mat for a win. I shouldn't have said you don't hurt your opponent. Choking someone is legit, and it happened to me once. Doug choked me out. And then I did it to a couple of others. You basically use the lapels of their fighting jacket, or your own forearms in a locked position over their carotid arteries for this. Painless and quick, it creates an immediate feeling of total submission and defeat.

The greatest *judoka* of all, Masahiko Kimura (d.1993) — about whom the Japanese say "there was no one before Kimura, and no one after" — sometimes specialized in breaking his opponents forearms in a match. Not intentionally, of course (well, maybe sometimes). It usually happened because he was so quick and forceful. He was Doug's teacher for a while. That didn't mean anything to me at the time. But it did a few months later. I was just 24 years of age and had done *a lot* of intensive training in athletics. At the time, I weighed a muscular 185 pounds, was bench pressing 300 pounds, and running the 400m in the high 48 second range. But I got destroyed by a 70-year-old judo teacher.

Doug came across the *dojo* — the gym: "Bill. You see that man over there?" A lean, grey-haired senior was standing by the wall. "Well," says Doug, who must have been enjoying what he knew was about to happen. "He is *hachi-dan*. Eighth degree (meaning, a highly respected teacher finished his competitive career). Go ask him for a little *Randori*" (informal fighting).

I was cocky enough to say, "Doug. I totally respect him. It's an amazing sport. But what does he weigh?"

"About 135 pounds."

"Seriously?"

There was no smirking. I just thought I had this figured out. So I said, "You know, I could actually press him over my head. With one arm."

"So, go ask him."

Against The Tide

With a kindly Zen-nothingness on his face, the old man looked like you could blow him over. Maybe he already knew why Doug sent me across the room? But I didn't.

*O negai shimasu*, and we got started. When I tried to get him off his feet, he vanished like a veil. When he attacked, I thought a python had wrapped around me, and I went down. He held me down at will, and started to laugh a little, I swear. And every time I tried to get out of his grip, he somehow managed to shift his entire 135 pounds to my weak spot, pinning me flat once again. Meanwhile, the entire room full of *judokas* had gathered around for an object lesson in *ne waza* (groundwork). He would use a certain grip, then tell the class exactly the move I would use to escape, and then quickly shift his weight, change his grip, pin me again, and continue with his lecture. All my strength was to no avail. After five minutes I was exhausted. It was a fine lesson for his students, and a lesson in humility for me. It also explained why everyone in Japan is always bowing. Back then, no one graduated from a Japanese high school without a year of intensive judo, kendo, or karate. So, you never knew who might be able to wreck you, like he did to me. It's why you never see Japanese people fighting in public.

These two fellows I met just walking down a laneway near where I lived. Mean-looking dudes who could probably slice and dice you in less than a minute. You can see I am bigger than them. But to them, that just means you fall harder.

But I am avoiding what happened today. Just after posting this photo here (August 16th, 2020), I surfed the web to see how Doug was doing, as I had spoken with him a year earlier. It was an awful shock to see the words *"Doug Rogers, Obituary"* on my screen. So, I had to take a break. I couldn't write about Doug and my memorable time with him in Japan right then. I needed a breather. Maybe tomorrow.

It's August 17th, 2020, the day after this bad news. I called his wife to offer condolences. I hadn't seen him for over 50 years. And given that we weren't exactly chumming around all that time, it just didn't make sense his obit hit me so hard. I couldn't figure it out, until I realized that while half of my spontaneous sadness — a mix of sorrow and grief — was for the loss of Doug. The other half was, should I say, selfish? Because a cherished part of my life fixed in the amber of memory which had been shared only with Doug, and no one else, suddenly evaporated. So, when he died he took half of it with him, so to speak. I mean, when I remember our time, he's not there now. My memory bank got disrupted, a little like, hey, you could have given me some warning!

Doug was a purpose looking for a cause. At 16, living in Montreal he earned his Pilot's licence, then fell in love with the sport of Judo and went off to Japan at the age of 19 to study with masters like Kimura. When I met him he was 23, six foot four, and 260 pounds. Formidable. There is an 18-minute retrospective entitled *Judoka* (a judo athlete) Canada's National Film Board did on Doug and his Judo life in Japan. In it you will see a bit of the Japan I experienced, much of which is gone now, torn down, highwayed over, and you will see some of the rough and tumble of actual judo. Not to be messed with, as I was to find out. You can find out more about Doug Rogers, *Judoka* by Doug Rogers, on the web. Very early in my training, Doug accidently broke my shoulder while giving me a lesson. He threw me hard in a move called *ippon seoi nage*, in which I basically went over his shoulders six feet in the air and hit the ground flat on my back ... but with him pulling hard on my arm. He was a big man. I knew how to break fall well, by then, so I would have been okay if he had just let me go. But in an act of sympathy aimed at softening my fall, he pulled so hard on my arm it came completely out of the socket with a suction-POP sound like a shotgun exploding in my ear. That sound filled the whole *dojo* (gym) such that a dozen athletes who knew what it was, stopped in their tracks. There I was, sitting on the *tatami* mat, clutching my shoulder, bewildered, in sudden shock. It hurt a lot, and I knew immediately it meant the end of my decathlon. Just like that. Bang!

Here is a picture of Doug, just as I knew him, on his way down a then typical Tokyo street to the Kodokan, still considered the world's Mecca of judo, where I trained along with him.

Against The Tide

This was the third disaster of my Olympic year, all in less than seven months. First the acute sinusitis that led to my back injury (and the on and off pain I have lived with ever since), then the bacterial stomach infection the night before the Olympic decathlon. And now, this, a broken shoulder. I guess I should say that exactly ten years later there was a fourth disaster, called shoulder surgery, that failed. Out of the sling, expecting a wonderful recovery and full mobility, I was aghast. So was the surgeon. I couldn't lift my arm even above my hip. So, two more surgeries followed to undo the first one, and then 25 years later I got a titanium joint replacement because of bad arthritis. I still can't raise that arm to shoulder level. Of course, I had no idea all this was ahead as I sat on the floor of the Kodokan.

I was very distressed, resolved immediately there was no way I could go back home with a broken shoulder and nothing to show for it. I had to get *some* kind of degree in judo, as a salve of sorts, and perhaps a face-saving matter of pride in the face of "What did you expect?" So I bound up my shoulder in a harness, changed to a left-handed grip, and worked very hard at judo for the next three months. The injury had no chance to heal properly, and even with a limiting harness it slid partially out of the socket about ten more times in the following three months.

In the final exam you have to perform to the commands of three judges by doing a whole bunch of *Kata* with a partner you have practiced with, intensely. These are slow motion, perfectly controlled judo throws, as well as a selection of groundwork techniques on the mat. The judges call out what they want to see. You perform it at once. No wobbling. Perfect throws. Perfect break falls. Perfect self-control. After this, you have to beat two Japanese black belts you have never met before, one after the other, to earn your black belt.

Somehow, I managed to beat them both, and ended up with *Sho-dan* — a first-degree black belt, to take home with my broken shoulder. It was the fastest black belt ever earned from scratch at the *Kodokan*. Here is a photo of the main *dojo*, a space mostly for Japanese *judokas*. The foreign *dojo* was a separate smaller space, a floor below. Separate but equal.

Here is that degree certificate, and the belt, still hanging on my wall. It's like a little shrine to my brief engagement with this fascinating sport. My name is on the belt in Japanese characters, and it makes me smile to see "BIRU GAWDONAH".

*Against The Tide*

Doug had a lovely Japanese girlfriend named Kimiko. The Japanese were, and remain, an intensely racially proud people. And yes, racial pride includes the feeling of superiority and ethnic purity. That is frowned upon these days, but I think it's natural to all races, and as long as you are not at the short end of the stick, racial pride is likely essential to national unity. I got the feeling most Japanese privately considered Westerners mongrels of a sort. Deep down. I was considered a nice mongrel and made friends easily with them. At the Shinjuku subway station at rush hour, when a sea of many thousands of black-haired people with almond-shaped eyes pours past you — and yes, "they all look the same" until you get sensitive to their differences (which can take a long time) — you can hardly pick your friend out of the crowd. He will see you first with your mongrel hair and face and will pick you out. We Westerners are called *gaijin*, which means "an outsider," or alien, and it has a definite odour of the pejorative.

The feeling of a threat to racial purity is particularly strong when it comes to fathers of Japanese girls who want to date Western men. In the '60s it was almost impossible to find a girl from a good family who would go on a date with a *gaijin*. Easy to find girls from not so good families. Doug's girl Kimiko was a nice girl. But he got a taste of the problem when her father, *Oto-San*, showed up at Doug's apartment one night looking to drag her home, the smell of *sake* on his breath, stumbling a little, Japanese invective pouring from his foaming mouth at a level of grammatical complexity too scrambled for anyone sober to comprehend, his hand on the grip of the samurai sword fastened to his waist. Doug slammed the door shut as the tip of the sword came through, he and Kimiko bolting out the rear sliding window.

Doug left Japan and Kimiko a year later, returning to Vancouver where he took up flying again and at the end of 37 years was a Boeing 747 pilot. He told me in confidence that "today's autopilot systems are unbelievable. Once, on a flight from Tokyo to Vancouver, I fell asleep. The autopilot took over, and I woke up 50 feet above the Vancouver runway." That was sobering.

My decision to return home came mostly because, much as I loved Japan, I felt I couldn't — shouldn't — get away with avoiding my own future any longer, and it was not the place for a future. Frankly, I was lonely for good female company but didn't want to fall in love with a fine Japanese girl and have to face inevitable complications. Distressingly, on self-examination there was still mostly profound silence in response to the question: "What are you going to do with the rest of your life?" The plan of staying in Japan to find myself, while a wonderful experience I still cherish, was a zero.

The turning point came in a single moment, in the dark, when I began to long for the deep culture of the West. A culture can be deep, or just skin deep. French food and movies (*Aran Deron*!), German cars, Italian clothing, and so on, are skin-deep things we love and live for, but can live without. But a deep culture is about all the things a civilization is built upon fine art, great and enduring literature, a musical heritage, great poetry, great political, religious, and moral convictions. Things we will die for.

I got hooked by luminous feelings of Western origin very young when singing solo parts to Handel's *Messiah*, and reading moving poetry, plays, and novels by great English authors. My deep culture was beginning to call to me now. You don't possess a deep culture. It possesses you. I remember so clearly that cold winter's night when, back from the baths, I was lying in my warm futon, thousands of miles from home, listening to my little pocket radio in the dark trying to understand a little of the Japanese chatter, and music that was alien to my ears. Suddenly, I got hijacked by the West. A heart-achingly mournful "*fado*" song by Amalia Rodrigues, a famous Portuguese singer, simply claimed me. I was overcome by a sudden powerful emotion as the West, and all it meant in my forlorn night took possession of me. Soul-penetration. A piercing of the heart.

After writing this, I searched YouTube and found that very song —it was *Algemas*, which means tied, or handcuffed (to a lover) — by Amalia. I can still feel what it did to me and my heart.

Against The Tide

The next morning, I arranged my ticket home, heading West instead of East, ready to finish my trip around the world.

## HONG KONG, BANGKOK, ATHENS, VENICE, FLORENCE, PARIS, AND HOME ...

While at university I saw French director Alain Renais' film *Last Year at Marienbad*. It was a time when young students searched for truth in artsy foreign films by Directors like him, Ingmar Bergman, Frederico Fellini, and many others — the more inscrutable the better. We felt you should have to suffer to find deep meaning, to figure it out. There is a scene in which the protagonists play *Nim* — "the match game." Individual matches are arranged in four rows of 7,5,3,1. You take turns and are allowed to remove any number of matches you wish but only from one row at a time. The object is to leave your opponent with the last match. I was intrigued when I saw it played and won needed money with this game. It is especially useful at a bar with an opponent well ahead of you in drinks consumed, and it paid for more than one meal for this hungry world traveller. After writing this I watched the scene from the film again, and was surprised to see the bad moves made by the guy who lost.

After a vast expanse of ocean and bare land from 30,000 feet, a towering metropolis bursting at the seams suddenly appears in my airplane window. Hong Kong. An eruption. An exfoliation in bricks, concrete, and glass. Tiny junks bent in the wind, heaving to and fro from Kowloon to Hong Kong. In its very essence Hong Kong is an architectural and financial rebuke to the viciousness and backwardness of international communism; indeed, to the entire murderous totalitarian history of the Far East. At the time, the one-hundred-year lease of Hong Kong to the British settled in June of 1898 was still in force. So, I was safe. No threats of prison or forced labour in a gulag. But since the transfer of sovereignty in July 1, 1997 ("the Handover") there have been mostly "two steps forward, one step back" brutalities by the Chinese Communist Party (CCP), and the banning and arrest of pro-democracy politicians, thus breaking the promise of "one country, two systems" that had been agreed upon to preserve freedom in Hong Kong until 2047. As I write, the freedom I saw there is all but gone.

Astonishingly, when I arrived in May of 1965 the GDP of this tiny island, with less than half of 1% of the Chinese mainland population, was generating the equivalent of more than a quarter of its GDP. This was a victory for freedom and free enterprise if there ever was one, as was the GDP of Taiwan (now called Formosa) the island refuge of the freedom fighter Chiang-Kai Shek, whose forces retreated there when defeated by the Red Chinese under Mao Tse Tung. I studied some of this history at CU and was appalled and stirred. I am still the only Westerner I know who has actually read Mao's Little Red Book (otherwise known as Quotations from Chairman Mao). It is interesting to see exactly how ideology empowers and blinds believers at the same time, easing the digestion of all sorts of illogical propositions, and I remain curious to know why it was that so many spiritually-grounded Asian societies such as China, Laos, Vietnam, and North Korea, swallowed whole such vulgar anti-spiritual materialism ("religion is the opiate of the masses"), along with the millenarian fantasies of a German Jew named Karl Marx. These tensions are quite visible — and deadly — in Hong Kong today. But in the Hong Kong of my visit, there was only energy, money, deal-making, and world-class production, and big projects underway. To immerse oneself there was to be sucked into a giant buzzing humanity-machine that never stopped.

I was still a little sick from my intestinal troubles but had no idea where to find a doctor I could trust who would give something stronger than ginseng. So, I walked into the Hong Kong Hilton hotel and ask outright, with feigned confidence, "Where I can find the hotel doctor?" That worked fine, and up to the top floor I went.

The doctor said he could write a prescription, and so I offered him cash. He said he would charge it to my room.

"I don't have a room."

Blank stare.

"I just thought the hotel probably had a good doctor, so I asked for you."

He liked the chutzpah and handed me his prescription with a smile. No charge. Hong Kong appreciation of the get-ahead way.

It was a bit of a shock to go from the modest, always bowing, hand over the mouth quiet populace of Japan, where behind every door one may find an aesthetically pleasing surprise of carefully kept gardens, tinkling water, and architectural proportion, in contrast to the ceaseless bustle of this place. The Chinese struck me as a noisy, outspoken, somewhat pushy in a lineup sort of people, frenetically busy, always hustling, buying, or selling anything that moves. No bowing here. Count your fingers after shaking hands. It was heady, fast-moving, a somewhat grubby marketplace feeling, hum, and bustle everywhere. I ate Chinese food, carefully of course, went to Kowloon by ferry, saw iconic Chinese junks sail past, tried to feel the somewhat inscrutable mystery of the Far East, unsure what that was supposed to feel like. Kind of a not-me feeling. I was definitely outside the Chinese fishbowl, looking in. I had seen the movie *The World of Susie Wong*, and I did catch myself hoping a

Against The Tide

young woman as lovely as her might suddenly appear and turn my brief stay in China into something memorable. But beautiful Susie was a prostitute, and that idea has always repelled me. So, I imagined my Susie as pure — she was a pure impossibility — stayed lonely in Hong Kong and made a note to come back some day when I had some money.

I had no way of knowing that although Soviet Communism was going to collapse of its own self-immolating weight by 1989 with the fall of the Berlin Wall, and therefore vindicate my strong anti-communist feelings absorbed from Professor Rozek at CU — the ghost of Mao would rise anew by 2020. Right here, on the very streets I was walking. More of the ceaseless clash of liberal-democratic, versus totalitarian ideology that has plagued the West for centuries — beginning with the English, then the French Revolution — and about which I would someday be writing serious essays and books. In a future that awaited, but about which I hadn't then the slightest intimation.

Bangkok was a bust. Terribly hot and humid. Plentiful open markets with customary as well as unrecognizably alien foods spilling off carts and tables under sunlit tent-coverings in a maze of open markets. My first day wandering I couldn't eat, at least couldn't afford to eat, in a nice place. So, I stopped in a small cubby-hole eatery and asked for a Coke, and something fried that looked safe. Drinking my bottle of the West, I wondered why there were large holes in the wooden floor and found out when a well-fed rat slithered over my sandaled foot and down a hole.

Most of the Thai women struck me as beautiful, like fragile dolls with perfect complexions; until they are about 50, and then they seem suddenly to turn 80 and have badly wrinkled faces. Lots of Western men have fallen for the graciousness, good manners, good looks, and yes, the traditional catering — it's not subservience — to the male, of Far Eastern women. And millions have married them by preference to loud-mouthed, angry Western feminists preoccupied with who does what percentage of housework. A young girl — or perhaps old, who knows? — kept knocking on my hotel door at night with the question whether or not I wanted sex, which she thought I should, because, she kept saying, "I virgin." Pillow over my head.

But in Bangkok, judo behind me and no energy outlet, I suddenly felt like running again, which I did, in 30°C weather on a beat-up soccer field. Since that restart, and not counting the occasional flu, I don't think I have taken more than two weeks off hard exercise in a variety of different sports for more than 55 years. That's a little crazy. When I got back to my modest hotel I gave the desk the last of my American Express traveller's cheques to lock up in the hotel safe. Unfortunately, I had made the mistake of countersigning two of them for a total of US $200. But they were safe, right?

In the morning when I asked for my cheques the countersigned ones were missing. So, I asked the clerk where they were? He played dumb. I asked to see the hotel Manager and asked him. Dumber still. So I told him if they couldn't produce the two cheques I was going to call the police. That word had a vigorous galvanizing effect on everyone within what seemed like half a mile, and they quickly produced US$200 in cash. When I got home, I wrote American Express with the serial numbers I had recorded of the lost cheques and according to their policy they sent me another US$200. That was probably unethical, but I couldn't see why, if it was. I figured the hotel paid a penalty for stealing.

My mom had introduced me to the music of India, which I loved, and so I wanted to visit India badly, but at the time there were so many vaccinations and visas required I passed over the land of Ravi Shankar and his *Sitar*, the Holy, and holy-dirty Ganges, the touchingly magical and mystical *Raga Misra Mand* which I knew by heart, as played on the *Sarod* by Ali Akbar Khan. Below is a version of this Raga by another fine Indian musician. Oh, those strings plucked; such plaints; it touches any feeling heart with a lovely mystical longing; notes that hang in the air, drift with the incense, red flower petals tumbling in the breeze and the dust.

This produced a minor heartache of sorts in a young man whose mind, feelings, and future were so unsettled, adrift like those petals.

So on to Athens, and the beginning of the world I knew. In a wonderful book of essays entitled *Mimesis* by the German scholar Erich Auerbach — which I didn't know yet, but in my soon-to-unfold future would be required reading — there is a seminal essay entitled "Odysseus' Scar," in which the Western heritage of philosophy and reason he saw revealed in Homer's *Odyssey* is compared and contrasted to the Old Testament story of Abraham and Isaac. Pure reason versus complex passions. Auerbach was a German-Jewish scholar who fled Germany prior to WWII with just a few classic texts in his suitcase and proceeded to write his seminal collection without any research apparatus, whatsoever. Soon, I was in Odysseus' world.

Sunlit, always sunlit, dry, sparse, and stony Athens, for centuries splayed and jumbled below the Parthenon; fresh-grilled sardines straight from the sea, blood-red tomatoes with basil and feta cheese, plenty of beer and ouzo. This is it. The home of Western philosophy. Of democracy. Of tyranny and intrigue, real and mythical. Of the civilization-crushing war with Sparta, of horrible plagues. Of Socrates, Plato, Aristotle, Pericles, and all those great dramatists. Much later in my life I would read plenty by these people, and write of them a little, too. But for now, all that lay in wait. Life lies in wait for all of us, doesn't it? For now, I sit still at the sunny and astonishing Parthenon,

Against The Tide

trying to imagine what it must have been like back then, what it meant to them, and what that meant now.

This photo was taken by Spiros, a kind, somewhat tragic and sad but handsome man my age wandering alone on the Acropolis in a dark trench coat, who struck up a conversation with me among the ruins. I worried he might perhaps, maybe, be a not so closet homosexual. I can't say a "gay" man, as that is a love that strikes me today and always has as not very gay at all, but rather a sad, desperate, and dangerous human activity. Dangerous to society and to its practitioners. But it never came up. He had a pained and poetic soul, and we wandered a little together, drank ouzo at *Plaka*, the oldest part of Athens and listened to typical *bouzouki* music in those narrow, winding, white-plastered pleasure-haunts. I had seen the film of Nikos Kazantzakis' novel *Zorba the Greek*, and imagined myself then a less naive Basil, the English schoolteacher in the film who was a sponge for the Greek mythos, summed up in what we thought was the wild, wholly unpredictable, even wonderfully free and wild character of Zorba. Who can forget the boat scene, those two huddled on that windy deck, when Basil asks:

"Zorba. Are you married?"

Zorba looks at him. The scales peel slowly from his eyes, and he says,

"Am I married?" Then a long pause. And then: "Wife. Children. *The whole catastrophe!*"

That got a laugh from all of us young students who took his reply as a pointed condemnation of the bourgeois life we snobbishly thought too tame for our wild spirits (but that would be ours sooner than we realized). Decades later I watched that film again and saw more clearly the deeply primitive darkness of Greek — or perhaps of all — life: the general incompetence, the insult of those shrieking, dark-robed women stripping the sad widow's home at the very moment of her death; the depthless, pitiable, wounded eyes of Lela Kedrova who made the mistake of falling for Zorba, and Zorba, with his ridiculous tree-harvesting project, logs speeding down the hill on his flimsy contraption, smashing his entire apparatus into the sea; the beautiful blue Aegean — the beginning and end of so much that is Greek.

Fifty-five years later my wife and I returned to Greece, by which time I of course admired again the stones, monuments, and sculptures, all very fine, extraordinary things. But now I felt the real monuments of Greece were its euro-generative ideas, its literature and philosophy. So, we took a taxi to *Pnyx Hill*, the place where thousands of Athenians gathered regularly over 2,500 years ago to hear great orators and leaders hold forth, and to vote on the laws handed down to them by their Senate (the *Boule*), which had what is called the law-making "initiative," but on which the people had the right only to vote Yea, or Nay. This was no democracy. It was class oligarchy in a slave-infested population.

On Pnyx Hill there is a large stone platform where Orators stood as they tried to win the hearts of the people of Athens mingling noisily, shouting

Against The Tide

approval, or not, sometimes dropping or drunkenly tossing away their clay wine goblets and flasks. Today, if you wander on the Pnyx after a very infrequent rain, as we did, you can pick up small shards of those very goblets turned up by rivulets formed in the dusty gravel; and if you do, you will feel the truth that your fingers are touching the smooth edge of a cup last touched by the lips of an ancient Greek, perhaps listening to Pericles.

For me then, and now, there is simply no explanation for the extraordinary works of mind of ancient Greece. What sacred wind blew over them to cause that explosion of intelligence and art for just a few short centuries, setting their souls to sail, we will never know, for I think such a concentration of the best of the human spirit has never happened since in human history. The Renaissance is a close second, and is astonishing, of course, but it would never have emerged as richly without the miraculous flourishing of the ancients. Anyone who has ever been, really been, heart and soul in Athens, and felt what it means still, never really leaves, except physically.

I had to get home now, to leave for Venice, which I wanted to see. But there was little money to travel except for a cheap train ticket taking me by night through communist Yugoslavia, wedged into a seat in a compartment of eight meant for six; between rough peasants reeking of garlic, gnarly-faced men with tangled, unwashed hair sleeping in patched, sweaty work clothes in narrow gritty hallways, almost atop one another, a cacophony of snoring, burping, garlic smells, fetid farting, thick cigarette smoke, the clickety-clack of slow iron wheels, all night. This train never exceeded forty miles an hour, and once in Yugoslavia stopped frequently to let big, ham-fisted, peasant-fingered communist guards aboard, in thick overcoats, a red star on their caps — it's true, a red star! They really did exist! Not just in books — flipping through every passport, time and again. Looking for spies, I supposed. Humourless and grim, they had the odor of the Gulag. Eyes front, keep your mouth shut.

After 30 hours on that broken-down train we limped into Venice. Beautiful Venice. Sinking, drowning Venice, where, after ducking under a medieval stone bridge on the way to a small hotel saw a sign pointing to "The Rialto," and my heart all but stopped. Really? This is the very place where Antonio met the Jewish merchant Shylock, in Shakespeare's wonderful 1597 play *The Merchant of Venice* that we had studied in high school. And I hear the bitter, memorable words of Shylock:

*I am a Jew. Hath not a Jew eyes?*
*Hath not a Jew hands, organs,*
*dimensions, senses, affections, passions;*

*If you prick us do we not bleed?*
*If you tickle us do we not laugh?*
*If you poison us do we not die?*
*And if you wrong us shall we not revenge?*

The conjuring power of words, here, in the classic plaint of all who suffer discrimination: *we are human, too.* Reading Shylock's words just now drives home the plaintive lines of the speech by James Baldwin, the eloquent, queer Black writer and civil rights activist of the '60s, in his historic debate with William F. Buckley Jr. at Cambridge University in 1965, the year after my visit to Venice, all reproduced 55 years later in author Nicholas Buccola's riveting book, *The Fire Is Upon Us.* I'll say it is. This book deeply interested me because Buckley, as mentioned, his ideas, and his person, came into my personal life in an important way, as I shall explain.

At Cambridge, where the audience was predisposed to favour him, Baldwin gave a powerful, personal and passionate speech concluding that American civilization can never mature until it confesses its historical and present racist sins. Despite the fact that American blacks, considered as a nation, were even by the sixties the most successful black nation in history, and that Baldwin himself was a much celebrated and well-paid literary star, he felt nothing had changed. America simply deserved to be destroyed, because *"I picked the cotton, and I carried it to the market, and I built the railroads under someone else's whip for nothing."*

Powerfully affecting words, just like Shylock's. But this was no debate. It was two powerful speeches, his emotional and compassionate, Buckley's a rational argument that despite the presence of racism, it doesn't make sense to destroy an entire civilization because it has made, and continues to make, grievously immoral or criminal mistakes, any more than it would make sense to trash the entire British Commonwealth because in the 17th century Civil War Cromwell's armies slaughtered a million Irish Catholics, many of them ordinary citizens, and sold 60,000 of them as white slaves in the Caribbean.

On the open taxi boat from the train station to this surrealistic floating city a very handsome middle-aged couple noticed the Tokyo Olympic tag on my bag, which spurred a few questions in broken English. By the end of the ride, they had invited me to their home in San Vito di Valdobbiadene, a hundred miles from Venice. So, on my second day, after wearing out my legs walking all over Venice, eating too much pizza, and still much elevated by the buoyant magic of so many beautiful buildings floating everywhere, I took a bus to San

Against The Tide

Vito. Better the life of real people than a crowd of tourists, the persistent smell of rancid water in Venice, and the mosquitoes it breeds.

Ducking through their stone gate, there was Signor Bagnani, busy, bent, and grey in his work clothes raking leaves. Startled, a soon-dissipated ripple of surprise passing over his face. Emerging smile. Oh, oh. Perhaps he had figured an invite was okay, because I was unlikely to show up? But I did.

The family lived in a small closed-off section of what was obviously once an enormous and thriving mansion built to work hundreds of acres of now desolate grapevines. I was entering a post-aristocratic world of the sort so common in Europe, where for many old families the dignity of the present survives parasitically on the dignity of the past. Annabella Bagnani. It had a nice ring. She was the last of their three daughters to be married off, a raven-haired, pleasantly plump girl of 18 with the soft, uncertain mauve eyes of a caged mourning dove. After a sparse dinner together, self-served where servants once bent, on a thick black oak dining table far too big for the four of us, under very tall windows nearly covered by dark drapes offering folded and faded scenes of past Italian conquests, I asked about the village. Could we walk there together? Annabella, and I?

It was getting dark. Mother raised her eyebrows. Dad frowned. Parental radar. Images of possible rape hip-hopped across the table; and worse … an unthinkable acquiescence in her own deflowering? Annabella looked as if, dying of thirst, she saw water. So, we walked to the tiny village in the dark — for a soft drink. Past dark forested hills in cool air. Past lonely orchards where she declined to sit with me on soft grass under an apple tree. "No, William. You know. The whole village will talk of this walking. For many months."

I slept on a lumpy mattress in a dark upper hallway on a small three-sided wooden bed-bench, a knight in a full set of medieval armour with a shiny metal lance staring down at me. The next day I made my way to Lugano-Montagnolo to see sister Norma at the American School in Switzerland.

There, among beautiful brooding Swiss mountains and sparkling lakes I could feel the stamping ground of Jean-Jacques Rousseau, of whom I knew nothing at the time but of whose political philosophy I would eventually learn sufficient to publish essays on how this talented author bewitched much of Europe with his peculiarly totalitarian form of democracy-talk. His book *The Social Contract* changed all of Europe, sparked the French Revolution, and was clutched to the breast of Robespierre, the main theorist of that disastrous event as he limped, beaten and bloodied to put his head under the blade of the guillotine, having sent so many before him to the same awful fate.

Norma and I took a train to Florence for a few days of steeping in the marvels of the Italian Renaissance, among them a fine replica of Michelangelo's *David* in the Piazza della Signoria, strained our necks upward at the astonishing *Duomo*, walked the charming *Ponte Vecchio* over a slow, sun-burnished Arno river, and I remember thinking then, and I still think, the head of David is too large for the body (as are his hands). Six months after this trip I offered Prof (who adored Florence) this opinion. He paused, and said, "William. I have always felt the body is too small for the head!" Hah. The athlete thought the head too big, the scholar, the body too small. I still smile over that.

After Florence, to which I have returned since, and which I would like to visit once more before I die, I went by train, with several stops, adventures, and misadventure across France to Paris. Oh, Paris … for so long the heart-beat of Europe. Where Caesar's army outwitted and defeated the Parisii at the battle of Lutetia and then made France much of what she is today. Astonishing Caesar has been a lifelong hero, as mentioned, ever since Appleby. I admired him then, but also felt great pity for his most wily and courageous enemy Vercingetorix, the feisty warrior who ranged the many tribes of Gaul against Caesar, but was captured and paraded bound in triumph, down the bellicose streets of Rome, jailed for years, then finally, his head cut off. Caesar was astute, daring in battle, compassionate to all who obey, cruel to all who betray, a man to die for, as so many enthusiastically did. He was an exemplar of the most singular trait of all great leaders: the courage and capacity to make the right decision, even in the face of inadequate information. I simply had no idea that four years hence, a different man in a very different condition of life, I would be steeping in this historically rich city for a year.

For now, I flew home with about 50 cents in my pocket to face the matura-tion music, and the next chapter of my life.

# PART 2

## FACING THE MATURATION MUSIC

## REALITY SHOCK

To arrive home one sunny day in spring without a clue how I was going to support myself felt unmanly and embarrassing. I was proud of my Olympics, of setting Canadian and Commonwealth records, loved Japan, and was happy to have done some European wandering. But the match-game was not going to cut it as a means to survive. I was as empty as ever about tomorrow, and worried avoidance was becoming a reflex. So, Dad kick-started "the talk," as he put it, "to get you off your ass," and took me to Toronto for interviews with some of his business colleagues at Gairdner & Company, which by then had 22 offices in Canada and 400 employees. A Gairdner son should want to seize this opportunity, no? What was with me that I didn't? I felt as if I was being driven to my execution.

I had no idea what a stock or a bond was, except they had something to do with making money. Hard work didn't scare me. At the lumber camp, then as a sailor stevedoring in the High Arctic, and so forth, I often got threats from co-workers to slow down, whence visions of my head on a pike pole, or pushed overboard into the cold North Atlantic sprang to mind. As an athlete, I could train my teammates into the ground. But honestly, the idea of doing something that to me at least, seemed ultimately meaningless all day long, unless you really *had* to? *Just* to make money? (Finger in the throat). Mark Twain defined "work" as "anything you don't like doing." Of course I felt very spoiled that I had never been *forced* to work. Like most people, I always chose it. So I had a mixed-up guilty feeling, too. That Russian official in Philadelphia carefully scooping an egg-yolk into his mouth because he had once nearly starved, did not have this luxury. Clearly, if I couldn't decide what to do with my own damn life real soon, falling into something of necessity was going to be next. The idea that hunger would be making decisions for me was really rock bottom. It was awfully quiet in the car on the way to Toronto.

We came out of the elevator near the top of a tower at 320 Bay Street. Barely two years after this visit, Gairdner & Co. would move to a 50-something floor of the spanking new Toronto-Dominion Bank tower, a spectacular building created by the famous German American architect Mies van der Rohe. There, Big Jim would oversee his business empire — about ten companies by then — seated at the large oak and leather desk I inherited after he died, and at which

I now sit, in his chair, to write these words. A crucial chapter in my own life — one that saved me, as I will explain in time — was to open 20 years hence in that same tower, two floors above Big Jim's old office in a cat-and-mouse financing game in which I would go up against Dick Thomson, Chairman of the TD Bank, and at the time one of the most respected and influential bankers in Canada.

But for now, there was mostly a hazy, lazy cloud of bluish cigarette smoke drifting above a half dozen glass cubicles where investment dealers were noisily making deals. Repugnance rising. Alright, Roger and I smoked in boarding school, escapees sneaking off to the woods on a fresh fall day, a bad-boy adventure that would end in a hell of a strapping if we got caught, and chancing that was part of the reason we did it. But to work all day, in *this*? My thoughts alternated between take it easy, Bill, give it a try, and oh jeez, I'm screwed.

Next were interviews of a sort with three stockbrokers, all of whom were clearly unfit, and overweight, tiny red blood vessels from too much booze meandering over their noses. Hmm. I knew that an investment dealer's lunch is mostly liquid, and I don't recall the first two interviews, but I remember the third with the Manager. You might say he changed my life.

"Close the door, kid. Lemee guess. You don't know what to do with yourself, right? And your family thinks it would be nice to have another Gairdner in the business? And that scares the shit out of you, right?"

Bending his prematurely balding head forward, a fatty part of his chin folding over the knot of his necktie, he sucked hard on the cigarette pinched between a tarred thumb and two fingers, knocked over one of the three phones on his desk, crushed the hot red butt in an ashtray, and peered straight through me. Drumming on the desk. Sizing me up. Letting me know he only does this job because it pays *really* well. "I make *a lot* of money, kid." With a wife and four kids, life had taken him by the scruff of the neck and shoved him into this glass cubicle. He was *never* going to leave (unless someone paid him *a lot* more).

"Listen. Whadda ya *really* wanna do?"

Nobody else could hear, so I took a chance.

"*Really*? A writer. Literature. Words that will move people, like, you know … Thomas Hardy." He broke into a smile, leaned back with shining eyes and a faraway look. "I remember Hardy. In high school. *Tess of the D'Urbervilles*, Right? I loved it. But I … *I loved Tess, more!* She was really a looker, right? Hah! Okay — we didn't see a lot of girls back then. But you know, kid?" — almost whispering now, a little anxious and leaning halfway over his big desk — "If I were you, I would get the hell out of here as fast as I could and go be a goddamn writer."

I never told Dad what that guy said. He might have got fired. But I still owe him, whoever he was. He wanted me to get the hell out of there for me. But for him, too. A happy little ghost of him was sneaking out the door with me. On the way down in the elevator I wondered if what he *really* didn't want, was another goddamn Gairdner in the business. But I took him at his word and got the hell out of there — with a profoundly happy heart.

That night I called Prof at Stanford, to tell him of my dilemma. One thing I knew was that I would like to get smarter, and maybe become a professor someday. Teach literature. Professors don't earn much. But they get summers off, right? There would be time to write novels. But … how to start down that road?

"Well, William. Why don't you come to Stanford, for summer school?"

Summer school? The thought had never occurred, and it hit like, well, a cliché ton of bricks. More like it lifted a ton of bricks from my chest. The next day I broke it to Mom and Dad that I had thought about things a lot, and for me, the life of a professor would be perfect. If I did well at summer school, maybe I could end up with a higher degree, and teach what I love? And (still cringing a little) become … a writer? Uhmmm … could they help with tuition and rent? I could earn a little money with part-time jobs, no? Grasping at any straw now.

Doom loomed as I announced this total rejection of the entire Gairdner family heritage, patrimony, whatever, and I feared I might be disowned. Mom was sympathetic. Dad less so. I figured the idea had to be close to his heart, though. Else, how could he quote Shakespeare with such feeling? They were calculating. One of our kids might get a Ph.D. from a great university, like Stanford? WWI had stopped Big Jim. WWII had stopped Mom and Dad's whole generation. The family would be proud. So, one week later, liberated at last from the prison of inherited expectations, my faithful Nash Rambler and I headed West.

Against The Tide

*Stanford Chapel*

## STANFORD, SUMMER 1965

When I got to San Francisco I drove a half-hour south, winding between golden-grassed foothills speckled with splayed shadows of cooling trees along Junipero Serra Freeway, one of the most beautiful highways in the world. From there, into Palo Alto and along the long palm-lined approach to one of the most splendid campuses in the world, where I saw once again the colourful façade of the Stanford Chapel peeking over those low sandstone buildings with red-tiled roofs, at peace in the warm California sun. I felt at home.

Then, straight to Prof's bungalow at 607 Mayfield Avenue for my marching orders to enroll "provisionally" in the Department of Linguistics, of which he was Chairman. I still can't say "Chair." He was a man, not a chair. But what the hell is linguistics? It was good to see him and his wife Ica again. And "Granny," Ica's Mom. She had fled Romania to come to the land of the free the year prior. Prof and Ica were born in Romania but left to study in France before Romania fell under the communist jackboot. When I got to know her, Granny told me there were spies 24-7 on every street corner in her town, dark raincoats, smoking incessantly. Censoring mail. Bugging phone lines. Watching. Watching. She was forbidden to leave Romania for 25 years until she got too old for the "caring" socialist state — which didn't want the expense of caring for Granny. So, they kicked her out.

Granny's stories personalized what I'd learned about Communism from Professor Rozek at CU and shaped my growing antipathy to all forms of statism, whether national (Nazi), or international socialism (Communism). I loved Thoreau's idea that the best government is the least. But I had not yet articulated my feelings, and I did not see the statism coming quietly in my own country, camouflaged with the term "liberal democracy." But one day I would, and in 1990 would critique it fully in my first political book *The Trouble With Canada*, an act that would make me a lightning rod for the Left for the rest of my life. At the time I didn't know the difference between left and right — or care much. But in Part IV, I will explain the national reaction of both gratitude and outrage that followed me and my books.

I found a very modest one-room shared clapboard cottage for rent at 745 Linden Avenue, Los Altos, shown below. Mine was just the right half of that modest structure.

It was behind the home of Signor Armanasco, a crusty Italian, surly but kind, living with his middle-aged daughter Margaret, a manless, longing middle-aged woman who handled his personal life and his renters (when she was not advancing haplessly upon them), and otherwise spent time as a dark-haired shadowy figure ironing behind a lace-curtained window. Their property had a small vegetable garden and three persimmon trees heavy with ruddy fruit that gave blessed shade over golden grasses I would watch turn green that winter, then blonde again in spring.

In a very fortunate and blessed life I still think of my time at Stanford as golden years. That first summer was ten weeks of hard work that included a heavy course in Japanese language and linguistics. I chose it because I needed a language major and was already speaking basic Japanese. I figured, get in or get out. This is it, Bill. Prove yourself, or you're done. I ended up with an A for the term, and that opened the door to full-time Stanford. I only filled out basic paperwork. At the time, Stanford had a deep commitment to favouring the most well-rounded applicants and seemed quite keen to accept a Canadian Olympic athlete doing straight-A work.

So I started training again for the decathlon and the 1968 Olympics. And training Prof, too. He wanted me to help him run the mile under six minutes, and that was going to be a chore, as he was a three-pack a day smoker, 35 pounds overweight, and when following me up only two short flights of stairs to his office had to stop to catch his breath. His future as a miler didn't look very promising. But we had a deal. I wanted to get smart. He wanted to run a six-minute mile. So I made him give up cigarettes, bought him some fine pipe tobacco and the first of many pipes he chewed through over the next 35 years, and showed him how to smoke them without inhaling. Just taste the lovely flavour. He never touched a cigarette or inhaled smoke again the rest of his life. His job was teaching me about intellectual matters in class, and in discussions over beer and burgers at Rossotti's Alpine Inn in Portola Valley[8] after workouts — our delightful and frequent routine. It was a pastoral place, built in 1852, with a sunny "beer garden" we loved, at the back. One of the Prof's first lessons in the meaning of "conservatism" (he called himself "a reactionary," which he had to explain) happened there. Zott's as we called it, was grubby. Peanut husks on a floor strewn with sawdust meant to soak up any spilled beer, every square inch of wooden walls, benches, and tables carved with countless initials; and always a lot of burger smoke in your eyes. Well, one day, I told Prof, "They ought to clean this place up a little." Oops.

He peered at me from under his tattered blue jogging hat, affected a hesitant, wounded grin, tilted his head, one hand in air holding the bowl of his pipe, squinted a little, just long enough for the signal I got used to that some fresh thought was percolating upward in the form of a mini-lecture. This was always suspenseful, and I and my dear friend Lowell Cohn (whom I met a year or so later) have always agreed that we learned more from running and drinking with Prof than from all other Stanford Professors combined.

"William," he began. "You want to change Rossotti's? I want Rossotti's *never* to change! The peanuts and carving? Smoke in my eyes? Sawdust? Beer and burgers? You change that, and you destroy what I *love*." And then came his lesson, which many years later I heard the great British philosopher Roger Scruton repeat as the speaker at a meeting of *Civitas Canada*, a national organization I was to create 30 years after that day at Zotts: "Conservatism is many things. But most of all, at bottom, it's about conserving what we love." He concluded his *bon mot* with a mock-injured look, "So, please, don't change Zott's."

He added that a *true* conservative (which he distinguished sharply, and with disgust from the *faux* liberal, or merely "fiscal" type of conservative), loves everything old: "Old books, old friends, old wine, old wisdom, old institutions, old traditions, old laws, old customs ..." It was a fine afternoon in which much more was digested than beer and burgers.

I soon learned that Prof was the Founder of the Stanford Conservative Forum, which was bringing great conservative speakers such as William F. Buckley Jr. (who, Prof?) to the campus, just at the point where Stanford was shedding its commitment to classical and objective learning and mutating under the pressure of intellectuals like the Frankfurt School Marxist Herbert Marcuse (cheered on by SDS — "Students for a Democratic Society"), into a temple of progressive — no, that's too tame — of extreme leftist revolutionary ideology. At the time, I had no clear idea what a conservative or a liberal was and didn't care for many years to come.

As for the decathlon, and the '68 Olympics? I was beginning to warm to that idea, and got strong again, put the 16-pound shot almost 50 feet (some kind of record, Prof said, for a man of only 182 pounds), and was running strongly. But with my Doug Rogers shoulder, I soon discovered I couldn't throw a ping-pong ball without my shoulder popping painfully out of joint. So, the javelin, one of my stronger events, was done. And I couldn't pole vault, either, because that needed both arms overhead. And academic work was piling up. So, the thought of giving up the Decathlon sprang to mind. I could stop all the weight training, lose ten pounds of muscle over the coming year, and run just the 110 metre and 400 metre hurdles. Why not? It would mean an hour and a half training daily, instead of three or four. So, Prof and I trained each other. He wanted to get fast, so I was his coach on the track. I wanted to

*Against The Tide*

get smart, so he was my coach elsewhere. He got *very* fast. Not so sure I got very smart.

## A SPRINTER IS BORN, AND SETS WORLD RECORDS

Spring of 1966, Prof was 20 pounds lighter and in good shape for his "assault" (his word) on the six-minute mile. Tension over that pregnant possibility was spreading all over campus. It even got an alert in the *Stanford Daily*: "Linguistics Prof to Assault Six Minute Barrier." Few Olympic events were ever laden with such expectation, mainly due to the unsubtle announcements of incipient athletic drama issuing at regular intervals, often with an impish grin it's true, from Prof's own office. And so, although a childless man, a half-dozen of his "sons" showed up to witness the big event. I held the stopwatch. Chris Lewis, another son, would step onto the track to pace Prof over the last half lap of his "assault."

Prof was left in the wake of the entire field of younger runners the moment the gun went off, all of them finishing while he was still half a lap behind. Chris was across the track waiting, with firm instructions from me: "stay just a yard ahead, and coach him home. Don't get too far in front."

Well, no one was more surprised than me at what happened next. No sooner was Chris alongside, just a little ahead, than Prof caught up to him. So, Chris had to speed up more. Prof caught up again. This scenario was repeated several times, each time at a faster pace, 'til they came into the last 100 yards engaged in a full-on race to the finish between Chris and Prof, whose stride seemed to open up, transforming him before our astonished eyes from a sluggish miler into a sprinter.

Red-faced Chris, as amazed as the rest of us, didn't like failing in his pacer's duty, or getting beaten by "an old man" in his mid-forties. Meanwhile, bent over, chest heaving like a bellows with not a little showmanship, Prof was waiting for me to tell him whether or not he broke six minutes. It was a moral dilemma.

"Prof, you ran 5:59.8"! That was a bit of "a stretcher," as Huck Finn would have said. But only by a few tenths of a second.

"Oh, gosh. Oh gosh. Let me see," says Prof, reaching for my stopwatch.

"Sorry Prof. I zeroed the watch."

Prof stared at me with the piercing air of a prosecutor, his mouth in a bit of a pout. Then, a fulsome smile broke: "I'll take it, William!"

"Take it, indeed. You just ran your best and last mile. I'm going to change your training. You are going to be a sprinter now."

Two years later, Prof was lighter by another 15 pounds, had a classic sprint technique, and held three Masters World Records for the 100, 200, and 400 metres, some of which stood for years. Here is a great photo of him on the way to victory, in perfect form.

The first sprint race he won seemed like the greatest achievement of his much-storied life.

"How did it feel, Prof?"

And him, with the smile of a happy child, "William: I don't need Mary *Whanna!*"

## HAPPINESS AT STANFORD

It's a paradox. If you want life to slow down, do everything that's boring. Stand in a long, painfully slow lineup for a movie, and when you get to the ticket box, don't buy a ticket. Go back and line up again. Time will come to a dead stop, and you will want to slit your wrist. My time at Stanford was just the opposite. The motto of this great institution is still *Die Luft der Freiheit weht:*

Against The Tide

"The Winds of Freedom Blow," and my life there went by like the wind. At the time, Stanford was a bastion of fearless free thought. But the wind of freedom and free thought soon got stilled by radicals, beginning in the mid-60s. There is no wind of freedom blowing at Stanford now.

Most people think the study of linguistics is about learning a lot of languages (being a polyglot). On the contrary. It's about studying the structure of language, how it works as a complex system of (unconscious) signs. The general field of which it is part is called semiotics, or semiology, the study of sign systems, whether of language, literature, folktales, anthropology — anything that relies on a sign system to express meaning. One of the most important and original modern works in this field was by the great Swiss thinker Ferdinand de Saussure (d.1913), who revolutionized how we understand a natural object like a language.

In high school we learned "old grammar." We were told that a noun is "the name of a person, place, or thing." Grammar was to be understood semantically, in terms of meaning. But any curious and confused child would ask: But teacher: "Love is a noun, but it's not 'a thing,'" and so on. So then came confusion and "exceptions" to a lot of "rules." But de Saussure said, no. A noun is a part of speech that fits into a functional position in a sentence, as follows. "The _____ ran away." Whatever fits into that blank space and is understood by a natural speaker of English, is a noun. And he spoke not of letters and words, but of *phonemes* (minimally distinctive units of sound) and *morphemes* (minimally distinctive units of meaning), and more. It still quite interests me.

One of the brightest and most inventive students of human language ever (although I think his later adventures in political writing have made him look naive), was Noam Chomsky. In 1957, as a grad student at Berkeley he published a ground-breaking short book on language entitled *Syntactic Structures*, in which he described the "system" underlying all human languages as Transformational, or Generative. All spoken languages rely on a system for generating utterances acceptable to a native speaker. The book begins with his now-famous sentence: "*Colorless green ideas sleep furiously*," which Chomsky offered as an example of a sentence any native speaker of English would agree is grammatically-correct, but nonsensical. He was making an argument for the independence of *syntax* (the study of structure), from *semantics* (the study of meaning). I was hooked. It was a revelation. Chomsky, like Saussure before him, further launched the study of language as a systemic science. One of the main points he argued was that if any normal child of two or three is able to generate acceptable original sentences that he or she has never heard before, there must be some kind of mental or biological device enabling this, no?

Otherwise, how is it done? He spent the rest of his life trying to discover what he called UG, the Universal Grammar device inherent in all normal human beings that makes this amazing feat — it is amazing, after all — possible.

The next leap into structural theory, which had to wait a couple of years until I was ready, was the notion that if it is true that all natural languages require a generative grammar of some kind to work at all, then what about larger language objects and sign systems such as poetry, folk tales, the novel, drama, all made of language? Is their existence, how they work, also made possible by some hidden structure? Thus began an intellectual curiosity, and a circuitous road that in time would lead me straight to the *École Pratique des Hautes Études* in Paris, to study under Professor Roland Barthes, then one of the stars of French intellectual life.

## THE VIII BRITISH COMMONWEALTH GAME⁹, JAMAICA, 1966 MEETING "THE DUKE," AND A MACHETE MURDER

"Stay on Princess Street, or expect to get mugged," was the first warning we got.

Jamaica was an unlikely spot for the British Commonwealth Games. It had gained Independence only in 1962, and just before the Games the government sent in a fleet of bulldozers to wipe out the poorest, most squalid sections of Kingston before foreigners like us got to see them. This was the first time the word "Commonwealth" was used to replace the word "Empire," due to a seismic shift in world sensitivities over supposedly oppressive colonialism. I have learned since from world experts such as Lord Peter Bauer that in fact colonialism — at least of the British sort — brought wealth, law, and orderliness, railroads, the telephone and telegraph, clean water, sound sewage systems, roads, bridges, public schools, viable courts, and much more, to previously backward countries. When I ask my closest Jamaican-born Canadian friend if Jamaica was better off under colonialism? He pauses to consider, then answers Yes. For sure.

On the second day my close friend (eventually my brother-in-law), Canadian team shot-putter Dave Steen and I thought we should get genuine and see "the real Jamaica." So, we jumped on the back of a rickety aluminum milk truck and were soon bouncing through what looked very much like dangerous territory. One right turn and we entered a hot, dusty tumble of wooden shacks with few windows, rambling, broken slat fencing, grassless, flowerless dirt yards, paper bits blowing about, but lots of small, happy black faces with shining eyes and very white teeth playing cheerfully, mindless of the larger world. Languishing black forearms, an occasional pretty face, stuck

Against The Tide

out of pane-less windows, squeezed out, as if by some pressure of humanity within, and … by now we just hoped to get the hell out of there in one piece. I was glad Dave was 6'5 and weighed over 260 pounds. But as one local warned, "that don't stop a bullet."

I qualified for these Games after my first year at Stanford by winning both the 110m high hurdles and the 400-metre hurdles at the British Empire Games Trials in Edmonton. At 42 inches, the high hurdles reached past my belly button, and how a guy 5'11" got over them fast enough, I can't say. But something was working okay. I beat all Canada's best high hurdlers and equaled my best time and matched the Canadian record again in 14.2" seconds. Mostly, I loved perfecting technique because I was slower on the flat than all my competitors. The trick was to get over and down off each hurdle before they did, running again while they were still in the air. After my 400m hurdles race, a 15-year-old kid named Johnny followed me around like a puppy. So, I stayed at the track for about two hours and showed him everything I knew, and that felt good. Little did I know I was to meet up with him as a grown man in a life-changing way, six years later.

The first thing you learn, the hard way, is that international competitions are designed to run efficiently for officials and spectators, not for athletes. For a fellow of ordinary talent like me, a perfect warm-up of the right timing was crucial to success. All international Games have a warm-up track outside the main stadium, but it may not be of exactly the same quality as the track in the stadium, and you have no way of knowing that in advance unless you can try it out before your race, which they won't let you do.

Our track shoes had spikes that could be changed with a little wrench in ten minutes time to short, medium, or long. In this oppressive Jamaican sun, how hard or soft would the dirt surface of the main track be? Anyone's guess. The final was at night after a long hot day. Maybe I could find out? I took a bus to the stadium and snuck in with a workman to find the track watered just right for my medium spikes. Perfect.

At the warm-up track that evening I felt very good and pumped. But when they marched us into the stadium with just minutes to peel of our sweats and get into our blocks, my heart sank. They had obviously stopped watering hours prior, so the track was like cement. Terror struck, I actually considered ripping my spikes off to run the race barefoot. Really. But no. This would need an exercise of pure mental control. Do what you can in the circumstances.

It was pain and strain on every stride, misery all the way. I doubt any Hindu walking barefoot on a bed of nails felt them more than I felt all 16 of my spikes that night as they drove up into my feet. You can see in the photo below (from Track and Field News), that I was in third or fourth place at the tenth hurdle, but I fell back to sixth place over the last 40 metres to the finish. Not so bad for my first international race in this event, but it was pure penury. There is a video of that race. I am in lane three.[10]

The next day I crossed paths, literally, with Prince Philip, Duke of Edinburgh, on a narrow walk of the athlete's village where he was ambling alone, but for an aide. We shook hands, chatted amiably, and I told him I had sung at the Queen's Coronation in 1953, and was on the mall watching his gilded carriage pass, and at Westminster Abbey a day or so after she was crowned.

"Oh? How swell of you. I wish I had been a spectator myself," he laughed. "That carriage was *most* uncomfortable." The duke gave a permeating sense of the centuries of dignified life vested in his role, at that moment a part of his every word and good cheer.

The next day, strength in numbers, four of us athletes went down the hill to Kingston in a small car. The locals had warned: stay on the main drag. Do NOT enter side streets. They were right. Princess Street was good for an hour's ambling, lots of foreign athletes and locals checking out a myriad of colourful shirts, hats, lots of cheap watches and bracelets for sale, mostly Paris or London knockoffs. Bright clothing, fresh vegetables splayed on tables, straw hats, green tarps for shade, life spilling into the street from all sides. Twice, a furtive black man walked straight up and pushed a genuine-looking "gold" wristwatch into my chest, asking — actually, demanding — 20 bucks. No thanks. We had George Puce with us, a huge discus thrower who won a silver medal here, and a few years later was third in the world. George had 17-inch biceps. We felt safe walking down one side street, just a little. But it got dark and seamy fast. So, we backed out.

On the way back to the Village we realized we were heading the wrong way,

Against The Tide

deeper into Kingston, and would have to turn back. George was driving and headed off the main drag into a side street too narrow for a turn. So, he cut into a deserted laneway between large banana trees, leaves drooping on both sides of us, scraping the car. Looking down to engage a sticky reverse gear, his massive left arm was resting on the open window-ledge with a very expensive watch on his wrist, real gold — a gift from his father. I got uncomfortable. The world was in suspension as George fiddled with the gear. I was hot, boxed-in behind him.

Suddenly, two long skinny black arms darted forth from the sap-green banana leaves and grabbed George's watchband. It happened fast, those two arms, like from a man-eating tree, a sudden stab of danger. A rangy teenager was tugging at George's watch, the gold bracelet stretching beyond belief a foot and a half from George's clenched fist. His arm froze stiff in resistance. The kid pulled harder. I was shouting at George, banging the back of his seat, "George. For chrissake! Grab him!" George could have got a hold of one of those skinny arms and snapped it easily with a twist of his wrist. But he just stared, stupefied, at his precious gold watch while the bracelet extended further, until it snapped. We got a freeze-frame of the kid's face, grimacing teeth, and worried, ganja-bloodshot eyes. As the watch sprang into his hands, he sank shadowy into a wrap of leafy darkness, bolting with frantic strides on long skinny black legs, the pink soles of his feet like fleeing tongues lapping, deep-throated laughing as he disappeared into a dark gulley.

Indignation, of course. Massive George upset to lose his dad's gift. I admit to a quickly dissolving moment of pity for that kid. Three well off Canadians on a prestige, international all-expenses-paid trip, while for this half-naked kid George's watch was going to mean food and ganja for a month. But hell, it was a keepsake. George insisted on reporting the theft.

So we made our way to the police station, a raised, one-storey wooden building surrounded by a high stucco wall with an open gate, and a sentry box warning NO ENTRY. But no police in sight. Anywhere. We weren't about to get shot for trespassing, but were still hotly indignant over the gold watch, so we walked hesitantly up the steps of the shadowy Kingston police station into a large rectangular hall filled with an array of school desks and chairs, several large fans turning slowly overhead. We wanted to report the crime and get on our way, but the place was empty. Except in the far corner was a dimly lit cubicle behind a wire cage. At the back three stacks of yellowed folders towered from floor to ceiling, as if hovering over the small desk on which a wrinkled old black man with curly yellow hair was writing, very slowly. We stood there until he looked up, pleasant enough, eyes glazed, oily yellow with age. His pen would be crawling through those files at his own pace, prisoners languishing in dank Jamaican jails far beyond their term until he damn well got to them.

The reality of Kingstonian justice was about to collide with white ignorance when a great din erupted at the entrance. Two detectives were pushing a reluctant black man in a rumpled blue trench coat forward, as he stumbled over himself. A gaping gash ran from the top of his head halfway down his forehead, blood trickling between his eyes, over his nose, dripping, spreading between his teeth, soaking into his white shirt, coming to a seeping stop on his grey trousers. One of the detectives held him down in a chair. The other pulled out a pack of Players' cigarettes, slid it open, and began asking the bleeding fellow questions, while noting his answers with a stubby pencil on the back of the pack. Due Process was taking a beating. We stood in the shadows, unnoticed, sensing the rapidly diminishing importance of George's watch by the moment. The bleeding man had just killed his brother-in-law in a machete fight over a prostitute. George's watch became collateral damage, a contribution to the underground economy of Jamaica.

## FIRST M.A., AND MORE FRENCH THAN I BARGAINED FOR

In spring of 1967 I finished a Master's Thesis, Master's Exam and Master's Graduation in something called "psycholinguistics," a cognitive science aiming to discover how the brain and human thought work, through the study of deep language structures. It was a chance to combine a bit of psychology with my interest in language, though still remote from my dream of literature. Also in May, and along with another grad student who almost slit his wrist when he found out, I failed my Master's exam. I was well prepared, so this was odd, but we soon discovered we had both been given the Ph.D. exam by mistake. I passed the second exam easily. Graduation was in June, and so another dead-end was looming, as I will explain. But prior to that came another unexpected turn in the pathway of my life.

In early spring my track friend Don Forbes came to my bucolic cabin for a visit with his girlfriend Mimi. She was in the Stanford French Literature program. Oh? I was quite single and sensed the possibility of something exotic. So, I asked, "Do you know any French girls?"

"As a matter of fact, I do." It was a fatal question.

Half a century later I still shake my head over how such an innocent question put to a friend casually with no expectation could have led so quickly to such a combination of romantic entanglement, marriage, cherished progeny,

*Against The Tide*

discord, and divorce. Fire is attractive at a distance but burns if you get too close. When Don and Mimi showed up the next evening and my French blind date, a dark-haired looker with engaging eyes stepped out of the car, I was a goner. You want exotic, Billy-boy? You got it.

Michele Lesavre and her family were *pied-noir* — the not altogether flattering name for a few million French-European citizens of Algeria, mostly Catholic, who were driven out by the bloody Revolution of 1954–1962, during which native Algerians, mostly Muslim, won their independence. In her halting English and my bad French, I got a picture of how her family were driven from their home and business in Bône (Annaba, in ancient times, once the home of Saint Augustine) by the Café-Wars, a couple of which she had witnessed while in high school. Rebels in stolen French army jeeps bristling with machine guns driving at high speed through town squares spraying everything in sight, terrified patrons and students diving under café tables.

So the Lesavre family lost everything and fled to Cassis, in the South of France, which I eventually came to know. Originally a charming fishing village on the Mediterranean Sea not far from Marseilles, redolent of salty air, the cries of stubble-faced fishermen, and the pungent smell of the day's catch, it is today a still charming, but somewhat overrun tourist destination with a diluted authenticity.

Michele had come to Stanford to visit her sister who was working as an *au pair* girl for a Stanford Prof who had taught in Marseilles the year prior. But the deeper reason was to flee her own sadness. Her boyfriend — from his picture a strikingly good-looking fellow — had recently been killed in a car accident. Indirectly, his death affected the course of my life because when I met her she was still in mourning. That sadness had a sweetening effect on what turned out much later to be an unpredictably volatile and haughty temperament. The engaging, still pained young girl I fell for was not the woman I ended up with.

At any rate, my sophisticated, stylish girlfriend had a sharp mind, a Fine Arts education from the École des Beaux Arts in Marseilles and was a good cook to boot. I think I was set up for the flair of this attachment because she had so many of the high-octane characteristics of my own mother. So, Mom set me up. A lot of sons end up marrying their mothers, and daughters their fathers. That makes sense, after all. Babies suckle more than milk. For a couple of years, we had a lot of carefree fun with friends, running around Stanford and the beautiful Bay Area. In the end many things good and bad came of this experience. You can't know in advance which, or when, they will be, because the trouble with life is you don't get to practice.

## L'AUDACE, TOUJOURS L'AUDACE. SAVED BY THE PEN!

Mom and Dad came to Stanford, met Michele, and attended my Master's graduation in June, a high occasion for the Gairdner family as I was the first in living memory to attend a Graduate School of any kind. In 1967 Graduation at Stanford was genuinely inclusive, a sharing of high achievement by all graduates without regard to race, gender, or any other differences. This was considered normal at the time and a vindication of Martin Luther King Jr.'s ringing statement: *"I have a dream that my four little children will one day live in a nation where they will not be judged by the color of their skin but by the content of their character."*

But a mere decade later, Stanford, and more than 100 other top American universities were hosting optional Graduation Ceremonies segregated by race. Which is to say, they had different grad ceremonies for blacks and whites, and sometimes for Asians and "Latinx," too. That's a phony term for a grab-bag of Spanish-speaking ethnicities. One college even began offering a *"blacka-laureate."* Ugh. Many also began providing racially segregated residences and fraternities described by some schools as "affinity housing." Euphemism is always a camouflage for the ideological manipulation of citizens, no matter the direction. Thus began a kind of mini fascism in America that ended my

Against The Tide

love of Stanford as it is today, but not for what it was before the progressive tsunami swamped reality. Those were golden years.

No sooner was graduation done and parents gone than the big life questions percolated again. A graduate degree in the mid-60s wasn't all that common. It had clout. Almost any university or college would hire a Stanford grad. I didn't regret higher education thus far. Who would? But, I was still in a dead end; living in a foreign country, a fine master's degree I couldn't see using from one of the great universities of the world, a deepening attachment to a girl from a foreign country, and no idea where that was headed, either. I was soon to find out.

Meanwhile, what to do? Poetry drifted in: "I wandered lonely as a cloud" (Wordsworth); then: "There is a tide in the affairs of men, which taken at the flood leads on to fortune (Shakespeare, Julius Caesar); and finally: "Two roads diverged in a wood, and I — I took the one less travelled by And that has made all the difference" (Robert Frost, The Road Not Taken).

I was much closer to my love of language. But not yet close to great literature. To maybe being a writer someday. Had I checkmated myself? A few days later I was wandering lonely as a cloud under the cool archway of Stanford's impressive Quad — a large open-rectangle sandstone structure with wrap-around cloister-like archways and a three-acre earthen courtyard in the middle planted with groupings of lofty palms that arch against a perpetually blue sky; past the beautiful, quietly dark and peaceful chapel, surprised, now and then, when turning a corner by a sunny nook of flaming red rhododendrons. Must I now say goodbye to this paradise?

Passing the inner sanctum of the English Department feeling rather like an outcast lacking formation in literature (Dad: "literature is something you do in bed before sleep"), my eye caught a small advert on the Department's Bulletin Board: "master's degree in creative writing." Whoa ... What's this?

When I lived penniless, jobless, training for the Olympics with Bill Toomey, I had secretly done some writing. That would be creative writing, wouldn't it? Sure. Or I wouldn't have tried it. Most people who dare to write fiction have a deep fear of showing it to anyone. I was no exception and never showed Bill or anyone else a word of it. Just the thought of someone seeing my writing produced a kind of emotional self-immolation. But I kept writing anyway, a couple of pages now and then about my experiences at sea, and the like, and ended up with 150 very private pages in a black binder that I kept hidden, and still had. Now, I'm walking past this advert, and I hear my dad again: "The squeaky wheel gets the oil"; and Prof: "*L'audace, toujours l'audace.*" And so, why not? Nothing to lose.

Stanford's creative writing program was already famous. It was run by

Wallace Stegner, a well-known Canadian author who lived as a boy for five years in Eastend, Saskatchewan, a poor, treeless, dusty village of a few hundred souls. Now he was known as "the Dean of Western Writers." A big man in the writing world. He was soon to win the Pulitzer Prize, and then the National Book Award. Some of his creative writing grads became famous, such as Ken Kesey who wrote *One Flew Over the Cuckoo's Nest*, of which a popular movie was made. Who can forget cruel, calculating Nurse Ratched? Stegner knew his own mind. He nurtured other famous "Wallace Stegner Fellows" too, such as novelist and poet Wendell Berry, the memoirist Tobias Wolff, and even Sandra Day O'Connor, who after she left Stanford became America's first female Supreme Court Justice, where I was much later to discover she wrote more than one legal fiction.

Anyway, I was immediately pregnant with the excitement of possibility as I wandered like a lost sheep into the Creative Writing office that Friday afternoon and asked Stegner's secretary — Betty, on her name plate — if I could have an appointment to see Professor Stegner?

"What for?"

Betty was cranky and tired. Nurse Ratched, staring bloodless at Jack Nicholson. Eyes just making it over the rim of her beat-up glasses. "Sorry. I mean he's busy and needs to be a little prepared." I had four little scars from a childhood terrier bite on my upper arm, and she was making them itch.

"It's about creative writing."

Tapping a pencil on her desk now. "Alright. He *likes* talking about *that*."

Tapping some more. Tapping slowing down. Flipping through her appointment book.

"Monday. Two o'clock. Don't be late."

That weekend was a blur of moral and spiritual agitation, disembodied wandering on a burnt-out planet. On Monday I walked into Stegner's darkened office gripping my secret black binder of stories with a hand that wouldn't dry. Stanford's god of creative writing was bent over beside a gooseneck lamp, writing slowly with a fancy black fountain pen, enthroned at an imposing desk scattered with small piles of books and manuscripts. He didn't look up.

"Sit down." He finished writing, stuck his letter in an envelope, looked at me with his tongue out as he licked, and put a stamp on it. "Who are you, and why are you here?"

University Professors tend to look like boys most of their lives, no matter their age. Maybe because their entire existence is cerebral, sequestered from the many shocks of real life. Not him. He was a gnarly, bushy-white-haired, plenty rugged and wrinkled, heavy glasses, no-nonsense man, and he was fixing me now in what I learned was the Stegner stare. *This better be good.*

Against The Tide

"Sir, I'm a student here from Canada. I just graduated with a Master's in Structural Linguistics. But I'm at the end of the road. I don't regret the Master's. I think structuralism is a coming field. Even in literary studies. I just can't see teaching it for the rest of my life. Sir, what I have always wanted, is to be a writer."

He wrinkled his forehead, a tickertape of thoughts running past, like, *Oh no, not again. Another goddamn dreamer.* But he obviously had a nose for good writing and knew it may be sniffed out in unlikely places. He was calculating. *Should I waste my time on this fellow?*

"So, Sir, I've done some writing. I've never shown it to anyone. Ever. Could you look at it?" When I think back, that was pretty brassy ....

He didn't drop the Stegner stare, still sizing me up, rolling his shoulders a little. And then ... "Leave it with me. Come back Wednesday. After lunch."

I walked out in a state of agitated apprehension and didn't sleep much for two days, just like before the biggest races of my life. But this was a literary Olympics.

Wednesday, after lunch, without looking up, cranky Betty waved me straight through to his office, a band-aided finger holding the phone to her ear.

It's hard to describe the feeling of having one's whole immediate future so completely at the mercy of another. That was me. He didn't start shouting. I'm just using italics because his words were booming like the gong of Big Ben.

"Well, I've looked at your writing. And ... I*t's not very good. In fact ... it's not very good at all.*"

Oh Jeez… darkness descending, and I'm not even out of the blocks.

And then, what a wonderful surprise!

"But… *it's good enough to get you into Stanford's creative writing program.*"

"Really. Sir?

"Go see Betty. Get signed up."

In that moment, in the sonorous thrill of his words, Wallace Stegner changed my life.

## MY INTELLECTUAL HOME, AND OTHER SURPRISES

Seriously, walking out of that office I couldn't feel the ground under my feet. I had just rolled the dice in the biggest crapshoot of my short life, and it worked. The warm sun, the blue sky, the floral smells, felt personal, felt mine, felt me, now. The Master's in creative writing degree required half of the course in creative writing and half in literature, plus a significant piece of writing at the end — a collection of short stories, or a novella. The next day I was mixing with students who had earned their way into Stanford with impressive under-graduate degrees in English Literature from places like Yale, Harvard, and Princeton. Most of them had already done intensive literary studies. Not me. I was as green as they come. And that turned out to be an advantage, for I had nothing to prove, everything to gain. I was home at last, and quiet, in unbounded emotional and intellectual freedom.

For each creative writing course, a half-dozen would-be authors would each write a short piece of fiction. The professor would then read each story to the class, and all would critique it. A raw experience, to say the least, in which good points felt good, and the bad ones, you took on the chin. Every piece of fiction I submitted for that year got very high marks for writing style and "voice," and lesser marks for "story." I hadn't learned story-telling yet, the art of hooking the reader with a crescendo of expectations crushed or fulfilled. Basically a story fails unless the reader eagerly wants to turn the page. This art comes naturally, or has to be taught. I had to be taught.

But the real surprise was my literature courses. I was surrounded by accom-plished Ph.D. hopefuls who had already studied many of the works before us. Not me. And they knew I hadn't. Compared to them I knew nothing of what makes great literature, except what I felt to be true upon reading. But this turned in my favour, for with no prior formation or established opinion to hold me back, unlike other students who fished in memory for whatever they had learned, and were now regurgitating, too fearful of their own novel insights, my untutored critiques emerged as fresh and unusual, to me, to the class,

*Against The Tide*

and to the Professor. I had entered a wonderfully new intellectual, emotional, and philosophical world where for lack of formation and accepted opinion, I could be creative and fearless. And I was rewarded. Almost all my papers and exams in literature at Stanford reaped an A, or higher — the coveted "+." One professor said out loud my paper for him was "near publishable." I think that piqued some of the other students.

After only six months of dating, Michele and I moved into a beautiful, half-suspended studio apartment attached to the home of Mr. and Mrs. Bacon, at 121 Escobar Rd., Portola Valley, overlooking rolling hills golden with wind-waved dry grasses and dark green shade trees. Sometimes deer fed just below our balcony. He was the President of Coca Cola (Northern) California. His wife was retired, doing saintly work raising the two children of her wayward, perpetually stoned, perpetually absent eldest daughter, who was lost somewhere in the hippie labyrinth of San Francisco, probably lying on the floor of the dark, strobe-lit Fillmore Auditorium, her psychedelic heart and mind one with the ear-splitting boom of The Grateful Dead. She was dead to her own children.

We no sooner got settled in this paradise than Michele told me her visa was about to expire. I was still in the grip of early attachment and hadn't thought once about her having to leave America. Leave me. Well now, there had been a few rough spots in our short time already. Mostly in the nature of her unpredictable temper when drinking, which I chalked up to the frustrations of culture, a latent French snobbism, and translation. In retrospect, trapped by my own self-regard, I was convinced that with enough exposure to me she would soon mellow, and those fiery moods soften and fade. Life was good.

Next day, we visited an Immigration lawyer in San Francisco. A big man in official blue shirtsleeves, a hot cramped office, large sweat-stains spreading dark blue under both arms. The outer flare of his nose that normally covers the right nostril was missing, so that we could see the pink fleshy ridge inside. It was hard not to stare as he spoke, because a small fly was making its way up the ridge and into his nostril. But he didn't seem to feel it. Just as the fly disappeared inside his nose, he dropped what felt like a muffled bomb, and the shrapnel hit.

"She can't stay in the USA. Her Visa expires in two weeks. She has to leave, then re-apply for another Visa once back in France... if she wants to come back. Which may take some time. The only way she can stay now, is if she's married to a US citizen. Or, to someone with a valid Visa" (looking at me).

I didn't want to get married to anyone, though it was probably time. In those days people married young. Mom (who married at 19) once hinted that maybe I had "feelings" for men? ("Mom. Puhleeze! How gross"). I just didn't feel ready to close off my wonderfully open life. I mean that's how I saw marriage, as a kind of trap (in which I had one leg in already). But I didn't want to lose this unusual woman, either. I figured gone would likely mean gone for good.

So we went home to talk about it, and the next day found a judge to marry us.

Prof was very upset.

It was the beginning of a long chapter in my life that was about to write itself.


## LOWELL

When I walked into my class on the 18th-century British novel — on the wonderful *Moll Flanders*, Fielding's ribald *Tom Jones*, Samuel Richardson's delicate, if windy 1740 epistolary novel *Pamela*, and more — taught by a genial, soft-spoken Professor, there was only one seat left at the end of the first row, and I squeezed in, invading somewhat the elbow-territory of the fellow on my right, who gave me a disinterested look. I was disturbing some private reverie. The Professor had Parkinson's disease, so his hands and head shook a bit, but his words and perceptions of *Pamela* seemed sensitive to the point of exquisite. It was all new. I loved it and was impressed. Having no friends in the English Department, I tried to strike up a conversation with the fellow on my right when the class ended.

"What do you think of the prof."

He looked at me with a wince. Really? Had I missed something obvious?

"He's a [expletive deleted] old lady."

I was unsettled by this jolt of candour and the implication I was a fool who had misjudged the shaking man. Maybe I should sharpen my assessment of the professor — and of the guy beside me, too? It was Lowell Cohn. That wasn't a great start, but he became a lifelong friend, and after we left Stanford, one of the world's great sports writers, who was surprisingly successful in persuading readers that a fat-bellied baseball batter was Beowulf *redivivus*, or that the reason a great football coach messed up was because he suffered the self-doubts of Hamlet, if not quite as eloquently. But the expletive was all I got out of him. He was either very in the know (and I was taken in by this prof's *shtick* — Lowell's word), or very rude and dismissive. I wasn't sure which.

A couple of months later I was walking through Tressider Union cafeteria and saw Lowell hunched in the shadows. We were indoors, but he was bundled in a blue winter jacket and a tight cap as if freezing ("a toque? What's a toque?"), eating a large cheeseburger. "Hey, sit down, guy." We got along immediately and laughed a lot. I have known Lowell for more than a half

Against The Tide

century, and every time we talk, we laugh a lot. He was a brassy, sassy, bright kid from Brooklyn — a long way from home. You can leave Brooklyn, but it never leaves you. Lowell became my first and only serious Stanford friend, my only Jewish friend, and one of my few close friends, ever. Drinking a great California wine with Lowell is one of the high points of my life, and we drank a lot of it together, because friendship made it taste even better.

Once we drove miles up a twisting redwooded road high into the Sonoma hills to the Annapolis winery, which specializes in Pinots so good you can't find them in a wine store. Private subscription only. There, after tasting a very special flight of Pinots served by lovely, dark-tressed Sophie, her black curls lying damply against her ivory neck when she bent over to fill our gasses, well, Lowell and I drew breath. My hand on my heart. No words needed. Lovely Tess was materializing before our eyes. So we bought a bottle of the best, and on a nearby bench under an apple tree watched the timeless golden grasses waving lazily in a light breeze, heard the distant Pacific, as we two sat, "Silent, upon a peak in Darien."

But I digress.

"I heard you're a runner!" he says. "Hey, I used to run." There was just a faint hint of a dare, as in, hey, you're not so hot, you know.

"You ran, too? When, what distance?"

"High school. I was fast. I *actually* ran in Madison Square Gardens. I did. No shit. On the relay team. *That* was fun." And then, quietly, an afterthought … "I heard you ran at the Olympics? Is that *true*? Hey. Tell me. How good were you?"

He was in a hurry, but we liked each other already. I told him I still run, and I go to the track at Angell Field most afternoons to train. "Why don't you come?"

"Nah. That's done."

"Lowell. They have all-comers meets. Every week. We could run relays."

"Nah."

"Lowell … *they give medals!*"

"They *do*? I'm comin'!" A burst of laughter from us both.

I became Lowell's coach. He got very fit and ran faster than he did at Madison Square Gardens. He even got some medals. Lowell, Prof, and I ran at Stanford together for a couple of years, usually going to Zott's for a burger and beer after, where, as mentioned, we discussed every important philo-sophical and moral topics under the California sun. Prof died suddenly from a subarachnoid hemorrhage in 2000. He was found naked on his living room floor with a wine glass clutched in his hand. But he is ever in my heart, and in Lowell's.

Once I was at someone's home for a small party with Prof, where we met a kindly Priest. Prof never went to church, and never spoke of God. I figured he was an elegant atheist. But one of the abrupt lessons of my young life was when I once said, "How could there be a just God in such an unjust world?" Prof fidgeted a little. Then he began asking me how I came to my point of view? I was cocky enough to tell him. So, he asked a few more questions about my line of argument. Before long, I got a cold feeling at the back of my neck. It became apparent that without using any arguments of his own, this master debater was hanging me with my own rope. I was duly chastened, for life. If you're going to raise a contentious point, you better have your logical ducks in order.

I wandered away from the Priest and lost track of Prof. Where did he go? I went looking. Through the glass partition of a shaded back room I saw him kneeling on a carpeted floor in front of the Priest, who had his hands laid, so very gently, on Prof's shiny bald head, in blessing. I was stunned, and deeply moved. My atheist's hero was in there confessing his private soul, through a glass darkly. The next day, when I described this intimately personal moment to Lowell, tears sprang from his eyes.

## TROUBLE TO COME

I started almost a year behind most of the Ph.D. students in the English program, but graduated well ahead of most by taking coursework year-round. Lowell and I were soon teaching Freshman English and shared an office where I was alone and lost in thought and feeling on a fateful fall afternoon in 1968, studying a beautifully-written page by Marcel Proust from his novel *Remembrance of Things Past* in which he describes how the smell and taste of a madeleine pastry just out of the oven at his aunt's home produced a near-mystical coincidence with that same sensual event as a small child, and therefore, with himself as he was in the past. That powerful, unsolicited invasion of all his senses by a small, warm, sweet pastry — he called it an "involuntary memory" — made all intervening time vanish, revealing the constancy of human personality, and of the soul. Of *his* soul. The fullness of that moment relieved the alarming transience of life and entranced him, just as his words were entrancing me now, happy, lost in my wonderful new world of literature, at last.

But I had a strange sense something was wrong, so I put books aside and left for home where I was surprised to see Lowell's car parked in the driveway. A nice surprise. Lowell is here. Time for a party. But once in the door I was shocked to see Michele slumped in an armchair in the corner, clearly not

Against The Tide

herself, drunk, overwrought, a large half-empty jug of white wine beside her. No knife, or razor blade in view. What the hell? I caught my best friend alone in my home, with my wife? They were drinking? They had a crazy fight? Lowell, stony-eyed, looked right through me as he made for the door, a man ready to jump without a parachute.

"Call me," was all he said.

Turned out Lowell had been in the office just before me, and Michele had called. She sounded drunk and distraught, and told Lowell, twice: "I don't want a *scandale*." Lowell bolted for our place and saw she was almost incoherently inebriated, and very upset. She blasted him: "I don't want a *scandale*. Get the hell out."

He fired back: "Sister; you can stand on your friggin' head if you want. But I'm not leavin' 'til Bill gets here."

And there I was. Worried she had tried to harm herself, and might try again, I took her straight to Stanford hospital. Dr. Richard U'Ren, the psychiatrist who saw her told me he had seen a lot of other French students who suffered a similar crisis, usually culture-shock and depression. "They really stamp 'em out over there!" he offered. Which was to say, France brainwashes every French citizen thoroughly from childhood with the feeling, "If I am not French, and surrounded by my French world, I am not me." But once rested and sobered up she seemed quite lucid, so he released her on condition of regular counseling, to which she agreed.

We English speak of those who move from their native culture to an alien one as "*up*rooted." When they change countries they take the tree of their culture, roots, and all. But the French, subjected to a lifelong belief that the French way of life — wine, cheese, art, culture — is best, describe moving away from France as being "*déraciné*" — or "*un*rooted"; they may take the tree, but the roots remain in French soil, forever. You couldn't dig 'em up if you tried.

Michele had sweetness in her that emerged when she was happy. But she spent a lot of time alone in those hills, and at a few parties I had seen the alarming effect of too much wine, along with a spontaneous anger that seemed out of proportion to whatever triggered her. I didn't much like the person who emerged, however briefly. But my inflated self-regard, combined with not wishing to forswear what I had so recently and precipitously chosen — only to appear even more foolish to myself — persuaded me that under my steadying influence she would drop all need for liquid oblivion. Would be softer and gentler more often, would lose the anger. But the easiest person to blind is oneself.

It seems strange to me now that we never spoke of this event, and I'm still not sure why. She did her counselling, and we never spoke of that, either, which was also a little peculiar. But in the aftermath, she was indeed gentler and more agreeable. Good times typical of college life, punctuated only occasionally by the feeling, still lurking, that I had probably, maybe, okay … I think … I jumped into this marriage too soon; wasn't fully certain what I had in hand and was now in a wait-and-see mode.

The months went by quickly completing course work. The final bit to earn the M.A. in Creative Writing required either the submission of a novella, or two additional courses in English Literature. I chose to write a 60-page novella in a Faulkner-like style, which had dramatic appeal in those days, but my "story" was weak, and my novella was rejected by … Wallace Stegner. That smarted a little. But by that time, I was doing top academic work and getting far more interested in literary theory and what was called the "history of ideas"; especially, in new and fascinating applications of certain ideological modes of analysis to bodies of literature, a specialty of my Ph.D. Thesis Supervisor, professor David Halliburton. A lot of exciting new work was coming out of Europe, especially France, and I began connecting the dots, for I had soon to pick a Thesis topic and take the dreaded Ph.D. oral exam, a three or four hour ordeal before a handful of Professors aiming to poke holes in the Candidate's work.

About this time, Michele was complaining of mild stomach problems, so I found her a local doctor. Two days later, I was alone when the doctor called asking for her. Not here just now. Pause. Then he told me, with a kind of suspended, paternal excitement: "Your wife is not sick. She's pregnant," hung up, and left me hanging.

I have never forgotten that novel mixture of amazement, dread, and a smoldering, confusing upset. Suddenly, I was the one with stomach trouble. Calm down, Bill. Calm down. No denying I felt excitement. A new life, part of me, would come into this world. Wow. But also, anger. Michele had already made herself of questionable tenure in our young marriage, and now, very clearly, had unilaterally decided, perhaps unconsciously, I grant, that she wanted a child. So, stop the pill. But without telling me? I felt put upon. More honestly? Trapped. There was also some pre-emptive shame in admitting to myself I felt this way over the miracle of my own child to come. I struggled to separate these opposed feelings. But there was no denying the trap. I didn't like the fact that another human being — it didn't matter who, it just happened to be her — had just morally-dictated the course of my life to salvage her own. I thought it was morally okay to resent the trap but love the outcome. Get used to it, Bill. Its checkmate now, for better or worse. You're gonna be a dad. I

Against The Tide

consoled myself with a verse from the *Rubáiyát* of Omar Khayyam that struck me in high school:

> *The Moving Finger writes; and, having writ,*
> *Moves on: nor all thy Piety nor Wit*
> *Shall lure it back to cancel half a Line,*
> *Nor all thy Tears wash out a Word of it.*

## STUDYING UNDER GOD

Michele wanted to have the baby back home in France. We were going to make the best of it. I was getting deeper into the philosophical side of my studies, which is to say, fascinated by *La nouvelle critique* and other European modes of analysis. One of the brightest critical luminaries of the day was Professor Roland Barthes, a sparkling intelligence whose commentaries on literature and culture seemed a combination of intellectual bravado, panache, and rare insight, an exciting departure from what was typical in the staid, merely analytical Anglo-American tradition, and it opened a panoply of fresh intellectual possibilities. I was hooked. As it happened, I saw a notice on campus that the French government was offering grants to foreigners to study in France. So I applied. Also, as it happened, Prof had connections with the *École pratique des hautes études* in Paris, where Barthes was teaching. So, he wrote and asked if Barthes would serve as my Thesis advisor while there. Very bold. To his surprise and mine, this letter arrived in January of 1969:

Cher Monsieur,

Je suis très heureux que votre demande de Bourse ait été acceptée et je vous en félicite. J'aimerais beaucoup vous rencontrer à votre arrivée en France, mais je dois vous signaler que je serai absent de Paris de Juin à Octobre prochain. Peut-être pourrons nous nous voir à l'automne. Je le souhaite et je vous prie de croire, cher Monsieur, à mes sentiments très cordiaux.

R Barths

Roland Barthes
11, rue Servandoni  Paris VI

You had to be there, as they say. In the world of up to the moment literary theory, this was like getting a letter from God. I would finish the rest of my Stanford courses, get through my oral exam in May, go off to France for a year of study with God, have our child in August, finish my Ph.D. Thesis, and come back home. Done. And I almost forgot, the next Commonwealth Games would be in Edinburgh, Scotland, July of 1970. Maybe I could make the Canadian Team in the 400m hurdles, and fit that in? Maybe.

## "WE ARE ALL ONE HEARTBEAT AWAY FROM DEATH"

One late afternoon, a week before my Ph.D. Oral exam our lofty eyrie was quiet as the tomb, stacks of study notes gathered in piles on the floor, divided by subject and author. I was seated in a comfy old armchair, wondering how I could stuff anymore knowledge into an already overstuffed head. Michele, seven months pregnant, the two of us comfortable now with the natural turn our life was about to take, came over and sat facing me on the ample left arm of my chair to ask a question about some notes she was typing for me. Big of belly, she faced outward, which I specify only because, had she decided to sit the other way it would have been fatal. I extracted myself from my focus on Chaucer to put my arm over her knees, my hand on her belly. Any kicking? At that moment, our life almost took a deadly turn for the worse.

Then came a booming, ear-splitting, window-rattling blast, an explosion so loud we were deafened momentarily; a sharp pain in my left elbow, the sleeve of my dressing gown flapping upward suddenly, shreds of cloth floating back down in the air; blood on my sleeve; nothing left of the shredded sleeve; our eyes locked in pure fright. A gas explosion?

A small chunk of skin and bone had been torn off the end of my elbow. What the hell was that? There was a blackened hole in the carpet the thickness of a thumb, fibres sizzled, smoke drifting lazily upward. Upward? There was another hole in the ceiling. So, from the ear-splitting boom I knew it had to be at least a 30-30, a bullet big enough to fell a grizzly, or pass through two or three human bodies before stopping.

Immediately upon the explosion the door below us banged shut, followed by the high-pitched, hysterical screams of a girl; footsteps; running. More screams: "Ah! … Ah! Ahhhhh …." trailing away. We sprang to the balcony to catch only a glimpse of fleeing, disheveled blonde hair swishing as the Bacon's granddaughter ran up the slope and out of sight to the main house. Someone just tried to *kill* us? Almost killed us?

That paralyzing possibility sank in, clothed in dread — and relief. Had that

Against The Tide

bullet passed five inches to the right — a mere five inches! — both Michele, and what turned out to be our beautiful daughter Christine, would have been killed instantly. Never mind the destruction of my left arm. The specter of near tragedy drained us completely.

A few minutes later came a knock on the door. Mr. Bacon, in a blue satin dressing gown, tangled white hair, grim in the dusky light, appeared at our door holding a bottle of vodka, holding peace and reconciliation of a sort, imagining, as he must have already done at some depth of panic, police sirens, lights flashing in spinning red circles at his home, his million-dollar job with Coca Cola fast losing its fizz, media stories about his grand-daughter's arrest, neighbours gossiping, and that quiet little stash of high-powered hunting rifles and ammo. Turned out this 14-year-old had rebelled at her curfew with emotional conniption, threatened to kill herself, snuck quietly to the store-room below us for a rifle, managed to get a large bullet in the chamber the right way, waved the rifle overhead, unintentionally pulled the trigger, and ran out screaming. Pretty sure it was unintentional. But not entirely.

We lost most of our hearing for a week. But neither we, nor Mr. Bacon, nor his grand daughter ever spoke of this again. The lesson was not lost as to how a concatenation of seemingly freak events at a single moment in time, resulting from a chain of strict causation that cannot be undone, may instantly change a life, or end it. In a deeper sense, this raised the perpetual God question once again, and the flukiness of a life.

## THE PH.D. ORAL EXAM – A HURDLE OF ANOTHER KIND

Ph.D. students uniformly tremble at the prospect of underperformance during the Oral Exam. It's an ordeal of several hours in which a handful of tenured Professors ask questions of the Candidate and expect them to be answered very well. General questions from anywhere in the history of English Literature and free translations of two pages, one in French, the other German. Then an hour or so of grilling in the student's area of specialization. In my case, exactly how was I going to apply some of those new European critical techniques to novels by … Virginia Woolf? This was sure to strike some of the profs as a little bizarre.

I had plenty of ordinary anxiety. But I got lucky. The exam was on a Monday in mid-May. As it happened, the Saturday prior I ran my best-ever 400m hurdle race at the Modesto Relays. This gave an injection of spirited buoyancy that lasted at least a week. Modesto is a small town in the huge flat Central Valley of California lying between the Coastal mountains and the

Sierra Nevada. It's where the only successful revolution in history has taken place, which continues to this day. I mean the Green Revolution in agriculture that with modern irrigation, fertilization, and smart-tech turned what was previously a semi-arid desert into one of the most productive food cornucopias of the world, shipping billions of tons of fruits, vegetables, nuts, and more to the rest of the world, all year round.

The meet is famous for the 30 or more World Records set there. I always figured you improve by racing better athletes, and that was a given at Modesto, where I had no chance to place, much less to win. I have lost far more races in my life than I ever won, and having spent so much time in the USA, the greatest track power in the world, I got used to it. Tough competition makes you tougher. On the dirt track at Modesto I got into the final and ran 51.9" for third place. When I drifted away with the stadium crowd after this meet, there was suddenly a loud — Crack! Crack! Crack! — pistol shots, behind me, and I ducked instinctively. Some guys ambling to their car said, "Relax. It's Saturday night in Modesto." Okay. At least it wasn't a 30-30. This was frontier country.

I was still race-high on Monday when I walked into my Oral Exam to see four Professors: my advisor, and three others waiting around a table, ravens awaiting carrion. Some small talk to relax me. Then, let's begin:

Translate this page of French from Camus' novel, *L'Étranger* (The Stranger). I did. Translate this page of German, from Troubetzkoy's *Grundzüge der Phonologie* (Principles of Phonology). Phew. I got through that, too. Then came an hour of general questions from the whole span of English Literature, and … why was I so interested in European critical methods? Finally, why, and how did I expect to apply any of those methods (a slight note of disdain in this question) to an English novelist like Virginia Woolf? Wasn't that a bit odd?

Frankly, I replied (at some risk) that her novels as stories did not interest me that deeply, but I admired her seemly unstructured prose style (was it really unstructured, or was the structure just hidden?) and thought it would be revealing to apply some of the new French "criticism of consciousness," as it was then called, especially as practiced by the remarkable critic Georges Poulet, and also some structural methods as displayed by Roland Barthes in his arresting book *On Racine*, to her corpus of novels. At that point, from the looks on their faces, it struck me that excepting my thesis advisor, they knew very little about all this. So, I asked them (*l'audace, toujours l'audace!*) … if I could step up to the blackboard, and explain?

Now it got exciting. I was in the blocks and the gun went off. For almost an hour I got enjoyably lost in sketching the various theoretical novelties of the day, most of which had not drifted as far as Stanford yet. When it was over,

Against The Tide

one of the senior Profs very kindly volunteered he had "learned a lot." I was sent up to my office in a fog to await their pass or fail decision. After a few minutes of sweaty palms, one of them came upstairs to get me. I sat for the verdict. Another fork in the road. Honestly, I was at a rare loss for words with the exception of repeating my gratitude when they told me I had not only passed but, they had decided, with a rare *Cum Laude* distinction. Holy. This was quite a distance for the young fellow who decided one day to try a little stumbling French with a nice-looking lady and her dog at the Stanford track.

## OFF TO FRANCE FOR A YEAR

I had bought a little blond Cockapoodle dog named Alfie to serve as a company for Michele in my absence. He set an unofficial world record for the 100 yards of 8.8 seconds in 1969. Lowell, holding Alfie's back legs behind the start line. Prof, running excitedly ahead as if in a doggie world championship. Alfie, barking and tugging his back legs like crazy to escape Lowell's grip. Me, at the finish line, calling "Alfie, Alfie, Alfie," timing him as he bolted past like a whirling dervish, tongue flapping, happy wild eyes, paws barely touching the ground. What fun we had. "And … *It's a … World Record*!" to laughter all 'round.

California was over for now. Big with child, Michele flew home to France. I drove the 4,300 kilometres to Toronto almost non-stop in 44 hours, Alfie perched atop my stuff. When we got out of the car at last on the green grass at Thornhill, he went a little crazy for a while. We were off to France for a year, so I asked my friend Roger and his wife Tinker to take Alfie; we would get him back in a year. But in fact, we never did. They fell in love with him, so we let them keep him. Years later Alfie came to his sudden end one cold winter night during a blinding snowstorm when he got run over while sniffing with his warm little nose along a train track.

Meanwhile, I drove my car to New York city to ship the car and myself to France on Queen Elizabeth II, just because there was a deal — you book a ticket, your car ships free. I arrived at Le Havre in the north of France a year after the Paris student riots of May, 1968, but had no idea that hundreds of thousands of students, leftist agitators and communists, had shut down France for a month, demanding the end of capitalism, free education for all, and so on, or that some of the main thinkers who stirred those riots were to intersect much later with my own intellectual life. The only inkling I had of similar unrest at Stanford was when a few students upset over the war in Vietnam broke windows at the ROTC cadet offices. I was a natural hawk: Communism has to be pushed back wherever found. So, I was in favour of that horrible war, hamstrung though it was by student protests, and therefore I was out of step with the growing leftist mob at Stanford. My Professor of American Literature, a credit-card hippie, walked into class the first day and told us "If you want to learn about American Literature, read my book. Now, let's talk about Marxism." We got cheated. Two years later he was arrested for walking across the Stanford campus with a loaded shotgun.

Michele delivered sweet Christine on August 22 at the Clinique Bouchard. Contrary to French expectations at the time, I wanted to be in the delivery room. I almost regretted that because the doctor was stuck in traffic somewhere, Michele was yelling, a window was open for air so there were a few flies buzzing around, and from the smell of ether, I almost passed out. Meanwhile, the miraculous sight of a newborn baby coming into this world altered forever the naïve thoughts I had been fed in classes about Darwin and how human beings came to exist. After that we decamped for Michele's parents' apartment in Cassis. I loved the scenes of gnarled fishermen in colourful, putt-putting blue and red sloops, the smell of gutted fish, coffee, baguettes baking, workmen stopping in for their *gros rouge* on the way home, shouting salutations across a picturesque glassy harbour to buddies in the sing-songy dialect of the region.

The breastfeeding ended far too abruptly, to my way of thinking, but I stayed out of that. Not my breasts. So, earlier than planned, we drove to Paris to find an apartment, and to meet Roland Barthes, while Michele's mother looked after our brand new bottle-fed baby. Her parents would bring the baby to Paris in a week or so. Okay. We found a small 2nd floor apartment at 4 bis, Rue Antoine Bourdelle, in the 15th Arrondissement.

Three things were remarkable about that trip. First, there was an immediate sense of being immersed in a very long, tragicomedy history, such as I, a denizen of the New World, had never palpably felt before. History became palpable. The victories of Caesar's troops over the Parisii in 52 BC are easily imagined when walking across the *Ile de la Cité* to the glorious Cathedral of Notre Dame; and dashing Charlemagne, whom we studied at Appleby; and the long line of philosophers and artists whose lives touched Paris, and whom Paris touched: Abelard, Aquinas, Descartes, and on into our own time, the lure of the robust Paris of the 20th century — "the lost generation". Impressionism in painting, literary symbolism, all mixed with a potpourri of philosophical styles that stirred the Western world. Hemingway, Henry Miller, Picasso, Sartre, existentialism, Camus, T.S. Eliot, Ezra Pound, and so many others. And most moving of all, surely, then and now, was the simple wording on the little ceramic memorial tablets one finds screwed to the walls of so many buildings in Paris, walls that still have machine-gun holes in them from WWII, and which give profound pause:

Against The Tide

*Ici, pour la gloire de la France, a tombé* [a name] *quinze ans, September, 15, 1943.*

*Here, for the glory of France, fell* [the name], *15 years old, September, 15, 1943.*

The second very odd thing was that after we got settled, a week went by. Then another. But no baby came to Paris. As it turned out, she was cared for by Mamie in Cassis until December, when she was driven to Paris the first time. Intense conversations ensued between Michele and her mother, while her father and I were sent walking. Then, I got the announcement Christine was going right back to Cassis. She finally came to Paris the first week of January, after Mamie complained of exhaustion.

The third thing that was very odd, and which left me wholly on my own to finish my Ph.D. work, was when at the end of September, I went to the *Écoles Pratique* to find God. Professor Barthes was in large part the reason I got a French Government Grant to study in Paris. It was time to meet him. His frumpy raven-haired Secretary looked at me dolefully over maroon-framed glasses, coughed a little, and said, "I am sorry, Monsieur. Professor Barthes has gone to Morocco for a year to live with his boyfriend." She didn't blink. Fashionable Paris.

To say the least, I was stunned. I had no idea Barthes was what the French call a *pédé* — slang for a pederast. My natural disgust at the thought of my intellectual hero buggering a young boy was confusingly mixed with my admiration for his critical mind. For boy-love, he hanged me out to dry? Jeez. "Stranded In France" might be a good title for my thesis now. Dear God …

## RUNNING IN FRANCE

One of the pleasures of life in Paris was taking a *café au lait*, and a buttery croissant as it seems only the French can make them, at a bistro where I could buy a copy of *L'Équipe Athlétisme*, a newspaper devoted to the world of Track and Field. It was run by a congenial sportsman named Robert Parienté who, unknown to me then, I was to meet in the spring and serve as his newspaper's translator for Bill Toomey when he would be coming to Paris to receive the *Prix coq d'Or* — a prize given annually by this newspaper to the person considered "the best athlete in the world." Stay tuned for me and crazy Bill almost getting arrested in Paris.

Alone in Paris mid-September, I was stranded for a place to run, and someone to run with. That day I read a story in *L'Équipe* naming all the top French track athletes of 1969 and saw that a fellow named François Huard was the French champion for 400m hurdles, and he placed 5th in the prestigious

European Championships in Athens, on … September 18th — the very week before I read this notice. With a best of 51.1." Better than me. Perfect. And he runs for a Parisian club called "Le Racing Club de France." What's this? A French sports club, with an English name?

Next day I took the Metro to Le Racing on the outskirts of Paris. Formed in 1882, it's still there. And how! Walking through the Bois de Boulogne in a fine tall forest I saw green fields, tennis courts, swimming pools, a rugby pitch, buildings for fencing, judo, gymnastics, and much more. It was a sport-emporium of a kind seldom found in North America. I told the club secretary I was the Canadian 400m hurdles champ, in Paris for a year, and asked if she could give me a contact for the French champion, François Huard?

She looks me over. Hmm. Not a *voyou* (a thug). She picks up the phone, and calls François' home. Then hands it to me. Talk about friendly …

*"Allo, Willy! Enchantez. Venez chez nous pour dejeuner un peu"* — Hello Willy! Come to our home for a little lunch! So, I did, straight to 109 Avenue de Saint-Mandé.

His father was Le Racing's team doctor, his mother charming, his sister beautiful. What a wonderful, warm family. Until I left France in July of the following year, François and I met several times a week at the large indoor track at INS, the *Institut National du Sport* in the Bois de Vincennes, on the other side of Paris.

François was a tough, genial fellow. We trained well together, and in spring, raced each other three times. After our tough, bury-each-other workouts, in lieu of showering in freezing water in an unheated locker room, we took a French-douche — no shower at all. Sweat will dry. Put your clothes back on and go home. In our three races, I beat him every time, in 51.6" — the same time, every time. That bit of news was picked up immediately by *L'Équipe*, and even by *Leichtathletik*, a German athletics newspaper, and that evidence won me a place on Canada's 1970 Commonwealth Games team to Edinburgh, without having to go back to Canada for the selection Trials.

Zwei in Frankreich lebende Ausländer dominieren in ihren Spezialübungen. Der Afrikaner Namakoro Niaré aus Mali führt im Diskuswerfen und hofft auf seinen ersten 60-m-Wurf. Der Kanadier Bill Gairdner, der in Frankreich studiert, ist bereits 51,6 über 400 m Hürden gelaufen und hat den besten Franzosen des letzten Jahres, François Huard, geschlagen. Colmar (17. 5.) ... ... Stein 2,00 — Paris-

It says, "The Canadian Bill Gairdner, who is studying in France, has already run 51.6" for 400m hurdles, and has beaten Francois Huard, the best French hurdler of last year." Well, they don't say "beaten." They say *geschlagen*, which has the ring of "thumped" or slaughtered. I liked that word :)

That spring, Dr. Huard gave both me and François a small bottle of "Danabol" pills — what's this, Doc? — and told us to take one pill a day (5mg). It would help us train harder. He was a doctor. We didn't ask. It was available over-the-counter at any drug store and was used by old people, and still is, to build muscle and fight bone weakness. "What's the difference?" he said, "between taking this for energy, and taking a cup of coffee for a faster reaction-time?" I dunno, Sir. So, we both took it for about three weeks. I ran the same time with it, as without, but I thought I noticed a little more pep the last time I beat François. Or was that a placebo effect, or was I just pumped from the pride of *geschlaging* him again?

François's coach, the kindly, white-haired Mr. Maigrot, laughed when he saw the 51.6" once more on the scoreboard at our last race, and said, "*Vous êtes abonnées*" — "You have a subscription! You must prepare for Munich, 1972." That seemed very far off. But I did try, and the Trials for that Olympics was my last serious race in Canada, for a gratifying reason I will relate. But I'm glad I didn't make it to Munich.

Tragic Munich. Intended as *Die heiteren spiele* ("The Cheerful Games"), it became instead the games of a hooded and bloody Arab assassination of eleven

Israeli athletes who were grabbed by Black September, an affiliate of the terrorist Palestinian group Fatah. They demanded the release of 200 dangerous radicals such as Ulrike Meinhof from German prisons. The aftermath was a debacle that ended with all the hi-jacked athletes freed, a few of the terrorists killed, and, disgracefully, some freed. Then came a messed up international manhunt by Mossad, the brilliant Israeli secret service, that got suspended when they killed an innocent man by mistake. Drop the "brilliant." But I digress.

Years later, steroids, by then taken in massive, damaging doses by many athletes — but not by me, I was on the way out — along with lots of other "ergogenic aids," were banned. The athletic world had gone a little nuts. Some athletes were creating more red blood cells by sleeping nightly in hypoxic (low oxygen) tents. Or injecting themselves with APO — artificial red blood cells. I read that East Germany was the worst offender (where female athletes taking male hormones were hyper-muscular and growing beards). A coach was caught injecting air into the anus of one of his swimmers "for better hip flotation" (but he couldn't keep it in). Another coach got an athlete pregnant, and then procured an abortion for her on the belief her body would be "boosted by natural hormones" from pregnancy. As for steroids? The whole sporting world acted surprised as if their use was something new when Ben Johnson, the Canadian winner of the 100 metres in the 1988 Seoul Olympics tested positive and was sent home in shame, a speechless, token sacrifice for the shame of all.

Ben's Coach was Charlie Francis, whom I first met at the Don Mills Track Club when I was 22. He was 16, a self-important, sour, mouthy young kid who came to train under the famous Lloyd Percival. Coach sent him across the track to run with me. Charlie looked at me and said my workout would be "no problem" for him. But he ended up puking after three reps of my fifteen.

Five years later I was surprised to see him appear at Stanford as an undergrad on a track scholarship — is this kid following me? — where his experiments with ergogenic drugs saw him balloon in two years from a moderately fast lean fellow to a 190-pound, very fast sprinter. He ended up making it to round two of the 100 metres at the 1972 Munich Games, and after that became a famous/notorious track coach. At the 1984 Games in Los Angeles his athletes won 8 of Canada's 14 medals in Track and Field. In the end, Charlie was disgraced for using drugs to boost all his athletes, which he admitted publicly at Canada's Dubin Commission in 1988.

He was forever chippy and kept it all very quiet; but he was direct and honest, if asked directly. He also said, correctly, that the use of drugs was widespread in track — that all the runners in Ben's final were likely on drugs — as well as in other sports, such as cycling. That turned out to be true. Six other finalists in Ben's race were on drugs. And the career of Lance Armstrong

Against The Tide

proved Charlie's point when Lance confessed to Oprah Winfrey, red-faced on national TV, that *all* his races were chemistry races. But ... all his competitors were on drugs, too. So, he was still the best rider. Right? I suspect all the drugs Charlie used on himself may have caused his early death from cancer at 62 years of age. I was fortunate to have participated at the Tokyo Olympics in 1964, which I still consider "the last happy Olympics," because there were no drugs, no money, and no politics.

## ROLLING THE DICE

My book-hunting was soon finished at the amazing *Bibliothèque Nationale de France* in Paris, where no one except staff is allowed in the cloistered stacks, and where if a pen so much as approaches the vicinity of a book, you get a harsh rap on the shoulder from a sour attendant — Voltaire in a janitor's jacket. I attended a few lectures in old stone buildings given by some of the rising French intellectual stars of the day in classrooms filled with lots of *gitane* cigarette smoke, rain-dampened coats tossed helter-skelter over chairs, or just dropped in a heap on the floor, students jammed together in every corner, sitting on the floor, on window ledges, on each other, breaking every fire-code in the book, the latest intellectual guru holding forth in high pontifical style in a spotlight, up front. Parisian intellectual life is public theatre. New stars emerge as in a cultural firmament, shine awhile, then burn out after newspapers tire of their vicious debates with other stars. Paris is a foment of rich ideas as likely to take place in a bistro over wine and a tasty *biftek pommes frites*, as in a classroom.

Barthes, the primary reason I came to France, was gone. So going back to Canada early was an option. But Michele seemed to be doing better with the baby, and it just meant I was going to have to write my Ph.D. Thesis alone, without guidance or correction, which had to be good enough to be accepted without objection, because the likelihood of my spending more time at Stanford if there were problems, was close to nil.

So, rather than write a typical thesis assessing, balancing, or correcting known critical interpretations of the work of some famous author or movement, I would do something original. Not a study weighing other critical studies, debating themes, or interpretations, but an original critique. At the time, English critics tended to see a work of literature as an object, and proceeded analytically, accordingly. But some of the new, and I thought more daring, French critics were writing about a literary text as a subjective, existential act, rather than as an object, teasing out a single voice that united a series of works by an author, and attempting, through an act of critical identification, to reveal the hidden patterns of perception and consciousness of the author. This seemed a profoundly original approach.

The second part of my thesis would be an attempt to apply structuralist methodology to Virginia Woolf's novels, as Roland Barthes had done with the whole body of work by Racine. So, the first half would be a subjective analysis of modes of consciousness in Woolf's corpus, the second, an objective analysis of structures. This would have to make a mark, because given the time constraints: compete in the Commonwealth Games in Scotland in July; start a job as a professor somewhere (where? I had no job offers, yet) in September. I planned to send bound copies of Consciousness and Structure in the Novels of Virginia Woolf to my three Thesis supervisors at Stanford in late spring. Having seen nothing prior, no drafts, they would receive it as a bound book, rather than in loose pages. The medium was part of the message.

When I started my grad studies four years prior, a Stanford Ph.D. could pick from a range of job possibilities almost anywhere. But there was now a glut of Ph.D.s on the market, and jobs were much harder to find. As it happened, I received a telegram offering an Assistant Professorship at York University. The pay was $10,300 a year. A letter from Stanford's Ian Watt, author of the seminal book *The Rise of the Novel*, had sealed the deal. And how. He was a dour, intelligent man of experience who arrived at Stanford the year before I did. There was an immediate mystique surrounding him, as a man among boys. He had joined the British Army and was wounded in the Battle of Singapore in 1942, taken prisoner by the Japanese for three years, and forced to work on the building of the Burma Railway (called the "death railway" because 16,000 prisoners died building it), where we heard that he and his buddies sabotaged and blew up the famous bridge that became the subject of the 1957 Academy Award-winning movie, *The Bridge Over the River Kwai*. No ordinary professor. And the movie fibbed a bit. They blew up the line, but not the bridge.

When I went to see him about possibly being my Thesis Supervisor, he went off in a little disquisition for an audience of one, *sotto voce*, about how "someone needs do a Thesis on Sir Thomas Browne" — a seventeenth-century author famous for exposing false beliefs in a high and witty style, about whom I knew very little. In short, he was more interested in his own interests, than in mine. While I was tenuously voicing my concern over this, his sandaled feet were up on his desk. I was a little taken aback to see him reach forward, tear off a clean piece of his big toenail, and pop it into his mouth.

I left, thinking, you get hungry in prison camp.

Against The Tide

# EDINBURGH AND THE IX BRITISH COMMONWEALTH GAMES 1970

Leaving France entailed regret and relief. I liked beautiful France much more than I liked the French, who at the time were off-putting to foreigners. The Japanese didn't like foreigners either, and thought themselves superior, too. But they would bow graciously, just the same. The ordinary French had an irritatingly dismissive haughtiness you could see in any store or restaurant, where they tended to treat even their own staff like peons. If they like you, which takes time, you can hang with them. But I used to say they have two dominant emotions — vanity and revenge. A Frenchman is unhappy if his tie doesn't match his socks.

French revenge was sharply underlined in 1967 at Canada's Centennial celebration when General De Gaulle, the last of the great and gifted Statesmen of the 20th century threw gasoline on the embers of separatism in Québec. From a lofty perch on the balcony of Montreal City Hall he lifted high his haughty chin, and said, in slow stentorian tones: *"Vive le Québec libre! Vive le Canada français! Et vive la France!"* That disgraced him in the eyes of all except Quebec revolutionaries, whence Canada's Prime Minister Lester Pearson sent him packing back to France as an ungrateful sot, reminding him that "The people of Canada are free. Every province in Canada is free. Canadians do not need to be liberated. Indeed, many thousands of Canadians gave their lives in two world wars in the liberation of France, and other European countries." So true. Shame on de Gaulle.

But this began my thoughts on a topic of my first political book of 1990, *The Trouble With Canada* (the farthest thing from my mind at the time), I eventually titled "The Revenge of Montcalm." Quebec paid for De Gaulle's words by way of an immediate massive exodus of Anglo talent from Quebec, and the rest of Canada (ROC) continues to pay by way of excessive federal subsidies to the Province of Quebec (about 3/4 of the annual total of federal subsidies to all provinces) to buy ongoing electoral support. During the regular bouts of separatist indigestion suffered in that province, France would regularly send thousands of agents they called teachers, observers, counsellors, whatever, who swarmed about fomenting revolution.

Meanwhile, after sending off bound copies of my Ph.D. Thesis to Stanford, I left France behind, ferried my car to England, and drove straight north to Edinburgh to compete in the 400 metre hurdles at the British Commonwealth Games (so-called, before they dropped the word "British" altogether from the name). After that, I had to ship the car to New York where customs officials, realizing the car had been in Marseilles, tore it to pieces because they thought I was a cocaine agent from the movie, *The French Connection*.

Despite the horrible mix of wind and rain at 40°F (about 5°C) in July! — and a strong starting headwind for both the semifinal and the final of the 1,500 metre hurdles — I managed to finish 6th at these Games, and again found myself lamenting I wasn't taller and faster. And here is a photo of the finish. The fellow on my right is John Akii-Bua, of Uganda, who barely beat me to the finish line for 5th place, but two years later won gold at the Munich Olympics with a new world record.

In the six months before the Munich Olympics he wore a vest weighted with 25 pounds of lead and ran 1,500 metres over five hurdles set six inches higher than race-height. He did that four times a day. Every day. No one could believe it. He became a policeman after winning gold at Munich, but because he was so famous, he was considered a flight risk, and so was denied travel outside Uganda. He was a member of the Lango tribe, a people purged by Dictator Idi Amin, surely one of the ugliest and most evil men in human history; flashing machetes dismembering Langos. Homes aflame in the night. Akii-Bua died mysteriously of an "undisclosed cause" at age 47. That's code for the likelihood this sweetest of men was murdered.

*Against The Tide*

The second fellow I bumped into was Menzies (pronounced "Mingus") Campbell. He was a lanky, lonely Scottish sprinter who had come to Stanford Law school for a year in 1967 and ended up training with our little group. I was the informal coach and took everyone to the Stanford Golf course once a week to run what became infamously known as "The Hill," a steep grass slope of about 200 yards that was the occasion for a lot of lactic acid production, sufficient, at least, to supply us with the unseemly weekly sight of someone retching behind a tree halfway through the workout. Who would it be this week?

Mingus had never trained as hard as with us, ever, and had certainly never run hills like that. But spring of that year he set a new British record of 10.2" for the 100 metres on a dirt track at a meet in Sacramento. So, he owed me. We had a "Hill" connection. He was strolling around the Games Village, reporting for a big Edinburgh newspaper in a dark blue pinstripe lawyer's suit of which he was so proud I figured he probably slept in it. We spotted each other simultaneously, as he sidled over with a huge Scot's grin. "'Ow 'bout a word, Willy boy?" Gosh, it was good to see him. He later became a liberal-democrat Member of the British Parliament for 30 years, after which he was elevated to the oxygen-depleted status of "Baron Campbell of Pittenweem." Not a joke. Though it brings a smile to my face, still. After retirement from political life, he also was knighted by the Prince of Wales. Oh, had we known he was destined for ... Baronhood! Knighthood! ... how he would have suffered our jolly ridicule as we tore past his spittle-frothed face up that Hill at Stanford!

Despite his possible ruination by privilege, you can see that "the Hill" and all it meant to us, was in him still in what he wrote below for his newspaper. Though I do wonder why a distinguished Baron who knew me so well, would misspell my name "Gairdaer"? Perhaps subconsciously he was claiming me for Scotland? Which wouldn't be so far off. The Gairdner clan came from Ayr, about 85 miles from where we two were then standing. His article, for a big Edinburgh newspaper, was entitled "Sprinting For the Hell of It".

## A PROFESSOR'S LIFE: BEGINNING THE DREAM

When I set out to York University to assume my new life as Assistant Professor of English Literature, I was quite pumped, as they say. But I didn't know where York was. I had imagined myself at the university's Glendon campus in a bucolic setting among ivy-clad buildings in mid-Toronto but was directed instead to the Keele Street campus, then barely ten years old, poured with a gazillion tons of concrete onto a huge empty field outside Toronto. Oh dear.

The English Department was on the 7th floor of the Ross building, an enormous rectangular grey cement bunker in the middle of the field. I got my keys to S765 and walked into my professor's life. York was no Stanford. No steady brilliant blue skies, waving palm trees, rhododendrons, brilliant scholars, and Stanford Nobel Laureates wandering all over the place. But this tidy little office was my world now, and it felt good. My name on the door. Professorship includes a built-in respect from students. I liked that. The Department needed someone to teach a first-year course in Can Lit. Can Lit? What's that? I was immediately handed a large box of Canadian novels and poetry by authors of whom I had never heard (except Leonard Cohen), much less read. I would need a new prescription for eyeglasses by the time I got through them all. I was also asked to teach a third-year mixed English and European novel course, and got another box of Russian, French and British novels, most of which I had never studied, either. A lot of late-night reading ahead. But I loved it.

By spring 1972 I published my first academic article in the *Journal of Canadian Fiction* (a new journal, with famous scholars such as Northrop Frye on its Board) on two Canadian pioneer sisters, Catherine Trail and Susannah Moodie, each of whom had written very different books about settler-life in Canada. They were both somewhat sleepy books, but I wanted to turn a sow's ear into a silk purse by revealing things hidden in their thought and imagery, and it seems to have worked. After its publication, the Editor wrote to say that he wanted to publish my article a second time, in a Special Edition of the journal, adding, "it is the only article we have ever published twice ... because of its profound and cosmopolitan intellectual reappraisal of these two long-abused Canadian writers ... it sets a standard for the criticism of Canadian Literature." That was a good start for a young prof.

There were no university presses in Canada that I thought had even heard much of the criticism of consciousness or the structural methods of such as Roland Barthes. So, I sent out my Stanford Ph.D. Thesis on Virginia Woolf to The Johns Hopkins Press, which had expressed an interest in such studies. That was probably a definitive career move. If they bite and want to publish, professorship is going to work out for me, probably for life. If not, maybe it's going to be a steep road, a red alert.

Eight weeks later the Johns Hopkins Humanities Editor Margot Schutt wrote to say she "found it a very interesting and enlightening study of an author whose works I do know quite well. However ... for reasons that are as much practical as critical, we shall not be able to publish your work ... sorry for the discouraging word ... [and so on]." Silly, but I was offended by this rejection. It was and is, *such* an original work, and had I been there, I could have helped her see why she ought to publish it. Maybe I would have to make

Against The Tide

some adjustments to make it read more like a book, and less like a Ph.D. Thesis? Hmmm.

As for teaching? I have always considered teaching a noble cause. But the 1970s were full on marijuana years, so teaching a first-year class at York was immediately problematic. At Stanford I had worked as a Teaching Assistant, and that was a delight because the students were uniformly bright. You could aim your remarks at everyone. You risked sending any Stanford freshman into a sudden psychiatric tailspin if you gave a C for an essay, which I once did. "But Sir" (very close to tears, riven with confusion), "I have never gotten anything but A. *All through high school!*" I liked the kid. "This is not high school. You're at Stanford now. I will reread your essay if you want. But you have to understand, your grade could go down, as well as up." He was in pain. So, I took him in hand and spent a few hours showing him how to write better. He ended up with a B.

But at York? A third of the class was unmotivated and maybe high all day on weed, there mostly because of family pressure to go to university. In the middle, were ordinary kids willing to think and work, but likely forever ordinary. At the top, were a small number of the very bright and hard working. So, as a Prof, do you try to motivate the unmotivated, and risk boring the brighter? Or do you aim at the brighter and lose the ones at the bottom? Or aim at the middle, and lose both ends at the same time? I never figured that out. But by 4th year the poor students had dropped out, or flunked out, and the ones that made it into my 4th year Honours classes at York were as sharp and motivated as any at Stanford.

On arrival at York there were many shocks. I had been out of Canada for almost eight straight years, in balmy weather. But in mid-October 1970, with some colour still on the trees, there was a freak dump of a foot and a half of snow in one night and we didn't see a day above freezing until mid-January. Holy, where am I? No palm trees. Just a barren, treeless waste of buildings in howling cold wind. At 30, I was still competing nationally, but indoor track facilities in Toronto were non-existent. We had to drive south almost an hour in rush hour to the CNE grounds on the shore of Lake Ontario to train on a flat rubbery track above the (wait for it) "Sheep and Swine Building." It was either that, or back to striding through deep snow on a nearby golf course, minus my long-gone dog. I can't say why I was still running hard and competing at 30, except that I still loved it, felt it gave my life a rounding-out in the classical sense of mind/body/spirit/, and yes — there was still that superiority thing. Not wanting to be fat and stupid like so many others. I was a body snob. Rage against the dying of the light, and all that. Fight frailty, sickness, and yes, even death — that ominous, but, well, be honest Bill — death was just a far-off philosophical spectre. More prosaically, what I was doing was selfish. It simply felt good to push the limits of self and body in a personal agony and ecstasy, doing what felt like manly battle in a soft and sucky well off world.

January of 1971, I won the Ontario Indoor Championship for 400 metres, two laps of the Sheep and Swine track in a fast 50.1." It was gratifying to beat a handful of younger star quarter-milers who were very surprised to get beaten by an aging hurdler. Tony Powell, the best 400m man around, was a curly red-haired, raspy-voiced, tough dude with a glass eye from a childhood accident. On the home stretch, still in the pack, I broke away, making sure to drill past Tony on his blind side. He had to turn his whole head around to see me — shocked, but too late. There was going to be an international meet between Canada and Italy in Sardinia that September, and though long in the tooth now — and older is definitely tougher — I wanted to make that team.

Another, and much longer lasting shock came while walking through the Ross building one day when I saw a crowd of mophead students gathered around the resounding sonority of a Frenchman's voice, and my education in Canadian politics began. There, in a spotlight, head and hair swirling in his own cigarette smoke, waving tarred fingers, gesticulating in arresting words and images, was a chisel-faced, white-haired man named René Lévesque. Who is this?

Though worse than ignorant of politics I was mesmerized by his powerful oratory. A shock, I say again, because I thought I had finally left behind all the annoying anti-war, peacenik agitation at Stanford, and the stale communist harangues of Paris, and was settled now in Toronto the Good, in peaceful, bland, unremarkable Canada, for the contemplative writer's life I had imagined. But here was a fellow speaking seriously about breaking up Canada? My country? About the "right" of French-Canadian separatists to "sovereignty"? The unilateral "democratic right" of a province of Canada to declare itself a new *nation* in our midst? What? Then, on a 50% +1 vote, what would be the fate of the other half, the millions of Canadian citizens living in Quebec who wished to remain Canadian? I immediately saw blood spilled, an angry terrorist throwing a beer bottle at an RCMP officer defending Canadian lives and property, and for the first time in my life I began really thinking about my country, and about my ignorance. About what Canada was, is, and should be. I had never taken, I had never been offered, a class in Canadian history or politics, either in high school or university.

On that day, too, I learned about something called the *Front de libération de Québec*, or FLQ, a terrorist group which had been agitating since the early 60's for Quebec to become a separate nation, had caused over 160 violent incidents, mostly by way of exploding about 200 bombs, and had already claimed responsibility for the deaths of eight Canadians — they killed eight people? — including a bombing of the Montreal stock exchange in 1969 in which 27 people were badly injured, while I was in Paris thinking about Virginia Woolf? Like, out of touch. All this made the commotions at Paris and Stanford seem like patty cake.

These revelations didn't stop. I'm minding my own business in peaceful Canada the Good when, just a few days after Lévesque's riveting, unsettling speech, two members of the FLQ "liberation cell" drove to the home of British diplomat James Cross disguised as workers delivering him a birthday gift, pulled rapid-fire rifles out of the gift, and kidnapped him, demanding the release from jail of a handful of their hooligan brethren and the immediate publication of their FLQ *Manifesto*, which was read October 8th on Radio Canada (French CBC). It's a poorly-written screed in *joual* (local French dialect) announcing a proletarian-socialist revolt against big government, big business, and the *maudits anglais* (accursed English).[11]

A few days later, the FLQ kidnapped Deputy Premier of Québec Pierre Laporte from his home, where he was playing football with his nephew on the front lawn. Negotiations ensued. Tension mounted throughout Canada (and at York). And I was shaken to hear Québec's labour leader Michel Chartrand announce cheerily, on CBC radio, that popular support for the FLQ was now rising, and *"We are going to win, because there are more boys ready to shoot members of Parliament than there are policemen."*

Seriously, I was ready to join the army instead of teaching novels. When a CBC reporter asked Trudeau how far he was prepared to go to stop this, he answered, famously, "Just watch me." Then, as promised, on October 16th his Parliament invoked the War Measures Act enabling the entry of federal troops into Quebec, and the arrest without warrant in the dark of night of about 500 suspected revolutionaries, all but 62 of whom were eventually released. It was gutsy, and just about the only thing Pierre Trudeau did that I ever applauded, for I learned and eventually was to write about the fact that in quieter but far more permanent ways he was on a one-man mission to change Canada forever.

The day after the army went into Quebec, Pierre Laporte was "executed" by the liberation cell of the FLQ. Strangled to death. His crumpled body thrown into the trunk of a car and dumped in a dark forest outside Montreal. This long episode ended with James Cross being released by negotiation in December, federal troops withdrawn from Quebec, and five of the original FLQ kidnappers flown to communist Cuba to spend their days with PM Trudeau's buddy, Fidel Castro. It's true, they were socialist buddies.

I still didn't have a political bone in my body. But the seed was planted. Two decades later I published *The Trouble With Canada* (1990), which became an immediate National Bestseller (despite the hurdles I had to jump to get it published, which I will recount in Part IV). The book became #1 within a few months, and made me a lightning rod for the left for the rest of my life.

## MR. DAYCARE

Meanwhile, what turned out to be another irony took shape. Michele, reasonably content living in Canada, was studying fine arts at York, and ended up teaching some first-year art classes. But I was getting concerned our daughter was spending too many hours in what was then a make shift co-op daycare in one of York's residence towers. So, I went to check it out. You had to be there. There were a few infants swaddled in the corner, and about 15 very young children running around trying to grab any one of a mess of toys from each other (but never seemingly happy with the one they had in hand). Three radical feminist mothers were sitting cross-legged on the floor in another corner getting worked up over the latest gender oppressions, while the cries and yelps of distraught children they were supposed to be tending rose in the background.

This was ironic, as I say, because if anyone had told me then that in a future book, *The War Against the Family* (1993), I would be including a shocking chapter on the behavioural and health dangers to be found in daycare centers, I would have said it was some kind of fantasy. But just now, serving my time on co-op duty, I barely managed to persuade those mothers that the profusion of toy choices was driving the kids crazy. I thought they would be happier with one toy at a time. So, let's give them one at a time. They listened (like, who the hell does this guy think he is), then ignored me. But after I left they removed the mess of toys, and began doling them out one at a time. Quiet descended almost immediately upon the place, and the women were so thankful, they asked me to help them further. The ringleader, Elody Scholz, needed a faculty parent to help her finagle a larger space from the university. So, I became the *de facto* head ("President" was a taboo male term) of the York University Daycare Center, co-authoring a proposal asking for an expanded daycare center complete with a fenced-in playground. Two months later we had our new space. At least now I didn't have to trudge through blowing snow to see my daughter.

In the process I learned enough about the health and developmental dangers of excess daycare — defined as more than 20 hours per week — to earn the everlasting ire of what felt like every feminist on the planet when I published this info in *War*. At the time, they were arguing that equality must rule even Rosedale moms in mink coats on their way to a tennis lesson should have "free" (tax-funded) daycare — just because they are, well, mothers. *War* got banned by several big bookstores for this audacity, and for a few other "incendiary" chapters, an event that led to open warfare between my Publisher and the Canadian Independent Booksellers Association of Canada — over whether or not booksellers have a right to ban books — which I will flesh out in Part IV.

## THE CRASH OF THE NOVELIST

Very few people get to design their life. But if you could, who wouldn't? Ever since undergraduate school, and despite the circuitous route, the obstacles, and the serendipity that led to this first job, one of the attractions of the professorial life was the shining promise of having three or four unobstructed months every summer to write fiction. I didn't realize at the time I may have become a better novelist if I'd had to scrap my novel together half-starved in a filthy hovel or get it down on bits of paper in a war-torn trench. But clear as day I remember driving to my office that first summer to begin my new life as a great novelist. Quiet. Undisturbed. A beautiful runway for this flight. Let's go.

I wrote, and wrote, and wrote some more. By the end of that first summer, I had 300 pages of fiction, but had no idea yet where it was going. So, I stopped. It was leading me down unexpected pathways. When the academic year got underway again, I spiced things up by creating a new Fourth Year Honours course called Contemporary European Criticism. I was known as a tough grader, but that course was always over subscribed. I didn't know then it was going to be a threat to my life as a fiction writer, for I was getting far more interested in the hidden ideological structures to be teased out of a good novel, than in the story, or the people, or in what the writer thought and said their characters were doing, or saying, or affirming, as distinct from what I actually saw happening in those books. What was wrong here?

But, don't give up. I mean this is why you rearranged your whole life until now. To do exactly this, right? So, by the end of the second summer, I had almost 800 pages. And although I was rather pleased with some of the writing, scenes, incidents, and so on, I still had a formless baggy monster on my hands. An interview I had heard in France haunted me. The popular novelist Natalie Sarraute, famous for one of the then-modish *nouveau roman*, advised

Against The Tide

all beginning writers to finish their first novel, put it in a drawer, and forget about it. Get on with the next one. Ouch. She was right, at least in my case.

Meanwhile, one of my Honours students graduated, went to work for a big Canadian publisher, and called asking if I could send her some of my novel. I did, and she called back: if I could shorten it, they would be interested. Trouble is, by that time I had lost interest in my own characters. That's fatal, of course. Writers often speak of how well-formed characters "take on a life of their own." They will write their story for you, so to speak. But I remember the philosopher Sartre, a novelist and playwright himself, observing that either the characters have free will, and the author doesn't; or, the author has free will, and the characters don't. Which is it? How could it be both? The fatal tipoff was that I was much more interested in this philosophical question than in what my characters were saying or doing.

Two other students in my new Honours course were Robert Lecker and Jack David, both very bright, very motivated. Well now, teaching anything you love is its own reward. The teacher always learns the most because of the effort needed to clarify what is taught. And you never know how many lives your teaching may touch. But sometimes you do, and it's always a satisfying moment when a former student reaches out, sometimes decades later. After graduating from York, Robert and Jack created the now very distinguished publishing company, Essays In Canadian Writing (ECW Press) which is thriving today, 50 years later.

Robert was hired as an English Prof at McGill University soon after graduation. So, I wrote while composing this bit to see if he is still there, and asked how is he doing? And this came in: "You are the person who most influenced me in my life and career. It is because of you that I wanted to become a professor. You got me into literary theory and the joys and nuances of literature. When you taught our class, I said to myself that I wanted to be like you." Well, that made my day. After my first marriage broke up in 1977, he came into my life by surprise, one snowy winter evening.

## MEETING THE MAFIA IN SARDINIA

At 30 years old I was still in top running form. But now this was feeling a bit odd. I had made a deal with myself when it all started at 17 years of age with Lloyd Percival, when I had no idea what to do with my life except to perfect Mind, Body, and Spirit: God gave me a body to look after and to use as well as I could. So, I will stop running when I get beaten, fair and square, with no excuses or injuries, by a Canadian, in Canada. About now, I was getting close to thinking: somebody, please beat me! But I was rather like St. Augustine who, when indulging himself physically, asked God to make him pure, but … "not yet."

The 1971 Canadian Championships — and Selection Trials for an upcoming International Meet against Italy — were held on a new synthetic Tartan track in Winnipeg. Have we seen the last of the dirt tracks? What a difference it made. At 30 years of age, I was considered the old dog in this 400m hurdle race, without much chance to win against the young bucks. Walking onto the track for the final on a beautiful windless afternoon I heard a familiar voice on the PA system. Unmistakably, it was John Hudson, former Irish cross-country champ and one of Coach Percival's athletes, who five years after this meet became the head of CBC Sports and hired me to work as a part-time Colour-Commentator for the men's field events at the 1976 Montreal Olympics. All this was ahead, and some strange things happened there, which I will get to. But I guess he didn't know his mic was live, so everyone heard the sound of a question to John from someone: "Who's the old guy in lane four?" [me]. I could hear John's reply: "If he's here, he means business." (With those words I felt the bonding of old teammates).

The gun went off, and by the fifth hurdle, tearing down the backstretch, I felt terrific, with a comfortable lead, when suddenly a horrendous shout — "AGHH! AGHH!" rang in my ear from the local race favourite, George Smith, in the lane outside me, whom I was just then overtaking. And gone. Turned out a bumblebee had flown straight into his mouth and stung him on the tongue. So, coming into the home stretch I was alone and had to decide whether to push harder for a PB under 51.0" for the first time in my life, or just run safe so as not to hit a hurdle and miss the Team to Italy. I decided to run safe, but still set a personal best at 51.3"

About 85 Canadian athletes flew to Italy for this meet, on Canadian tax dollars. But no one knew. Your tax dollars at work! We went to Rome for three days of training prior to shipping out for separate men's and women's competitions, the men to Calgiari, Sardinia, the women somewhere else. As it happened, Prof had been teaching at the Stanford campus in Florence and came to Rome for a few days pleasure and to meet with me before catching a flight home to California. He took me to one of those dark little bistros on a narrow cobblestoned side street deep in Rome somewhere, dried fruit, tomatoes, figs, onions, hanging from centuries old sooty rafters, pizza smoke wafting, carafes of blood-red wine, and a flavourful *Bistecca alla Fiorentina*.

The next day we flew over the gorgeous blue Tyrrhenian Sea to the *Golfo degli Angeli* (the Bay of Angels) near Cagliari to compete against the best of Italy — *gli Azzurri* — or "the blues," as they were called — on a dirt track in

Against The Tide

a large soccer stadium before a rude crowd used to heckling and throwing popcorn bags and empty drink cups at the enemy.

When I got back home, Prof told me he was just about to catch the train from Rome to the airport, about to miss the train, Ica urging him to walk faster, when he spotted me on TV in a bar at the station. "Ica" (blood in his eyes). "I will miss the train. And the flight, too, if I *have* to. Here is William, about to race." She kept going, "see you on the train." The 400m hurdles was the first race of the meet. Prof told me a year later that the camera moved in for a close-up of the enemy (me). "And there was my William, head lowered in the blocks, gun up." Prof saw the whole race and my victory, then sprinted for the train with a smile all over his face and made the flight home.

The Canada vs. Italy Dual Meet began at dusk, and right away it was raucous. The crowd was mostly soccer fans used to harassing foreign enemies. When the Italian pole vaulter was on the runway getting ready to jump, they fell silent. But when our man Bruce Simpson was on the runway, they started whistling, heckling, and throwing popcorn boxes and empty cups at him. Bruce won anyway, with stoic pride.

Next up was the 400m hurdles. For Canada, it was me and George Smith — he of the bumblebee in the mouth at Winnipeg. The wind was strongly in our faces. The Italian hero and a high finisher in the preceding European championships was Giorgio Ballati, in the lane outside me. From the gun, we two led the race, leg for leg on each hurdle, pushing into that wind, and at 23" at the fifth hurdle, this was a very fast pace. Going into the bottom turn, still leg for leg, I began to pull ahead a little, which no one expected. But sweeping around the bottom turn, the wind, strangely, never became favourable, and so it felt surreal until I realized it was blowing into the huge opening at one end of the stadium and circling against us the whole way to the finish. It was *never* going to help. Suck it up. Bear down. Then, came a loud \*\*\*CRACK\*\*\* sound: the eighth hurdle smashing. Ballati disappeared. I'm all alone now, their number-two-man Giovanardi, chasing me. Here is a photo of me passing over that ninth hurdle alone.

As described in the press the next day, Giovanardi *ha tento invano di contrastare il finale di Gairdner* ("tried in vain to counter Gairdner's finish"). It was a sweet victory for me and for Canada, as I was one of only three Canadian men to win his event at that meet. Ballati disappeared without a word or a handshake. The next day a sore-loser Italian Press described how the *poco elegante Canadese* — the "not very elegant Canadian" — had beaten their elegant loser.

After this, my last international race for Canada I laid down on the sweet evening grass to recover, coveting my flimsy silver-plated trophy cup. Very relieved it was over. But that didn't last long. I was still recovering when an out-of-breath, worried-looking Canadian team official came rushing over, belly bobbing: "*Man down for the 4 x 400 relay!* We need you to run! In second spot."

What?

"*Soon.* Fifteen minutes. Get up."

"Me? I just got off the track!" A blank stare. But Canadian honour was at stake. There was no on else. He nodded at me as if to say, "We die for our country, right?"

I love a relay because from the first step there is an immediate out-of-body feeling that permeates one's whole being, a selfless feeling of devotion to others rarely found elsewhere in life. I love sport for that. You run for your teammates and your country, not for yourself. Pain? What pain? But 15 minutes? I would be up against Giacomo Puosi, a tough 46.5" 400m man on a dirt track, like this one. My best on dirt was 48.8" in Brazil. So, no contest. We all knew I was going to lose at least 20 yards to the guy. So, the pressure was on our first man to get me the baton well ahead. The gun went off and I was pumped, watching our first man neck and neck with the Italian on the backstretch, then, rounding the last corner, he got a little ahead to bring me the baton in first place by five yards. Now the pressure was on not to lose more

*Against The Tide*

ground. A nice pass and get the hell out of here. I was alone for about 30 yards when Giacomo, shown here, went by me like a rocket on the first turn.

But as he went by, I latched on, his Jetstream sucking me along the back-stretch. I was running out-of-body mentally, so to speak, and thought I was going to blow up, but I lost only ten yards, finishing in 47.5" to his 46.5." Tired, but happy with the best 400m of my life. Our next two men lost another ten yards each, so Italy won easily.

## OLYMPIC TRIALS, 1972 – MY LAST SERIOUS RACE

Okay. I said I would stop competing when I got beaten fair and square with no excuses or injuries, by a Canadian, in Canada. That seemed like a God-given duty because you shouldn't frivolously squander your talents. Stopping took a while. 1972 was a long, bitter winter, and part of what made life outside work exciting, was training and racing. I was still doing well in races and was certainly the only 31-year-old English Professor ever to run the 400m hurdles in Canada. No one at York University knew of this part of my life. It was a private passion I wouldn't have minded giving up. But not yet.

As it happened, I broke my deal with myself just a little because while training on the loose track at Varsity Stadium in spring, I stepped in a pocket of loose cinders and pulled a thigh muscle. It took weeks, but it healed sufficiently to enter the 400m hurdles at the 1972 Olympic Trials at Scarborough Stadium in August. It was a stinking hot and humid week, and just before my race came up there was a violent rainstorm, and a strong wind that held. No one was going to make Olympic Standard in that wind. Alas, although by convention the fastest runner — me, in this case — is always given the middle lane, for reasons I could not fathom they put me in lane eight.

So, the gun went off, and going like a bat out of hell down the backstretch I couldn't see any of the other competitors until the eighth hurdle, when I saw a leg swing up beside me. The race really began now as we both did all we could to get to the finish line first. But I lost by about a foot. On the infield, still bent to catch my breath, I glanced up at the tall fellow who beat me.

"Who the hell are you?" and extended the handshake of the vanquished.

He caught his breath, then smiled, a little self-consciously.

"You remember Saskatoon, 1966? The Canadian Championships, where you won both hurdle races? You stayed afterward to help a 16-year-old boy for two hours. That was me. John Konihowski." And he extended his hand. A flood of gratitude and pride washed over me. This young boy, now a 22-year-old man of 6'3 and 190 pounds — and this evening the new Canadian Champion — rose to beat his teacher. I loved it. Another reason why teaching is a noble calling. What a great way to go out. John went on to become a star receiver for the Edmonton Elks and then Winnipeg Blue Bombers football teams two years later.

Something else, unknown to me at the time, marked this meet. On the same track, in a race just before mine, was a beautiful, talented, 17-year-old girl from Vancouver named Jean Sparling, whom I was to meet three years later and who would change my life profoundly.

## THE CEMENT SARCOPHAGUS

One day, spring of 1973, the end of my third academic year, as I turned into the York University Campus the sight of that monstrous cement bunker called the Ross Building caused a pall to descend upon me.

Three years had been very good. No regrets. I loved teaching. It's a noble calling. But next year would be much of the same. And the year after that. Until I was an old man. Trudeau's burgeoning socialism was taking an unexpectedly large chunk from my monthly paycheck, and I knew some very old

Against The Tide

professors who were still paying off their first mortgages. Not what I had planned. Student papers had begun to resemble each other, and I was already tired of them.

I still had no interest in political ideas, but after the FLQ crisis, my antennae were sprouting. Quite a few of the Professors at York were among the many American draft dodgers who fled to Canada — estimates are from 30,000 to 100,000 — all a radical leftist or revolutionary tilt, all quite happy to have a leftward-bound Canadian government controlling more and more of citizen life. I just shut up. But I figured that morally, you can't run from your country when it calls for help after taking everything it has given you your entire life — the argument of Socrates before he drank the hemlock. Unless it is doing something evil, which arguably was not the case. You may not want to kill in war, which I understood. But conscientious objection is the option, not abandonment of brethren. You can do troop laundry, wash dishes, make boots, whatever. Quiet and uncomfortable with them, was my position. I agreed with President Nixon:

> *"I can think of no greater insult to the memories of those who have fought and died, to the memories of those who have served, [than] to say to them that we are now going to provide amnesty for those who deserted the country ...."*

I was getting uncomfortable passing refusenik colleagues in the hallway.

On this day, as I drove toward the sarcophagus, a panic was erupting on the top floor. Word had leaked that student enrollments for the next academic year had suddenly dropped — more than 9%! York's income was based on the BIU, or "basic income unit": every enrolled student was an income unit accounting for a lot of hard cash from government. So, the panic fire spilled down every stairway and by the end of day had spread to the ground floor and every department of the university. Faculty accounted for 80% of all York's expenditures, so unthinkable thoughts were circulating: *some* faculty would have to go. But who, how, and when?

Immediately, I made an appointment to see Dick Ewen, Chairman of the English Department, a calm, portly, sweet man of learning, but not one to rock a boat. A couple of Professors had once told me they thought I might stand for Chairman someday. I asked them how it worked? They explained that a Committee of Profs votes on actions to be taken, and the Chairman executes. I said, no thanks. You'd be better off with a puppet. I already disliked the aversion to merit, and the virtue-signaling phony egalitarianism of the Professoriate. The Prof had warned me.

So, to Chairman Dick, thumbs circling each other on his lap, I said, "Sir, we have all heard that due to this financial crisis, the University may be faced with letting faculty go. Is that true?"

"Possibly."

"So, if that happens, how will it be done? Because if it's based on merit, I would be happy to stay, and take my chances."

Dick looked down at his thumbs, for a long time. Then he managed a wan look, and said, barely audibly, "Well. All I can say is it will not be based on merit. All Professors at York are considered equally meritorious. So, it will be *last to come, first to go.*"

"Well Sir … we both know the equal merit story is not true. And *I* was the last Professor hired by the English Department, in the last year you hired anybody." This drew a look of mild, tenured pity, as if I'd just told him I had a terminal disease.

"Yes. You were."

I left his office with barely disguised disgust over the equal merit comment. It was a knife in the heart, a manifestly weak-kneed, false notion, simply because no two human beings are ever equal in themselves, or in their achievements, and because merit should always be the cornerstone of excellence unless you are describing the denizens of a jail or a holding-tank for weaklings. He had confirmed I was employed by a weakling institution, and the weakling Chairman was proud of it. No Ian Watt types here, defying their captors, blowing up enemy bridges in the jungles of the Far East. I felt like spitting. But for me, the writing was on the wall, and I was not about to wait for the guillotine. Politics is personal, and it had just entered my life for the first time.

Against The Tide

## A TURN OF THE WHEEL

For the years I was away at Stanford and then in France trying to get smart, Dad and my old coach Lloyd Percival had become close friends. I was the initial reason for this connection. Lloyd told *Executive Magazine*, in August of 1971: "Coaches often dream of finding an athlete with a wealthy father who makes their dream project come true. Well, in my case, it actually happened."

Dad was still a heavy drinker at the time, but for more than friendship — he cared — Lloyd designed a personal fitness program for him to use every day in a small space Lloyd was leasing at The Inn on the Park Hotel in North York, one of the renowned Four Seasons chain of hotels. He called it The Fitness Institute (FI), because he'd always had a serious interest in getting people fit, and so this new operation was to have a medical and scientific basis for health and exercise. Soon, everyone was amazed that Dad stopped drinking, cold-turkey, and became the fittest 50-year-old ever. One of the gentlemen who served as a Director on the Four Seasons Board and also the FI Board, was Murray Koffler, the dynamo druggist-businessman who created the national chain eventually called Shoppers Drug Mart. I had no idea that way down this road he was going to all but knock my office door down and storm very briefly into my life a very angry man, for reasons I will relate.

The consequence of their friendship was that dad got so evangelical about the fitness that was changing his life, he persuaded Lloyd to plan a much more ambitious, world-class version of The Fitness Institute — the world's first-ever scientifically serious fitness operation. Dad would handle the building, and the business end of it. Lloyd would handle the PR and fitness technicalities. Here they are, Dad on the left, signing the deal for this ambitious project.

It was a 50,000-square-foot fitness club to be built at 255 Yorkland Boulevard, in North York, with 40,000 square feet of office space for lease on the second floor. It opened in Spring of 1969 with all the latest trimmings: a large gym with indoor track, tennis and squash courts, a gorgeous large swimming pool, serious fitness-testing facilities based on the scientific protocols of the famous Swede Per Olof Åstrand — the "founding father" of modern exercise physiology, a cardiac-rehab program, and more. Here is a photo of Coach Percival standing in front of Dad's brand-new building.

All previous fitness operations were small, low-cost-high-volume, retail operations like Vic Tanny's. They sold thousands of memberships every year — more than they could ever accommodate if all members actually used the facility — and hoped members would not come back. The FI was different. You had to follow Lloyd's "fitness program" designed personally for you. This was so novel that *Time* magazine came up from New York, February 9,1970 and did a short story on it.

Everyone was proud. Except Big Jim. When Dad showed him around the building for the first and only time, he was very quiet. Then he turned and said, "You're a little nuts," and never came back. Not what you call a supportive father. Maybe it *was* a little nuts. But one night a few years later, Dad told me he had heard from the grapevine that my job at York was in jeopardy. And so, he said quietly, was The Fitness Institute. He had sold our family home in Thornhill, purchased for $25,000 in 1952, less than two decades later he sold it for $750,000 and bought a 350-acre farm in rural Caledon. Now 55, he

Against The Tide

didn't want to be coping with business problems at the FI. He wanted to be a gentleman farmer, bring in the hay, and raise Black Angus beef cattle. There were "lots of problems" with the FI, he said. Mostly — it was losing gobs of money. "What about coming to work for the family. You're an Olympic athlete with a Ph.D. Pretty good credentials." But they weren't, really. I didn't know how to read a simple balance sheet.

I went to bed with a swimming head. Did I really just agree I would do it for five years, and see how things went? Privately, I was naïve and cocky enough to think that running a business just couldn't be *that* difficult. Not as difficult as getting a Ph.D., right? I would solve all his business problems and turn things around, in five years or less. And move on to what I *really* wanted to do — write books.

But events proved otherwise.

## HEALTH
## On the Frontiers of Fitness

The urge to exercise, as Educator Robert Hutchins once observed, is most easily overcome by lying down until the impulse passes. A better answer would be to enroll at Lloyd Percival's Fitness Institute in Toronto, where one of 4,200 forms of physical exertion might be prescribed. Sprawling over 4½ acres of Northeast Toronto, the $3,000,000 health emporium boasts the most complete set of fitness-testing equipment gathered anywhere under a single roof. In fact, to drop in merely for a quick workout would be rather like checking into the Mayo Clinic with a cold.

The institute's 32,000 sq.-ft. laboratory can give Percival's clients the kind of physical going over usually reserved for returning astronauts. Beside the usual tests, technicians check the glucose, hemoglobin and cholesterol in a subject's blood. There is a treadmill on which athletes are run into a state of complete exhaustion while staff members measure blood pressure, respiratory rate, oxygen intake and heart beat. There are gadgets to analyze lung capacity, muscle contraction and the speed of reactions as well as a dolorimeter to sort out the difference between an athlete's complaints that he is being pushed too hard and genuine pain. Says Percival: "If a man has a low pain threshold, the odds are he won't make a professional athlet-

*Cross-country skiing changed my life …*

# PART 3

## A TIME OF TURMOIL

## THROW YOUR KID IN THE WATER.
## AFTER FIVE MINUTES, IF HE'S FLOATING, HE CAN SWIM.

Dad threw me in the water with pride and the best of intentions. I continued teaching my course in European criticism and publishing occasional academic papers for a few more years because I couldn't just drop the richness of intellectual life, cold turkey. It made the practical world of business tolerable. After managing my own life for so long I was a little shocked to find that the list of daily problems always seemed to get longer than the day before. In business, it's easy to drown in problems created by others. I was struck, and a bit cowed by a saying from then Minister of Justice John Turner: "If you're always taking work home at night, the job's too big for you." I was prideful enough to think nothing was too big for me. So, I had to learn to organize and prioritize quickly. "File 13" became a necessity — a drawer where I put the most non-pressing issues and found that weeks later, many of them had taken care of themselves.

And there were feelings. Key staff, whispering: "There's nothing like starting at the top." The optics were bad because Lloyd's adopted daughter Jan Percival was the Manager of the women's division and thought she had a right to be running the whole show. She felt usurped, which I understood. But it was a Gairdner family financial crisis now, no longer a Percival fitness adventure.

The biggest mistake I made out of the gate, was my faith in Dad and his informal management team of himself, Lloyd, a crusty retired engineer named Aubrey Montgomery, and Ted Simpson, a gentle, elderly long-term accountant for the family whose negative advice on most suggestions could usually be counted as a positive vote. In my first week Dad told me they were one day away from signing a lease for a new 50,000-square foot club to be built in Mississauga by FI member Leo Goldhar. What did I think? He spread out the plans. It looked amazing. With even a little business experience, however, I would have said STOP! STOP! Give me a chance to examine the lease, the location, the market, launch plans, and so on. Instead, I said, "I don't know enough to advise you, one way or the other. I can only assume you and your colleagues have done the necessary homework." He was sure they had. I was proud of my dad and figured it must be true. So, the next day he signed the lease that almost sank the family and put a millstone around my neck for 15 years.

Meanwhile, my heart had already begun to sink. Memberships were almost sold out, but the business was losing big money. The combination of taxes, overstaffing, labour-intensive methods for fitness testing, programming, and counselling, wasted space allocations, lack of budgets and projections, and no sales strategy or staff (Dad didn't want "fitness hucksters"), was lethal. All we had was the considerable promotional value of Lloyd's fame (or press-worthy notoriety) — and a club full of members, half of whom thought nothing of cancelling a membership to go play golf in summer, then cheerfully rejoining in the fall, leaving the FI to find bridge-financing every summer just to stay open. Yikes.

After Dad signed that lease I drove to the Mississauga site only to find a muddy, neglected apple orchard in the middle of a low to medium-income housing area right on the noisy Queen Elizabeth Highway. As a trickle of rain ran down my neck, I'm thinking this is a heart-sinking, dismal location, Then I drove around the entire area, which did nothing to suggest we would find members for miles around at the fees we needed. This club should be built in a wealthier area such as Etobicoke, or Oakville. What have I done? I might have been better to take my chances at York. My learning curve steepened as the new club, planned to open in fall of 1974, rose from the ground. Lloyd would be our entire Sales and Marketing program. He could make a few calls and a half-dozen media mavens would be on location, cameras, and mic in hand. It would be big news: the FI praised in *Time* Magazine was now expanding with a brand-new club in Mississauga!

Meanwhile, for the prior year or so, Lloyd had wholly withdrawn from the daily operation of The Fitness Institute to run a publishing arm called FI Productions from an office on the second floor. He had gathered a dozen employees to do research into fitness and sports articles that he and others under his oversight would write and publish in a homey newspaper he created called *The Sport and Fitness Instructor*. It was a busy little hive of earnest activity — papers and books all over the place — where the questions any naïve businessman might ask, such as, "Where do you make your money?" or, "What are the monthly expenses?" got happy shrugs from would-be writers and researchers and a gushing talk about the next exciting Percival project. There was always another, just around the corner.

Part of the deal that was supposed to help finance FI Productions had been made with Murray Koffler and his string of Drug Stores. Each monthly edition of *The Sport and Fitness Instructor* would be distributed in bulk to each Shoppers Drug Mart manager. I was a little skeptical. So, I drove around to three of Murray's Drug Stores. At the first I saw copies of the newspaper blowing around the parking lot, trampled underfoot. At the next I asked the Manager where the newspaper was. What newspaper? He had no idea. I persisted. Upon searching, he located a two-week-old bundle still bound in a back storage room. I had to share this with Dad.

By now I had a swirl of betrayer emotions about Lloyd. If we passed in a hallway, "the little man," as we athletes affectionately used to call him, could barely look me in the eye. It hurt. He had been my surrogate father. He was most of the reason I made it to the Olympic Games. He was the reason I won that Public Speaking contest at Appleby, speaking on — yes, on *his* brand of fitness! What an irony. My goodness. And here I was, slipping around him, quietly questioning his publishing adventures. Concomitant with this, were the various "consulting" arrangements with mysterious or entirely absent financial implications for the FI, that Lloyd was busy arranging with such as the Detroit Red Wings hockey team — implications that smelled to me like FI money was probably being spent, or at least costs to the FI charged, without oversight or budgeting, to satisfy his hunger for fame. Gordie Howe was a big Percival fan, as was the whole Red Wings Team, which Lloyd had famously beat into the best shape ever. He often travelled to Detroit with a few of our fitness staff, but I didn't have the nerve to question him or what he was doing there. I was too new to further rock the boat.

Quite astonishing, was the fact that one night late in 1972 Lloyd went to a bar in Detroit for drinks, heard a band called Special Delivery, and fell for Connie Graham, their beautiful, torchy, 25-year-old lead singer, she of the raven locks and wickedly attractive eyes. He was 60, but he went back there a lot. It was a kind of love, or perhaps more likely the powerful infatuations of a frustrated old man, vain conjuring's of imagined romance and the bliss of youth. Before long, Lloyd began working his charismatic coaching on this unknown band in search of fame. He promised them promotional help, and lured them to Toronto, where I saw Connie sing once, and understood. You had to see her. Listening wasn't enough. She had a powerful sweet voice that rang with rock and back-country-blues sadness from a sultry body. I figured Lloyd was a goner, and this was going to mean trouble.

True to style, he got so motivated by another elusive dream of possible fame that by spring of 1973 — just when I was brought on board — he had created a whole new kind of fitness regime set to music called *Rhythmics*. He talked the band into writing original music for exercising at home, then had them perform at places like Sherway Mall in Toronto to walk-by crowds, where he hawked his fitness-to-music exercises recorded on tape. Then he renamed the band Olympus. This was another Percival revolution before its

Against The Tide

time that preceded the coming Jane-Fonda-style aerobics craze. People could get fit at home while having fun exercising to hot music. Imagine! He was no Jane Fonda, but he now had his band, somewhat to their embarrassment, outfitted in faux-Greek Olympic tunics and headpieces meant to broadcast the classical pursuit of the balanced life to passersby scratching their heads.

## THE BUY-OUT

Meanwhile, I had been very busy rationalizing and streamlining the entire operation, cutting costs, trimming staff. Making myself unpopular. I had never fired or let anyone go before, and the thought almost made me sick. The first fellow was 63-year old Ken Hibbert. When I informed him, frozen in his chair, he wept, right there, in front of me. (Dear God, let me go back to teaching). Then he slouched mournfully out of my office, holding his forehead. I felt terrible for days and couldn't get that image out of my head. Then he called back to say he thought we should have a Night Manager, and he could do it for half of what he had been costing us. He was right, so I hired him back, and felt like Jesus. Phew. I also got an unsolicited inside reputation as a feminist of sorts because I noticed on pay slips that two or three young women in our employ were being paid less than the guys for precisely the same work. Why? Because they accepted that amount, was the answer. I didn't think it was right, so I raised their pay immediately.

This was ironic, because a few years later Ontario Premier David Peterson issued his "Green Paper" on so-called "Pay Equity", which was not about equal pay for equal work (what I had done). It was a socialistic scheme to give women equal pay for "work of equal value." His bureaucratic toadies were already creeping around our operation with complex charts ticking boxes to indicate that the cook in our cubby-hole restaurant was doing work of "equal value" (they could never answer the question: value to whom?) to the work of our maintenance man, who was paid way more than her. In their view, cooking great hamburgers was equal in value to getting called out of bed at three in the morning to fix a gas-leak on a rooftop heating unit with pipe wrenches in a high wind at –25° Celsius. It was the dangerous camel's nose of egalitarian statism under the tent of a free society. So, I called Premier Peterson, and in Part IV I will tell of my conversation with him and of his slippery, evasive defense of his "Green Paper". But the hardest trimming was still to come.

I made an appointment to see Dad when he came in from the farm and told him I was certain FI Productions was costing us a lot, that the newspaper was blowing around malls or just tossed away, that notwithstanding some very good practical pieces, it was largely a promotional venture for Lloyd himself. And anyway, I couldn't see why it took a dozen people to turn out a small monthly newspaper. And to make matters worse — Lloyd has gone a little crazy over a hot young girl and her struggling band. So, I think you should buy him out. We are still losing gobs of money. So, his shares are worth nothing. You will have to pay him personally for his contribution — for the Good Will — and lure him to leave.

Lloyd agreed immediately, because he had no options. So, Dad wrote him a significant personal cheque, Lloyd surrendered his shares, and agreed to operate FI Productions personally. He never looked me in the eye again after that meeting, and I felt like Machiavelli.


## A PARRICIDE

On the afternoon of July 23, 1974, I was planning how to hire Lloyd to publicize the fall opening of our new club in Mississauga. He was the media star, all we had, and all we had thought necessary. But everything changed suddenly in a shocking way, and I reacted as if someone had suddenly poured sulphuric acid over my head. Doug MacLennan strode into my office with dread in his eyes, shut the door abruptly, leaned over my desk, and announced unemotionally (because he felt too deeply what he was about to say): "Lloyd just dropped dead in Montreal."

My mouth was stopped with incredulity; a sudden hot sweat broke all over my chest, soaking through my shirt. Doug repeated what he said. Lloyd was at lunch with some sports promoters and collapsed, dead. It was never clear whether he choked to death or was felled by a sudden heart attack.

But a wave of guilt washed over me as suddenly as the sweat. It was I who had become suspicious of his activities. I, who had to choose between loyalty to my father, or to him, my second father — a double jeopardy. I did feel intensely disloyal as I engineered the buy-out, because it surely plagued him with anxiety. Anxiety can cause a heart attack. Oh dear ...

Then came a second wave as doom-like as the first: it was all on *my* shoulders now. Only mine. This business, this building, all these employees, the family loans, the upcoming Mississauga operation, and Lloyd Percival, our famous media-magnet, suddenly gone. Gone! Combined with the guilt-feeling of a parricide was a kind of irrational anger that he had just orphaned me, and I wasn't ready for that. How *could* he ...?

Compounding this dread — even though I felt selfish thinking such thoughts the day he died — was the piercing realization that at the very moment his

Against The Tide

new conception of personal physical flourishing was gaining ground in the public mind, the nation's "fitness" guru had dropped dead prematurely — at sixty-one. What? This was a negative for the business. Obviously, fitness is no guarantee of protection against heart disease, or anything else, would be the public conclusion. So, why join a fitness club? Especially, one built on Percival's ideas? Why work so hard to get fit when it doesn't help?

I didn't attend Lloyd's funeral. I just couldn't, out of respect for his daughter Jan and his wife Dorothy. Jan had already left our employ, indignant, furious, at me and the Gairdner family whom she felt had stolen her family's right.

It's a national disgrace that this remarkable, talented, charismatic, kind, and quixotic man, plagued with dreams of personal success far beyond his capacity to manage them, and responsible for the stellar careers of so many fine athletes in so many different sports, was so unappreciated by Canada in his lifetime, and now lies buried in Toronto's Mt. Pleasant Cemetery.

Strangely, in spring of 2020, almost 50 years after these events, I was called by a CBC radio Producer in Edmonton who was preparing a one-hour episode on "Ace" Lloyd Percival, to be aired on its nationally respected *Ideas* show, in which I agreed to participate.

## THE GRAND OPENING ... WHERE NOBODY CAME

In panic conditions we did our best to publicize the coming Grand Opening of our Mississauga Club. Willowdale was now at capacity, with 1,900 members, but was still hemorrhaging money. At that point I was still not fully aware of the lease implications for this new club. When I asked a bright accountant to examine the lease, which contained a COLA (cost of living adjustment) clause, he showed that in 20 years the rent could be over a million dollars a year. But worst of all, at a time when "fitness" was still of uncertain value in the public mind, the sudden premature death of Canada's "Fitness Guru" amplified public skepticism about the value of exercise in general. Some members could be overheard mockingly suggesting maybe it was better to take it easy and enjoy life to the full like their long-lived fat friends — no exercise, and lots of fine scotch and cigars. Some argued we all have a finite number of heartbeats. Why use them up faster, with exercise? At any rate, Lloyd's unexpected death made fitness a very hard sell.

Opening day was early October 1974. The club was fully staffed, ready to handle a flood of excited and motivated new members. At Willowdale, our "Early-Bird" members were ready to kick the doors open every morning by 6:30 a.m., so I arrived at our spanking new Mississauga club for Opening Day at 8 a.m. all set for the excitement and pride of showing people around our beautiful new facility.

But nobody came. By day's end at 8 p.m., 12 tire-kickers had wandered in to take a look around. But none of them bought a membership. I went home in a turmoil. Worse, home was in a turmoil. After a few good years, Michele had grown even more temperamental, and unpredictably angry, without apparent triggers. This was emptying our marriage of any reasonable motive to continue. So, I sat in the garden with her at our lovely home in Unionville one sunny April day in 1974, and told her things were going to have to change or our marriage would not survive. I confessed that it takes two to tango. But that doesn't mean both share the blame equally. One day in our kitchen she all but ripped the telephone from the wall and threw a souvenir nice plate across the room, jugular veins popping from her neck, enraged at me for something I couldn't remember. But I did remember a terrible night in Cassis when she had behaved exactly this way in a horrific shouting match with her dad. So, I shouted back, in an effort to stop her:

"Why are you angry at *me*? *I'm not your goddamn Father!*"

It was like watching air come out of a balloon. The veins in her neck suddenly relaxed, her look turned pitiable, vulnerable, and she sank onto a chair as if her legs had given out.

"Oh my God," she whispered. "*What you just said …*"

I have oft suspected that some traumatic chain of childhood events between her and her Father were responsible for so many of her erratic leaps from a mood of enjoyable pleasantry to a senseless outrage she could somehow broadcast, thereby making everyone in the room feel responsible for her anger. She and her dad had tempers that set fire to each other.

So, I said, "If we want this marriage to survive, you have to get a grip on the underlying problem. Get a therapist. Find out. And I told her, after she threw her shoe at a fellow on TV one night, for being "a male chauvinist pig": "You know what? I think you need to stop your rants and get into being a full-time Mother. Get in or get out. Christine should have a sibling." So, she found a therapist, and we made a beautiful sister, Emilie, who was born January 14, 1975. The baby got more beautiful. But Michele — all that wasted potential — got more temperamentally difficult.

She found two children tougher than one, and her therapist seemed to have persuaded her that the road to better psychological health was a more defiantly authentic individualism. Be your most genuine self. You have trouble getting along with others? Thrive as your *true* self! For a guy who was used to managing his life very well, it was plainer than ever I was sitting on a slow-burning powder keg at home, and at the business. Both were in a state of

*Against The Tide*

imminent collapse. Worse, I felt in recent years I had been retreating slowly inward, maiming my own self in an effort to keep the peace, going quiet in fear of domestic discord. It was simply easier to retreat, to self-corrode, than to resist. But it was not me.

## FAKE NEWS AT THE MONTREAL OLYMPIC GAMES, 1976

In midsummer of 1975, I got a call from John Hudson, the fellow who had been Lloyd's Assistant Coach at our Don Mills Track Club when I was 17. John was now head of CBC Sports, responsible for broadcasting the 1976 Olympic Games to all of Canada. Would I like to be a "Colour Commentator" for the men's field events? "Colour" meant adding human and sporting interest to whatever was being broadcast. The other Commentator would be Jenny Wingerson, another of our Don Mills Track Club athletes, who would add Colour for Women's events. Then we had the venerable CFL Announcers Don Wittman, and Tom McKee, the latter a jaded, cynical, but very funny man, who delighted in responding to microphone tests just before going live on air by speaking in falsely interrupted sentences as if his mic was failing, which caused immediate panic throughout "the Mothercorp," as he called it. He also got a chuckle every time he described the CBC Logo as "the exploding anus" (though he used a more basic terminology). He was so simultaneously sad and jovial, a lot of CBC personnel on the loose after work ended up in his room, which quickly turned into a boisterous casino.

We worked high in the stands in a special media box in the midst of 68,000 cheering fans in that beautiful, scandal-plagued stadium. Initially budgeted at $250 million, it was left unfinished by the French Architectural snob Roger Taillibert, already at $1.4 billion, and financed with so much borrowing it would take the scandal-plagued Mayor of Montreal Jean Drapeau, more than 30 years to pay it off.

A large colour TV sat in front of us on which events were being shown to the nation either live as they happened, or as captured on tape to be shown later. Beside this was a smaller black and white screen showing concurrent events that were being taped all day long such as swimming or judo, which the nation might get to see later in the day or in the evening. Some shadowy broadcasting eminence higher up had to choose whatever upcoming events they considered hot at the moment to show Canadians live.

Typically, Don or Tom would announce an upcoming event for the live national feed, and either Jenny or I were expected to tell the nation all the intriguing, sweet and sour emotive stuff about the athlete(s) millions of fans were now watching live on their home screen.

Here I am with Jenny and Tom in the box, ready to roll, as they say.

"Well Ladies and Gentlemen, here we are, at the start of the Men's Long Jump, with Suleyman Gongong, on the runway. He's a humble shoemaker from Indonesia, with 17 siblings. Amazingly, he overcame polio as a child to train himself for these games in the alleyway behind his shop, where he dug a pit for jumping. He's never had a coach. And he's on the runway … right now!"

That sort of thing.

It was plain exhilarating to comment on an event like Greg Joy's surprise silver medal in the high jump, an entire nation silent in suspended expectation as he ran up to the bar. On his last of three tries, Greg cinched the silver medal, and as I shouted for, well, for Joy, the stadium shook for ten minutes.

Then came a mini trauma — my first experience with *really* Fake News. The men's 200 metre race was ready to start on the far side of the track. With so much crowd noise it was hard to hear what was coming through my earphones. But the men's javelin event was about to start, too, and I knew that a husky Hungarian named Miklos Nemeth, though little known outside Europe, had a chance for a big upset win. He might even break both the Olympic and World Records! But the CBC was at that moment broadcasting a nothing swimming heat. So, we were going to miss the javelin. Really? I got anxious.

Against The Tide

"Tom! Tom! The men's javelin is about to start. We *have* to grab this guy on camera. *Live*. He could win. I think he's going to break the Olympic record! He's that good. What the hell are we doing, showing the swimming heats for nobodies?" Tom grabbed his mic to talk to central command.

"Guys. Guys! Hey! Wake up! Billy says this dude from — where did you say he's from? — Okay. A sausage-eater from Hungary. Hey … get your camera out of the goddam bathtub. Nobody gives a shit about swimming heats. Billy says your gonna miss this; goddamn it. You're gonna … Oh jeez …"

Nemeth was on the runway, ready to throw. He ran. He threw. You could feel it. His javelin just took off, maybe got lifted by a small breeze, I don't know, but it was soaring like a beautiful still-winged hawk the whole length of the stadium, more than an entire football field — it landed over 310 feet away to set a new Olympic — and World — Record! And … we missed it. Aargh! We felt pretty stupid missing the only sensational World Record of the day.

Tom irrupted in a fluid arc of verbal conniption, his special brew of salacious language, epithets, and curses so colourful our whole broadcasting team bent over with laughter, until … until … on my right earphone I heard a garbled command from central:

"*We got the throw.*" And, Tom, grabbing my shoulder, says: "They're coming to *us now, Billy. Quick. The black and white monitor.* You have to do this *as if it is happening now! Got it?* NOW!" Tom has to shout over the pounding crowd noise, because the gun is up for the 200 metre race on the far side of the track. It's chaos all around us. "So [he cups his hands over my ear] *don't give away that it's already happened. Got it? You can't say the goddamn truth!*"

*Can't say the truth?* Holy, anxious. Tom and I are staring at the black and white monitor. The techie from Central is yakking in one earphone. Tom is yakking in the other. I can hardly hear. I put my hand over one ear to hear Central.

Central: "Billy, the sausage guy is walking to the back of the runway. *He's fiddling with the friggin' spear.*" Tom hears this in his own earphone and can barely hold back a laugh.

But ... Yikes! There's nothing on the black and white screen!

So I start to panic. Twenty-five million people will be listening to me freak out?

Tom looks at me, then shouts at Central: "You're gonna have to talk Billy through it. He'll do voice-over, on the black and white monitor, but *with no picture.*"

There I was, the men's 200m getting into the blocks on the other side of the track. This Central guy doing his jokey blind description for me, live, for millions of people all watching something *I couldn't see*, waiting for me to start describing what they were watching.

Central: "He's still fiddling with the spear, Billy." So, I just jumped in and faked it.

Me: "*Ladies and Gentlemen, get ready for what may be a once in a life-time event. This is Miklos Nemeth from Hungary on the approach for the men's javelin.* [the approach was empty]. *This fellow is not well known, but he's a real comer, and I think he could win — maybe even set a massive new record — maybe even on his very first throw!*" [which we knew he'd already done. Oh, the lie!]

Central: "He's starting to jog."

Me: "*Nemeth is looking very determined now, almost grim ... moving very fast ... he's into his five-step cross-over pattern now. Watch him lay back, ...* [I could only guess that's what he must be doing now].

Central: "He's leaning back kind of screwy looking now."

Me: "*There's the five-step lay-back ... the throw is away. And how! Just look — at- that!* [I couldn't see anything]. *It's floating higher, higher still, maybe caught by a breeze!*" And it's ... It's ... Wow! ... It's." [I'm waiting for Central to tell me if it's landed yet].

Against The Tide

Central: "It's coming down, Billy."

At the very moment that throw was high in the air, the crowd was beginning to go crazy over the men's 200m race sweeping around the far corner into the home stretch. So I had to SHOUT, just as Central said *"It's stuck. It's in the goddamn ground, Billy."*

Me: *"Unbelievable! Nemeth has just broken the Olympic and world record, with a throw over 310 feet! Longer than a whole football field! (I still couldn't see anyone on my screen. Nothing.) His competitors are just staring at it, mouths open, astonished. The crowd is astonished, too!"*

And just as that javelin landed, and I was shouting "It's a world record!" the men's 200m runners were in fact crossing the finish line, and the crowd was roaring like crazy, a roar that flowed into my microphone and was broadcast to millions of Canadians as a roar for a World Record javelin throw. But it wasn't. It was for the 200m race. The whole thing was fake.

Meanwhile, Lowell had come to Montreal to spend a little time with me and see the Games. Michele came, too, and we three stayed in my hotel room. It was a delight to see Lowell. Despite the growing fractiousness of married life, there had been some peaceful interludes and I had hopes for a great time in Montreal now. But it was not to be. We went to dinner, finished late, and I was anxious for sleep because we were to be On Air at 8 the next morning. But Michele couldn't shake the conviction she had come to Montreal for special attention. Back in our room late, she suddenly demanded some barhopping, and launched into a petulant, demanding, deeply embarrassing scene in front of me and Lowell, whose appearance alternated between flushed embarrassment and a painful paleness, with lots of wincing eyeblinks (a Lowell trademark). After more of her loud protestations I took her by the arm — it was now almost 1 a.m. — and marched her around two full blocks of downtown Montreal in the dark, at an angry pace. We happened upon a half-dozen bars, all firmly closed for the night. Are you happy now? That was not the first time she embarrassed me so deeply in front of a dear friend, again broadcasting an indiscriminate anger, as if Lowell, too, had done something wrong. She crossed the line, and I didn't like the me that emerged. Clearly, her penchant for eruptive anger was getting worse, and in reaction, I was changing for the worse, which had me confused, and a little bitter, as if I had lost control of my own self. To quell a justified anger was to be false to myself; to express it was to feel manipulated, a pawn. I was trapped and couldn't see my way out. This is my life, for 40 or 50 more years?

# THE HUG THAT CHANGED TWO LIVES

In late Summer of 1975, Jean Sparling — the girl from Vancouver who raced the hurdles just before me at the 1972 Olympic Trials, and subsequently won four gold medals at the Canada Games — came to Toronto to study and train. She was a bright, beautiful young woman, and a top athlete in just about any sport she tried. But she didn't have a coach, so her boyfriend called to ask if I would I coach her? The reply was, "No." I am just too busy with family and business. But if she wants to tag along and run with our little group, she is welcome. At the time I still liked to train and compete, mostly because physical exertion and the peace that follows it served as somato-psychic medicine: the body improving the mind, rather than the other way around. In my new, stressful business and home life I needed the endorphin-hit for emotional and mental equilibrium. But in truth, it was the one thing I alone controlled.

I was now casually coaching a small diverse track group. There was Hamlin Grange, our one black athlete, whom I had already coached to a Junior Canadian Gold Medal in the 400m hurdles the summer before, then found him a full scholarship to the University of Colorado. And Dave Elbaum, a wandering Jew and funny guy who wanted to make it to the Maccabiah Games in Israel. He had no chance. But I told him if he could run as fast as he talked, he would make it for sure. Now we had a female runner, so would have to watch our language, and filter our jokes. Almost 50 years later I am still close friends with Hamlin, and cycle with him a lot. He was the first of a half-dozen, usually fatherless young black men I coached and for whom I worked hard to obtain full track scholarships at American universities.

But the most amusing headline in the lost and fatherless black kid who made good category, has to be Nyjah James. I met him when coaching three of my own kids in track: "Dad — you have to help this kid." Nyjah was an amiable, fun-loving, incredibly gifted jumper who was also completely irresponsible, but in no way outright immoral. He just had a different, "sometimes misunderstood" moral code, as he liked to think. A mixture of payback and revenge on the system. I liked him. He was flunking out of Grade 12 with four subjects incomplete. So, I called his English teacher after he failed to show up for a meeting about a term paper he failed to submit. "What did you do?" I inquired. She replies, "I didn't react. It's up to Nyjah to meet his commitments," and so on. High School teacher was lecturing this Stanford Ph.D.

So I told her, carefully, she was way off base. This kid has lacked authority all his life. When you told him it was up to him, well, he had figured that out already. But he also figured if it was up to him, you just didn't care, or you would have chewed him out like no tomorrow. These kids sense that when

*Against The Tide*

you're angry with them, it matters, and if you're not, it doesn't. Next time he tries that, you show him how gawdawful angry you are, and see what happens. So now … he's not passing this course? What does he need to do?

"He skipped half my classes and has to write a B paper to pass. On the aboriginal situation."

I tell her, "No one has ever taught him how to write a good paper. If I teach him, will you accept a tutored paper?" She agreed.

For two days, Nyjah sat by my side, and I showed him how to write a paper, do the reading, main argument, objections, answers to objections, footnotes, and so on. Sentence by sentence. I coached him, but he reasoned out the arguments I taught him to see which were the best words and sentence options, and so on. And he handed in the paper.

A week later I call the teacher to ask how he did? "It was the best student paper I have ever had on the subject. I gave him an A."

"Don't give him an A," I said. "Give him a B+, because by skipping so many classes he failed to honour you." So that's how that incident ended.

Next, Nyjah was working at a pet store as part of another course, and he decided he liked a small goldfish. So, he stuck it in a plastic bag with water and put it in his knapsack. But he got caught at the cash register. Not a good thief. And he got fired. Turns out Nyjah kept goldfish as a hobby, and when one of them got too big for his home tank he gave it to the store owner as a gift. "So Mr. G," he pleaded, "I gave the guy a huge fish. He owed me. I just took a small one in return." So after scolding him: "Don't you ever let me catch you doing that crap again. All you had to do was *ask* for the damn fish," I called the owner to explain that in Nyjah's world, moral standards were very touchy-feely. No fatherly guidance, and all that, and he felt he was owed a fish. He understands now. Please hire him back. So he did.

Then I coached Nyjah through four more subjects which he passed with flying colours; attended his High School graduation; and then spent about a 100 hours phoning lots of American schools to get him a full scholarship. Then, I took him to the Toronto Airport for a flight to enroll in a Kansas Junior College, where, against the rules, he almost burned the residence down by cooking on a hotplate in his room. But he graduated two years later and left the school with a Conference record in the Triple Jump. It's a great story. Then Nyjah joined the army, where he says he always carried our paper for that teacher ("our" paper) around in his knapsack. And he got the job of Chief Editor of the Army Base newspaper. Now he's out of the Army, which is paying for him to continue university studies.

But back to Jean. For two years we all ran together, competed, and joked around a lot. But she was a little unhappy with her performances, and maybe with a few other things in her life, and I wasn't a very good coach. But I did what I could to prepare her for the World University Games for the summer of 1977. For the entire two years prior we had a purely arms-length, coach-athlete relationship, no more, and no social contact outside track. I saw her at her best, and her worst. And I got to know her sweet and gutsy spirit.

The Trials for the World Student Games in Bulgaria were to be held end of July in Edmonton. I knew I would be very busy doing CBC Colour Commentary there as prep for the World Track and Field Championships in Dusseldorf, Germany, mid-August. I would try to catch her race anyway. But I missed it. The meet ended. Oh dear. Maybe I should go looking for her? That would be right, if just to salvage some semblance of reputation as the coach who (oops) missed her race.

But the stadium was empty. I hustled to the dusty parking lot where the last team bus was idling. The last athlete, blonde hair loose in the breeze, was about to climb aboard. It was her. I waved and, oh my, not a very happy wave back. We walked toward each other, no joy in her face. A few feet away she said, "I missed the team by one hundredth of a second." And tears of disappointment sprang into her eyes.

I had never seen her cry, and it pained me immediately, my heart in my throat. And I felt guilty I had let her down, too. But the words just came out: "C'mon, give me a hug." It was a reflex offer of comfort I didn't have time to think about. But when she came briefly into my arms I got ambushed by unexpected warmth and peacefulness. It was a simple gesture, after all, without presumption or expectation, but it took fire of itself in a pristine beauty and softness that sparked a grounding return to myself I had not sensed for so very long, and feared was lost forever. This was not something I intended; it was something that happened to me, and I surrendered.

Here is Jean back then, in a happier moment. What's not to hug?

It took a while to realize I was feeling the sudden, profound release of a badly constrained heart, and I knew that no matter what might come of this moment, this now, this feeling, it was the beginning of a reset of my whole being. I was going to have to free myself, from myself as I then was, and so — from my married life.

To this day she says when she got on the bus, she felt uplifted. Forgot altogether about making the Team. That hug changed her life, too. We went to dinner, and I saw that this 22-year-old woman whom I had known for two years only as a runner, and hardly knew in any other respect, was as beautiful inside as out, with a depth of maturity and intelligence far beyond her years. Two weeks later I went to Dusseldorf, and she made the relay team to Sofia, Bulgaria, for the World University Games.

Against The Tide

When I got back, regardless of what might have come of me and Jean, I felt a deep, intense desire to leave home with just the clothes on my back, and my books. I rented a small, caretaker's cottage on a 300-acre property just south of Newmarket. This is it, Bill. At 37, *you're starting over.*

I wasn't exactly an automaton at that point. But despite a lingering guilt about breaking vows, I felt justified. And also, a little as if something larger and as yet inexplicable was taking hold of me. I didn't know exactly what would come in time of that hug, but if nothing else it was a soul-moving moment that served a vital purpose. It helped pry me out of a bad situation. I had a faltering business I couldn't seem to fix, with financial disaster looming; a failed marriage; but two lovely daughters, Christine and Emilie, eight and two and a half, whom I would now see on regular weekly visits, and for alternate weekends. It was a pathetic show at 37 years old. An Olympic athlete with a Ph.D. from Stanford, no money, no savings, no home. I could hear Lloyd's voice: "Cheer up kid. No place to go, but up."

When I was eight, living on Rural Route 3 south of Newmarket (now Mulock Road) we used to walk home the mile and a half from Alexander Muir Public School in the dark of late winter afternoons, turning on our snow-drifted impassible road to play our way home, tunnelling and sliding, for hours. But we always felt safe in the pitch dark because half a mile away, on the north side, we could always see the beckoning bright bulb shining at our back door.

On the first evening of what I was already calling my "new life" alone, in the dead silence of that empty cottage, free, but forlorn in chilly darkness, still unsure exactly where I was because so much of the area had changed, I decided to go for a five-mile run in softly falling snow. A mile or so along I was ambushed by involuntary memory, as Proust called that powerful feeling that all of us have when a moving past event reappears exactly as it was and makes the past very present. In the distance, on the north side of the road, a small bright light was shining warmly from the back door of our old home? Could it be? Yes! And those 30 years simply vanished, slipped down a black hole; and were replaced by that old childhood sense of profound safety. For a moment in time, I was a child again, running alone in the dark in an adult body. I knew where I was now. You're gonna be okay.

## SHARK SKIN SHOES

A year later, my divorce under way, Jean and I were "an item," as they say. She had met my two girls and took to them warmly whenever they came to visit, and they to her. Meanwhile, I was still trying to figure out how to make The Fitness Institute successful, but there just didn't seem to be a sufficient market for our product at the prices we needed in suburbia — Willowdale and Mississauga — where our two clubs were located. Those clubs should have been right downtown where the population density and money are. I felt doomed by the imponderable weight of the challenge, my neck in a millstone I had chosen until I died. In some despair, I told Dad and Jamie I was

Against The Tide

ready to throw in the towel, because it was simply an impossible business. But just saying this made me feel like I was abandoning ship, leaving the family to sink. Let's pull the men together and sort this out. Could I go back to my former life as a professor? Not much chance of that.

Dad, Jamie (who was then the owner of the very successful Johnston & Daniel real estate firm), and I, had a crisis meeting, and Dad brought in Uncle Jock, his younger brother, who had joined Big Jim to form Gairdner & Son, Investment Dealers, but was now retired. I took the floor and explained I had tried my best. But we were still in big trouble, still struggling to pay off loans. We needed other answers. And we soon got them.

Jock, who was very sharp with his pencil and had made his calculations, proposed we create a plan to sell 20 year debentures instead of charging initiation fees. A debenture is a loan, so it doesn't count as income on a financial statement. Jock imagined that this clever Bay Street idea — which came with Ted Scott and Bill Clarke, two of his former investment sharpies, whom he proposed I should now hire — would be attractive to hundreds, perhaps a 1000 new members, who would be repaid their "loan" in 20 years. The company would gain a million dollars, tax-free.

Silver-haired Uncle Jock, deep in his soft chair, legs crossed, shark-skin black leather shoes bobbing a little in the air before him, was soft-spoken but decisive, his warm, light green, passionless eyes preying, circling every problem like a, well, like a shark. It was quite a spectacle for this young professor to watch him command the immediate labours of several big lawyers at Toronto's big Fraser & Beatty law firm, who snapped to attention whenever he called. Oh Boy, this was going to be exciting!

But the debenture idea was a big flop. Ted sat in his office most days, pencil fiddling with exotic numbers, smiling awkwardly like a grad student in physics hoping to come up with the big formula that would explain the universe. Bill Clarke came in every morning, read the financial news, then walked around musing on what could be done to improve this damn business, but forever striking out (I don't think so, Bill. We tried that).

In a year, less than 20 people bought a debenture. So, I called another family meeting and told the men of the family the Bay street plan, to be kind, was a failure, and had cost us a lot of money. What I didn't say in exactly these words was that watching those two big shots from Bay Street dither about gave me renewed confidence in myself. I was now certain I *would* eventually find a solution; one that would make the company successful and (I didn't share this) enable me to create the meaning in my life I badly craved. I was ready to give business one last shot.

# A LIBRARY ANGEL

I was not used to failing, and time was passing. So, to save my sanity I continued teaching part-time at Atkinson College, a division of York University offering courses for mature students, and made long head-trips into the world of ideas, pouring all I had learned and thought into a manuscript for a book I thought might be worth publishing someday. If all else failed, there would at least be something of my thoughts left in the world of ideas.

Then, on a cold and dark winter night came a knock on my door. It was a library angel in the form of my former student, Robert Lecker, of whom I spoke earlier, by now a co-founder of ECW Press, shivering in the windy darkness on my front porch. He had heard I was writing a book and showed up, contract in hand, offering to publish it, sight unseen. The book I eventually gave him, *The Critical Wager: Essays in Criticism and the Architecture of Ideology* was a long way from my first dream of writing novels, but I had got thoroughly hi-jacked by the lure of complex ideas. Honoured, Robert. Honoured. He left. The winter wind howled.

I got to work on that book, which took a while. It was published in spring of 1982. The motive for it was a statement by Roland Barthes, my illustrious queer professor *in absentia* from Paris/Morocco, who wrote: "it is virtually impossible to deal with literary creation without postulating the existence of a relation between the work, and something besides the work." All the intellectual effort I made then, and since, has been devoted to figuring out and articulating what that "something" is with respect to the world of ideas.

Generally speaking, it's always an "ideology," which I loosely defined as "an autonomous system of interdependent ideas" — either consciously chosen and deployed, or pre-conscious — which shapes as a kind of filter the outcome and conclusion of *all* one's thinking and actions. However articulate or inarticulate, all intellectuals, artists, writers, and yes, all politicians and social theorists — see the world through their own particular ideology, and the astute critic learns how to decipher those thoughts and actions accordingly. This meant the great mass of humans — the man in the street, too — live unconscious, or (a term I prefer) pre-conscious — lives. Great critical thinking converts preconscious to conscious. I was fascinated with the thought that I could learn to be a perceptive analyst of complex, mostly unexamined underlying realities and relations of truth and fact hidden from others — an act of revelation. Good critical analysis is like a scalpel revealing the hidden soul of great literature, of art, of any chain of ideas, and, as I was to discover, of political philosophy — what the American Founder James Madison called

Against The Tide

"the greatest of all reflections on human nature" — because it has to do with who we are, and how we shall live together ... or not.

## DIVORCE, MARRIAGE, AND INSTANT FAMILY

I have always felt badly the cookie crumbled the way it did, because a broken marriage unavoidably breaks the lives of the children, no matter how sweetly (an adverb rarely found in any divorce) it may have been done. Despite our almost 15-year age difference, Jean and I fell passionately in love and dated for months before she went back to British Columbia to try what was present on her pulse in the context of her own family life, trying out the painful prospect of leaving that beautiful, bountiful place for good — commanding mountain peaks looming, over briney salt-sea — where she had grown up. What would it mean to leave BC and her family, to make a life with an older man and his two children? Her Great Uncle, Bert Hoffmeister, one of Canada's finest Generals in WWII, who had led Canadian troops onto the boot of Italy, took her to lunch and warned her: "You can't build happiness on a foundation of unhappiness."

He was correct to warn her; and I did not want another mistake. So, I went to Stanford to visit Prof, who took me to the Faculty Club for lunch and gave me a stern lecture on how I must not "mess up" again. I was one of his favourite sons, so those words hurt, for I had previously failed his expectation of good judgement. But while there, I couldn't sleep for love of Jeanie. Knowing her, even as little as I did, almost had me believing in angels. My favourite truth about her then, and now, is that she is as beautiful inside, as out. A year later I took her back to Stanford just to see the place I loved so much. I wanted her to meet Prof, and after about five minutes, he fell in love with her, too. So, I had permission.

Leaning over the back fence at the farm where I lived one moonlit night, hearing the cows beyond the fence munching as they drifted over dewy grass, she popped the question: How did I feel about having more kids? Oh, jeez. Kids? I hadn't even asked her to marry yet. Marriage terrified me. Under inspection, in the cold moonlight. "I would be okay," I answered (hypothetically, but with trepidation), and took the risk of saying "*as long as you look after them.*" I didn't want another faux-feminist wife on my hands. What was she going to say, at what she just might think was this male-chauvinist condition? She was astonished: "Of course. Of course. Who else?" But she was already ahead of me (as she so often is) and understood my panic. "You're terrified."

We got engaged without a ring on the roof of her parent's boat under a starlit West Coast sky when, after observing again that I was terrified, of making another mistake — to which I freely admitted — she almost broke my arm asking me to say I wanted to marry her. Which I did. And so, I said it. And because her dad had run out of wine, we toasted the occasion with her parents over a glass of milk. We married in Vancouver on September 15, 1979, at her parent's home by the ocean overlooking Howe Sound, by an Anglican Minister — because I wasn't catholic — who later became the voice of gay rights for his capitulating church. Huge redwoods towered over us in late afternoon sun. When Jeanie came down that spiral staircase in the same gorgeous soft Chantilly-lace wedding dress her mother had worn, eyes melting my world from under her lacey, wide-brimmed cream-white hat, to the garden where I stood, I was sure now she was an angel, glowing in a warm light.

The tide was out. So later that evening we got lowered on a small flower-garlanded bench-seat to her dad's boat for a short ride over a moonlit ocean to Horseshoe Bay marina, from whence, by taxi to a Vancouver hotel, and next morning a flight to England and France for two weeks of cycling. Once on the deck we looked up at all the guests silhouetted on tiered decks by bright lights and heard Jamie's loud voice:

"Willy! You forgot the champagne!" He was certainly three sheets to the wind when he decided to throw a heavy bottle of Dom Perignon down to me, tumbling, spinning, glinting green glass catching the porch lights in the dark. Oh dear … This is going to kill me, or my bride. Or shatter on the deck. But in the luckiest reflex of my life, I managed to catch that spinning bottle. The guests roared with delight. I wiped sweat from my brow. When we got back from our honeymoon I called Jamie to say, "What about that catch?" His immediate reply was: "The catch? What about the throw?" To the same question, Jeanie's dad said: "The catch? What about my boat!" It was a good laugh.

## OUR FIRST $75

Our marriage got a financial blessing of sorts when after our first year together the business made a profit of $75. It was a kind of fiduciary salute to our marriage, because two months earlier our accountant had soberly counseled me to take shelter in bankruptcy. But I kept saying we had worked so hard and made so many positive changes; just give me a few more weeks, you'll see. But it was like turning a ship with a toothpick. I still felt shackled by Dad's mill-stone and was becoming desperate. I had painted myself into a corner in terms of the meaning of my life. Even if the business became sound, made good money? Well, supporting one's family is number one, of course; and having

*Against The Tide*

decent money is a lot better than not. But no amount of money can define the deepest meaning of a life. Will I just live and die without a mark made on my world? The French, when I was living in Paris expressed this daily meaninglessness with the expression: *Metro, Boulot, Dodo*; which translated roughly means "Commute, Work, Sleep." OMG. If you can't arrive at a satisfying deep meaning, what's the point? By now I was taking refuge in reading books and filing away articles on all sorts of important political, social, economic, and moral issues of the day; intuitively connecting them, jumping from them to the larger ideological and moral questions I wanted to write about some day. I had a growing worry my country was asleep. A hunger was developing to synthesize, to write about big ideas. But, like Augustine swearing to correct his sins — not yet.

At the time this hunger was developing I was ever more dissatisfied with seeing my kids by appointment only. Then, one day, after dropping them back home I saw a beautiful 1852 colonial home for sale at 124 Main St. Unionville, around the corner from my first house, and the thought suddenly popped up: If Jeanie and I bought that home, the kids could just walk a block and see us, right? There would be no need for more appointments. They could stay with us awhile, or go back to Michele, as we all found convenient. Maybe that could work? It was logically and emotionally persuasive. Maybe it would actually ease tensions? Maybe Michele would be easier to get along with? As for Jean, who had taken to the girls as if her own, I was anxious not to upset her. Moving a stone's throw from my ex-wife might be a crazy idea, after all. But, I pitched her. And after a moment's reflection, she said, "I'm shocked I'm not shocked." Which shocked me.

Jean was just 25 and two months pregnant when we bought that 1852 home in the summer of 1980. It had been lovingly restored to its original condition by Toronto antiquities collector Peter Krohn. Walking in was like a trip into pioneer Canada; high wainscotting, rippling glass windows, authentic painted pine floors, two large fireplaces, some hand-stenciled wallpaper. We moved in expecting an easier arrangement. No more appointments to pick up the girls. The prospects for amicable détente seemed at least possible. The day we moved Christine announced to her stony-eyed mother, "Daddy and Jean bought a house. Right around the corner!" Then shrank when she saw the electric daggers in her mother's eyes.

Thunder booming. Lightning crashing. Flocks of startled starlings erupting from treetops. A gossip-tsunami soon washed over town: (*Her ex-husband moved in next door. With a beautiful younger woman. Can you Imagine?*).

The kids were very happy with this cross-visiting arrangement. But Michele had a fit of emotionally advantageous outrage. She had always wanted to live in Toronto. But not me. All that concrete was, still is, a kind of death. But it was soon apparent her non-stop emotional fury was providing what she felt was justified moral cover for leaving her children and moving away. But time was of the essence. She had to sustain her outrage and act quickly before everything got normalized. The danger lay in waiting too long, for then it would look like she was abandoning her children, rather than being driven out by an outrage she thought anyone would say was justified. For what reasonable woman could, should, abide an ex-husband dumping her, then moving in right next door with a beautiful younger wife? Better get moving. She was dating a psychologist at the time, whom I am certain took it on the chin, for the very next day, he called to discuss "the situation." She can't bear it. Who could? You understand, Bill. So, what is to be done? You can't expect her to put up with it."

I offered to get the house she was in appraised by three real estate agents, would show her the appraisals, and we would agree on the middle value. I would write her a check for half, which I figured would be about $60,000. But she demanded $100,000, regardless of value. Her boyfriend agreed to $90,000. I had no money left after purchasing 124, so I arranged a bridging-loan at our bank for that amount. Michele left town in less than a month, Jeanie suddenly had "two ready-mades" on her doorstep, and we had two sizeable mortgages.

There were feelings of deep gratitude as we worked together to clean up that empty house, scrubbing floors, windows, and bathroom, hoping to sell it privately to avoid agency commissions. Those times were full, full of joy, and work. We had agreed on having more kids. Soon. Especially, I said, "A man should be able to say, 'my son.'" By the end of our third year of marriage young Jeanie, ever generous, ever loving, had our children Ruthann, Billy, and Franklin in bottles and diapers to look after, along with her two step-kids.

As anyone might imagine, there were some rocks in the overflowing river of our life. And I was one of them. There were minor frictions, some misunderstandings, or rather, mis-appreciations. I didn't seem to appreciate how very tough it was for her to handle our growing, blended family, and when she just wanted some empathy, I seemed too indifferent to her efforts. I was grappling with the business and came home tired. She was working 24-7, and at times I thought, was going under. Wanting so badly for it all to work out, I was afraid to admit how tough it was for her.

One day, a bit of chill in our feelings, she wanted to know why? Why was I behaving as if there was nothing to it? And then it struck me, and so, worried that even to admit such a thing might give her the idea of it, I blurted, "I'm terrified that if it gets too tough, you'll send the girls back to their mother." To prevent that possibility, I had been stupidly sending the message it can't

Against The Tide

be *that* tough; lots of women do this sort of thing. Mine was a self-protective stupidity.

"Never," she said. "I have never for a moment considered sending them back. That's why you're so head-in-the-sand? It *is* really hard. But I love those girls. You don't have to worry. I'm committed to this marriage. And to you. And to *all* our children?" She was almost insulted by what I said, but she saw me ambushed by my own damp and panicked eyes upon admitting it.

Honestly, the moment she said those words, the tension drained from me, and an immediate, profound happiness filled my heart. For that, I have been ever grateful in the bonds of love. Thus began some of the fullest, busiest, most wonderful times of our life together. Our new home had three doors at ground level, one or more of them always banging, open or shut, the kids and their friends running in and out, laughing, chasing each other, all the pleasures and trials of a full family life, now combined with lots of work and good times pulling the company forward, inch by inch, until it began making a decent return. Crowded staff Christmas parties at our home in candlelight, holly, and red ribbons, redolent with laughter, singing, drinking, and good food in a pioneering home and mood. Five children asleep upstairs. Jeanie, beaming and fulfilled. I was a happy man, all but restored from the near-catastrophic condition of what "my old life" of five years earlier when running alone and penniless in the snow and wind toward that lonely light bulb.

But the meaning of life itself? Why did this question still bother me? I don't know. It doesn't seem to bother many other people. I was no longer a snob about the business culture. But the more secure we became, the more I felt a yearning to address the larger questions of human existence, whether political, moral, economic, or philosophical, especially under Prime Minister Pierre Trudeau, whom I was later to characterize as our first true "libertarian socialist." I mean, here was a man, so his biographer wrote, quite fine with stripping and swimming naked at a mixed party (very "libertarian"); but also, eager to enchain Canadians in his version of a unique Charter-controlled, French-style social-welfare state. He had said publicly that Chairman Mao was his hero. Really? Canada was already succumbing to his big government statism like that frog in the pan of water who never jumps out because it's heated so gradually, he doesn't notice, and so is eventually boiled to death. Canadians are getting slowly boiled, was my suspicion. Someone has to tell them to jump. I wanted to tell them — when I figured out how.

Jean had given me a Christmas gift of a book by the American author George Gilder, entitled *Wealth and Poverty*. One night I went down to our library at 4 a.m. to give a bottle to our youngest son Franklin who was sleeping there, began reading it, and got immediately hooked. When Jeanie came down and asked how I was enjoying the book? I said, "It's wonderful. Someone has to write a book like this about Canada!" I didn't know until a decade later that the "someone" would be me, or that because of her and her gift, my life would soon change forever.

## HOW SNOW DANCERS KILLED RUSSIANS

When I first arrived back in Canada after eight years away, I thought it was a frozen hell. An hour in Toronto on a bitter January day under gloomy dark skies and bitter wind, cars splashing grey slush, was enough to turn anyone off Canada. But this was my native land, my roots. So, my fightback was, if you have to live in a winter country, you better figure out how to enjoy it.

By the mid-1970s I was done with track. But after two decades of high-intensity physical training under the illusion it will help perfect the whole person in some way, you can't just stop, cold turkey. Sport as self-perfecting is a little crazy, I know. Selfish and egotistical, too. But that was me. Self-perfection *was* undeniably part of the unconscious psychic allure of running until you drop (or rather, until the other guy drops). How else would you, or could you overcome your imperfect body (too short, not enough natural speed)? At that level of extreme fitness, to stop hard training even for a few days, meant having super-charged muscles straining on a leash, and a lot of compensatory fidgeting. To cope with bitter, soulless winters, I needed a new sport to make them beautiful; beautiful to *be* in.

One winter day I was trying my hand at downhill skiing at Blue Mountain, Collingwood, bundled in heavy ski jacket and pants, strapped into rigid plastic boots, helmet, goggles fogging up, blowing on painfully cold fingers. I felt like some goon being pulled up a long slope, a J-bar under my butt, skis in the track, wondering why am I doing this? A huffing, puffing machine — at considerable expense per ticket — was doing all the work to pull me up the hill, and gravity was doing the work of pulling me back down. I wasn't disabled, so something seemed very wrong with this picture; like all of us spoiled dudes in expensive clothing and skis were chickening out of the real challenge, which was getting up the hill and down by ourselves. Then, suddenly, my winter life changed forever.

Gliding down from the top of that snowy hill, agile as a seagull turning in flight against a blue sky, long telemark motions side to side, fluffy white snow spraying up and away from his legs, coming toward me, was a man dressed in a bright red skinsuit so thin you could see his muscles working. Oh jeez … about to run into me? But at the last moment, with a smile, and "Excuse me

...," he carved his final turn as he jumped between me and the guy in front, niftily placing his skis in the track, and — I was *very* startled — he began skiing powerfully *up* the hill. What? I am stiff with cold? Being pulled by a friggin' expensive machine? And this guy is skiing *uphill*, under his own power, at the same speed as me? Stunned by this display, I shrank with shame watching the forward thrust of his lilting motion. I was an immobile slug. He was a snow dancer. I almost got right off the J bar to hang my head. Beg forgiveness. I didn't want him to see me. How does he grip snow, and glide uphill? Right there and then I wanted to do that, to be like him. To shed my burdensome clothing, to be dressed in almost nothing, gliding uphill under my own power, hot vapour steaming off my shoulders. It was physical magic, and I could see right away this was to be how I was going to fall in love with winter, to have the play-joy of a child in snow again, but with manly courage and grit, with the gravity-defying use of my own body in raw nature.

He was Kauko Riihiaho, formerly the Junior X-C Ski Champ of Finland, which is to say he was like our Wayne Gretsky to the Finns, but had emigrated to Canada. Leathery-faced, taciturn, unsmiling at first, but then, you'd catch a twinkle in his eyes. He is "yust training liddle bit" at this downhill area because there is artificial snow here, and not enough on the trails yet. Yes, he would teach me how to ski.

A carpenter by trade, it wasn't long before he made me a track setter and we cut a beautiful 2.5 km track through the forest at Dad's farm in Caledon. There, it was magic to watch him glide along a sunlit snowy slope past dapple-shadowed cedars and white birches, delicately but powerfully sensing his own perfect kick and glide over every modulation in the ground. A snow dancer, for sure. He had a legendary kick, like a mule. His competitors thought he had a secret because he could grip and kick when all the rest were slipping.

In those first happy winters, so in love with this new sport we yearned for good snow to come early in fall, I trained with a lot of hardy Finns. Some of the older ones had served as snipers on Finnish ski-patrol units in WWII, skiing from one strategic place to another to kill Russians who had occupied Finland during the coldest winter in memory. They worked in units of a dozen skier-snipers, hands, clothing, and faces chalked white. No walkie-talkies allowed, navigating by compass alone through still forests at dusk, without shadows, until they saw their target: a Russian supply-train frozen, eyeless and still in bitter cold. One sentry every 100 metres; six guarding this train.

Ski and kill. Then ski and kill again, in a winter that stayed at −30° below Celsius for three months. Six of those Finns, rifles on their backs would drift silent and shadowless downward from the hills toward that train, each zeroing on a sentry. About a 100 yards away, they fall forward and lie on their skis in deep snow, rifles on their backs. Kauko said without a scope, those guys could put a bullet in the eye of a man from a 100 yards. Each hand gripping the tip of a ski, they shuffle closer lying flat on their skis to within deadly range. Left-right. Pause. Left-right. Stop. Check if the Russian has noticed; brace for a gunfight. Not this time. So, left-right. Pause. Left-right, again. Closer. Then, quickly and carefully ready your rifle. Then: Crack! Crack! Crack! Six Russian sentries shot in the back, falling, crumpled, face-first in the snow, altogether. A morbid minuet.

Then, our Finns are up, disappearing as white ghosts into the bush whence they came. Angry Russians pour, shouting, from their frozen train, giving chase on hopelessly clunky Russian skis; with no chance of catching these snow dancers. Once reassembled, the patrol skis another 30 kilometres or so, to attack another frozen train, and kill again. The Russians thought the Finns had dozens of patrols. "But" Kauko said, with pride, "It was same guys."

They never went inside a human habitation that winter of −30°C for four months — except to beg for food. So how did you manage? After skiing so hard to attack, and attack again, you would be sweaty, and hot. How did you get dry? Where did you sleep?

"We ski one more hour, slow, to get dry. Then, with 'spessial' blanket, sleep under snow, like dog." They were my new heroes, these fellows, manly, a *spessial* breed.

Against The Tide

# HOW CROSS-COUNTRY SKIING CHANGED ME, AND HOW I CHANGED THE SPORT

When racing on skis began there were almost zero opportunities for an older skier to race. Sometimes a regular competition would offer a half-hearted event for what were pejoratively called "Old Boys" — skiers 40 and older. That name made us feel like rejects. So very few Old Boys came. I never saw more than six of various ages, and they competed feeling as if they shouldn't be there. I was determined to change that.

Before fiberglass skis were invented, we used gracefully shaped, inexpensive birchwood skis made by the Finnish company *Jarvinen*. Those bases had to be treated with a coat of pine tar to prevent water getting into the wood. When the snow was gone, a whiff of that wonderful smell would trigger memories of gliding past snow-laden pine boughs along a lovely, lonely ski-trail. It sounds a little fanatical, I know. But, I kept a broken ski-tip in my car so that in summer, whenever the longing for winter and skiing welled up, I could pick it up for the smell of pine, and swoon for ski-dancing.

But the term "Old Boys" ticked me off. I just knew there were lots of men and women over 30 like me, who would love to race again. But I could see the problem right away, and it linked to my growing interest in political philosophy. This was a chance to push back against big government in my own little way. By the 1970s the Government of Ontario had taken another step toward statism by taking control of all amateur sports. "Sport Ontario," a government agency, had a collection of tax-funded offices and staff in Toronto from which most sports in the province were being administered. This was incredibly offensive to my sense of independence. Citizens who enjoy sports should be running their own damn sports. Why do sportsmen need tax-fed government officials to control what they love? Here was an opportunity to create something new for skiers on the model of Masters Track and Field, which by then was highly organized, in the USA at least.

So, I grabbed an art pen, created a logo and letterhead, and opened a bank account for "*The Canadian Masters Cross-Country Ski Association*." Why not? And I named myself the President. That made Jeanie laugh. "You made yourself President? That's funny." It was. But why not? Someone had to do it! I also drafted a simple Constitution providing a Director for each Province of Canada. Our main function would be to organize an annual Canadian Masters Cross-Country Ski Championship, to be rotated among willing provinces, and each Director's job would be to stimulate Masters skiing competitions within their own province. This was all prior to the internet, so it was done by word of mouth and snail mail. It worked wonders.

In January of 1980 I organized the first-ever "Masters Cross-Country Ski Championship" (no more "Old Boys") at Dagmar Ski Resort, northeast of Toronto, and over 120 men and women showed up from across Canada to race in five-year age groups from 30 to 80. I also talked Carling-O'Keefe Brewery into sponsoring the meet, and they made a half-hour movie featuring many former champions who, like Kauko, were all excited to be back in shape and racing again. I still have a copy of the results and remain proud that in the 10km and 30km events where I finished third and fourth respectively, only Finns beat me. So I almost felt like one of them. This Association has been active now for over 40 years, and as one top national ski coach said recently, "you changed a lot of lives." You can see it as it is today, at http://canadian-masters-xc-ski.ca/about/

Contemporaneous with this, The Viking Ski Club of Morin Heights north of Montreal was busy organizing a wonderful competition they called the "Gillette World Masters Cross-Country Ski Championship" for February of 1980. Skiers, 104 of them, came from nine nations, and we had a wonderful time. Here is a photo of my 30-kilometre race at this meet, where I got beaten soundly by Norwegians and Swedes.

Something new was happening. But what, exactly? At the banquet afterward I asked the organizers, "When, and where is the next one? We really loved this." That question drew mostly a blank look on exhausted faces. There were no plans for another event. Nothing at all. I could see the problem. Masters skiing, unlike track, had no organizing world body. Something had to be done. Meanwhile, inspired by the meet at Morin Heights, Sweden arranged for a similar one-off Championship in Uppsala, in 1982. I skied it. Two hundred and forty skiers loved it. But again, no one had any idea what would be next, if anything.

## THE WORLD MASTERS CROSS-COUNTRY SKI ASSOCIATION – A VISIT FROM THE INTERNATIONAL SKI MAFIA

A German friend once told me of an old German saying about anything that needed doing: *"If it's not by me, it will not be."*

After pondering this I decided to form a new international organization, to be called *The World Masters Cross-Country Ski Association,*[12] or WMA. This would be an Association of National Directors, one from each nation wishing to join, rather than an association of skiers. Not a democracy. Next, was to draft a simple Constitution, design a logo, and create letterhead and a business card. Oh, and I named myself the President (Jeanie laughed again: "Now you've named yourself President of the world?"). Again, I replied, "Someone has to do it!" — and a year later I asked the German masters skier Dieter Heckmann, to serve as Vice-President.

Then I talked a nearby design company into creating our logo for nothing, from which letterhead, business cards, and eventually a super good-looking home were made.

Next was the challenge of creating a World Masters Cross-Country Championship and developing a bidding process for other nations to do the same. I didn't know much about organizing such a world event, so I asked Tony Wise of Telemark Wisconsin to do it as part of his annual American Birkebeiner, a famous race in Wisconsin that draws about 8,000 competitors every year. He agreed, and we were in business for spring of 1983. Except …

Late fall of 1982, I got a call from Ottawa. It was Marty Hall, an American coach recently hired by Cross-Country Canada, a talented, crusty, bull of a man, if there ever was one. But likeable, too, because if he wanted to stab you in the back, he would tell you first. He was coming to Toronto to see me with a couple of Canadian ski officials, because …

"We got wind of this here World Masters thing you are trying to do. *Forget it. You can't do it. Period!* FIS [*Fédération Internationale de Ski*] is the goddamn world governing body, and you know that. See you tomorrow." And he hung up. He's 84 now, but even then, he was a legendary coach. Here's a photo of him in his sixties. Crusty Marty was coming to Toronto to chew me out.

You see what I mean. He looks like if you hit him over the head with a baseball bat, he would just scratch his chin, and ask, "what the hell you doin'?" When he was hired by the US, he coached Vermont's young Billy Koch to America's first-ever Olympic medal in cross-country skiing — a silver in the 30km race at the 1984 Winter Olympics in Innsbruck. That was the first and last American medal in this sport for forty years.

Against The Tide

At any rate, FIS, with a membership of 118 nations, is based in *Oberhofen am Thunersee* in Switzerland, and it controls *all* Olympic skiing sports and World Championships (except Biathlon): cross-country, alpine, ski jumping, freestyle, snowboarding, rules, regulations, facilities, course specs, infractions, penalties, the whole shebang. It's a *big* deal on a world scale. Marty was FIS's hired gun — both priest and executioner — for Canada. I had some sympathy. I mean they do have to police their standards worldwide, and all that. So, let's see what happened to *"You can't do it! Period!"*

Marty walked into my office with the two honchos from Cross-Country Canada in Ottawa, who were just as concerned about usurpation of their authority in Canada as he was about undermining FIS authority worldwide. A sour beginning was rather likely.

Marty: "We heard about what you're tryin' to do and came down to see for ourselves. Like I told you. FIS is the *sole* world authority for *all* skiing competitions. So, what the hell were you thinking?" You can't just up and create a goddamn new world skiing organization!"

Me: "Why not?"

Marty: "Because it's not gonna fly."

Me: "Why not?"

Marty; "Because FIS is the sanctioning authority for every ski competition in the world. You can't hold an international meet without our sanction.

Me: "We don't need your sanction. We're just having a good time. Why do we need a sanction?"

A little disturbed now, Marty began shifting in his seat. "Because of regulations. The rules."

Me: "If you want to share your FIS rules with us, we'd be happy to look at them, and see if they work for us older guys." [I was 40 at the time. Marty was 45].

Marty: "Sure. But still, like I said, you can't just organize a world ski event without our sanction."

Me: "As I said, we are older skiers. We don't need a sanction. But we would be happy to co-operate with FIS, and if you want to give us a sanction we don't need, that's fine, too, as long as we can do everything we want to do, and you don't try to block us. We aren't kids. We aren't going to be ordered around. We are going to run our own world championship, and our first one is set for spring of '83 in Telemark, Wisconsin. In four months. So, you better get moving. Because we figure, if we have to wait for a huge bureaucracy like FIS to get something done, we'll all be dead."

Familiar with sluggish bureaucracies, Marty allowed himself a bit of a knowing smirk.

Marty: "So, what's this 'World Masters Cross-Country Ski Association'? Do you have an office?"

Me: "You're sitting in it."

Marty raised his bushy eyebrows very high now.

Marty: "Do you have, like, a logo? Letterhead? Business cards?"

I was ready for that question and slapped a clean sheet of our handsome new WMA letterhead, and the business card of the President [me], on the table, right in front of him. He was a little startled, but also a little impressed, and he smiled, sort of …

Marty: "I see. Okay. So, you aren't waitin'. Got it. We still can't allow it, like, on your own."

Me: "Gentlemen, as I said, if you want to *help* us, we would be happy to work out some kind of simple affiliation agreement between FIS and WMA. We'd be happy to co-operate on agreeable terms. But you're going to have to get moving. Our only activity will be one world championship every year, which we plan to rotate between the Scandinavian bloc, North America, and Europe. Our first *World Masters Championship* is going ahead in four months, in Telemark, Wisconsin, with, or without FIS."

Marty and his gang conferred worriedly, but briefly.

Marty: "First problem is: You can't call it "*World Masters Championship*," because we already use a name like that. In German, It's *Weltmeisterschaft*, which means "World Masters," exactly like the title you want to use! You see what I mean?"

Me: "Right. So, what about we call it *Masters World Cup*, instead? That name just leapt into my head.

To make a fun story short, they liked that, and liked our immediate willingness to change too, and left our WMA "head office" (!) quite happy, promising to draft an Affiliation Agreement between our two organizations, which was concluded a year a half later in Zurich and negotiated by our VP Dieter Heckmann.

By 1985, for our *Master World Cup* in Hirschau, Germany, 1012 competitors from about 18 nations paraded through that magical village in the dark of evening, holding candles, singing, and celebrating this great sport, lots more candles burning in the windows of every home and shop. It was so charming. Bengt Eric Bengtsson, Race Director of FIS, came to check us out. On that night, he stood before the crowd of over 1,000 Masters skiers in the public square, and said, "This is the way all sport should be." It was vindication.

I just loved doing all this. Today, more than forty years after that meeting, the WMA has 30 member nations, and every *Masters World Cup*, rotated between those three regions of the world as originally planned, regularly

Against The Tide

draws about 1,000 international competitors. Take a look at our website. You will see a lot of happy faces!

## "MORE THAN A GREAT PLACE TO WORK"

By 1983 the business was finally making decent money. I should have been happy. Relieved. We had put away about $500,000, so were no longer teetering on the edge of bankruptcy. But looking back, I'd say those ten years scarred me. Correction: that's baby talk. I chose that life, and as a man, you deal with what life serves up. Not your fault if you get knocked down, but it's your fault if you don't get up, and all that. I guess you could say I knocked myself down. But hell, I knew plenty of guys who got into going-concern businesses. Their challenge was just to keep it going or make it better. That's a slam dunk, really, and maybe a lot of fun, too. At least, I could say, listen, my friend, if you haven't ever had to pull a badly failing business from the brink and turn it around, you haven't ever done business. It was a painful, pride-damaging experience. Distrust from suppliers; cash only for deliveries suspicion; no cheques, thanks very much; uneasy staff, always worried about losing their jobs. And I knew that half a million can disappear in a hiccup in a bad year. So, at 43 my life likely more than half over, I was still exposed to what I thought privately is the ultimate failure: living a life without significance. Without real meaning. Despair at the last ding-dong.

On our rare vacations, Jean and I would spend heartfelt time talking about, making lists about, what we *really* wanted to make of our lives. We were both deeply happy with our love, our marriage, and our blended family. And we knew this mattered most of all. So, our lists were about unfulfilled personal ambitions, longings, fulfilling hobbies, the thirst to learn, self-educate, get wiser, and so on. On my list, making the business successful was essential but I saw it as a means to an end, one of about 20 ambitions, almost every one of which meant more to me than that. If we had been making lots of money, well, sure, I would have been very proud, mostly because we had a great product. We were improving people's lives with somatopsychic medicine, as I thought of it. That was noble, and the only meaningful reward of that business. Like, bumping into Henry, who had joined our club a year ago when he could barely walk around the block without puffing; then seeing him now. "Henry! Is it you? I hardly recognize you." Henry: "I'm just great. I'm down 50 pounds. I'm training for a half-marathon. I sold my business, and I divorced my wife. It's been a *big* year! I owe you a lot!" Well, I guess it wasn't *all* good. But we did change his life, right?

At any rate, most of the other things on my list had to do with engaging the big questions; about writing important books; maybe teaching again, a noble calling I dearly missed; but mostly, I longed to engage once again with profound ideas. There were lots of *big* and creative ideas in the business world, but precious few *profound* ideas. Very few business people are interested in profound ideas, especially if they might rock the boat of public opinion. In fact, I'd say that disappointingly, a lot of large corporations have become public-opinion whores. Despite obvious ideological conflicts with the premises of a free society and the legal and moral rights that guarantee and enable free enterprise, they will support whatever opinion polling tells them will sell more product. That was causing concern, and a somewhat desperate desire to fight back, to address my growing meaning-emptiness. Clearly, I needed to figure out how to make the business so strong I could sell it for what a friend called screw-you money, and then write books about meaningful things, challenging ideas, question received opinion, create deep insight for myself, and for others, teach through writing. Live exactly as I had always wanted to live, be who I wanted to be.

One day that fall of 1983, just a little despondent because I still couldn't see a way out, wondering if that would *ever* happen, I walked into my office, flipped open the *Globe and Mail* and saw a full page advertisement for "The 4th Tower" of the Toronto-Dominion Centre, with a photoshopped image of the tower already in place. Under it was a proud corporate slogan: "*More Than a Great Place to Work.*"

Just to see this triggered an immediate image of possible salvation and a fast-rising heart rate. What about putting one of our clubs on top of that tower? This could be a way to make the business sound and valuable. Holy … grabbing the phone, I called Cadillac-Fairview, the builder, and asked to speak with the Project Manager for the 4th Tower.

A voice came on the phone in a soft South African accent: "David Weinberg, here."

"Hello David. I just saw your advertisement for the 4th Tower. I think I can help make your TD Center *'More Than a Great Place To Work'*." He laughed, amiably, at the chutzpah. "How so?" I told him "We run the finest executive fitness and health operation in the world, and you should think about putting one of our clubs on top of your new Tower." Just like that.

An hour later, this affable, articulate gentleman, a curly dark-haired, warm-eyed straight shooter, who had come to Canada, like so many successful South African citizens to escape the deadly politics of apartheid, was in my office, and we got along at once.

He left very enthusiastic and asked me to send him specs on what one of our clubs would need in terms of facilities and square footage. I did. All 43,000 square feet, with gym, restaurant, squash courts, swimming pool, the lot. He had it all by the next morning, but he called me back a lot less pumped.

"I'm sorry to say, your club is just too big. Maybe we could put a smaller version in the basement? And anyway, it turns out the top floor is already allocated for storage space."

"Storage?"

"Yeah. You know, documents, and the like. Paper. We rent a lot of storage to our tenants. You wouldn't believe how much."

I was shocked. Nothing could be more meaningless than storage.

David asked, "So what do you think?"

"I'm trying to imagine what it will feel like to show your international guests around your storage space, instead of around the most stunning sport and fitness club in the world?"

"Right. Well, personally, I'd like to see the club. But it's just too big. Clearly, we don't have enough space. We could try fitting it in below ground level, beside the garage."

That seemed to end it. But I didn't want to let it go. Suddenly, the idea came that turned my whole life around.

"What about adding a floor?"

That got a long silence. And then, "Are you kidding? This building's already been approved by the city. We are only allowed so much office space."

"It's not office space. It's recreational space."

"You know," David said, pausing, mouth open in suspended calculation. "That's true! It's true." A longer pause, David thinking … "Maybe. You know, it's worth a try. I'm going to take that idea to the Committee of Adjustments and see what they say."

The next afternoon David called, clearly surprised and delighted, to say the city had immediately approved an extra floor for recreational use atop the 4th Tower.

If you get knocked down, you get up.


## THE TWO DICKS

So, what is such a club going to cost, and how are we going to finance it? I had no idea. I just thought the idea was super, and I had to make it work. However, there was a big gap between my enthusiasm and practical possibility. So, I said to David Weinberg … you've got the plans. Please ask your Cadillac-Fairview experts — structural, electrical, HVAC, and so on — to estimate the full cost of building this club. I have to figure out how to pay for it. He did. It didn't take long to get an estimate of $3 million. This was presented as a very close estimate from one of the world's top construction companies. We had only $500,000 to put in. They had better be right!

There were two Dicks that mattered. Dick Davies, Senior VP, oversaw TD loans and financing. Son of a United Church Minister, he had caution and a twinkle in his eyes at all times (just about right for a loan expert), loved a good cigar, and was involved with the Arthritis Society. So, he was delighted when I told him my Grandfather created The Canadian Arthritis Society, and was its first President. He told me he played the saxophone, too, and in a bit, I will tell how he tried to play me.

Dick Thomson, his boss, began work as a lowly ledger clerk in a branch, and in just over a decade rose to President at age 39, then Chairman and CEO of the TD Bank (then the number 2 bank in Canada with $290 Billion in assets). He was one of the most respected bankers in the world, and at the helm of TD Centre development. I didn't know it then, but I, me — little ole professor me, it's true — would soon be heading for unanticipated crises and deadlock with both Dicks. But I'll start with the positives.

Cap in hand, with draft plans to unfurl on his desk, I made an appointment to see Dick Davies about financing this club in the sky. Okay, it was a bit of a sales job. I felt so passionate (and maybe a little desperate, too) about this project that I managed to make Dick feel and see it, too, and our hour ended with a vigorous handshake. If we put our $500,000 in, he would eagerly

*Against The Tide*

finance the rest — he just wanted to, uh, "clear it with his Credit Committee." But he sincerely thought — wow — this would be a terrific plus for the whole Centre.

I walked — floated? — straight from his office to Women's College Hospital to see dear Jeanie, who was to bring our third child, son Franklin, into the world the next morning. She was in early-stage labour, upright in bed, rosy-cheeked, slightly flushed, the perfect image of maternal beauty on the brink of creation, a fit study for Leonardo.

But after I outlined what I was trying to do, with whom, and asked her opinion? I mean, I wanted her to buy-in to what was going to be an additional load on me, and so, on us (maybe I should have explained it more before getting in this deep?). At any rate, I worked up to asking her what she thought? What she said brought me up short, but I wasn't going to argue just before she gave birth.

"Don't do it."

"Pardon?"

"It's too much. This will be child number five. You have enough on your plate. So do I. All these negotiations, long meetings, and ... I can tell ... they're not even *feeding* you! We're doing okay. We don't *need* more." Of course, she was right about that. She's still the one person on the planet with whom I would endure any hardship.

But it was the first and last time I ever quietly ignored her normally insightful advice, chalking it up to pregnancy hormones and, well, a reasonable anxiety over both of us getting buried by a too-frantic business and home life.

She might have been right.

## CADILLAC-FAIRVIEW LOOKING VERY INCOMPETENT

She certainly seemed right a few weeks later when Cadillac-Fairview did their final costing (as distinct from their first "firm" estimate) for what we were already excitedly calling our "TD Club." I almost fell over. It came in at $4.5 million — fully 50% higher than the original estimate! Fifty per cent! What? This was simply shattering news; or a bad joke, or some kind of world-record incompetence. One of the best builders in the whole world was erecting huge towers all over the place —at the time they were building a half dozen towers in New York city — with every talent and skill at their fingertips. And they *actually* miscalculated this small project — by 50%? I got dizzy with disbelief. I had just arranged financing on their $3 million upper limit. So, what now?

Oh dear. Get up and fight. I called David Weinberg and asked for an immediate special meeting with him, and everyone involved: architects, structural engineers, HVAC, electrical, construction manager, the lot.

The next day I walked into that meeting. They were all around the table, likely figuring they just had to get rid of an unfortunate screw-up, the egg on their faces, and me. But I had nothing, or rather everything, to lose. And so, I never felt as free. I wanted to pump them up with pride in what they were doing. That meeting was about coaching, and I have always felt comfortable coaching; I mean, inspiring the best in others.

"Gentlemen, really? Think of your slogan. If we are going to make the TD Centre 'more than a great place to work', and not just a lot of empty words; if we are going to *honour* those words, give them *meaning*, we have to collectively roll up our sleeves and knock the hell out of these costs. I'm sure it can be done, but it's going to take everyone in this room. Everyone. So, I'm asking, let's go around this table quickly, one by one, and see how much we can knock out."

We started with the HVAC fellow. He put big numbers on the table. About heating and air conditioning — especially for the gym area, which took up half of an entire floor of the building,

"Where's all the cost?" I asked him, point blank.

"Duct work. So much and so many air vents. It's an exercise space, not an office, so, extra venting, temperature controls, closing up the ceiling, and so on. Lots of fussy detail."

"It's a gym. They like cool air blowing on them," I told him." And not much heat will needed. A lot cooler than an office space. And upstairs are the squash courts, so no heat needed there, either. So why not leave the entire gym ceiling open? Why not just have one big tube blowing cool air over the whole track? Same in the courts?

"The air will blow right in their faces when they're exercising."

"They'll love it."

He wasn't expecting that, and his bushy eyebrows went up skeptically, caterpillars climbing up his forehead. This was a guy who made a point of never sweating.

"So ... how much can you reduce costs by doing what I ask?" He got his calculator out and worked for five minutes.

"Could be as much as $300,000."

And on it went. By the end of that meeting we had knocked big costs out of the club in every area. By the end, inspired by this little exercise, Bernie Ghert, President and CEO of Cadillac Fairview — a fanatical cyclist who had

Against The Tide

his assistant drive alongside on his rides to hand him his cellphone, came on board and offered to put in $600,000 as a leasehold improvement. That contribution came to under $14 per square foot, which, relative to what they were giving other tenants, wasn't so much. We were still over the original estimate on which the TD financing with Dick Davies had been arranged, but not far off. Our lawyer and theirs could now put a lease together. I wanted zero rent for five years, and after that to pay an agreed percentage of net cash flow. We were going big, about to build the most professional sport and fitness club in the world, and the highest — 37th floor, and upward, into the sky!

## THE FIRST DICK DROPS A BOMB

My life, at last, seemed to be turning in the right direction. The fitness industry in general, is terrible. Most of the operators back then were Vic Tanny style: low fees, high volume, high-turnover, storefront operations. You walk in and ask about membership. They put a chair against the door so you don't think about trying to get past the T-shirted muscle-boy in the chair until he has sold you a lifetime membership "deal" (hoping you will not come back to use it much). About 80% of their members never renew. It's a sales grinder.

Lloyd Percival and The Fitness Institute changed all that by insisting on the medical screening of members, on fitness testing for all, and a full facility, high fee, low volume, high-retention, membership-based club. More than 80% of our member renewed, every year. Nevertheless, it was hard to shake the cheap public image of a "fitness" operation. Our new, high-in-the-sky TD Club was going to change all that by serving a downtown professional clientele and their out-of-town guests from other cities where this same concept could spread. I actually found myself thinking of how we could do the same thing in New York, London or Paris? Asking myself, how would you like being an international businessman? Stop it, Bill. Focus on what's real.

What's real came two weeks after that meeting when Dick Davies dropped another bomb in a two-minute phone call.

"Bill. I'm sorry to say, our Credit Committee has just declined your loan."

"Sir! What do you mean? We just did the deal! I thought we agreed!"

"I did, too. But they disagree now. And I can't interfere. When the overall cost went up, they decided you just don't have enough equity in the deal. You need to put more money in."

"We don't have more money. We've putting in everything we have."

"I'm really sorry. But my hands are tied. You'll have to come up with more equity."

And he hung up. A feeling of something close to rage rose in my throat; curtains down, the last, sad note of his saxophone trailing away as he hung up, and the millstone got heavier. I just said goodbye to a dead person. Maybe Jeanie was right?

That night, she gave consolation, but may have been secretly pleased that our life could now go back to what it was. Be thankful, and all that. Of course. But I was still in shock. My best chance to escape, Houdini-like from the chains of a sluggish business had just evaporated. I told myself, you're just not a big business guy, a wheeler-dealer; you're just an intellectually hungry dreamer. You let vanity puff you up. You stupid son of a bitch, was all I could think.

But in desperation, in my slow-burn, and as a last ditch, I called the other Dick, the Chairman and CEO of the whole TD empire, Dick Thomson. It was a pity call. He already knew what the first Dick had done. So basically, I implored him: "Sir, you and I have never met. I have never had an opportunity to explain what this Club could do for the whole TD Centre. You shot me down without us even meeting. I'm asking for a brief meeting." That was Thursday afternoon. He agreed immediately to a meeting at 9 am the following Wednesday.

## I WAS JUST LOOKING FOR NEW SHOES

The day after my call with Dick Thomson I figured I should de-stress and go do something I enjoyed. At the time I was in love with orienteering, or what some call "cunning running," a sport where you run for best time through wild hilly forests with a compass and a map, just like in a car rally, checkpoints and all. I needed orienteering shoes with spikes for running up the hills. Whenever under stress, go do what you love. So, I found a supplier and drove there, trying to keep my mind off Davies and his damn call, off how I would have to tell our pumped-up management team the bad news and let them down. How they were going to wish I had never pumped them up. I bought the shoes and sat in my car, very alone, rain snaking down the windshield. The inside of a car is a small world, but about now it felt just right. Weighing the future. Weighing my life. The years ticking louder. When I looked up, there was a tall wet building staring at me with *Continental Bank* plastered across it. What the hell is the Continental Bank?

I couldn't dial brother Jamie fast enough. At the time, he was the big-shot owner of Johnston & Daniel Real Estate (J & D), a successful, handsome figure

Against The Tide

around town — and with the ladies — in his wolfskin winter jacket. J & D was the brainchild of my mother's brother, our elegant, white-haired Uncle Bobby Johnston, a man whose adult hobby was trying to figure out how magnetism works. Not what it *does*, but what *is* it? He used to buy us kids little wooden soldiers with cloth parachutes that we would throw out of high windows, then lean out to watch them drift to ground. I was calling Jamie for a parachute.

"What the hell is the Continental Bank? Do you know anyone there?"

He did. David. A VP. So, I called David. He already knew of our high reputation in the fitness world. So, I asked: "How would you like to finance a new club we are about to build in the Toronto-Dominion Centre, right downtown? There was a very pregnant silence.

"I'm coming over to see you." I put away my new shoes — what a fluke — and met him and his credit guy at my office.

I'll just say it was another coaching opportunity. I spent two hours spilling my soul, describing the whole frank, sorry financial history of The Fitness Institute, of Lloyd and his shocking death, of family loans, of how the location for the Mississauga club was a mistake we had to live with, but also — what a great professional model we had now, ready to go big. How, whenever the North American Association of Fitness Clubs has its annual meeting in Toronto? Why, they all line up around the block just for the chance to get in and see how we do it. We *are* the standard for the entire North American industry. When I finished, I was flushed and exhausted. No more to give. My future was hanging on their reaction. Succeed, or die.

"So … what do you think?

An ominous pause. Then: "We think this is going to be your best club. By far. We'd love to finance it. But … we also think TD will never let us do it. The Continental Bank? Financing a corporate magnet like The Fitness Institute in their new Tower? Uh, uh. They'll smarten up, and come right back in." I was delighted they liked it but crushed and stopped short by what he just said. Think on your feet, Billy.

"I think that's true. They will have to come back in. So now what?"

"No idea," spoken with forlorn sympathy.

I had to offer something.

"Then here's what I think. I have a meeting already set up with Dick Thomson for next Wednesday morning. What about you go ahead and arrange a matching line of credit, and I'll make a promise to you, here and now. This Club is going to be a world-beater, and we will likely expand to other cities. So, I am giving you my word: the very next Club, no, every club we do after this one, the Continental Bank will be our banker of choice."

"Thanks. Appreciated. Really. But a normal approval for a job like this takes our credit guys about two weeks. Why would we put the effort into it for nothing?"

"I'll pay. What will it cost me to have you approve a matching line of credit by Tuesday evening?"

"By that time? A couple of guys working over the weekend? That's a tough call. Five thousand."

That stopped me, for a second. "Please. Go ahead. If you get it done by Tuesday afternoon, and the TD Bank is forced by this move to come back in, you're right, we will have to go with them. But if that happens, I will happily bring you my promise, and a cheque for $5,000 on Wednesday, before the close of business. They agreed, and there were smiles all around in anticipation of rubbing the nose of the TD Bank in their own poop for beating up on the little guy.

But confirmation didn't come over the weekend. Not on Monday. Not Monday night. I couldn't reach anyone at the Continental Bank. Not Tuesday morning. Or afternoon. Now, I'm panicking again. It's gonna collapse. How embarrassing. I'll have to cancel with Dick Thomson, last minute. Really? Oh, please, just call. I went home late Tuesday, despondent; emotional cliffhanger, was an understatement. Then, just when I was about to give up, feeling deeply cynical, a phone call came at 8 p.m. from David, at the Continental Bank.

"You have your line of credit!" I could hear the smile in his voice as he read me the terms. It was perfect. A wave of happiness happened.

But what now? This was a moment for considerable strategic delicacy. I didn't think it right to walk into a meeting with the Chairman of the TD Bank and red face him with news we just got funding from his competitor. So, I called Dick Davies at home. He was surprised to get a late evening call at home from someone he had just shot down; but he was genial, bracing himself.

"Dick … I don't want to ambush you, or Mr. Thomson, tomorrow morning. So I thought it best to let you know we have just arranged financing for this club on terms equal to, or better than yours, with the Continental Bank."

He gasped, "Oh my God." That was all. Then came a studied pause, wheels grinding. "I have to call Mr. Thomson, right away. Thank you, Bill. Thank you for calling me." And he hung up. I think he really was thankful.

But I couldn't get the grin off my face, and the sense of incipient victory, combined with knowing I had behaved honourably in alerting the enemy I was about to crush. Jeanie understood I had to get out of the house to avoid the risk of baby Franklin keeping us awake. So, I booked a room at the Sheraton Hotel from where I could walk to the first of the TD Centre's iconic black towers (the architect, Mies van der Rohe: "black is a noble colour"). Then,

*Against The Tide*

an elevator ride to just two floors above where Big Jim used to be sitting at his desk at Gairdner and Company, the year after that tower went up. I was whishing upward past his spirit and felt a little ache of regret he couldn't see me now. Would have been great to share this moment with him, this imminent coup. He would have been so proud ("Even if you're going to be wrong, for Gawd's sake, speak up!").

Then came a short climb up a concrete, bunker-style private staircase to the Sanctum Sanctorum of Canadian financial eminence — the TD Board Room, with its daunting 36-foot English oak table resting on slabs of creamy Italian Travertine marble, anchoring a scene of elegant, executive solemnity, floor to ceiling black-framed windows giving breathtaking views of the city, and of those black leather seats — the largest one at the head, for Mr. Thomson.

Here is what the Heritage Toronto website says about it:

Just about every important decision made by TD Bank has been made around this table. It's made from five sections of solid English brown oak sourced from the Broadlands estate in Hampshire, England, the home of the Mountbatten family where both Queen Elizabeth and Prince Philip and Charles and Diana honeymooned.

As I was going up the final stairs, David Weinberg was coming down, fast. I was peeved. We had worked closely on this project together, but he hadn't returned any of my panic calls. What the hell?

"I couldn't call you. I was in a bad position. What happened? You really threw the cat among the pigeons."

I told him about the Continental Bank, the matching loan, and the deal to pay $5,000 if TD came back in. With a barely perceptible grin, he said, "It's the best $5,000 you ever spent," and went on his way, shaking his dark curly hair, and added, "I'd love to be a fly on the wall."

## CORPORATE THEATRE: WE ALL HAD TO FAKE IT

When I entered the Board room, Mr. Thomson was standing stiff, emotionless, in thick, black-framed eyeglasses by his big black Chairman's chair at the end of the table. Cadillac-Fairview's President Bernie Ghert, TD finance VP Mr. Davies, and their head marketing man were ranged alongside, with my own VP John Wildman, who well knew what I had done and could hardly stand keeping it all bottled up. Soft morning sunlight almost painful to the eye filled the room. At once, I extended my hand to Mr. Thomson, and spoke words to set the tone for a meeting I knew I had to genuinely fake, so to speak, as if he held all the cards for our financing, when in fact, I did.

"Sir, would you mind if I take the head of the table?"

His chair, at his table.

It was an audacious move that arose spontaneously and put me in mind of Big Jim, who replied once to colleagues who offered him the head of the table at a meeting: "Wherever I'm sitting, *is* the head of the table." Take charge. Mr. Thomson didn't blink. He extended his arm toward his chair like a bullfighter waving a cape, fully aware, I suspect, of the symbolic significance of this little flourish, and I took it.

Thus, began almost an hour in which I was expected to sell those big executives a convincing reason why they should finance a club in their tower for which (as they all knew) I already had a draft lease from them, and a firm commitment to finance from a competing bank. I had to fake the real motive for my enthusiasm, while disguising the underlying irony that this club was all but a *fait accompli*. As for them? They had to behave as if they held all the cards and were now seriously examining whether or not they should finance the club. Even Voltaire could not have written a scenario as fake as this, into which not a sliver of truth could be allowed. The key to passionately persuading and selling them on the concept was first to persuade myself this

*Against The Tide*

meeting was real. Somehow, I had to fake it was not fake; to get them so genuinely excited we could all, including me, forget the fake, so to speak; I didn't dare give even the slightest indication we were all being false, or their loss of face would be exposed.

When I was finished, passion expended, vision completed, I placed my hands on the table as if it was *my* table, and asked Mr. Thomson what he thought. Now, he had to do a final, executive fake. He turned to his key people, one by one, asking each a qualifying question. Bernie said he was already a member of the FI, and so was biased, but in principle — "in principle"! — he was in favour. I loved that bit of executive delicacy from a man who was about as delicate as a heifer in a china shop. Then came the marketing fellow, who was reasonably concerned about how business people in business suits in the elevators would feel about a sweaty jogger from the club standing close to them? I replied we could always put a nice track on the roof and get rid of that problem. Their eyes lit up at the idea of jogging in the sun on their own rooftop, up in the sky.

Finally, Dick Thomson turned to Dick Davies, the man who told me so sincerely his hands were tied, that he couldn't interfere with his credit committee, and asked: "What about the financing, Dick?" But he already knew. He already knew all about the financing, he had been forced to concede the evening before, but nevertheless, was speaking now with just the right degree of practiced circumspection.

That was the moment on which everything was hanging. Conversion of fakeness into reality was imminent. I will never, nor would ever want to forget that delicious moment. Dick Davies, eyes lowered to the tabletop, rather sheepishly reported:

"It's all in order, sir."

All in order! I felt a huge inner smile I could not reveal.

At which, Dick Thomson looked around the table, and announced:

"Gentlemen, I think we have a club!"

With his "I think," he signaled the clear, subtle preservation of his personal corporate dignity, the right to authorize publicly what he had already conceded privately.

Thus began the last chapter of the book of my life, the lifting of the millstone, the first intimations of possible financial security, and soon, to my surprise, my first taste of the unforgiving, double-dealing world of public and media opinion I would be facing for the next three decades.

That afternoon I took a cheque for $5,000 to the Continental Bank.

## MY MESSAGE TO PM BRIAN MULRONEY:
## *"YOU'RE TOO PINK!"*

The Club we built up in the sky was a dream come true. Below is a mock-up shot of the whole complex before the tower was completed, but you can see our floors on top of the 4th Tower, and the planned track on the roof!

THE DOWNTOWN FITNESS CLUB
FOR MEN AND WOMEN

The first day we opened this amazing club I met a member exercising by the large windows in the corner of that gym, and asked her how she was enjoying the club? She exuded joy when she said, "I feel like I'm flying!" I did, too. We caught a bit of flack, however, from 25 Bay Street big shots who refused to be medically screened and fitness tested prior to using the club. So I told our VP Technical, Rick Johnson, "go visit every one of them with our company check book, and tell them they can't use this club unless they get medically screened and tested first. I don't care how much they paid. And if they refuse, give them all their money back." Within two weeks they all agreed. One of them

*Against The Tide*

was a 36-year-old millionaire. We had to stop his fitness test and send him to hospital for immediate open-heart surgery.

Meanwhile, I was now on my launch pad to become a writer, and the first of many occasions of serendipity was about to arise. After ten years of reading deeply in political and moral philosophy and amassing large files on lots of topics, I felt a growing need to start expressing my developing views publicly, and forthrightly. Canada seemed riven with moral and political confusion and contradiction, having abandoned its moorings, and founding principles. At the time, PM Brian Mulroney, in name at least, a "conservative," (an indistinct political species I could not define) had been all over CBC News for years, pushing for a socialist style "national daycare" scheme that was estimated to cost the nation "only" about $4 billion. Not chicken feed in 1987. Not chicken feed today, either, when PM Justin Trudeau is doing the same thing.

This was not a national child-care scheme for the truly needy — a plausible notion. It was a very radical feminist scheme to fund "universal daycare" for every mother in the nation — even for Rosedale moms in mink coats with tennis racquets. Something was very wrong. I could see Karl Marx, and his bitter sugar daddy Friedrich Engels, co-author with him of the 1848 Communist Manifesto, grinning from the tomb. I had a copy of Engels' shocking anti-family tract advocating "to bring the whole female sex back into public industry." For what purpose? So that *the monogamous family as the economic unit of society be abolished.*" What? Where is Canada heading? Was Mulroney then (and Trudeau junior now), what Marxists call "useful idiots," promoting the Communist system by another name? Mulroney's daycare scheme was the thin edge of a policy-wedge aiming not to "liberate" women (as Engels imagined) but to lure them out of the home and into the market, thus converting homemakers into taxpayers to help fund the utopian welfare state.

The underlying, if unspoken justification (as when introduced to all the Scandinavian nations before us), was not liberty, but "equality." The classical virtue of liberty before the law and the natural differences and merit this ideal permits and shelters, creates very natural inequalities. With a national daycare program, the biological "penalty" of motherhood that makes the lives of women so naturally "unequal" to those of men, could at last be eliminated. That was the underlying policy aim. I knew at the time that this exact scheme was proposed by Plato for his utopian Republic more than 2,500 years ago, when he advocated national daycare such that all children shall be raised by government, and "no child should know his parent, nor parent his child." At the time, a Calgary Board of Education Chairman (and law professor) Alex Proudfoot, was even more blunt than Plato when he told a meeting of astonished parents: "The child is not your child. Canadian children are the property of the state, like our oil, our gas, and our pipelines."

With every bone in my body I felt I needed to fight this insanity. I wanted to cry out: is no one reading history? Is Canada just going to roll over like a sick dog and surrender its deepest principles? Someone had to shout, "beware!" In effect, I was angry, and a little frightened for myself, my family, and the millions of people sleepwalking through their busy days unaware of what was being planned for them. So when I got a fund-raising letter from Brian Mulroney I wrote back immediately:

*"You're too Pink; If you don't get more Blue; You won't see any more of my Green!"*

That letter was leaked to the press, and a week later, serendipity happened. I got a call from Mr. Colin Brown, President and Founder of *The National Citizens Coalition* (NCC), who had got a great chuckle from it. I knew of the NCC because back then, initially in response to the massive public spending initiated Prime Minister Pierre Trudeau (unequalled for excesses until his own son Justin, who as I write is busy smashing his father's record for public debt), the NCC was well-known for publishing very funny cartoons showing a lot of big-spending politicians (it didn't matter from which party) as gloating, fat-cat beneficiaries of "The Great Canadian MP Rip-Off" who were enjoying huge pensions ordinary citizens couldn't imagine.

I had been sending the NCC a little money to keep their riotous cartoons going, and so when Colin called, I invited him to lunch at our new Club. He was tickled and wanted to use my Mulroney letter. Meanwhile, we had a list of unofficial Honorary Board members at the FI, so I asked if he would like to join? He agreed. Then I added my condition. He would have to get a medical and then get fitness tested like all our other members. Only then did I noticed he sometimes bent his head as if to scold his own hands when they trembled faintly and was occasionally slightly slurring a word. I thought our test would be a great start in getting him healthy. Meanwhile, he asked if I would consider being a member of the Board of the NCC? I thought that would be fun, and maybe a way to put some of the political views I was slowly forming into action. But I was naïve.

I went to my first NCC Board Meeting, and Colin went for his medical. The first went well, the second not so well. One of the members of the NCC Board was Jack Leitch, who attended Appleby with "Jumbo" — that was my dad's nickname — and it made Jack smile, for he admired Dad in the way young boys fawn over their manly elders. Jack was the wunderkind owner of Upper Lakes Shipping Company, whose grandson Jordan — this was more serendipity — was to marry my eldest daughter Christine, many years later, a marriage that produced three fine grandsons. Jack was a staunch defender and practitioner of free enterprise, and the hidden gunner helping to aim NCC ammo at oversized government targets.

Following his medical, Colin called me to say he had very bad news. He had seen the doctor, and "they found a tumour in my brain. I go for surgery in the morning." It was a heart-sinking moment, for hadn't I precipitated this bad news? It was soon worse than I imagined, both the news and the feeling, because Colin went under the knife on March 4, 1987, and died on the operating table. This felt like another parricide, for clearly, he would have lived a little longer — a few days? A few months? — if I hadn't urged him with my health-puritanism attitude to see the damn doctor, right?

I called Jack to lament the situation and said maybe he should Chair the NCC now? He declined. He didn't want to be expose himself as "a right winger." I thought that was strange, for I always had Dad's motto in mind: "Know what you think, say what you think, do what you say." Was Jack afraid of his own views? And if so, why? You couldn't find anyone more sincere. I was naïve, as they say, this was my first exposure to a Canadian specialty: a widespread fear of openly expressing and defending one's own deeply held convictions if they go against the tide. This struck me then, and more so now, as a kind of moral fear — even more strange to be found in a war veteran and hugely successful man. So, Jack, what about you Chairing the NCC behind the scenes for six months, giving us time to find someone permanent? That suited Jack, and the hunt was on to replace Colin. I had no idea it was going to be me.

## CHAIRMAN BILL, AND THE MESS I MADE OF IT

At the time, the President of the NCC, a dark-haired, mustachioed man named David Sommerville, erect in a soldierly fashion, struck many as so deeply fervent, even rabid in his commitment to freedom and small government that he had become a little joyless. But not quite. A good joke always sparked a brief, transformative chuckle. But he was definitely a crusader. The motto of the NCC, then and now, was "More Freedom Through Less Government." This struck my amateur promotional sensibilities as a clever, libertarian sort of line that was more or less true, but not entirely. There is nothing in history that says a small government cannot be tyrannous, or that in the absence of appropriate citizen self-discipline and law and order, "more freedom" won't lead to moral and political chaos. Those are discussions I thought worth having, and I would have them aplenty in my first political book some years later.

But not with David. Alas, he became morose under my leadership because I got too excited and began behaving as if I were the President. A mistake. The NCC had some 40,000 members, and I thought it ought to have 400,000. When I offered that opinion, David stared at me dispassionately. I smelled the opportunity to put my incipient political and moral views together as a kind of promotional manifesto for the NCC, but David cautioned: "once you put it in writing, you will be stuck with it." But feeling what must have been some primordial desire to write, I drafted a small booklet outlining NCC principles, we sent it to a large sampling of members, and waited. In silence.

At that time we held the first NCC "Colin Brown Freedom Award" Dinner — a memorial night where I met some of Toronto's politicos. Barbara Amiel, whose journalism, with elegantly-barbed language and cutting insights I greatly admired, was at my table, leaning, snuggling, into her fur wrap, her piercing and engaging feline eyes a study in practiced nonchalance. She was just out of a marriage with George Jonas, a remarkable and gifted writer himself, and the man who told me some years ago — it's worth repeating — that when he fled communist Hungary for the freedom of Canada: "I thought I was fleeing a disease, but … it followed me." Sobering words, and more true now, than ever. The disease is here.

I was counting on a flood of new members from that mailing to NCC members. But the silence just fell deeper except from a few dozen who called

*Against The Tide*

or wrote to say they loved it. For most, I soon realized, Colin's jolly, in-your-face cartoons were all they ever wanted from the NCC, and certainly not mini lectures on politics and other intellectual challenges. I was duly chastened without another word spoken. David got more morose, and pale; nothing was funny anymore. So, after six months I resigned as Chairman and let him go back to running things. Clearly, I was not cut out for politics on the ground.

Meanwhile, the TD Club success turned our business around, and fast. We sold out our capacity membership of over 2,000 in the first six months and paid off all our loans. Some years prior to this, and due to the existence of the onerous lease at Mississauga that we had calculated would sink the family eventually, I talked Dad into using his holding company to buy the Mississauga property so that we could control that lease. So now, having seen the success of the downtown club, Dad and my siblings started talking about how they wanted to cash out. To sell both properties — Willowdale and Mississauga — in which two of my large, but lackluster suburban clubs were located. I said I wanted to stay out of the value question, and asked them to go to market for buyers, but to give me a right of first refusal. My accountant, who had seen us through all the near-bankruptcy years, warned: there is no way this can be done. The bank, he said, would never provide the size of mortgage I would need. I knew it was a lot to entertain with only one strong year under my belt. But with a combination of commitment to a large down payment to the family, with staged installments to follow for five years, and a pledge of the membership cash flow from all three clubs to back up the mortgage needed, I managed to raise sufficient financing to buy both properties, thus, to control my own leases.

## THE GAIRDNER FOUNDATION

As mentioned already, Big Jim, in part surely to compensate for his disappointment that WW1 had stolen his medical dreams, created The Gairdner Foundation in 1957, an entity dedicated to rewarding medical discoveries from anywhere in the world and aiming, in his own words, at "the relief of human suffering." He wanted to give pure cash awards for the greatest discoveries in medical science *without regard to nationality, ethnicity, gender, or any other feature of the winners or their circumstance.* As of 2023, the Foundation had handed its Award to 418 Winners, from 40 nations, and 96 of them afterwards won the Nobel Prize. Big Jim would have been ecstatic about this achievement. If you go to the Foundation's website "Our History" you can read a bit about it and see a happy shot of Big Jim painting a scene near his fishing lodge on Blue Lake, in northern Quebec.[13]

It was about the time we opened the TD Club that Dad resigned as Chair of the Foundation and I was asked to take over. So, I did. At the time I had 200 employees operating three large fitness clubs with over 6,000 members in total, owned two significant commercial properties in which two of the clubs were located, with about 50 small commercial tenants; was running The World Masters Cross-Country Ski Association with 15 of its eventual 30 nations already signed up, and we had five rambunctious kids at home. Life was very full. And now comes this Chairmanship; another duty, but a proud one. I'm not sure I did a great job, but it was strengthened a little during my tenure.

After I resigned a half-dozen years later, the Foundation decided to expand beyond its style as a closely held family-run foundation under its new President, Dr. John Dirks. He was a bright and effective leader who worked so hard no one else could keep up, and the Foundation's growth redounded to his credit like a work of personal salvation.

Now the Foundation wanted to find big government money. But I didn't, so I tried to fight it. My argument was that once you take government money you structure and expand the organization around that expectation, are then exposed by the need to keep funding the programs such money has enabled, and to economic downturns and changes of identity and policy that may be demanded by government. I knew that Big Jim would have detested the idea of taking government money — he said so, and vehemently — because no government will give money without something in exchange, such as a name change promoting the government, and will eventually insist on a whole gamut of politically correct objectives of the kind now plaguing all democracies. Such as: what about a Québecois Awardee? Or, what about a winner from Western Canada? What about more women Awardees? What about blacks, and other minorities? Maybe we need a homosexual winner (and the ludicrous extension: who is also Black? Female? Disabled? Transgendered?). I found this trend deeply offensive to the pure scientific purposes of the Foundation, and most of all, a betrayal of Big Jim's profound belief in the importance of the merit principle, the only standard he cared about! To defend him, I had to fight.

But Board members felt our Award was not big enough, each award being about $30,000 at the time. So, they insisted we needed more cash to give bigger Awards, or the Foundation would lose its considerable international prestige. I disagreed. The Greeks and Romans throughout their long rule gave an enormously prestigious laurel crown (or a palm leaf) to all sporting, artistic, and intellectual champions. "It's not about the money, dammit, unless you *make*

308       *Against The Tide*

it about the money. So, stick with the symbolic honour of the achievement," was my point. Honestly, I tried hard, but I got worn out, gave up, and surrendered the Chairmanship to other willing family members because, as my dear Jeanie, said, "you don't own it." So, I left, whereupon the Foundation turned turtle on its founding ideals of financial independence, self-sufficiency, and the pure merit principle.

Leaping forward now to 2006, I got the feeling that our future Prime Minister Stephen Harper — a man I knew personally well before that date (as I will explain in Part IV) was following me around surreptitiously. In the 1990s, after my writing career began, I had got to know him casually as a political operative and adviser to Preston Manning (with whom my life also intersected meaningfully — and I will explain the good and bad of that, too). Now, where was I? Oh yes … I felt like Stephen was shadowing me because right after I resigned as Chairman of the National Citizens Coalition … *he* became Chairman of the NCC.

And now, thanks to special pleading, Stephen's long — and arguably generous — arm was about to be felt right in the heart of The Gairdner Foundation, which felt that in order to sustain its prestige a significant one-time grant from the government was needed. Not incidental was the fact the Harper government would look very good in the eyes of Canada's medical science community. In the end, Stephen agreed to a one-time grant of $20 million, and the value of the five annual awards shot up immediately to $100,000 each. By the Gala Fiftieth Anniversary dinner in 2008, the influence of big government was clearly at work. In exchange for his grant, Harper wanted the name of The Gairdner Foundation, which had stood for 50 years, changed to "The *Canada* Gairdner Foundation." That was immediate, and exactly what I had warned of, to no avail.

I had also warned that next we would see government pressure for the Foundation to conform to political correctness policies, such as EDI ("Equity, Diversity, and Inclusion"). Which it has done. By 2019 the angry, resentful language that always accompanies radical EDI virtue-signaling was exhibited on The Foundation's website. And this, despite the fact that "equity" as used in the present neo-Marxist context always has an historical and political charge that assumes a class of oppressors, and a class (or classes) of oppressed, in all human activities, even in the field of medical science, and therefore assumes the existence of a myriad of invisible injustices. The Foundation had now taken the plunge into the murky waters of affirmative action. At once the flimsy, angry notion of invisible injustices permeating medical science pointed an invisible finger of accusation at the Foundation's historically merit-based Awards, and at the same stroke threw the prestige of all past Gairdner Foundation winners under the bus of suspicion. For if invisible systemic injustices exist everywhere now, they must always have existed, correct? Which implies that all past winners of the Foundation's Award were somehow bogus. This unavoidable conclusion made me feel sick, and still does.

So-called "diversity", another dishonest political principle, is also damaging to excellence because it leads straight to representational population-balancing quotas that undermine merit by their very existence, and assumes, again, that all awards given prior to a diversity-balancing regime were either racially- or gender-biased, or both, and therefore wrongly bestowed.

As for "Equality"? Before the law and in the eyes of God, this is a necessity, and a foundation of Western civilization. But as the cockamamie, but clearly erroneous notion that all human beings are absolutely equal in capacity, intelligence, effort, and achievement, and therefore all awards ought to be proffered in exact proportions to a population's social, wealth, racial, and gender mixture, is another direct threat to true excellence; another form of corrosive affirmative action (in truth, it's simply a reverse form of discrimination) that creates an immediate suspicion in any sensible person that winners have been chosen for political rather than purely scientific reasons. But this is the road the Foundation has taken, blind to these harms, and once the larger public begins to suspect the tokenism and race and gender (etc.) pandering for which even a hint of EDI calls, high reputation will be a goner. Recently, the Foundation has added the cute term "accessibility" to its slogan, giving us EDIA.

A year after I resigned, I attended an annual awards banquet under the new regime and saw the changes of which I had disapproved on display. This was clearly no longer an intimate family foundation event, a warm and wonderful celebratory dinner where all the guests were known to each other, and long-term friendships rekindled, such as we had by tradition at Big Jim's favourite spot, The National Club. It was now a show-event like those on the big-charity circuit. At those National Club dinners, I knew everyone in the room — usually about 120 of them — by first name. But I didn't know any of the guests at my table now. Not one. So, I turned to the fellow on my right, introduced myself, and asked him, "Why are you here?" He replied, "I have no idea. My boss bought a ticket and told me to come." I winced, with a sense of immediate alienation, and was quite certain Big Jim would have raised the roof. I had let him down.

At the end when guests were rising to leave, I felt a tap on my shoulder and turned to see Mark Cameron, a highly placed staffer in the Prime Minister's Office, whom I had met casually a couple of times.

"I was in the PMO office," he beamed, "during Dirk's fundraising visits to Harper."

I thought it gracious to thank him for the grant, though I didn't want it, so I did.

Against The Tide

Smiling with satisfaction, despite my somewhat damped delight, he said, "It didn't hurt at all that your name was connected with that grant."

Oh, irony …

## THE KINGS OF KETCHUP

Back now, to 1988. After three great years of solid business profits I found myself longing more than ever to be free and to speak out concerning the deepest moral and political changes taking place in my country, and so felt a growing urgency to sell the business, because I agreed profoundly with Thoreau who wrote in his 1846 essay "Civil Disobedience": "The best government is that which governs least." And now, almost as if in rebuke to all free spirits such as his (I was one), government was stepping in to control my business. They were telling me who to hire (via "diversity" legislation), how much to pay my employees (via "pay-equity" legislation), and the latest restriction was an Ontario law making it illegal for clubs like The Fitness Institute to charge more than twice their annual dues as an Initiation fee. Meanwhile, nearby golf clubs were allowed to charge their members Initiation fees ten times greater than their annual dues. The state was everywhere now. You can't run a business if the government is telling you who to hire, how much to pay them, and how much you are allowed to charge customers. So, I wanted out.

I had recently finished a book by Alain Peyrefitte entitled *The Trouble With France*. He was a grand fellow, and French Minister of Justice. The year I read his book he survived a bomb-assassination effort in front of his own home, in which the driver of his car was killed, but not him. His book was an autopsy of a once-great nation born in revolutionary liberty, now choking to death on its own slimy socialist entrails, gorging itself with immense tax harvests, and stumbling through an inebriated chase after a huge underground *maqui* of tax evaders. In short, France was in a war of survival with itself, too much government, too many laws, and permanent structural debt. Much like Canada.

Like clockwork, civilizations rise, run very well for a while, and then fall. But why? When the course of history is obvious to all who have spied it — from Polybius, to Toynbee and Spengler, and so many others — why can this mutation not at least be slowed, if not reversed? France was already what I thought of as a Tripartite State, in which one third of the people work to create wealth, one third work for government at some level, and one third receive significant state support in cash or in kind. So, you end up with two wolves and a sheep debating what to have for dinner. Game-over for the sheep (Baaaa …) — and for the nation. So, what duty do citizens have? I felt the call and duty to try to warn Canada. I badly wanted to write the book I was to call *The Trouble With Canada*, about the national mutation at work in my own country. Why not? I could do no more. So one day Jeanie told me, "Stop complaining. When you wake up at 4:30 a.m. fretting, forget coming back to bed. Make yourself a tea and go start your book." It was the best advice ever, and I plunged into the book, happy as could be.

Excited to imagine the life of a writer at last — this is how I want to spend the rest of my life! — I began putting out feelers to sell The Fitness Institute. Our long-time accountant Gord Beattie, was stunned. "What the hell do you want to sell for, after so many years of struggle? Why now, when it's making such good money?" My reply, was: "You can't sell it for much when it's *not* making money." He went silent, and I put out more feelers. I have reason to be very thankful now that I didn't keep it, because COVID would have severely crippled, if not shut us down.

My first try was a well-known American company called Club Corporation of America (CCA). I got President Jim on the phone. I knew CCA was an arrow-in-the-back specialist (and Jim more or less said, "that's our MO"). They scoop up poorly run failing clubs for a dime and turn them into profitable, very well-run operations. We were different. Already well-run, and profitable. So, Jim flew to Toronto to see our operation. I liked him. But after he left, he sent us his operative Walter Altholz, a swanky, swaggering urbanite in a black suit and tie, who started off telling me about his black Porsche. Then, he said: "We just want to give you a cheque." I knew right away this was his little puff of seller's tranquilizer, and nothing much was likely to happen. He just kept talking.

After he left, promising to "seal the deal" when he got back to Houston, I didn't hear from him for a while. So, I called and got one of his co-workers who warned me that Walter was, well, Walter. He said the standing joke around CCA was to ask: "What's the difference between a porcupine, and Walter Altholz' Porsche?" And the answer was: "With the Porsche, all the pricks are on the inside." That ended things with Walter. Jim called to apologize, and said, "I should have handled this file." I guess so.

The next interested party was a Toronto dental corporation named Tridont with had big ideas about developing a name in all sorts of health care. The head fellow had a black Mont Blanc fountain pen (but no black Porsche). His team was affable and seemed interested, so we actually penned an agreement in principle to sell them the company. At the signing, there were handshakes, and the fellow with the black pen, speaking of the coming change of ownership, said in the most sincere tone: "We'll make sure it's a smooth transgression."

You have to imagine the look Jeanie and I gave each other when we heard

Against The Tide

him say that,realizing that *he* hadn't heard himself. He called back the next day to say that instead of the cash part we had agreed on, he wanted us to take shares in Tridont. That just gave me a bad toothache and ended his transgression.

So, I kept writing. I had thick files spread all over the floor of my study, one for each chapter of "the book," yellow stickies all over the place, each file subdivided; an expanse of organized themes crying out for expression. This book wanted to write me. So, I put selling the business on hold for a while. But then, one day, while admiring the view of Lake Ontario from our amazing sky-high Downtown club — tiny sailboats like toys scooting over fluffy Lake Ontario, white sails zig-zagging in the wind — I was called to the front desk to meet a fine New York gentleman from the H.J. Heinz Company.

"We are basically a fat farm," he began, "and we want to change that perception." He was a pinstripe suited slight gentleman, with aquiline features and warm, kindly eyes. I liked him at once. No Porsches, no toothaches.

"Heinz is a fat farm? I thought it was a food company. Like, ketchup."

"Food is the main business. But ten years ago we bought *Weightwatchers*. They were doing weight-loss classes for, uh ... fat people. Diets, food recipes, and the like. Today, we run classes in over a hundred countries, 16,000 classes, every week. It's a great story. But we want to change the fatness image to fitness. We like what you are doing. The way you do it. Very professional."

Then, he launched into the backstory. "Weightwatchers got started by a very heavy Jewish lady from Queen's, named Jean Nidetch. She was fed up with being fat — we don't use the word "fat" officially — so she goes to her doctor for help. She say's to him, she is fed up with trying to lose weight. He's not the most compassionate guy, and tells her, 'You gotta stop eating so much.' She is already on the edge of tears, and says, 'I eat like a bird!' Well, you can imagine the scene. The doc looks up over his big glasses, and says, "Eat like a smaller bird." You had to laugh at that.

"So now, she breaks down in tears and stomps out with a few choice Yiddish words for him in her wake. And then? And then, she goes home, calls her fat friends, and they come over, and she says, 'Docs are useless. We gotta do this ourselves.' So, she basically works out these weekly weigh-in and talk sessions. Like a club. You know, true confessions, like Alcoholics Anonymous, diet and food talk, and so on. It becomes a kind of team effort to lose weight, and she calls it *Weightwatchers*. No charge. Just a bunch of people trying to solve a common problem."

"Well," he went on, "It so happened this overweight man was in her first class, and he thinks she is dynamite and has a terrifically motivating format. So, after class one day he says, 'Jean, I think you ought to charge for these sessions. They're *very* good.' She is shocked, and says, 'Charge? Charge for what? What would I charge?'"

"He looks out the window, where he sees people standing in line to buy a two-dollar ticket for a movie, and says, 'This is at least as good as a movie. Charge them two bucks. Better yet, I'm a retired advertising guy. What about we form a partnership? You do the motivating. I organize the business and look after publicity.'"

"Well, by the time we bought Weightwatchers, she was the poster girl, weighed 75 pounds less, and it was a roaring success."

"Today, Heinz does a lot more. Frozen food portions, cooking classes, magazines, licensing the name, and famous recipes. We even have a *Weightwatchers* chef named Franco, who lost 105 pounds with us, and now he's world famous. It's very funny. We call him '*the chef who lost his pot!*' That was a good one.

"Now," he says, "Heinz does $4 billion a year in revenue, and Weightwatchers is $1 Billion of that."

I was thinking this could work. I told him I was interested in selling because I wanted to change careers and become a writer. He liked the fact I was an Olympic athlete (and not fat). At the time, his boss, Heinz CEO Tony O'Reilly, was a Hall of Fame Irish Rugby star who studied philosophy in college, developed the famous Irish butter brand *Kerrygold*, was knighted by the Queen (so now, it was "Sir" Tony O'Reilly), was friends with Henry Kissinger, and that ilk, and headed up all sorts of charities, artsy institutions, and foundations. A powerful man. During his reign he took Heinz from a $908 million company to $11 Billion in annual revenue: not chicken feed. Everything he touched — not just Irish butter — turned to gold.

Soon, O'Reilly sent us his acquisitions man, Chuck Berger, who came to Toronto with his M&A guys to buy The Fitness Institute. He was short, midfifties, with white curly hair, softly inquisitive eyes, and a depthless curiosity. Chuck and I got along fine. Right off the bat when he learned I attended CU in Boulder, he shared that his daughter went there, too. But she had to drop out in her sophomore year because walking home from class one very windy autumn day — the same sidewalk I had walked — a small branch fell on her head (now, Chuck's eyes are watering), and she suffered brain damage. Besides his grief over his beloved daughter, what Chuck couldn't stand, I mean philosophically speaking, was the arbitrariness of the accident. Why her, just when that branch fell? Why *that* moment, under *that* tree?

He shared that terrible news like an old friend. We often got sidetracked in worldly discussions completely ancillary to buying the company while his lawyers and accountants waited patiently for us to get back to business. His wife was a large ("we don't use the word fat"), raven-haired woman with too

Against The Tide

much lipstick who couldn't stop talking and interrupting him, or me, which annoyed Chuck. When he and his wife came to our home for dinner, Jeanie and I sat with them by the fire for after-dinner drinks, lost in discussion, whence his exhausted wife leaned back in her chair, mouth open, and snored herself to sleep. Chuck was not embarrassed. He looked relieved. But he felt a prickle of need to explain why, for good manners, he wasn't waking her up. He just looked at her open mouth, at her big red lips, and said, "She needs to sleep." A sweet man.

Six months after completion of the sale to Heinz, O'Reilly invited me and Jeanie to an all-expenses-paid Heinz Corp gathering in Ireland. We rode rented bikes (followed by a Heinz chauffeur) on winding paths through Dublin's beautiful, sleepy Phoenix Park, a herd of deer in the shady distance, grazing under dark spreading oaks, heads, and ears smartly up as we passed. The next day, back to Phoenix Park to watch horse races; pipe-smoking gents in muted Irish plaids, women with dark black hair and shiny black Irish eyes, half looking at charging horses, flesh and flank rippling, and half at who was watching them.

This memorable visit included a sumptuous party with 200 guests at Tony's 18th century, 50-room Castlemartin Chateaux in County Kildare, about an hour from Dublin on the river Liffey, where it sits on 750 acres of gorgeous land and forest and busies him with a Stud farm of 155 brood mares and 350 Charolais beef cattle. What a life he had. Here is a shot of his estate.

The much-loved Liffey winds down to and all through Dublin, and through James Joyce's famous novels, *Ulysses*, and *Finnegan's Wake* (*"river run, past Eve and Adam's, from swerve of shore to bend of bay"*). Here it is running through O'Reilly's estate, where it looks a lot nicer than when it becomes sewage-infested in Dublin.

I had read Joyce's book, with a guide to its multi-layered meanings, and figured he ended "the novel" as an art form, because he tried everything he could possible with words, and better than anyone since. Molly Bloom's stream of consciousness soliloquy, page after page with no punctuation, was striking, mesmerizing (and also the closest young men and women got to literary sex in those days). At any rate Joyce transformed the river Liffey from an ordinary stream into a vital poetic symbol of life, time, and human history. So, the Liffey winds through our life now, too. And it's a Liffey-lesson, of river running and winding, that Tony O'Reilly's bright sun has darkened. In his eighties, he has been sued for very big money by creditors and forced to sell off many of his properties — including Castlemartin, on the river Liffey (for 30 million Euros). The river ran through him.

The sale of The Fitness Institute was completed fall of 1988, three years after the TD Club opened. So now I owned only the properties in which two of the three clubs were situated, but at 48 years of age, I was suddenly mostly retired, free from running an aggravating, problem-intense, day-to-day business; free to write now, and say what I thought needed saying. I immediately ordered a half dozen cans of Dunhill *Aperitif* pipe tobacco

*Against The Tide*

for the pipe I saw myself smoking as I wandered free, free at last, and fully contemplative under the stars, pondering that "*le silence eternal de ces espaces infinis m'effraie.*" I have never figured out the silence of the heavens (though I bought a big 14-inch Celestron telescope right after this sale, to try). Back-yard astronomy brought me closer to God. (I mean the feeling and wonder of what God must be, as I find few other explanations). It's not a real knowledge of God, which I think is impossible. The finite cannot possibly comprehend the infinite. But you can't look really deep — millions, no, billions of light years — into the cosmos, at entire galaxies and star-clusters with a big tele-scope like mine without feeling an immediate sense of insignificance and humility. Bow down, my friend, drown in wonder, is the feeling. Now, free at last, could I focus on saying something meaningful about this earthly life?

I didn't want to die saying nothing.

It was during this time that Murray Koffler, who indulged when he came to our club in what some of our staff described as "a Jewish workout" (some light jogging, very little exercise, followed by a full massage, whirlpool, and sauna), very excitedly he told Jeanie and me about Canyon Ranch, a walled health and fitness spa in Tucson, Arizona that he loved. Too much, as it turned out. He had sold his Shoppers Drug Store chain for many millions of dollars and was dreaming of recreating Canyon Ranch in King City, where I now live, as King Ranch Health Spa and Fitness Resort, which his son Adam, would run. What did I think of the idea?

We needed a vacation, so we flew to sunny Tucson to check this out for him, at our own expense. The first thing we saw in the beautiful Canyon Ranch Garden was a few white-gowned guests smoking by water-tumbled rocks under a shady saguaro cactus, some of them Murray's friends from Toronto escaping winter; supposedly cleansing themselves of over-indulgence in the good life. We tried a few fitness classes, which for us two athletes were just too easygoing. Neither of us liked massages, and the meals seemed like elegant, leafy-green rabbit food. Neither of us needed to lose weight. What we needed was a really good meal that we didn't have to cook. So, on our third night, we went "over the wall" to a local French restaurant for a *coq au vin* and some great red wine, and snuck back after dark like truants.

Murray was a friend of Dad's and had served on the FI Board, and I owed him true conclusions about his dream project. So, I laboured over a ten-page analysis of why his idea was never going to work, and my secretary walked it to his office. Two hours later Murray stormed — literally pushed his way — through the doorway, very red in the face, barged past my astonished secre-tary, straight to my desk and pointed his finger at … me.

"You!" he began, spitting angry, "You! I have spent almost $200,000 on marketing studies by the top firms in this city. They all *love* this concept. You're *the only one* I didn't pay. And you're *the only one* who says, don't do it."

"I'm the only one you didn't pay?"

"That's right, dammit."

"What does that tell you, Murray?"

Well, there was no point reiterating my reasons, so he stormed back out. Let's just say there were many, including "stick to your knitting." Sadly, Murray stormed ahead and built King Ranch anyway, an architecturally beautiful Arthur Erikson project in a gorgeous summer setting of rolling hills, trails, and forest. But at –30°C with two feet of snow, King City gets very little sun, and has no palm trees or saguaro cactus. So, nobody came, and less than two years later he sold it off at bargain basement prices to the Bank of Commerce as an executive training centre. Today, after several commercial iterations, it's the Kingsbridge Conference Centre. I'm not sure Murray got over the insult of that disappointment before he died.

## A FEW LAST, EMBITTERING EVENTS OF MY BUSINESS LIFE

Right after the business was sold I got sued personally for a million dollars by a cuckoo member who insisted one of our staff had "broken her back" by manipulating her legs in an exercise class. Really? This was a ridiculous accusation by a practiced court beggar moving in for her share of the pot. My pot. As a lifelong athlete I knew that to actually break someone's back in an exercise class you would have to whirl them around your head by the feet at least three times, then throw them into a concrete wall. But she was, our lawyer said, a "credible" witness (he meant practiced enough at the pity game to fool the judge and screw you).

We had a published company policy that our gym staff must never touch a member; and we were able to prove that the part-time staffer she accused *by name* was not even on the premises that day; and the court was told she had a history of collecting money by similar means. Nevertheless, the feckless judge, having heard all this, said "well, somebody did it," and ruled in her favour. How's that for evidence? I had to write her a large check. Smaller than a million dollars, but significant, and embittering. That made me happier than ever to leave the business jungle, at last.

On top of that, I got deceived by one employee, and defrauded by another. And those two experiences made me wonder if that's just the nature of business — eat or be eaten? Or was the loyalty I assumed, and had thought sincere

Against The Tide

merely a feeble front for their personal gain? Or was there something wrong with me that two employees I trusted a lot, turned against me so easily?

The deception was by an Officer of the Fitness Institute who was a go-getter at everything he tried and did a good job helping to make the company successful. However, After the Fitness Institute was sold to H.J. Heinz Company, I was now his landlord, and he immediately began asking for more leasehold improvements I thought were unreasonable. So, we negotiated for a while and eventually agreed on a new five-year lease term and signed a Landlord-Tenant agreement. But at the very same time, he was secretly negotiating an alternative lease to move the FI a mile down the road to a new business tower. In other words, he signed an agreement leading me to believe he was happy to stay for five more years, but the day after that he exercised an escape clause to terminate his lease and move out. In other words, he was dealing in what the law calls "bad faith" because there was "no meeting of the minds" when he signed our agreement. And he knew it. So, I sued Heinz. And they didn't like that. But they knew they were in trouble and would lose if it went to court. So, they asked me to drop the suit in exchange for an above-market rent for the Mississauga club lease (which I had told them I would not renew if they didn't settle first). This move enabled the eventual sale of our Mississauga property for a higher price than we otherwise might have received.

The fraud was perpetrated by a fellow we hired to manage the tenants at both our properties. He had done a good job for years and in retrospect, was amusingly loyal, for he often said, "I always treat your money as my own." And in the end, that's exactly what he did. My mistake was trusting him too much. Alas, our accountant trusted him too, and had approved us simply funding his personal management company to handle the expenses he submitted to us monthly, for the payment of which he would render cancelled cheques and receipts. This went very smoothly for many years. But when this Manager got into personal financial trouble he decided to divert our management funds to pay his personal expenses. He also took a cheque for $150,000 with only my signature as my dad's sole Executor on it, for deposit to my dad's estate account at the local TD bank, and then asked the Teller for a Bank Note in the same amount, which he took to Manulife to buy $150,000 worth of Manulife bonds made out in his own name.

He also told us some of our tenants were having trouble, so we needed to forgive them a lot of rent. But in fact he had asked them to stop making their rent cheques payable to our company, and instead make them payable to his own. So, we called the police and sued him for "fraud over $5,000" and had the goods on him. But the Crown Prosecutor was so inept we gave up in the end when, after a day of testimony as a witness for the Crown I was made to feel like a criminal myself. At the end of the day, I went after the TD Ombudsman for the Bank Note amount of $150,000, and was repaid, mostly. And then … the TD Ombudsman called me to say that our property manager had called him and personally admitted he had stolen from us, because he felt we owed him. This fellow had fooled the TD Bank, too. But his fraud against the Bank initiated a revision of TD's bank teller security protocols across Canada. So at least some good came of it.

Looking after some 35 different tenants in a dumpy neighbourhood was a real pain. I still get flashbacks of that first rainy day standing in the orchard, rain dripping down the back of my neck, with that sense of doom. There were constant worries in the night about break-ins and vandalism. On one occasion our cleaning staff opened the door of our tenant, a psychologist offering "Lifestyle Management" — and there he was, sprawled, dead by his own hand, on his office floor, blood trickling from his head over the carpet. Not exactly lifestyle management.

In 2001 we got a call from Mississauga police that the well-known boxer, Eddy Melo (24 knockouts in 38 fights) who was sitting in his car in front of Amici Sports Café — one of our tenants — was shot dead in the head point-blank along with his friend Johnny Pavao, by a 20-something contract killer named Charles Gagne. Gagne had already committed twenty armed bank robberies for which he was never caught, and said he just wanted "to move up in the underworld," with a contract-killing to his credit. When Melo's wife arrived on the scene her husband and his friend were stretched out on the black pavement covered with a tarp, firemen hosing their blood down the storm sewer. Gagne, who got a one-day escorted parole pass in 2017, told the parole committee, that when he pulled the trigger he saw the empty child car seat for Melo's son, and said, "I'm still haunted by the sight of that child car seat."

All of which is to say I worked hard; I got lucky; in business I loved making people healthier and fitter; and so on. But my original view of business life itself when my dad took me to the offices of Gairdner & Company, and I chatted secretly with that trader about Thomas Hardy, was as I felt it then. It's a difficult, somewhat dog eat dog world, that promised zero in the realm of the deepest ideas that mattered most to me. So, when the time came, and because I had no intention of still paying for my first mortgage at retirement like most of those York University professors, I had to take the gamble of going into business in the hope of making enough money to retire early, and write books. That's what happened.

And it caused an unexpected storm of reaction in Canada.

Against The Tide

# PART 4

## THE PATH FOUND:
## FAME, INFAMY, OUTRAGE

*Question: "How do you feel about having spent the last*
*35 years as a conservative author?"*

*My Reply: "like a man who has been standing on a rock in*
*a leftward-drifting sea. In the foggy distance,*
*I see leftward-drifting ships, and I hear*
*voices on deck saying, "Look, look — there's*
*a man out there ... drifting to the right!"*

Why would you do this to yourself, Bill? You had an early retirement and a nice, quiet life, the envy of many. Why make yourself a target for liberal outrage and media flack? Well, that's hard to say. A lot of praise and ego-pumping came with it, the instant public figure part. And who isn't susceptible to that? From the countless enthusiastic snail mail and email letters received over the years, a large number of grateful citizens have heard at least some of the moral and philosophical side of the story I wanted to tell. But you certainly need a thick skin and the courage of your convictions to do what I did.

This is a memoir, not a book review, so I will explain only the core motive for a few of my books, and some of the gratitude of readers. There has been a lot, most of it from the silenced majority. That's not a cute phrase. It is meant to describe the millions of Canadians who do not subscribe to the egalitarian-leftist direction our country has taken over the last half-century. I still have a binder full of their passionate and often very articulate handwritten snail mail letters. These people did not hit a few computer buttons. They had to get a decent pen and paper, write their thoughts out, find an envelope and stamp, find the publisher's address, and get it into the mail. I was very moved with every letter, and still am. And I guess you could say we still have a decent country, because hardly any of those letters were cranky or angry beyond the normal upset over the regime change they saw, and their frustration that it seemed inexorable. But there were no angry, fulminating letters damning me to hell. What I will outline below is some of the surprisingly prickly outrage my ideas immediately sparked from various media figures such as the CBC's Peter Gzowski, whom I met in his personal echo chamber on *Morningside* gripping a national microphone tightly for the manufacture of leftist opinion in Canada. Your tax dollars at work! Below is just some of the trouble with Canada.

Research for *The Trouble With Canada* (Stoddart, 1990) — a book revised 20 years later as The *Trouble With Canada ... Still!* (Key Porter Books, 2010) — made it manifestly clear that along with so many other Western democracies Canada was suffering a long cultural and moral regime change engineered by highly placed progressive radicals such as Prime Minister Pierre Trudeau, that was seeping into every aspect of civil society. This included a frontal attack on the moral and legal basis of the natural family, so I fought back with *The War Against the Family* (1993). Then, when the dismembering of the national moral fabric as a whole began through the spread of moral relativism, I wrote *The Book of Absolutes: A Critique of Relativism and a Defence of Universals* (McGill-Queens, 2008). You can hear an interview on that book with the CBC's then house historian Paul Kennedy.[14] Who knew? After this interview I suggested to Paul that what Canada needed from our "national broadcaster" was a truly open-minded talk from opposing perspectives. What about a show in which he speaks as a modern liberal on the issue of the day, and I from the true conservative position, then we open the lines for questions from the public and listen to the fireworks? I was worked up and enthusiastic about this notion. But Paul got up quickly, closed his office door, sat down hard on his chair, looked at me with a kind of eyeball angst, and said, "At the CBC? Not in a million years!"

At any rate, all my books have been part of one man's resistance to the ongoing assault on our historically common moral, family, sexual, and intellectual standards, an assault that has accelerated acutely and continues aggressively to corrode the foundations of our civilization as if propelled by some invisible, irrational, and bitter — though far from arbitrary — vengeance of the West upon itself. There is an ancient, perhaps apocryphal story that when surrounded by inescapable danger, a scorpion will arch its stinging tail toward its own head and kill itself. Just so, there is a perverse, potentially fatal inner logic to Western cultural and moral decay that I have made it my mission to reveal as clearly as possible.

The most moving and meaningful aspect of this work is the "voice" these books have given to millions of the more conservative, freethinking, patriotic, tradition-loving people who constitute the silenced majority of Canada. The most common response received, whether from business people, academics, wives, husbands, students, tradesmen, or artists, in countless handwritten letters, phone calls, and emails, still makes the hair stand up on the back of my neck: *"You put into words all the things I've been thinking and feeling."*

In those words, I found my happiness as a writer. When you dare to speak out in a leftward-drifting country like Canada, where most citizens don't have a clue, nor care, as to the history of their own nation, or the meaning of basic terms such as "liberal," "conservative," or "socialist," and most commonly are either drifting through life in an unexamined way, or — the converse — are blindly ideological and intolerant of all counter-argument, no matter how clearly expressed, you have chosen to swim against the tide, big time. Enjoy the appreciation from whatever quarter, but expect a tsunami of unreflective indignation, repudiation, and, in today's bizarre language — cancellation — from the unreflective.

I got cancelled lots, long before that term became popular. And I didn't mind. For as I say, when the pig squeals, you know the knife is in the right place. When *Trouble* first appeared, went into eight printings, and ignited a media bonfire across Canada, it felt very strange. Why did it become number 1, as quickly, while creating such a storm of immediate upset? This suggested a badly bifurcated nation, a country where the public is still sufficiently free to buy such a boat-rocking book — where it only got selectively banned, as I shall explain — but where politically incorrect attitudes are increasingly filtered, suppressed, and policed by a dominant liberal outrage. This suggested the people of Canada had been lolling along under a kind of national attitudinal anesthetic for a very long time, and those manufacturing and controlling their opinions didn't like me waking them up.

Today I have more respect than ever for what our Founders thought Canada ought to be, but less than ever for what it has become, and a much deeper concern due to our present tsunami of political correctness as to what's ahead for my five children and 16 grandchildren. They will have every right to point their fingers at *my* generation (but hopefully, not at me) for the closing of the Canadian mind. At any rate, I still tell them what my dad told me: *know what you think; say what you think; do what you say*; that they have a duty to speak up forthrightly and, as the diminishing number of freethinking citizens we have left are inclined to say, unafraid.

What follows is about some of the pleasure, and the price I paid, for speaking out.

## A STREAM OF ANGRY REJECTION LETTERS. THEN, A BIG SURPRISE!

I had a full head of steam and was half finished *The Trouble With Canada* when I began sending out a few chapters to some possible mainstream publishers. Before long, I got sharp snail mail rejections saying, or rather, shouting: "How can you say such things?" — along with other choice expressions of indignation (often poorly written). That was the first figurative cup of acid in this

Against The Tide

writer's face. I loved my country and was pouring my heart out in a sincere citizen warning. In fact, the subtitle I chose was "*A Citizen Speaks Out.*" And I didn't include "Ph.D." letters after my name because I wanted to address the intelligent public (not an oxymoron), rather than scholars. So, I called one of those outraged publishers and asked to speak to the woman who threw the acid. When she said, again, "How can you say such things?" I replied: "I *did* say them. What's your point? I can debate your arguments. I can't debate your emotions. What are your arguments?" She didn't have any, and hung up, with a sarcastic, "Good luck with your book."

That was my first indication that Canada was rapidly shutting down intellectually and morally. Our entire publishing industry and media, and almost all academics, were by their own admission in the hands of self-righteous left-leaning idealists with the same rigid views. They were shockingly anti-free enterprise (it's all greedy profiteering); opposed to traditional family (any combo of any two persons — or more — is "a family"); thought the legalization of homosexuality (and eventually, gay marriage) was "a must" (even though our own Parliament voted against it twice); and very pro-socialist (although back then they still wouldn't use such a label for themselves). As for the clear and bloody evils of communism? They simply ignored and excused them, said it wasn't done right, and behaved in general as if they thought that when the Berlin Wall came down all the Germans ran to the East.

They were all very supportive of taxing more highly anyone making more money than themselves (except for their favourite movie stars, athletes, and singers), ignorant of the fact that the top 20% of earners in most democracies already pay about 50% of all income taxes, while the bottom 50% pay around 9%. And of course, the term "corporate greed" issues from them like black blood oozing, even though a so-called corporate tax is actually a pass-through tax on consumers; on them! And of course, no entity in the entire country could be more "greedy" than our tax-gobbling, and manifestly wasteful governments. It is a bit stupefying that many of them think giving a vote on the laws to criminals (people who have made a career of breaking laws), is a good idea; and that we should be sending millions in foreign aid to "poor" countries, many of which spend more than we do on bombs, tanks, and fighter planes.

I was a classical liberal, even a libertarian in economics, and a Burkean conservative in morals, and tolerant enough to say that toleration and normalization should not be confused. I'm fine to tolerate a lot; but please, stop normalizing the abnormal and unnatural and pouring it into the heads of my kids and grandkids in the schools. To me, the world has seemed upside down for more than a half-century, and a small minority that has succeeded in capturing control of media, universities, and publishing, is now calling the shots and forcefully shaping public opinion; many of them doing things themselves once widely considered morally wrong and shameful, and shaming the rest of us for shaming them. It's a shaming war out there.

I didn't like any of this because it was intellectually weak and factually unsupported, and I felt I had sound arguments against all of it. Arguments, not just emotions. Still do. So, I decided to hell with them. I will have to spend some money and publish *Trouble* myself — if I could just find the right free-lance editor. The job could be done for $5,000, right? I could do my duty, then wash my hands of people whom I considered deeply misled, some of whom were manifestly radicals devoted to the revolutionary overturning of my country. Most of them are good people. But good people with bad ideas. Very bad. Ideas very harmful to civil society, to the building and preservation of our moral community, and so, to my country — and my children and their children — long term. And a lot of this demolition was being done in the name of "democracy," which people on opposite sides of so many questions were regularly citing in defence even of radically contradictory ideas. My job was to show why we should dump their bad ideas, for better ones. I had to offer better ideas. Maybe my book would engage them? (Boy, did it ever!)

The best freelance editor in Toronto at the time was a man named Fred Wardle. So, I sent him a few chapters to see if he might be willing to do my book. Fred called back three weeks later, and my heart rate jumped to 180 bpm. Toughen up, Bill, you can handle another rejection. "Bill. I liked your book. In fact, I liked it so much, I took it down to General Publishing. They're Canada's largest trade publisher. They want to see you, at 11 a.m. tomorrow."

"Really? Would you mind repeating that?" He did. I was stunned. This was every new author's dream. When I walked into that meeting with Fred, stodgy Jack Stoddart (President of General Publishing, since deceased), his Managing Editor Don Bastian (still a friend), and his design man, and his international rights fellow, Nelson Doucet, I felt absolute authenticity was the only way. *L'audace, toujours l'audace.* There were the usual pleasantries. Then Jack opened up.

"We don't have any idea who you are. Maybe you could start by telling us?"

At the time, and as mentioned previously, Mulroney's universal, tax-funded government daycare plan starting at $4 billion a year, was still in the air (and everyone knew he was lowballing it). So, I thought I might as well be direct, no beating around the bush.

"Let's just say you'd have to drag me stark naked across Canada behind a team of wild horses to get me to agree that government daycare is better for a child than a loving parent in the home."

Against The Tide

Eyebrows were raised as one, followed by a deep quiet.

Jack just stared. Then, a comforting relief seemed to settle upon the room because now they knew who they were dealing with, right out of the blocks.

"You know," Jack began, "we're liberals around here. But it's good for us to do a book like this once in a while. To show how open we are. Welcome to General Publishing!"

More than 35 years after that meeting, Don Bastian and I are still friends. As a conservative, Don was a round peg in a square hole, but a brilliant Managing Editor who was to see my book through the publishing process for Stoddart Publishing [a division of General]. When I began this memoir a year ago, he told me something I didn't know: "After you left that meeting, Jack turned to me, and said: 'This book won't sell a 1000 copies, we should do it anyway.'"

Then Jack sent me an author's contract which had all the paragraph-headers printed in gold. The gold print meant: "accept these terms, as written." A bit bold, the gold. So I bought a little guide for authors on how to negotiate a book contract, and sent back a very gently worded note, asking for a few minor changes. The next day it was pouring rain when a man in a turban driving a grimy yellow Toronto taxi pulled up at our home in Richmond Hill and dropped a large wet envelope on the doorstep. What's this?

Oh jeez, it's my manuscript. They didn't like my letter? I called Stoddart immediately, and got his cantankerous design guy, who sniffed, and said, "You been seein' a friggin' lawyer! Screw you. We don't want lawyers." I protested. "I haven't seen a lawyer. I just did my research and asked for a few simple changes. You're making a big mistake. This book is too important. You *have* to do it. Forget the changes. I'm bringing the manuscript back, right now." Which I did, and they went right to work on it.

## WILLIAM F. BUCKLEY TO THE RESCUE

At the time, Prof, that wonderful Prof, was the Founder of the now defunct *Stanford Conservative Forum*. He was a duck out of water at Stanford, which had just executed the most fatal miseducation move of its long history, in scrapping its venerable and mandatory year-long Freshman course on Western Civilization. And what a course it was — all any university student ever needed to get grounded in America's founding facts and truths and those of "Western Civ" as a whole. It got tossed and replaced by dozens of openly discriminatory affirmative action courses, all reeking of what two Stanford grads in a well-researched and damning book called *The Diversity Myth*.

Stanford University is now America's premier engine of cancel-culture, woke-ness, and the closing of the American mind. Shameful.

Prof's Forum was pushback against this trend toward intellectual and moral self-immolation. He began inviting top conservative speakers, writers, and philosophers to speak at his Forum, which regularly filled all 1,700 seats in Stanford's Memorial Auditorium. William F. Buckley was one of them. He was a hugely prestigious presence for all who knew his work and had some kind of Amazonian energy. He could write a sparkling, elegant, word-perfect opinion piece for the *New York Times* while having drinks with friends hardly aware he was scribbling his article under the table whenever there was a lull in the conversation. That is, when he was not crossing the Atlantic on a small sailboat.

When the increasingly leftist Stanford student body got wind of Buckley's impending visit, outrage ensued. The *Stanford Daily* newspaper ran excoriating articles condemning his views on everything. *Palo Alto Daily Post* did the same. And Stanford Radio couldn't shut up about how upsetting and "hurtful" it would be for Stanford students to hear Buckley speak. Poor things. Threats to shout him down ("deplatforming" and "cancelling" were not yet popular terms) were blared from radio. Posters sprang up like prickly weeds all over campus calling Buckley a racist, a capitalist pig, a homophobe, and so on. I was unaware that in the future I was going to get some of this treatment myself.

When Buckley showed up, Prof warned him of the ruckus. There could be violence. Maybe we should just go for dinner and cancel the speech? But Buckley, never one to back down from a good debate, refused. This was a man who, as a Yale undergrad, published a bestseller called *God and Man at Yale*, about how Yale had been repudiating its own classical and Christian roots. At the same time — as an undergrad! — he was debating important world leaders like Henry Kissinger, in front of sell out crowds, and trouncing them. His TV show, Firing Line,[15] which debuted in 1966, was a national arena for American and world debate that ran for 33 years — the longest-running public affairs show in American history. Here is a typical Firing Line discussion with the brilliant black political thinker Thomas Sowell, a man trained in scholarship by the great Nobel economist Milton Friedman. Sowell has been endlessly picketed at Stanford by black activists and labelled "an oreo" — black on the outside, white on the inside — for expressing opinions contrary to radical black ideas (if you can call them ideas). What a poised and elegant man.

So, Prof and Buckley formed a plan. Prof would go to the podium first, and briefly welcome everyone. But he would skip introducing Buckley altogether, so as to take the sold-out, but assumedly radical-infested audience, by surprise. Let's not give them time to react! Buckley would stand off in

*Against The Tide*

the wings behind a curtain, and at an agreed moment, would stride forward briskly from concealment and jump right into his speech.

For many years afterward, Buckley said he was never so delightfully surprised. He always spoke from a written text, and when he sped to the podium while pulling the speech from his jacket and opened his mouth to speak, he couldn't hear his own voice, because the entire audience of 1,700 people jumped to their feet and gave him a ten-minute standing ovation. What a moment!

After this, Prof told me the lesson learned: "All the negative fuss over Buckley was created by just four students — two editors of the student newspaper, and two announcers at Stanford Radio." They had learned the Soviet lesson for taking over a target population: get immediate control of all media, the universities, and airwaves. I was aware of this technique from my studies in the very bloody communist takeover of Eastern Europe, and never forgot it. Here was soft totalitarianism in action, where reputations are killed first, and then people. Here is a picture of Buckley with Prof's wife Ica at the Stanford Faculty Club dinner held in his honour after that speech.

When Prof told me of this interesting turn of events I asked, tenuously: could he approach Buckley for a blurb for *The Trouble With Canada*?

So, he wrote Buckley, who agreed, but was travelling a lot, and I would somehow have to get my manuscript to him on the go. There was no such thing as email then. Just phone, snail mail, and fax machines. So Stoddart copied the book and fired it off by courier. But hitting Buckley was like trying to hit a pigeon flying across the horizon with a .22 rifle, and we kept missing. So, another copy was sent to Hawaii to head him off, but we missed again. Finally, we got a copy to him, somewhere. But no blurb came, and Don Bastian was pressing me. On January 20, 1990, he said Stoddart would hold a space on the back cover until 5 p.m., then would have to go to press without Buckley. I sat staring at my fax machine for quite a while.

Then, *mirabile dictu*, the unmistakable sound of chipmunks chewing frantically began as the fax machine revved up, and Buckley's name jiggled forward with his to-die-for blurb. In all the years since, with 18 published books and many other blurbs, this was the best possible gift — from the man who all but single-handedly began the modern American conservative revival. Prof … I love you!

> Buckley wrote:
> "Dear Mr. Bastian, sorry I couldn't meet the deadline. I read most of the book, and it was quite wonderful. Herewith, a blurb":
> Mr. Gairdner sees bright and clear what Canada so greatly needs, and his mobilizing passion wonderfully animates an analytical precision that should be the reason for national — binational — celebration.
> — William F. Buckley Jr.

With this, Stoddart immediately ordered a first print run of 2,500 hardback copies of *The Trouble With Canada: A Citizen Speaks Out,* to be released in a month. I could hardly wait. But there was one more potential roadblock. Virtually all books published in Canada have a statement of slavish gratitude on the flyleaf acknowledging the support of the Canada Council, the federal Canada Book Fund, and — in Ontario — of The Ontario Arts Council, the Ontario "Book Initiative," and so on. Clearly, Canadian publishers and authors were up to their armpits in government aid, and I had criticized such capitulation to state-subsidization of the arts. In fact, in my book I quoted the then well-known author John Metcalf, who sat on a Canada Council jury.

Commenting on the state of culture in Canada, he complained:

> The big commercial publishing houses are subsidized. The smaller literary presses are subsidized. The smaller regional ogresses are subsidized. The writers are subsidized. The literary critics are subsidized. Translation is subsidized. Publicity is subsidized. More bizarre perhaps than anything else: the Writers' Union of Canada is subsidized!

In Metcalf's view (and my own, then and now), "the acceptance of subsidy means that consciously or unconsciously the writer is joining the State's enterprise. However arm's length the relationship, the writer is entering into a partnership with the State." And, he went on, the money is not given to promote literature. It is given "to promote books which the government vainly hopes will foster a greater sense of national unity — a national identity," an identity, I add, almost indistinguishable from the State itself. No thanks. I argued that all literature — all books — need to be taken away from the State and given back to individuals.

In short, I was disgusted by the grant-seeking effect subsidies had then — and certainly still have — on publishers, and on the choice of what books get published — or not. So, I called Jack to complain: "No book of *mine*, called *The Trouble With Canada*, is going to be published with government money!" For Gawd-sake, *this is part of the trouble*! If you need money, I'll give you a cheque myself!"

Jack never asked for a cheque, and to this day, that first edition is a collector's item because it's the only book by a Canadian published in the last 50 years that DOES NOT have those fawning government-subsidy statements on the flyleaf.

This wall-to-wall subsidization by the state of books and other literary works, only got worse. A year later I was invited with Jack to a 400-seat dinner celebrating the entire Canadian publishing industry. It was quite clear that the work of every single person in the room that night: authors, publishers, cover-designers, illustrators, editors, poets, and poetry mags, and too many others to mention — all except me, the only one — was government-subsidized.

## AN EXPLOSION OF INDIGNATION

*Trouble* was "released" on a Tuesday morning in March and requests for interviews poured in immediately from all across Canada; from CBC, CFRB, CHUM, and a lot of other radio and TV stations and newspapers, big and small, coast-to-coast, too numerous to mention. I was on talk radio live for 14 hours total in the first four days after the book's release — a shock to this citizen. And it didn't stop, for months. Actually, it went on for a few years at a slowly declining pace and changed my life radically. Suddenly, I was a public figure, a hero to the right, a lightning rod enemy to the left.

After a while, I heard that Peter Gzowski, the host of the CBC's national radio show Morningside was so upset with *Trouble* his producer wouldn't return Stoddart's call, even though the book had jumped immediately onto the *Globe and Mail* Bestseller List. I figured that as the CBC's head socialist, this was his way of killing my book, but I wasn't giving up.

Half the hosts were amazed and delighted, and said so: "Finally, someone is saying things about this country that *had* to be said!" The other half had a "How *dare* you?" attitude — "How can you say these things?" — and would have thrown tomatoes or eggs had they been able. French radio hosts were apoplectic about the *maudit anglais* [accursed Englishman], because I included a chapter called "French-Fried," criticizing Quebec as a soft-socialist state, within a larger socialist state. I argued that in a kind of "revenge of Montcalm," Pierre Trudeau's *Charter* had imposed a French-style Code Law system upon Canada's ancient English Common Law and free Parliamentary system, and thereby had infantilized Canadians by transferring the people's sovereignty to unelected (mostly leftist) judges of the Supreme Court, who cannot be removed by any power in the land.

Worse, since Confederation, Quebec, with its 24% of the population at the time, had been holding Canada to ransom by block voting in elections, and recently, for billions of dollars in "transfer payments" — a form of federal vote-buying (which is ongoing: $13 billion went to Québec in 2021, $0 to Alberta). A journalist from *La Presse* flew straight to Toronto for an interview with me (which, to his surprise, we did in French), and began by telling me I was "public enemy Number One in Québec." Good, I thought. Very good.

Andy Barrie, an American far-left radio announcer who became a conscientious objector, and so was trained as a combat medic instead of as a soldier, deserted the US army when they called him up for active duty in Vietnam, and fled to Canada where he ended up with CFRB Radio. He interviewed me, once, as if to shut me up. But he was a lousy debater who lost every argument we had, mostly because he was more interested in his own ideas than mine, and to say he was apoplectic and tongue-tied, was the least of it. He was frightened I was trying to turn Canada into the USA, when in fact, I was arguing Canada should return to its own roots in British liberty and follow Prime Minister Laurier's ringing declaration of 1896: *"Canada is free, and freedom is its nationality."* That's what I was doing with my anti-statist book. But he saw it as antithetical to his beloved soft socialism. So, I was immediately Andy's nemesis. And it got more pathetic. Six months after our show he showed up at a public event where I was just one of a number of speakers. I watched him approach the media table. When he saw my name on the list of speakers he spun around and left in a huff, like a kid. For his career in Canadian leftism, he ended up with an Honorary Doctorate of Laws degree from York University, and got the Order of Canada for his "achievement in Canadian broadcasting" (but also for his advocacy for those suffering from Parkinson's disease. So, he wasn't all bad. A medic, after all).

Against The Tide

But, what goes around comes around. Some years later I received this email from a book fan:

Many years ago I was listening to you being interviewed on CFRB in Toronto by Andy Barrie. Up to the point of that interview, I had always enjoyed listening to Barrie. He was educated, well read, and the interviews were interesting.

You were on as a guest to discuss *War Against the Family*. I seem to recall Andy Barrie trashed your book and was very antagonistic towards you as his guest. I wondered why he ever decided to invite you if he ended up carrying on the way he did?

Two things happened. I went out and bought the book. I grew to be suspicious of Andy Barrie. He moved over to host the CBC radio Metro morning show, for better than 10 years. Then, because of him I became suspicious of CBC. Anyway … All the best. Mike Brennan

## MY NUMBER 1 BESTSELLER, AND "THE PIANO MAN"

By August 4th, 1990, my book had been bouncing around near the top of the *Globe and Mail* Bestseller List for a few months, and had risen to a high of number 2 for a week or so, then started to slide slowly downward, on its way to booklist oblivion. Oh well, it was a fun ride. Stoddart paid for a bunch of my book trips to Vancouver, Calgary, Edmonton, Winnipeg, Montreal, and many other cities. I was supposed to have one of their "publicists" along to help. But I didn't want the company. From Toronto they would organize a half-dozen radio and TV interviews for each day of a three-day trip, and I exhausted myself doing interviews, grabbing cabs to the next radio or TV station, putting makeup on, taking it off, signing books by the box-load, and swimming against the leftist tide everywhere. I wish I'd had a cellphone camera, because one day at the Pearson airport bookstore I saw a stack of *Trouble* piled eight-feet high and just as wide from floor to ceiling like a big pyramid. By then, just a few months in, Jack Stoddart had sold 30,000 copies and my book was going into its fourth printing of eight total, for an eventual 50,000 sold — and still counting today.

On August 4th of 1990 Jean and I were sitting in our car at the ferry terminal in Nanaimo, ready for a trip back to Vancouver, seagulls flitting about pecking spilled french fries, the smell of kelp and moss in salt air. Jean went walking. I got a copy of the *Globe and Mail* and, figuring my book must have dropped off the list by now, I flipped straight to the Bestseller page and started reading from the bottom. Not there. It's gone, like I thought. The fun is over. I consoled myself by reading every title, moving slowly upward. It was an impressive group. *A Brief History of Time* by Stephen Hawking; *Wonderful Life*, by Stephen Jay Gould — such a fine writer, he was. There was even a book on that list — *Toward A Just Society* — by Pierre Elliot Trudeau and Tom Axworthy, both notable leftists.

Then, in a rush of surprise and joy I could hardly describe, but still feel today, I saw this:

## THE GLOBE AND MAIL NATIONAL BESTSELLER LIST

| THIS WEEK | NON-FICTION | LAST WEEK WEEKS ON LIST |
|---|---|---|
| 1 | The Trouble With Canada, by William Gairdner (Stoddart, $29.95). An essay on a country hurtling toward economic, political and cultural ruin. | 8 / 16 |
| 2 | Father, Son & Co., by Thomas J. Watson Jr. and Peter Petre (Bantam, $27.95). The story of the father and son who built the IBM empire. | 9 / 6 |
| 3 | Barbarians At The Gate, by Byron Burroughs (HarperCollins, $29.95). The story of the $25-billion takeover battle for RJR Nabisco. | 1 / 24 |
| 4 | A Brief History Of Time, by Stephen W. Hawking (Bantam, $24.95). The Cambridge astrophysicist attempts a coherent theory of the universe. | 7 / 27 |
| 5 | Towards A Just Society, edited by Tom Axworthy and Pierre E. Trudeau (Viking, $29.95). Essays by Liberals examining their last government. | 4 / 19 |
| 6 | The Sea Is At Our Gates, by Tony German (McClelland & Stewart, $39.95). A popular history of the Canadian navy. | 10 / 8 |
| 7 | Read For Your Life: Literature As A Life-Support System, by Joseph Gold (Fitzhenry & Whiteside, $27.95). Bibliotherapy: reading books as the new wonder drug. | 6 / 4 |
| 8 | Wonderful Life, by Stephen Jay Gould (Penguin, $27.95). An examination of bizarre life-forms in British Columbia 530 million years ago. | - / 10 |
| 9 | Megatrends 2000, by John Naisbitt and Patricia Aburdene (Macmillan, $29.95). The future predicted by viewing broad social phenomena. | 2 / 27 |
| 10 | My Traitor's Heart, by Rian Malan (Little Brown, $23.95). A white South African exile comes to terms with his country, his tribe and his conscience. | - / 6 |

Pure, unadulterated joy and pleasure is rare in a life, but this was certainly it. Wow. Not just the pleasure of topping such accomplished authors — and especially the pleasure of topping Trudeau, the arch-villain of my book — but seeing in black and white before my eyes that the biggest gamble of my life had actually turned up an Ace. After all those years I had actually found myself, and my happiness, couldn't get the smile off my face, and won't ever forget Jeanie's look when I showed her the list.

Against The Tide

Then, it was onto the phone with her sister Teresa to plan a celebration dinner at Il Giardino's, our favourite Vancouver restaurant. This was going to be such fun! Il Giardino's (relocated since) was a wonderful Italian restaurant run by the famous chef Umberto Menghi, and to walk in was to walk into Tuscany. Large burnt-umber tiles underfoot, the sound-swell of 50 happy diners chatting and laughing in an open-air courtyard, red-brick walls dripping with bougainvillea and hibiscus, glasses and tableware tinkling, the smell of wonderful pasta sauces (as you walk, ducking under hanging red peppers, dried corn cobs, and onions), see red wine splashing and swilling in sun-glinted goblets. And there, in the middle of that happy crowd was a white-clothed table with four chairs, waiting. There was already a buzz in that happy space. Teresa's husband at the time was a well-known emergency physician in Vancouver, and the woman running reservations was one of his patients. So, we got that special table, and special treatment, other guests already wondering: who is this for? Unknown to us, there was a famous fellow already seated right beside our table.

A lot of great food and wine kept arriving, and that wonderful mood is preserved in memory. I was watching, my soul peaceful, life is good, when Jeanie nudged me to tell me about the famous man beside us. "Don't look now — but the fellow sitting to your left is the singer, Billy Joel." I didn't know what to say. She was used to my non-reaction. I have never much liked popular music unless it happens to be joined with a memorable event or woman. But Jeanie loves it and loves to tease me whenever I tell her I haven't heard a song that everyone else seems to know, or when I can't say the name of even one (apparently) hugely popular singer such as Billy Joel. Raised as a choirboy singing difficult classical compositions, often *a capella*, and as a lover from boyhood of fine tenors like Di Stefano and Pavarotti — and yes, of that shirtless, grimy, but oh-so-happy Italian stevedore belting it out on our ship in Montreal — well, I figure that compared to them, most popular singers can't actually sing. It's cheating. Microphone-amplified singing, where even a sultry whisper can be made to sound awfully good. But put them on a stage without a microphone, walk 15 rows back, and you'll hear mostly very strained voices.

Anyway, I didn't look. At least not in an obvious way. I just turned my eyes slightly leftward. But Billy Joel caught me. A nice-looking dark-haired man with a tan, puffing on a big cigar (Oh my, what do I say to a famous singer?). He hitches his chair toward me, just a little, and bends over, near my ear. Right away, I thought, maybe his nose was a little out of joint because he was so used to being the center of attention himself, and obviously we weren't celebrating *him*. But no, he was just real curious. He asks, "What are you celebrating?"

"My first book hit number 1 on the national Bestseller list today."

"Oh?" he says, with a pleasant smile. Like, he really appreciates a winner. "Congratulations. What's the name of the book?"

"It's called *The Trouble With Canada*."

And this moment happens. Billy Joel looks up from his chewed, damp-ended cigar, waves a little smoke away from one squinting eye, looks around at the wonderful setting in that beautiful walled garden at Il Giardino's, takes another puff, and says, still squinting, "I don't see any trouble."

By this time our table was watching me and Billy Joel, and they heard what he said, and the laughter burst from us, and from him, like water from a dam.

I told him, "That's a riot. I don't see any trouble, either. At least, not here!" But he was very pleased with his observation, and the laughter he drew. It was one of the funniest things he could have said, and whenever Jeanie and I remember it, we still laugh.

We also laugh, because she tells me that on our way out of the restaurant later that evening, my face in her sweet blonde hair, I whispered, "I thought that Elton John fellow was *really* nice."

## PETER GZOWSKI'S *MORNINGSIDE*

*The Trouble With Canada* bounced around between number 5 and number 2 for months before it hit number 1, and during those months I had done interviews with just about every big radio and TV show in Canada — except Gzowski's Morningside. It was no secret to anyone inside the leftist vacuum that Peter was "Mr. Canada," a man whose great-great-grandfather had a hand in building the Welland Canal and did a short stint as Lieutenant-Governor of Upper Canada. Peter wasn't building canals; he was the CBC's house socialist (though not sufficiently frank to use that term), helping to engineer the progressive state, and he was damn well not going to give an anti-statist book like mine any of *his* airtime. Stoddart's publicity folks had tried, but no potatoes.

So, I figured I'd try myself. I called his Producer once a week or so for a couple of months, and to her I was soon like a fly she had to swat. She would chuckle a little. "It's You? Again?" But when the book hit number 1, I just wanted to hear her turn me down. So, I said, "C'mon. It's number 1 in Canada, and you're still not going to do an interview? You're gonna embarrass yourself." She replies: "Peter can't interview everyone who thinks they have a good book." To which I say, "number 1 in Canada is more than good. It's the best. It's what the Canadian people think. C'mon. You're Canada's public

Against The Tide

broadcaster." And Low and Behold, after a moment or two, she relents, and says, "I'll try." And she did. And soon I had a date with Peter Gzowski.

When I walked into his darkened CBC studio, I saw the famous man sitting bent over in his high-backed chair behind an imposing desk, black microphone waiting. Already looking at me askance. He had a not very kempt beaverly gray beard, was half-done smoking a cigarette, one eye wincing from a curl of grey smoke moving up his cheek. Without looking at me directly he made a limp-wristed, dismissive hand motion that I should sit down in the cushy victim chair in front of his desk. "Down" was the right word. I was at least one head level below Hizzoner and could see he loved this positioning: me looking up at our National *Eminence Grise*.

Peter was known (at least when he wasn't simply begging for more government funding for another favourite left-liberal arts cause, or more affirmative action for something or other) as a sensitive interviewer. And he was. I love nuanced thinking and speaking, and he was always such, though always in the same damn pro-government, pro-public-funding vein. Anyone who wrote or spoke against the Canadian welfare state, or against the visions of Saint Pierre (Trudeau) that danced in his head, or who disagreed with Peter that America is a burning hell compared to peaceful, generous Canada the Good? Why, expect to be shunned. Peter was the gatekeeper voice of statist Canada. But I was on his show now, and we did a 20-minute interview you can hear right here. It's worth a listen, and part of our history now.[16]

It starts calmly. But after a while you can hear Peter getting heated. The old beaver begins to gnaw furiously at the tree he really wants to fell. I could feel his yellowed teeth on my knees. He gets much more interested in fighting his version of the arguments in my book, than in telling his audience what I *actually* said. In a while I will tell of my second "interview" with Gzowski a couple of years later over my second book, *The War Against the Family*, where he really went ballistic and lost a lot of fans.

## MY CHAT WITH PREMIER DAVID PETERSON, ON SO-CALLED "PAY EQUITY"

It so happened that a few weeks after *Trouble* hit the street, a tweaky-nosed, thin little man in a dark suit with a briefcase showed up at our company door with a Government of Ontario "Pay-Equity" Checklist. A what? He had been sent by Ontario Premier David Peterson's liberal government to assess whether or not all the jobs at The Fitness Institute satisfied the government's revolutionary new standard for pay-equity. Very few understood that while equal pay for equal work seems logically fair — you should pay a man and a woman, anyone, the same for doing exactly the same work. But so-called "pay-equity" is not about that. It's a radical feminist scheme to increase the pay of women who happen to choose, or simply end up in, lower-paying jobs. The Checklist compares the demands of typical female-chosen jobs to higher-paying jobs men tend to choose. This nattily dressed government twerp incensed me with his inane Checklist, because I had just researched the whole topic and published a critique eternally shaming the pay-equity scheme in *Trouble*. You might say I was ready for this dude.

He began by telling me his Checklist would compare say, the job of Maureen, our female cafeteria cook, to the work of our maintenance man Austin, to see if they were of equal "value." To whom? I asked. Blank stare. It didn't matter. He would decide job value according to his job-scoring system, and if he decided they were the same, he would order me to pay Maureen, whom everyone loved and who did a great job preparing breakfast, and soup and sandwiches for lunch, $10,000 more per year to match the pay of Austin, who had a gas licence, and was often hauled out of bed in winter at minus 25°C to climb up a ladder onto the roof in a 50km wind to fix a frozen gas pipe.

I complained: "When we advertised for a cook at her pay, 25 women applied. But when we advertised for a maintenance man at the same pay as her, nobody applied. No one wanted his job until we raised the pay to what are paying him. You are intruding into the free market for labour, then dictating

Against The Tide

false job values to private owners. Get the hell out of here." And I all but pushed him out the door.

Then, very upset, I called Premier David Peterson's office, and was surprised to get him on the phone. His second in command was Ian Scott, Attorney-General of Ontario and an out homosexual, which I mention only because he was a force in the destruction of our traditional marriage laws (which he called "discriminatory") and was deemed a so-called "intellectual soul" of Peterson's leftist government. In other words, he was a reasonably intelligent lawyer who, at the urging of the far-left NDP with whom he had negotiated a coalition enabling Peterson to become Premier, drafted and published a "Green Paper on Pay-Equity," likely at the pay-back urging of radical feminist Dippers such as Judy Rebick, a self-confessed former Marxist whom I was later to debate on air.

Shame on Peterson. He hadn't a clue, intellectually speaking. When he came on the phone, I raked him over the coals by turning his own points against him.

Premier Peterson: "Our pay-equity policy is justified, because we know there's a 30% wage-gap between men and women in Ontario.

Me: "That's because of marriage. Canada's own StatsCan tells us (I cite the file for him) that never-married men, and never-married women, make exactly the same pay at every stage of life. Except in the first few decades of working life, never-married women actually make *more* than never-married men. But once women get married, once they choose family and children over working; they either quit altogether, or they choose to work part-time; or they refuse more demanding higher-paying promotions so they can spend more time with their children. Averaging all this, is how you get the 30% figure."

Premier Peterson: "Really?"

Me: "Yes. Furthermore, we have a lot of other "wage-gaps" in Ontario. Are you going to legislate against those, too?"

Premier Peterson: "Like what?" Spoken in disbelief (now, he sounds worried).

Me: "Like StatsCan also tells us we have a "bachelor wage gap." Bachelors make about 30% less than married men in Canada. And StatsCan also tells us there is an "ethnic wage gap;" which is to say, there are significant gaps between every ethnic group in Canada, from top to bottom. Jews are at the top by a wide margin, followed by people of Japanese origin, English origin, and so on, down the ladder, maybe a hundred ethnic wage gaps, all the way to the bottom. Then I read him off some of the actual numbers (shown below), and then ...

"So, Mr. Premier, Sir, what do you plan to do about the Bachelor wage gap, and all those Ethnic wage gaps?"

**Wage & Salary Differences in Canada, by Selected Ethnic Groups, 2005**

| Ethnic Group Average Male Employment Income | |
|---|---|
| Jewish | $ 72,311 |
| Japanese | $ 51,988 |
| English | $ 48,088 |
| Greek | $ 45,612 |
| Chinese | $ 38,307 |
| West Indian | $ 37,261 |
| N.A. Indian | $ 31,681 |
| Inuit | $ 29,967 |
| French | $ 42,142 |

*(Source: www.12.statcan.gc.ca/english/census06/data)*

Premier Peterson: (You could hear the silence), "You know Bill ... it's just politics."

Wow. The smooth-talking fellow leading us had no facts on hand or intellectual substance. He was just another clever finger-in-the-wind politician. Liberal-Democratic systems seem to attract this kind of personality like flies to honey. At any rate, this was my introduction to deeply cynical grassroots politics.

One night not long after this experience I was minding my own business and happened to flip to CBC TV, where I was shocked to see Wendy Mesley on the screen, livid, and fulminating about *Trouble*. What's this? She's talking about *me*? We had never met or spoken. She never called to discuss her problems with my writing. But there, right before my eyes I see a full-on, full-screen, personal attack on me. Not on my book; but directly on me, and broadcast to the whole nation. She starts as an outraged, indignant, virtue-signaling, talking head, then shows the nation a full-screen banner yelling that author William Gairdner is anti-feminist, anti-immigration, and anti-French.

But none of it was true. She didn't like (but couldn't answer) my argument, above, that "pay-equity" schemes are in fact radical feminist pay-gouging scams interfering with the liberty of all free citizens, male or female, to pay as much, and work for as much, as they choose.

And ... I wasn't against immigration, either. I just didn't see why any elected government — here today, gone tomorrow — should be allowed to suddenly change the ethnic composition of an entire, historically

*Against The Tide*

majority-Euro-Canadian nation, without asking the people if that's what they wanted? They clearly didn't. I wanted to know, how does that square with "the will of the people."

And I love French culture and (unlike Wendy) am fluently bilingual. But I get annoyed to see Quebec issuing big fines to English-speaking business owners under draconian language laws, while holding ROC (the Rest of Canada) to vote-ransom for unconscionable billions in handouts every year paid by the rest of us. Like, hey, Wendy shouldn't Canadians at least discuss these things?

But Wendy helped me see I was now deeply engaged willy-nilly in a long-term civil war of values. With Ontario's Premier. With the CBC. Correction; not a war of "values" (a mushy, relativistic word), but a war over underlying *principles*. Clearly, the national discussion had to be elevated, sharpened, on every topic I wrote about. But so far, my book wasn't elevating anything. It was causing pea-brained people like Wendy to harden their positions emotionally, rather than clarify, discuss, and defend their arguments rationally and factually.

A fitting irony to the Mesley story is that in June of 2020, a new, self-abasing, virtue-signaling Wendy got de-platformed herself! And (this is amusing) — by her own troops, for using an "insensitive" word in a private meeting. The word was apparently so outrageous that all present went into immediate adrenalin-shock, and when asked to convict herself by repeating the word out loud, Mesley couldn't. No one could. As if the word was so toxic it destroyed itself in a puff of smoke, leaving just a rancid odour in the room. Then, Canada got treated to her supine, begging apology: "I was careless with my language, and wrong to say it. Regardless of my intention, I hurt people, and for that, I am very sorry. I am also deeply ashamed." This is really juvenile, finger-in-the-throat stuff.

Then, in early July of 2021 she admitted publicly that she did, yes, really, indeed, use "the N-word," and resigned from CBC altogether to refashion herself as "a free-range journalist" — a variety of free-range chicken. Then, on July 10, in an act of vengeful self-justification and fault-finding that included further self-abasing apologies, she wrote a *Globe and Mail* article attacking the CBC, complaining that free-speech advocates were now supporting her (the horror!), and — a delicious irony — whined that CBC had missed an "opportunity for sparking meaningful discussion." Instead, "I was shamed, blamed, and cast aside." But Wendy … frank discussion was all *I* wanted when I published *Trouble*; and instead, you shamed, blamed, and cast me aside. Hmmm.

Some years after she attacked me on air, Wendy married Peter Mansbridge, the CBC's highly respected, prematurely balding news-Buddha, probably Canada's most famous high-school drop-out — he of the kindly, passionless eyes, monotonous voice, and stumble-free, ruffle-free self-assuredness. He was the perfect straw-Canadian; every damn night for 29 years; Canada's newsman in net, at whom no one ever took a hard shot. But I had a run-in with him over the Sikh Turban, which I will tell of soon. And I took a shot.

## LUNCH WITH THE OMBUDSMAN OF THE CBC

Call it a public duty. I didn't think Canada's national public broadcaster should get away with carelessly smearing an honest citizen and his book. Boy, was I naïve! I guess when you get $1.2 billion of public money every year to shape public discourse, you can smear whoever you want! So more from a sense of citizen duty than a desire for revenge, I sent the then CBC Ombudsman, a brief description of what Wendy had done (he had seen the tape), and my complaint that it was an unintelligent, uninformed smear job. It was just bad journalism. I didn't mind being criticized. We needed to elevate public debate. Couldn't Canada's public broadcaster do better than this?

The Ombudsman responded at once by inviting me for a nice lunch. A little Canadian white wine, pan-fried Canadian trout, and Canadian maple syrup on a dollop of ice cream. He was perfect for the job of unruffling the feathers of a CBC audience or, you might say, for pan-frying complainers. He began with a tortured exculpation of prickly Wendy's words. The CBC is over-worked, and underfunded, and so on. He didn't exactly weep at this point, but his head went down and his voice went up; he was holding back (he wanted me to know), a *genuine* concern. If the CBC just had more money, it could be much more thorough. I waited for the word "fair," but it never came. Wendy's perhaps hasty apprehensions were, he thought, well, understandable (given the public mood); she didn't really misspeak; the incident with me was more, perhaps (if you agree), a possible misunderstanding of her underlying intent. She was a little "too surface," he thought; after all, you can take political ideas either way, right? And the CBC should have, well, made *that* very clear. It was as if he was reading an invisible script from some lazy communist agency specializing in the saccharine mollification of distressed citizens, easing their way, making public discomfort comfortable. My Stanford Ph.D. in English Literature and Philosophy was entirely inadequate to decipher what he was getting at, because he wasn't getting at anything — except a wrinkle-free continuation of the CBC's moral and political hegemony, funding, and devotion to a certain kind of public-broadcaster psychobabble. Jean-Paul Sartre spoke of certain problems having a built-in "coefficient of adversity" — an

Against The Tide

innate measure of difficulty — that appears immediately upon attempting to resolve them, and that will always defeat you. I finally knew what he meant.

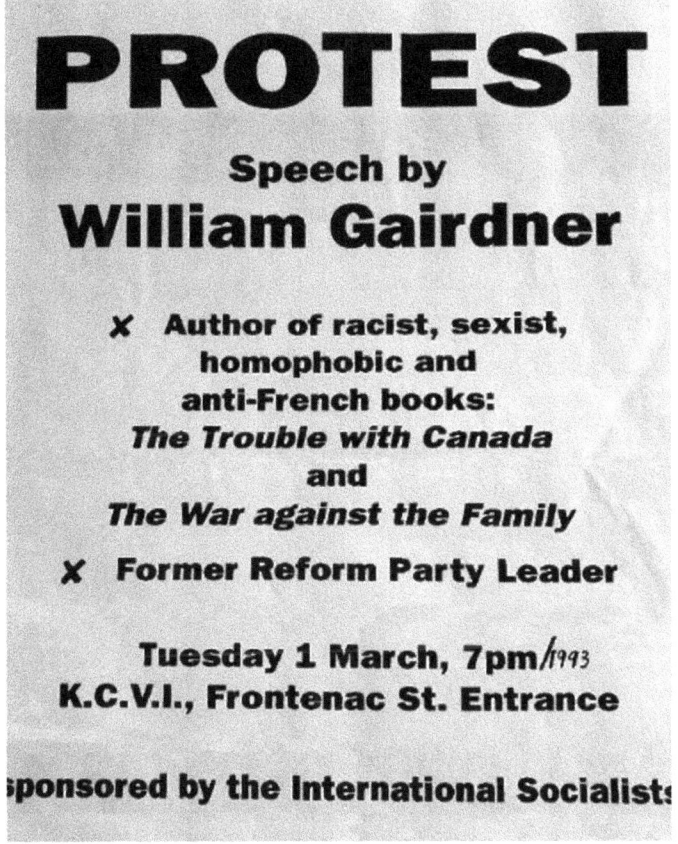

## PICKETED BY "THE INTERNATIONAL SOCIALISTS" – A RARE DISTINCTION!

In spring of 1993 I received a phone call from two student members of the Law Students Society of Queen's University inviting me to debate a notoriously smug leftist law professor — they described her as a tenured feminist radical — named Sheila McIntyre. They despised her teaching but feared debating her publicly because … they wanted to graduate. So, would I come to Queen's? The topic would be "Equality."

When I walked that evening with my hosts toward the debate venue, a wondrous sight unfolded before my eyes. We had about 50 yards to go on a concrete sidewalk lined on all sides with picketers making quite a racket, chanting leftist slogans, handing out leaflets, and jiggling placards. What was this? Who were they picketing? But then — I can still remember the slight shiver of apprehension and delight — I was astonished to see *my name* plastered all over those signs and leaflets, produced by (really?), *The International Socialists*! What? In Canada? The Socialist International? Was this some kind of political groundhog day when all the socialists come out of their dark holes?

I had a distinct sense of sleepwalking a gauntlet through a fantasy, for it was immediately clear they had no idea who I was. They were shouting and protesting a "speech by William Gairdner," but weren't aware it was me walking slowly past them. This was just too funny to believe, so I chatted briefly with a few of them, extending my hand which they took and shook vigorously, and went on into the debating hall. Now, very few Canadians have been picketed by the dinosaurs of international socialism, so from its place of honour on my study wall, here is the leaflet they handed out. You couldn't buy this.

But you could hardly imagine the reality-warp this produced in my mind and heart, for I am probably a racialist (a patriot, and proud of my own race, if not of everything we have ever done) like every other human being, but certainly no racist (someone who hates another race); and proud of my sex, too, but unsure what a word like "sexist" is supposed to mean, as I have loved lots of women, starting with my mother and sisters. As for homosexuality? I am for toleration, but not for the social or moral normalization or promotion of gross homosexual practices, especially to children in schools. Alas, Canada has never had an open public discussion about whether or not homosexual practices, even if we think they do no harm to consenting individuals (which is not proven), should be normalized and promoted as good for society as a whole? At the time, Ottawa had a special bureau publishing Canadian Statistics on AIDS and was on the record that about 80% of all AIDS deaths in Canada were of homosexual men. So, this didn't strike me as a healthy behaviour to normalize or promote to the nation or to kids.

And as mentioned above, I am fluently bilingual in French, and love French culture, literature, philosophy (and food — yummy). So, all of these ignorant charges were rather off-putting. Couldn't these lump heads at least read the friggin' book? Just my thoughts in passing that poster. Oh, and … I was never a member of the Reform Party, either, let alone a "Leader" of it. So, the entire poster was a lie. But I grabbed a copy of it as a rare souvenir and went forward to our debate. *The International Socialists*! … I loved it. The dagger was in, and they were squealing aplenty.

The theatre held about 400 students, with more jammed in (illegally, someone shouted) up and down the stairs on all sides, and extra speakers were set up in the large foyer outside the auditorium. Professor McIntyre made it clear she was openly dedicated to the destruction of our historical and constitutional concept of law, arguing that the differences between people

Against The Tide

and groups in society are not natural, circumstantial, or merited in any way, because "systemic" oppression (racism, discrimination, inequity, etc.) exists throughout society. This was 1993, and although that thoroughly envy-based notion, critiqued today as neo-Marxist, has by now permeated all Western democracies, it was then a newly emerging complaint about "inequality" and anything and everything an angry and envious person could think of that could be deemed "privileged" and "systemically" oppressive.

Now inequality before the law should offend any reasonable person, but inequality in the outcomes of people's lives? Oh, so compassionate Sheila began our debate by saying she wanted all her (mostly male) oppressors to "get your foot off my neck." She wanted the law to create equality of outcome by treating people differentially; by handicapping those with privileges of income, birth, skill, merit, class, and so on, and bestowing compensating advantages on those without such things. In other words, she wanted professors, lawyers, judges, and Members of Parliament to be social engineers. To engage directly in the very sorts of discrimination banned in our *Charter*, to arrange the future egalitarian utopia of which she was dreaming.

I argued that the normal concept of law in the West has always struggled against radicals like her by insisting that in a free country, all people, rich or poor, smart, or stupid, strong or weak, without distinction, must be judged by the same apolitical Rule of Law. That by and large, and despite natural or circumstantial inequalities and outcomes, that's more fair. But radicals like McIntyre amuse themselves with the observation of the French socialist Anatole France, who quipped that in a free society the rich and poor alike are free to sleep on park benches. Her complaint was that formal law can produce only "formal equality" (all citizens are free to sleep on the benches), as distinct from a "substantive" equality under which everyone will have roughly the same material outcomes in their lives. She was still naïve, and unaware that in thoroughly socialist societies where there is an equal distribution only of misery, everyone is going to end up sleeping on park benches — except the professionals, like her, who run the equalization scam.

Freedom-lovers — I am one, reply — and I did, that if the law is anything besides formal, it becomes the rule of men, rather than the rule of law. Then, left, or right and overnight, the law becomes a political weapon. Freedom from this kind of law, I argued, is more important than forced substantive equality, because as forced equality goes up, freedom must immediately go down. So, the law should tell us what we cannot do, but otherwise leave us alone, and free. There is a real danger in switching to her kind of substantive law, because throughout history, whenever the law gets seized by social activists like Sheila (who may themselves have good, if misguided motives) it soon thereafter gets captured by much stronger political activists who, as we have seen in all prior revolutions, quickly shove the soft intellectual types like her aside. And then, with all customary legal safeguards gone, anyone, and any institution, may be eliminated, and any person considered a source of oppressive inequality, liquidated. Not just the rich aristocrat, but also the baker who sells him bread. That's how the logic works. At this point, revolutions devour their own founders (bye, bye, Shelagh) who, slowly realizing their mistake, begin to resist the most radical measures. That's how Robespierre, the original egalitarian theorist of the French Revolution, the "prophet of virtue" who ordered thousands of his own citizens guillotined, got guillotined himself — for not being sufficiently radical. There was no system of formal law left to protect him.

Near the end of our debate — and knowing there were at least a halfdozen Queen's professors in the auditorium — I felt a special curiosity to find out how the students would respond to my most telling question: "Please answer as honestly as you can: how many of you have ever been afraid to voice an honest personal opinion in a class at Queen's?" After a moment's hesitation — students looking around to see if a professor might be watching them — at least half of them raised a hand. Immediately, some of the professors began to fidget. I couldn't resist saying, "Shame. Shame" — the single most important word spoken in that debate.

In closing, there was no small pleasure to be had in reminding Professor McIntyre that it was her, not me, who had her foot on citizen's necks. She had a privileged, tax-funded high-salaried job as a tenured professor (with four months off every year) and could not be fired. It was she who got her radical articles — more politics than law — published in state-subsidized journals, not me. It was she who was the privileged power broker and stakeholder, exerting a radical influence and power over her students, most of whom prefer a free society to a tyrannical one, but — as we just saw — were afraid to speak their minds openly in her classes.

A week or so after this debate, writer Rob Martin published an article in Ontario's *Lawyers Weekly*, citing Donald McCrae, Dean of Queen's University Law School, who said "The idea of equity is that everyone should get the same advantage." But it has apparently never occurred to the good Dean that at such a point the whole concept of advantage can have no meaning. So, on the heels of this, Queen's invented a "discretionary" admissions policy justified by the argument that academic admissions standards are "systemically oppressive." The new policy stipulates that up to 30% of all those admitted to first year law studies may be admitted with below standard marks. In addition, because many of those inferior students will not do well on exams, Queen's will offer them "examination accommodation" (they can have twice the allotted time

Against The Tide

to write exams). After one year of this policy, however, it was discovered that more than half the students who received accommodation were in fact not members of any disadvantaged group. So, to solve this new problem, the "Equity Committee" recommended that *all* students be granted accommodation. Lowering standards for everyone was how "equality" would be achieved.

## THE REFORM PARTY, AND PRESTON MANNING

My father-in-law Bill Sparling was a dyed-in-the-wool Vancouver liberal when I first met him. But after reading *Trouble* he slowly converted to a conservatism of a sort, and one day invited me to go meet an Albertan named Preston Manning, who had formed something called the Reform Party of Canada. It was a small meet-and-greet in a private West Vancouver home, and it was there I first saw Preston's soon to be ubiquitous Blue Book outlining the policies of his Party. In most respects they echoed everything I had recommended in my red book, *The Trouble With Canada*. I liked Preston Manning. He had a twangy Western voice and twinkly eyes that squeezed almost shut when he laughed. A passionate citizen of a country he loved; he was clearly as committed to fixing its troubles as I was. So even at that first meeting we joked about the many similarities between "Your Blue Book, and my Red Book." Preston could laugh with you, and study you at the same time from deep within those smiling eyes, and you never quite knew which he was doing in the moment. What about joining Reform? I told him I loved what I saw of the Reform platform and would help in any way I could, but I wouldn't join any political party because as a writer I wanted to be free to criticize if necessary.

The following spring I got a call from a fellow named Mark Magner, telling me he had read *Trouble*, and was very excited. He and his family enjoyed sitting around the dinner table discussing it. He saw overlap with Reform, and wanted to organize a recruitment event in Markham, Ontario, for six weeks hence, and was hoping to draw 100 people. Could I come and speak? He couldn't pay much. I said "forget the pay. I want to help." So, we sealed the deal for my first political speaking event.

Two weeks later Mark called, pleasantly flustered, to say they would have to move the event to a larger space because he already had 300 people signed up. This was exciting for the party, and for me. Then a few days later came another call to say he had 500 signed up. The new room was at capacity. Another week later he called to say he had 1,000 people "banging the door down." Could I speak twice, on the same night? I said sure, why not? This would be fun. Grassroots fun. Was I getting interested in politics? I wasn't asking that question to flatter myself. Only because, after so many radio shows on which not a few Canadians frustrated with big government said: "You should run for politics. You got my vote," the thought did cross my mind, in a foggy way. I confess that for just a little over a minute I imagined myself as Prime Minister. What would *that* be like? The second thought was, it wouldn't work — how would I get my long bike rides in? I imagined myself cycling around Ottawa at 30kph followed by a couple of breathless RCMP officers with their tongues hanging out, and I caught myself smiling.

On that big Reform Party night, I spoke with the requisite passion to the first 500 potential reformers. Then Mark ushered them out of the room to his waiting team of recruiters and opened another door for the next 500. But during that 20-minute rest, Mark took me aside for a serious corrective chat. I was still a year away from writing *The War Against the Family*, in which there would be four chapters on education and the schools. But I was already persuaded that the whole idea of public schooling — of government control of education — was an anathema to genuine education because the government is the paymaster, instead of the parents, and I saw that too many teachers considered themselves "change agents" whose duty it was to change society through radical education of the young — *often against the values of their own parents*. So, my remedy was to change the paymaster. And you could do this by issuing education Vouchers to parents for a specified amount per child, which they then could spend at any school of their choice. This would not only change the paymaster, causing teachers actually to *listen* to parents and what they wanted for their children, but it would also force schools to compete for Vouchers, and thus weed out bad schools.

When Mark took me aside, he said, "Bill. Vouchers are not part of the Reform Party platform. Please don't discuss that with our next group." I just looked at him and he knew what I was thinking: So, you invite me to speak, twice in one night, for free, and then tell me what I can't say? This got me dropping any Prime Minister gig. My entire passion was first to know, then to freely discuss, and express, facts and truth. Mark wanted to muzzle me. I could see that politics would be a lifelong muzzle, and truth discouraged for political gain. So, I spoke again, and told the audience that Vouchers were not yet a Reform Party idea but should be.

## FRANK STRONACH'S SILK TIE

One day that winter I was cross-country skiing on the winding forested trail at my parent's farm in Caledon, crisp clean air filling my lungs, striding past

Against The Tide

pine boughs bent heavy with glinting snow, and on passing their stone farmhouse I saw Mom at the door, beckoning, "There's a call for you from Frank Stronach." He was one of Canada's richest and most powerful businessmen, and I had bumped into him once at *Le Connoisseur*, a fine dine-and-dance restaurant he once owned in Toronto where I took Jeanie when we first found love. Frank could be seen there late on the occasional Friday night sitting on a chair — holding court, really, with friends and admirers — very rosy-cheeked from too many glasses of Austrian Riesling, plucking fresh strawberries from a dish of rich cream, and the night I saw him, with a 20-something beauty on his knees.

As a poor young machinist from Austria, he came to Canada to seek his fortune, a precision guy who got his first job easily because Canadians were sloppy machinists. He had no place to live, so he slept on the factory floor his whole first year. And went up from there. And down a couple of times, but mostly up. His philosophy for success in business (voiced from his perch at *Le Connoisseur*) was starkly simple and effective: "Just make something a little better than the next guy, and a little cheaper, and they will come to your door." It's true. And he did. And they came, and they made him a billionaire. It was his secretary inviting me to "Have lunch with Mr. Stronach, at noon today." You bet. This was going to be interesting.

When I arrived at his office in Markham, he was sitting at a large Board table, his hands on an open copy of *Trouble*, and at once began giving me his own version of the trouble. This continued non-stop in a chauffeured car to his favourite restaurant, but I had a little trouble concentrating on his theories in the car.

When we got seated Frank ordered a salad with lots of oily dressing and began his table talk on the fix. First, he handed me a short paper he had written on how to change our political system, which I tucked away for later. Then, armed with a red felt pen and a pad of legal-length yellow paper he began to make diagrams to illustrate his personal theory of government. During this concentrated display he would frequently pause for a forkful of salad; then talk a little more — it was a lecture, actually — and then would come another red slash across what quickly became a complicated graph on the yellow pad; and then, oops, he splashed a little salad oil on his beautiful $300 silk tie — like, one I could never afford in those days — paused to scrape it off with a linen napkin, and made it sink in deeper. Back to the yellow pad. Meanwhile, I am rather astonished listening to all this, and could see it was pointless to offer a comment (he wasn't asking). This was pure Stronach on Stronach. I was the #1 bestselling author of a book on Canada. But he considered himself the #1 expert in political theory. *This* (!) is how to fix Canada.

How? Frank spoke (and wrote and drew more graphs) about how liberal democracies were strangling themselves with endless bickering discussions, useless compromises, and stalled initiatives. That seemed true. So go on. What we needed, he insisted, was "a new system" altogether (*new altogether, ja?*). This would work by allowing just a little debate from all parties on whatever the issue might be. Then, we tell each party to submit its own best solution. Then, we get to study each solution for only a limited period. A couple of days perhaps. Then, the House has to vote for *one* of those solutions. You see? No further discussion! This was Frank's way of forestalling what he thought, with some justification, was a brewing Weimar Republic situation in Canada where parties squabble fruitlessly and problems multiply, until Parliament is immobilized. He was a man of action, like Big Jim. With this kind of man, you shake hands and count your fingers afterward.

That lunch wasn't the time or place to tell him that the glory of a properly functioning Parliament in a free society is having contending parties that through open discussion and debate arrive at solutions none of them had ever imagined. It's a creative process that limits government to ruling between the forty-yard lines and frustrates one-party tyranny. Oh, no. He wanted "efficiency" in government. I didn't tell him that I have always warned against a too-efficient government. They are in our faces enough already. God help us if they ever get super-efficient! The point is to make sure they don't. A super-efficient government makes the sound of tank treads on the move.

Then came the real reason for the lunch. "If you want to run for politics, Bill, *I will back you. Money will be no problem.*" That got my attention, to say

*Against The Tide*

the least, and I thanked him for his generous offer, but I would have to think about what it could mean. Holy … one of the richest men in Canada just said he was willing to back me? Unlimited? Imagine! I confess, I got an immediate brain-flash again of myself sitting in the PM's office without ever having to run for power. Frank and his millions would put me there. Yeah, well, who's kidding who? It would not be me running. It would be me as a Frank surrogate. I remembered Churchill's statement about the Germans: "The Hun is always either at your throat, or at your feet." Frank was a Hun, and at my throat already; and was not the kind to be at my feet (which is where I would want him). Our conversation ended in a more or less permanent silence, and I left thinking my damn book was causing all sorts of stir.

## "YOUR BOOK MADE ME SO GODDAMN MAD!"

In spring of 1991 I was invited as one of several Keynote Speakers to a big Reform Party Convention in Saskatoon. The first indication that my red book was stoking the fire of Reformers everywhere was word from Stoddart that the Reform Party had just ordered 400 copies of it for this convention.

The party and I were of one mind on the need to reduce the size of government, and our massive debt; to rejig Canada as a union of equal provinces — no more favouritism for Quebec — (or any other province); to rejig immigration policy so it would not threaten Canada's traditions, institutions, and historically ethnic composition (unless the latter was an expressed wish of the people), to introduce some tools of direct democracy such as Recall, and Referendums (in the manner of the Swiss); to open free trade between provinces; to protect the traditional family; to vote against legalizing gay "marriage" because, as Reform leader Preston Manning himself once publicly stated (I could not agree more, then, or now): "homosexuality is destructive to the individual, and in the long run, to society."

I was to follow Reformer Stan Waters the morning of my talk. He was the real thing. A man who on December 3rd, 1943, used ropes for his men to climb the vertical cliffs of *Monte La Difensa* during the Italian Campaign's "Operation Raincoat" against German forces. Just imagine that! My wife Jean's Great Uncle, Major-General Bert Hoffmeister, was at the time leading a fierce battle not far from him.

But now, Stan was using political scaling ropes to mount an attack on Canada's traditional appointed Senate, promoting a so-called "Triple E" Senate (equal, elected, effective), about which I had not said or written much as yet, because I wasn't sure what to think. But in the main, I thought making a Senate elective in a democratic system with two Houses creates an inevitable conflict of democratic legitimacy. For in a conflict of opinion, which democratic House was correct? My clearest argument for keeping a Senate appointive was published 25 years later in June of 2015 in *The National Post* in which — so many years after Saskatoon! — I refute directly what Preston Manning had been saying all along in support of an elected Senate.[17]

At any rate, when I walked into the auditorium at 8 am … it was empty. Just 800 empty seats staring mutely, and so I thought, oh my, this trip has been a waste of time. Who wants to hear a speech about *The Trouble With Canada* at 8 in the morning? So, I got lost in my notes for a while. But the next time I looked up, I was amazed to see 800 people in those seats. A full house. Stan Waters gave his talk — Reformers were already persuaded about changing the Senate to elective — then I gave my talk, and from their vigorous standing ovation, I was pleased to feel this trip was far from wasted.

After the talk I went back to our hotel to lie down for a little and asked Jeanie, "You think I have to go back for book signing?" She said, "I think you better go back." Of course, of course. We walked, and a few hundred yards from the convention centre saw a line of people on the sidewalk stretching all the way around the block. What's this? No idea. But when we got inside, we saw a large table with those 400 copies of *Trouble* stacked four feet high for purchase. Those people were lining up to buy my book! What a shot in the arm. I was a little ashamed I had even considered not showing up and got right to work. You have to be very careful signing books. Shake every hand, ask a little about the person buying, try to concentrate on what they are saying, ask them to spell their name clearly, because one slip of the pen, or a misspelled name and their book is ruined.

At that table was a quiet, shy young man named Scott Reid, who said he enjoyed my book, wanted to meet the author, and to help out. Near the end of the book is a chapter recommending Canada adopt some features of Swiss-style direct democracy, which he liked a lot. I can say now that whatever else may have come of my writing life, the most rewarding has been meeting young people like him whose thinking has been changed in some measure by my work. Two years later, Scott published *Canada Remapped*, a fine book about the possible partition of Quebec in which he recommended a Swiss Cantonal system of government that would have kept Quebecers and Anglos separate, but together, in Confederation. Then he became a distinguished Member of Canada's Parliament for the Kingston area, and still is.

At any rate, the signing went on for almost four hours, and I was eager for it to end when the last buyer, a very old man with ruffled white hair and a knobby hickory cane, military medals slapping and clinking on the breast

Against The Tide

of his blue jacket, shuffled up to the table, leaned over with fire in his eyes, pointed directly at me, and blurted, "Your book! Your book made me so goddamn mad!"

Oh my, here's the last fellow to buy a book, and he's angry? With me? Could this be the only socialist war-vet in Canada, and he has to show up here? Out of respect for his age and service, and upset I had offended such a frail old man I stood bolt upright and stuck out my hand, "Sir. I'm so sorry. It wasn't my intent!" He straightened up, cleared his throat, wiped one damp eye with the back of his bony spotted hand, and said, in slow lamentation, "No, no. It's not you. It's your book. I started reading it this past winter. And I was halfway through, when I got so goddamn mad at what's happened to this country, I just had to go for a walk, to cool off. Well … goldarn if I wasn't half a mile down the road, when I realized I still had by bedroom slippers on!" With those words, he broke into a laugh that shook him from head to toe and made his medals jingle. I took his bony fingers in my hand in thanks, and he bought two more autographed books for his grandsons. The memory of this old patriot, who went to war for liberty, like my dad and his buddies, getting overheated about the growing leftism in Canada, then storming into the cold wind and snow in his bedroom slippers, still moves me a lot.

## YOU'RE FIRED!

After the Reform Convention I was invited to speak to a half dozen of their meetings around Ontario in the next half-year. Always free of charge. Always before an enthusiastic full house. Then, suddenly, I got de-platformed from all future Reform meetings.

A somewhat negative article got published in *Alberta Report* about *Trouble*, which was rather odd, because *Report*'s writers, being Western freedom fighters, were normally quite favourable to my ideas. The writer, Ken Whyte, who is today himself an author and publisher, took aim at my chapter criticizing immigration, but didn't deal with the main question: Why was the ethnic composition and cultural inheritance of Canada (the same process was underway in most other western democracies) suddenly being unofficially altered through non-traditional immigration, by direction of a here-today, gone-tomorrow elected junta at the top that made this drastic change without national discussion, or permission of any kind from the people of Canada?

It came down to a question of democratic right: does any small, temporary government of a free society have a right, much less a mandate, to ethnically re-engineer an entire nation without its consent? I thought not and had said so. After all, the dominant "ethnicities" of the nations of the world are just a token for something much deeper and more significant than ethnicity, which I call "deep culture." This is made up of a dominant race of people (the ethnic part around which all modern nation states have been organized); but more importantly, by a common language, a common religion, common traditions, laws, morals, and symbols, common manners, customs, habits, and so on. There would have been less objection from me, as mentioned, if the Canadian people had at least been offered a full and free discussion and their approval sought for such a radical alteration of their country. But we weren't. It was and continues to be a major scandal.

Not long after that piece came out, the CBC TV found Preston Manning at Toronto's Pearson Airport, and all but accosted him with a rabidly excitable CBC reporter who stuck a microphone right in his face, on camera.

Reporter (quite heated): "Do you support William Gairdner's views on immigration?"

Preston: "You'll have to discuss that with Mr. Gairdner."

But no one discussed it with me. That reluctance to engage in honest and meaningful debate with opponents of one's ideas in the hope of changing their views, or perhaps having one's own views changed by better arguments, seems now to be a persistent and continuing failure of Canadian public life.

The next day I received a call from Preston Manning's second-in-command to say that Reform was cancelling my upcoming speech to the Reform Party in Belleville. So, Reform lights went out, and I sorrowed for a country too lamentably frightened to openly discuss the reasons it was so blithely participating in its own cultural and ethnic demise. To repeat: I don't own the country. And if after full national discussion of the consequences of such a radical policy Canadians decided by, say, a national referendum (the matter is that serious), to change profoundly and forever their own ethnic and cultural mix and traditions? Well, good on ya, mate. So be it. What I mostly deplore is the heavy hand of a know-it-all temporary government making such a nation-altering decision without discussion, permission, explanation, or apology. What kind of spineless people allows that?

When I found a moment, I called timid, squinty Preston and told him that after all the time and effort I spent helping Reform, without any speaking fees, he could at least have called me himself to say thanks, and to explain that our leftist media were hammering him so hard over my views that he hoped I would understand. And I would have said, "Yes, I do. And I enjoyed helping you. Good luck." But he didn't say much, except goodbye.

*Against The Tide*

# ANOTHER PUBLISHER BITES THE DUST

After almost 25 years of fun and tribulation following the publication of *Trouble*, and a week or so after a review article I wrote for the immensely cultured New York journal *The New Criterion* that was very critical of the liberal pleading by the American writer Alan Wolfe in his new book *The Future of Liberalism*, I got an unsolicited call from Jonathan Schmidt, Managing Editor of Key Porter Books in Toronto. That company, one of a vanishingly small number of publishers of conservative books then still surviving in Canada, was the brainchild of Hungarian immigrant Anna Porter, who fled the Communism of the Hungarian revolution about the same time as George Jonas, and like him, was worried it was a disease that followed her to Canada. It followed them both. In resistance, she created Key Porter Books in 1979, and published many writers interested in defending the liberty, and political and moral traditions of the western world, then sold it in 2004 to H.B. Fenn publishers.

Jonathan had read my review of Wolfe, liked it a lot, and wanted to meet — which we did over beer — and said if I was looking for a publisher, he was interested. I was. The book I prepared for him, released in 2010, was an updated version of *Trouble*, so we published it as *The Trouble With Canada … Still!* and sent an autographed copy to Prime Minister Stephen Harper, and individually to all 330+ MPs in Ottawa, including Justin Trudeau, then a smooth-talking about nothing pretty boy candidate for Prime Minister, himself. He was the only one besides Prime Minister Stephen Harper who wrote me a thank-you note; very classy, by hand, with a fountain pen.

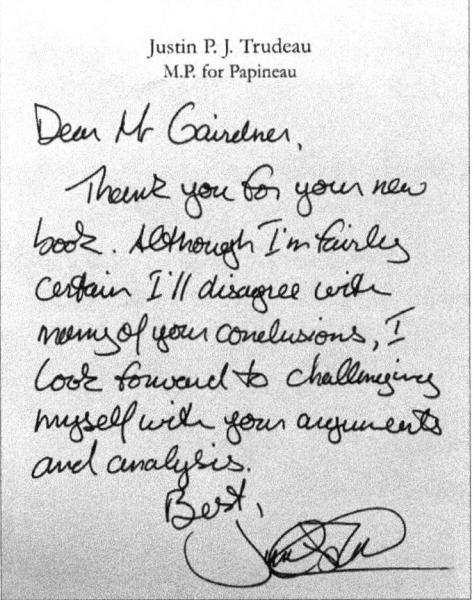

Justin P. J. Trudeau
M.P. for Papineau

Dear Mr Gairdner,

Thank you for your new book. Although I'm fairly certain I'll disagree with many of your conclusions, I look forward to challenging myself with your arguments and analysis.

Best,

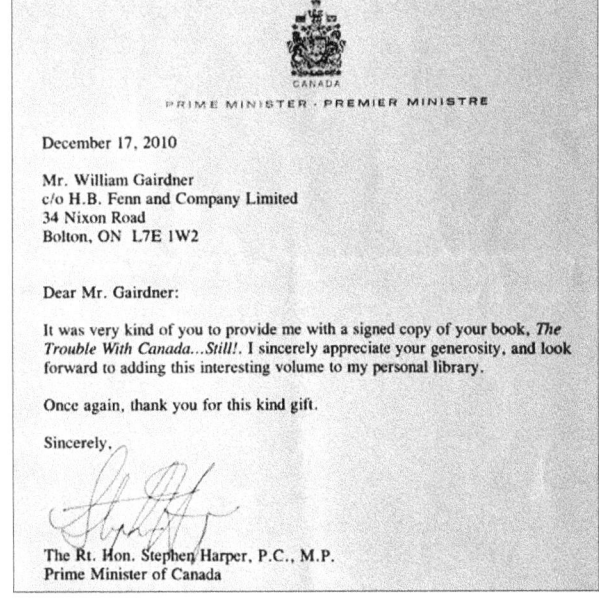

CANADA

PRIME MINISTER · PREMIER MINISTRE

December 17, 2010

Mr. William Gairdner
c/o H.B. Fenn and Company Limited
34 Nixon Road
Bolton, ON  L7E 1W2

Dear Mr. Gairdner:

It was very kind of you to provide me with a signed copy of your book, *The Trouble With Canada...Still!*. I sincerely appreciate your generosity, and look forward to adding this interesting volume to my personal library.

Once again, thank you for this kind gift.

Sincerely,

The Rt. Hon. Stephen Harper, P.C., M.P.
Prime Minister of Canada

Three months later I wrote to ask him if he had challenged himself as yet? But he never replied. From his performance as Prime Minister since, I would say not.

Fall of 2011, not even a year after that book came out, I got an email note from Jonathan telling me they had to lay off most of their employees, immediately. Why? Because Stephen Harper is Prime Minister and "is not interested in subsidizing Canadian publishers any longer." OMG … another of my publishers going belly up? I called Jordan Fenn, who told me the Harper government had not come through with a promised grant of $600,000, so he could not continue to operate. Then he sent me a letter reverting the rights to my book to me.

I had already met and chatted with Stephen Harper personally, many times in the ten years prior to his becoming Prime Minister of Canada, he was one of the original members of an organization I created for the national discussions and debate of ideas, called *Civitas Canada*, which I will tell about below. I knew he had a copy of *Still!* in his hands, and likely sympathized with most of it.

It was a pleasure to get this coded message. My book was not being received officially and filed away in the Library of Parliament. The Prime Minister of Canada was adding it to his *personal* library. It was, nevertheless, a kind of poetic (in)justice that one of the complaints I discussed in that book — Canadian publishers sucking too hard on the government teat — had come around to sting me once again. From now on, most books about conservative moral and political matters of Canada in would have to be self-published.

## WATCH OUT! YOU WANT TO DEFEND THE FAMILY? EVEN "CONSERVATIVES" WILL RUN FOR COVER

"You didn't write enough about the family," was a common observation about *Trouble* from book fans who recognized that from abortion on demand, to gay rights, to euthanasia, to pornography rights, to the end of the contractual basis of marriage by unilateral divorce, the family in all the Western democracies was under considerable attack and had been for some time. So, I shut myself away and wrote *The War Against The Family: A Parent Speaks Out on the Political, Economic, and Social Policies That Threaten Us All* in six months, in a white heat, and often with a tear on my cheek. It's true. The most memorable of many causes of emotion was when I wrote about a quadriplegic boy named Matthew Van Geffen who had a tube in his mouth when being unplugged from his life-saving devices and so, killed against his will by euthanasia at St.

Against The Tide

Michael's Hospital in Toronto. He kept shaking his head — "No, No" — for the doctors to stop. But they didn't stop. I say without the least exaggeration that *War* is the most complete autopsy ever written on the destruction of the natural family. Best to read it sitting down, though, or you might fall over.

Plato, in his book, *Republic*, in 375 BC was the original villain, for in it he presented a complete totalitarian program for the destruction of the natural family, which I define, at minimum, as *"a married mother and father living together with their dependent children."* Why would he do such a thing? Because the natural family is a difference machine, so to speak, a key generator and incubator of differences in talent, social skill, equality, property, and wealth (and therefore also the key producer — if one is so inclined — of human envy and unhappiness). He wanted to replace it forever with a permanent police state on the model of Sparta. And his anti-family screeds had a powerful copy cat effect on Rousseau, and then Marx, more than 2000 years later.

He began by urging that the institution of marriage be ended, and private property banned, that all women be held in common by the men, that there should be a selective-breeding operations in "mating festivals" to produce only the best children. For eugenics, inferior kids were to be euthanized by the state, and "No child should know his parent, nor parent his child" (because all will be taken from their parents and raised by the State), and so on. *War Against the Family* climbs from there quickly up to modern times to explain in great depth how and why the modern democracies — originally all free Christian states — have been abandoning their original bottom-up foundation in family, community, and liberty, to embrace a new, top-down radical foundation rooted in egalitarian statism. Canada was already way down the road on this platonic journey.

I began that book citing the words of the American Fisher Ames, spoken in the mid-18th century, which are even more true today: "we are sliding down the mire of a democracy which pollutes the morals of the citizens before if swallows up their liberties." And then, on page one, I wrote the words that move me still because they are eternally true: *"When all is said and done, there is scarcely any love more fierce than the love of children, nor any death so mournful."* I was quite convinced that too many politicians and intellectuals in the modern democracies had been striving mightily to dissolve the most basic social unit we call the private family and replace it with the most basic political unit we call "the individual" — all the better to organize wraparound, top-down control by the nanny state.

*War* included four damning chapters on the failings of state education, excoriating chapters on radical feminism, on women at war; and on the homosexual lobby (I was even mocked by liberals at the time as an alarmist for saying Canada would one day legalize homosexual marriage); on the invisible holocaust of abortion; on the coming euthanasia movement (it is here now); and on the many attacks by radical legal activists claiming the natural private family is a "discriminatory" institution. They were correct — each family discriminates fiercely in favour of the nourishing and flourishing of the children produced, and in this sense the family is the world's most profoundly anti-egalitarian institution. A battle to the death was clearly underway, and I was badly outnumbered.

Deep gratification was felt, but also the sharp realization that Canada as a whole was badly split over the significance of the family and its place in the social order. There were many hundreds of pro-family magazines, organizations, and media outlets that expressed profound relief someone was finally speaking out in defence of the family. Here is a province-wide defence of the message of War, from Alberta Report, Calgary, a stronghold of traditionalist values.

But from the first day this book hit the streets, there was also a violent reaction from progressives across Canada, a lot of it directed against me personally, rather than against my arguments. This was the first sign of our national dialogic sickness — which is much worse now — and it had the immediate effect of smoking out a lot of folks calling themselves "conservatives," who were in fact merely "fiscal conservatives." In effect, it exposed them as just a different kind of modern liberal or libertarian who happens to have a special worry about the size of government and taxation but has no particular worries about the preservation of the nuclear family or other socially and morally cohesive institutions that bolster our civilization. Edmund Burke would have spat on their ant-like convictions. As did I.

## STEVE PAIKIN'S AMBUSH – INTERVIEW ON TVO[18]

Steve Paikin, a fixture at TV Ontario for time out of mind, is a smooth-talking, mostly left-wing, amiable fellow who likes to give the impression he is always fair and balanced but is in fact far from neutral in his views, at least when he's with true conservatives. Strictly by virtue of a pleasantly negative reaction of voice, and a raised eyebrow he quietly promotes his personal views and is very good at teasing fair comment from a guest while loading the deck in his own favour through the wording of a question, or an example he chooses. One of his favourite techniques is to pre-select and show on-screen quotations from an author's book, absent any surrounding context from the book's larger arguments, or any advance warning to his guest, then drop a question with a rather too self-satisfied gotcha smile, while urging a response the guest has had too little time to think upon.

He had made a beeline for my office, with sound crew and cameraman in tow to get an interview on *Trouble* when it was flying high on the charts in 1990, and that went fairly smoothly, given that he seemed a little perturbed that a completely unknown author was trying to sink his boatload of comfortable opinions. He was on a personal plug-the-dam mission. We got along fine with the understanding we were clearly on opposite sides of every political and moral fence. Twenty years later, when *The Trouble With Canada … Still!* came out, he did another. Steve can't help digging for faults if he is in ideological conflict with his guest, in sharp contrast to interviews he does with people whose work he admires. There was not a single word of praise. But it went very well, despite this, has had about 9,000 views to date, and can be seen here.[19]

In between those two episodes he was the host of a province-wide show called "Between the Lines." *War* was already high in the national bestseller charts within a few months of appearing in 1993, but it never found steady legs because it was an explosive book, every chapter of which went off like a bomb to rock citizens from their civic and moral complacency. The leftist soldiers in that war were mainly radical feminists, homosexual activists, utopian, Social Justice Warrior, pro-choice and pro-euthanasia enthusiasts, and others of this ilk employed mostly in bookstores, newspapers, radio and television media, and universities. In other words, there was a platoon of enemies ranged against every chapter I had written, and other than Christian groups who liked the book a lot, and some secular true conservatives of the Edmund Burke sort, *War* revealed a deep, theretofore unarticulated civil war of values and principles in Canada and in the West at large.

I often found copies of *War* in bookstores and libraries with black marker-pen slashes through various pages, or with pages entirely torn out with a knife. This told me I had hit the mark. Once again, there were at least a hundred radio and TV debates and newspaper interviews over this book, and I may have lost ground occasionally by refusing to raise my voice and shout back; but I don't think I ever lost a debate on the merits of the case at hand. And I enjoyed that immensely, though I must say, it is always a strain because you never know what dirty tricks a host is going to pull.

Steve pulled a dirty trick, though if he ever happens to read this, he may not agree. But he did. He greeted me at TVO as usual, for what I thought would be his regular personal book interview. But he walked me to a different room than his usual small studio. I was expecting the usual set-up: two microphones, a round table, just the two of us. Instead, he showed me into a large room with about a dozen people seated facing the front and motioned me to a high-backed black chair facing them, where his sound-techies were about to wire me up. There was no time to object. Hey, you could have warned me! Who are these people? We never talked about this format! Although taken by surprise, I buckled up and decided to consider his ambush as backhanded respect because it meant he figured I could handle a gang-up.

The format was obvious: three of those people were stooges for the right; an earnest evangelical Minister with a dark wart on his nose that moved around when he spoke, whose sincerity was painful, as he fed Steve exactly the religious lines he expected, and thought would make his mostly secular Ontario audience wince. Next, was a sweet, soft-spoken, grey-haired 75-year old woman who was Steve's stand-in for the archetypal family matron with children. Finally, there was a sad-seeming 30-something divorced woman at the back of the room who looked so frail she seemed close to tears. All the others were firmly — you could say defiantly — on the left: two strident,

Against The Tide

youngish radical feminists, two ardent pro-choice types, one Marxist student, one gay man, one family lawyer, and so on. And let the fun begin.

And begin it did. For an hour, Steve would walk with his cordless microphone to one or another of those guests whose opinions he was coaxing, then to me for answers. The Minister was so biblically sincere he made me wince; the matronly mother gave strong answers you would expect of a good mother; in between, various of the radicals present would be called upon to approvingly glue-down some left-leaning answer Steve was chasing.

The highlight for me was when the tables turned on Steve. He was very hip, even groovy, on his idea that "a family" is whatever you decide it is. "So, Mr. Gairdner, please tell us your definition of a family." He was actually smiling in anticipation of my fall, but I gave him no such satisfaction: "A family is a married mother and father living together with their dependent children."

"Well, then," — Steve smiled, as he jumped on this comment, striding quickly to a young married couple, then spun around like a figure skater in a pre-triumphant way to face me with the mic held straight-arm in front of them. "These two have been married for a few years, Bill. But they decided not to have children. What kind of family do they have?"

"They don't have a family. They have a marriage. And probably a lovely one. But it's not a family until, and unless, they have children; of their own, or adopted, whatever."

Steve was crestfallen and really piqued now. So he strode over to the family lawyer who was sitting alone near the back, looking in control of something or other. Steve told the room this fellow was a family lawyer with a lot of divorce experience. "Let's get his opinion. Sir ... what would *you* say a family is?" He accused me of promoting an out-of-date Ozzie and Harriet model of the family.

At this point I wanted to interrupt and say, "Excuse me. This fellow is a divorce lawyer? He has no right to speak, because he has a vested interest in family breakdown."

Now Steve is fishing for help. He scoots over to the 30-something woman with a child and asks her what kind of family she has? She looks up at Steve, close to tears, I swear, and says, "I was married for five years, but am divorced now, with one child."

And Steve Pounces. "Okay, Bill. Tell us what kind of family *she* has?"

"She has a broken family."

Well, that was like a gunshot, and the room went heavily silent. Beaming in anticipation of a rebuke, Steve moves the mic a little closer to her face. Did you hear what Mr. Gairdner just said? That you have a *broken* family? Everyone expected her to react angrily.

But instead, she looks up at Steve and tells the room she agrees she has a broken family. When it was all over, she said she wanted so much for it to be whole again. I could have kissed her for speaking truth.

In 2022, almost 30 years later, I secured a copy of this interview and posted it on my own YouTube site.[20]

It's refreshing, actually, to see a lot of people trying hard to have a decent discussion.

## DEFENDING THE RIGHT TO BAN BOOKS

A few weeks after the TVO gang-up I realized *War* was really touching a nerve nationally, when I woke up to see that the *Globe and Mail* had published a frontpage story that Duthie Books in Vancouver was "banning" my book. What? Book banning? In Canada? The book trade in Canada, and perhaps in most other free nations, is an odd duck. Booksellers have a lot of books lined up on their shelves which they purchase with a 30 day promise to pay. What's odd is that they get up to three months to return any unsold books to publishers for a full refund. Some of them pay very late — or never if they want to send their books back. In other words, bookstores rely on publishers (who don't want to own and operate their own chain of bookstores) to produce top-selling books for them, and publishers rely on bookstores to sell them.

Duthie's was a family bookstore chain that at one time had eight stores and controlled about 40% of all book sales in Vancouver. So, if Duthie's banned your book it had almost no chance to succeed in that market. The Duthie daughter currently in charge was a well known leftie so I wasn't surprised she didn't like it, because I was attacking just about every loopy anti-family value, I figured she and most of her staff likely supported. But she was fine with selling books such as Hitler's Mein Kampf, and Marx's Communist Manifesto, which between them have ideologically — and morally — justified the slaughter of at least 70 million human beings. And she was okay with selling radical feminist books supporting the "choice" of women to kill their perfectly healthy unborn babies in their own wombs. But … you get the idea. She was not exactly a standard-bearer for freedom of speech, the right to life, or the open mind. I got the knife in.

But this situation (justified in the subsequent, very heated *Globe* letter-exchange as a "refusal to carry" as distinct from "banning"), really riled Jack Stoddart who, as mentioned, was running the largest Canadian-owned trade publishing company at the time. *Trouble* had made a lot of money for him (and I was sent some decent royalty cheques, too). So, when The *Globe*

*Against The Tide*

front-page story appeared, Jack went right up the beanstalk and fired off a letter of complaint to the *Globe*. Then, the Canadian Independent Booksellers Association (CIBA) got into the act, defending the right of a bookseller to refuse to carry any book as a matter of bookseller liberty. There was a conflict between the liberty of booksellers, and their obligation to observe the rules of engagement between themselves and publishers. In the end, I was told that CIBA gave its annual essay prize, which included a significant award, to a member who wrote an essay justifying the banning of my book.

It seems a little weird to have a nation of independent booksellers who see themselves as *de facto* censors filtering what the public gets to read. That, surely, is a recipe for the slow ideological takeover of a nation. This may be conscious when perpetrated by an avowed revolutionary like Karl Marx, who thought "the purpose of philosophy is not to understand the world, but to change it" or unconscious, when perpetrated unwittingly by such as the operators of Duthie's Books whose minds have been taken over by a feel-good ideology they have never questioned. That process is precisely what all my books have sought to examine and expose.

## MORE BANNING OF *WAR*, MADONNA, AND PORNOGRAPHY AT THE PARK PLAZA HOTEL

When *Trouble* came on the scene, no one knew who I was; booksellers had no idea what I was arguing for. But by the time *War* came along two years later, and even though pretending to open-mindedness, lots of them tucked my book away on a low shelf at the back of the store. Or put it behind other books so it couldn't be seen. They didn't want to see themselves as censors, but figured they had no obligation to promote, either.

I was still Chairman of The Gairdner Foundation in those days and the year that book came out we held our annual Awards Dinner on the top floor of The Park Plaza Hotel. All five International Winners and those 125 guests — the cream of medical science in Canada and the world — were, like me, in black-tie formal attire, and a few had brought their teenage children to this event. There was a break in the proceedings, and I suggested to Jeanie we go down to Edwards Books Store on the bottom floor of the hotel to see how my book was doing, because it was #4 in Coles Books National List by then.

When we arrived looking rather special — certainly Jean was the only woman in a formal dress and I the only man in a tuxedo — we looked for *War* but couldn't find it in the relevant section. So I went straight to the genial sales clerk on duty at the front of the store.

"I'm the author of *War Against the Family*, and don't see my book in your store. It was number 4 this week on the Coles List. Could you tell me why it's not available?" He didn't know and couldn't say. Unknowingly, I had placed my hands on a stack of about 20 copies of the pop singer Madonna's pornography book, and as he was speaking, I saw one copy of *War* behind the clerk, perched on a windowsill, quite obviously taken out of circulation.

"Oh. There's a copy right behind you," I announced, pointing to the window. He turns to look. Now he's unsure what to say and gets a little red in the face. A few customers are lining up behind me to buy books. "Could you tell me why my book is on the shelf, instead of out here, where interested people can look at it?" He had no idea. But I obviously wasn't going to move until he did, and so he picked up the phone to call his manager. I felt badly because he seemed to know nothing of the situation. But now, eyes lowered, very flushed, he listened for a minute, then hung up.

"It seems someone *complained* about your book."

"Someone complained about my book? So, you took it out of circulation? You're censoring my book?" Now he was all but hiding under the counter. So, I said, "Forget it. It's not your fault. But ..." Now I was speaking louder, so all behind could hear: "Do I understand correctly that at Edward's Book Store, all you have to do to have a book taken out of circulation, is to lodge a complaint?" He was staring, helpless now, so I finished with, "If so, I am lodging a complaint about Madonna's porn book here," and lifted the stack for him to see. "I would like you to place it on the shelf beside my book and get it out of circulation."

At this, he all but collapsed, so I put Madonna's book down, told him it's okay, not to worry, and went on my way. But at least he and his customers got the gist of how selective censorship works in Canada. Edward's Books is gone now. And good riddance.

When we got back up to our room and were getting ready for bed, Jean called out in her panic voice that "There's porn. On CBC!" I couldn't believe it, and walked into the bedroom, certain she was kidding. There, I saw a full-on porn scene of two women tangled in various indelicate positions with a guy. "What channel did you click? Did you buy this?"

"No. It's CBC. Regular TV!" So, I told her to change the channel to CTV, and she did. And other porn scenes appeared, with more so-called sex workers *in flagrante*. Porn was on every regular channel. We called the front desk immediately, and heard,

"We apologize. We've have a *technical* problem."

Neither then, nor the next morning did they at any time apologize for having raunchy, super-explicit porn available on all TV channels on 13 floors

*Against The Tide*

of their first-class hotel, where teenaged children of our international guests got exposed to it. Henry James would have loved the irony. How, with the practiced affectation of an open-minded, sincere sympathy, the Manager apologized, repeatedly, for "the *technical* problem." But not for the porn. Not at all. His mind was so open his brains fell out.

## BACK WITH THE BEAVER:
## ALL HELL BREAKS LOOSE AT THE CBC

There was a little less resistance when I called Peter Gzowski's *Morningside* Producer for an interview on *The War Against the Family*. It was almost too easy, as if they were lying in wait, setting a trap. They were.

When I walked into his *Morningside* office things felt a little icy, but Peter was alerted — "your guest has arrived" — whereupon he came striding out of his darkened lair and stopped right in front of me with a large book in hand. It wasn't my book, which anyway, I figured he would only have flipped through to rile himself into a fit of pique.

Sure enough. There was no "Hello, how are you doing?" Or "Thanks for coming in. This will be interesting. You know, there is so much controversy these days over family, marriage, and so on, I'm really looking forward to what you have to say." You'd expect something like that from a national broadcaster over a Bestselling book, wouldn't you? Instead, he just said, "Here," and thrust the 400-page book he was holding into my hands.

"Okay," I said, "But there's no time to read this."

"It's by a Professor of Sociology at the University of Manitoba. He'll be on the show with you today," upon which, Peter hurried back into his lair — a crab scuttling under a dark rock. The book in my hands was an attack on the "subversive" concept of the traditional heterosexual family by an openly gay Marxist Professor, and that was irritating enough. Here I was, again, in an ambush even more off-putting than what Steve Paikin had pulled off. Peter obviously didn't want to take me on single-handedly. I felt like Billy the Kid, fending off two bandidos shooting at me from their cover behind big boulders. I would have to pick'em off, one by one.

We were barely settled in our chairs when Peter introduced the sociology prof, who was clearly ready to blow up over what he thought was his "right" to "marry" his much younger boyfriend. In fact, Gzowski brought him in to blow *me* up. It went something like this:

Gay Prof: "So why shouldn't I have a right to marry someone I love?"

Me: "Well, first of all, I don't think states have any right to be involved in marriage at all, except for one huge reason. Namely, the survival of the nation itself through procreation. This justifies the many laws and benefits encouraging and protecting heterosexual marriage. But homosexual couples cannot procreate with each other; they are a zero when it comes to procreation. So, I don't see why the state should care about what they do, or don't do, except for illegal stuff."

Gay Prof: (Getting angry now) "But, we *love* each other!"

Me: "I'm sure you do, and that's better than hating each other. But with respect to the state, love has nothing to do with marriage. If it did, the state would have to withdraw support for marriage when love evaporates. So, clearly, the state's interest is not love. It's figuring out how to produce more children. Everyone knows that if you throw enough men and women together, protect and bonus their unions financially, basically, luring them to marry each other with tax goodies and benefits, there's going to be a lot of children. But if you throw a lot of gays together, there will be nothing. Just one hand clapping."

By now Gzowski had spittle on his lower lip and the Prof from Winnipeg was apoplectic. Especially when I added, "And further to my argument, anyone who has studied the moral and theological basis of Western civilization will understand that one of our core teachings is that we have to distinguish between good love and bad love." This went off like a bomb in the studio. "I mean, human beings love lots of things that are bad for themselves, and bad for society. For example, self-love — narcissism — has always been considered bad love. So has love of money, love of pornography, sexual love of little children, love of adultery. And so on. The psychiatric manuals are full of definitions of hundreds of kinds of bad love. And homosexual love was one of those, until yesterday."

Gay Prof: (Apoplectic now. Shouting. Gzowski, red-faced, chirping-in to support him).

"You're saying the state should *discriminate*? That's outrageous, unfair, and undemocratic ..."

Me: "All government policies discriminate in whatever they do, in an effort to influence human behaviour. They are *for* some human behaviours, and *against* others. That's what makes a policy a policy, instead of just an indiscriminate handout to everyone. We give old age security only to the old; child benefits only to those with children; veterans benefits only to soldiers; and marital benefits only to heterosexual couples. Policies are aimed at encouraging or discouraging specific behaviours, and if they don't do that, they aren't policies at all. They're just vote-buying government goodies."

This was the gist of our "discussion" at first, but in a maelstrom of frustration

Against The Tide

and apoplexy, it went rapidly downhill — something close to a shouting-match between myself, and the Marxist professor, with curmudgeonly Peter chirping in whenever he thought his man was losing ground. It was all I could do to reply to both of them, one after the other, or both at once, and it was certainly the most turbulent and distasteful media experience of my entire book life. And I wondered, why? Perhaps no human being can be neutral about all things, at all times. But surely the mandate of a national talk-show host funded with tax dollars should be to air opinions that may be of interest to listeners? And surely, any bestselling book could claim that description? So why was I getting this angry grilling from Gzowski and his gay guest? Because they didn't like my arguments. They both saw *War* as a serious threat to the urban liberal values they considered unimpeachable. Okay, so I say, deal with it. Let's hear your clear counterarguments. But they didn't have any. None. Just emotional flack. It was a demonstration of what the distinguished philosopher Alisdair McIntyre called "emotivism" — irritable performative outrage — instead of cool and decisive argument.

After Gzowski died in 2002, the Editor-in-Chief of *The Montreal Gazette* wrote the following as part of a dark but deserving eulogy:

> "There may have been crueler bullying of a guest on Canadian airwaves than Gzowski inflicted on author William Gairdner when the latter published *The War Against the Family* in the mid-90s. I have yet to hear anything, though, exceeding that exercise in unrestrained, unwarranted and utterly outrageous verbal abuse. When not arrogantly belittling a man clearly his intellectual superior, Gzowski displayed ill-tempered impatience to get him off the air. Why? Because he considered him a conservative, and therefore unworthy of the most basic courtesy."

But the Donnybrook didn't end when it ended. When I walked out of his studio, I extended my hand to thank Peter. He just stood there, frozen, beside his aghast Producer, and refused to extend his hand. It was a rude, awkward moment, and I could feel my face getting warm. Peter, in his trademark shabby grey beard was staring through me with soulless eyes, as if it was perfectly normal for a CBC radio host to refuse a basic courtesy to a guest whose taxes were extracted to help pay him.

But the story continued. About two weeks later I got a call from another CBC Producer, who said the CBC had received "an avalanche" of mail in reaction to that vitriolic show, and as a result, they were now going to do another show, for a whole hour, dedicated to reading a lot of the letters, good and bad, they had received after the first show! And they did. And I listened.

In fairness, of all the letters read on air, quite a few scolded Gzowski mildly. But I had received carbon copies by mail of some they did not read on air, that really lambasted him. Some said that although they had been fans of *Morningside* for more than a decade, his behaviour was so ill-mannered, they would never listen to him again.

So … I bundled those copies up and sent them off to Peter.

## WHEN POPPIES TRUMP TURBANS

In spring of 1994, at the exact point in a busy family life (kids and their friends running all over our farm; a horse breaking through a fence; helping with schoolwork; driving kids to sports (sometimes to three different hockey rinks on the same night), when the prospect of ever writing another book seemed far too daunting, there came a library angel. I got a surprise call from Murdoch Davis, Editor of *The Edmonton Journal*. He said he was tired of his golfing friends calling him "a leftie," and referring to his newspaper as "The Edmonton Urinal." That was amusing — but not to him. So, he wanted a little more "balance" on his Opinion page. He seemed sincerely interested in a broad range of well-considered views and figured my work would do the job for the conservative side. I would have preferred it if he'd said he wanted a "corrective," because in any battle of ideas, there has to be a best idea lurking somewhere. Debate should not about "balancing" opposing opinions just to appear "fair" and make people feel good. It's about drilling down to find the truth. At any rate: Would I be willing to write a weekly column for $300 per column? He was offering a Trojan Horse to take the fight right inside the fortress of Canadian political correctness.

This was new. I told him I had never written anything that I knew with 100% certainty would meet the fate of all newspapers the day after printing: the garbage can, or the fireplace. I had sufficient authorial ego to think the idea of disposable expression was not that appealing. The title of the opinion page for which he wanted me to write was "Perspectives," and I thought it a grand irony — lost only on the most committed pluralists — that he wanted a man who believes there are in fact discoverable truths, to offer only perspectives.

So, I gave him my perspective: What about $800 per column? Immediate silence was followed by a counteroffer of $600 per column, and I committed for one year. On hanging up the phone I called Stoddart, told them what I was about to do, and that I thought a book of short pieces on a variety of topics (not perspectives) would be popular with readers. So, they sent a

Against The Tide

$5,000 advance to publish my columns a year later in a book titled *On Higher Ground: Reclaiming a Civil Society.*

One of those columns, was entitled "When Poppies Trump Turbans," describing a national uproar in 1994 over a Canadian Legion Hall rule that commanded anyone entering the Legion's war memorial room — a space dedicated to Canada's dead Legion heroes — to remove all headgear as a sign of respect. I had a lot of feeling for those willing to risk their lives for Canada, and feelings of appreciation also for the Canadian Legion itself, because the very year I began training for track at 17, the Legion started mounting a lot of the track meets in Canada as a public service, and is still doing so today, more than 60 years later.

As it happened, before I got that call from Murdoch, a Sikh fellow was once again denied entry to a Legion Hall in Ontario because he refused to remove his Turban. He knew that Sikhs have been great fighters and allies of Canada and the Commonwealth in so many wars, that this refusal would create a national conflict of loyalties and an uproar construed by scandal-hungry media as racist, bigoted, unfair, and discriminatory (I'm running out of adjectives). Immediately, a lot of leftist journalists were writing anguished columns urging Canadians not to buy Poppies (sold by the Canadian Legion across Canada) on Memorial Day. Here was very good column material. So, I wrote about it, and our wary national man-in-net, Peter Mansbridge and his CBC team, got wind of it, and pounced.

I got an emergency call from Stoddart publicity staff asking if I could leave, *right now*, and drive two hours to a remote Legion Hall in Southeastern Ontario where this apparent offence to the assumed egalitarian rights and dignity of all Canadians, had occurred. Peter Mansbridge and his TV Crew for *The National* would be waiting for me there, already set up to interview me, along with a U of T Professor of Eastern Religions.

I was, and remain a property rights and religious rights enthusiast, and figured that whether owned by Christians, Sikhs, Muslims, or anyone else, you have a right to set the rules for your own private home or temple. Those who don't like the rules, don't have to enter. It's still a free country.

But I did wonder what Sikhs themselves had to say about this? So, before leaving, I called to speak with a representative of Toronto's Shromani Sikh Society and asked what would happen if I showed up at his Temple with the Canadian Charter of Rights and Freedoms in hand, demanding my right to enter his Temple wearing shoes, and bareheaded? Horrified, he said, "It is absolutely forbidden! All must take off their shoes and cover their heads [whether with a Turban, bandana, a hat, or some other covering] as a sign of respect." I knew that taking off one's shoes at a Muslim Temple is also required and strictly enforced. No one was fighting Sikhs or Muslims over such things. Least of all, Peter. You don't mess with folks who think you are an unbeliever infidel. Good Heavens, even Christians object if a man wears a hat in a church, for as Saint Paul wrote, "a man indeed ought not to cover his head, forasmuch as he is the image and glory of God."

When self-righteous Peter got going on why I supported "discrimina-tion" against a Sikh, I said, "I don't. I support the right of Legionnaires to set their own rules on their own property, for their own sacrosanct beliefs. And I support the same rights for Sikhs." I mentioned my call to the Shromani Temple, and Peter put on the brakes. He was frustrated now, because he saw his project to pin me as a bigoted author melting before his eyes. So, he turned to the U of T Professor on the show with me and asked him, could he explain the religious significance of the Sikh Turban? Things quickly went even farther south when the Prof told Peter and the nation on live TV that the Sikh Turban was originally cultural attire, and not actually of religious origin; there is nothing in the Sikh religion that says a man is *required* to wear a Turban. And many Sikhs do not. I interjected to tell Peter that I ran hurdles in the 1960s against a Sikh Indian champion who always wore a Turban. But he took it off to run his race against me, no problem. And he put it back on after the race, smiling as I watched him wind it back on his head, asking him how it felt to wear it all day, and so on. Peter's ever-motionless eyes were now doing a little jiggle.

So, I struck: If a Sikh can put on or take off his Turban anytime to suit himself, or to run over hurdles, why can't he take it off to follow the rules of respect for our dead soldiers at a remote Legion Hall in his adopted country? He will certainly become outraged if anyone insists on entering his Sikh Temple bareheaded, with shoes on! And I would agree with him. So, if he doesn't feel like respecting our rules regarding soldiers who died for Canada, why can't he just go home for supper, and forget about it, instead of causing a fuss? In 2023 I made contact with the Ottawa Legion and asked if headwear is still forbidden in their memorial rooms? He said in some Halls all headwear is forbidden, in others, not. The rules of each Hall are up to each Legion district membership. Amen.

Against The Tide

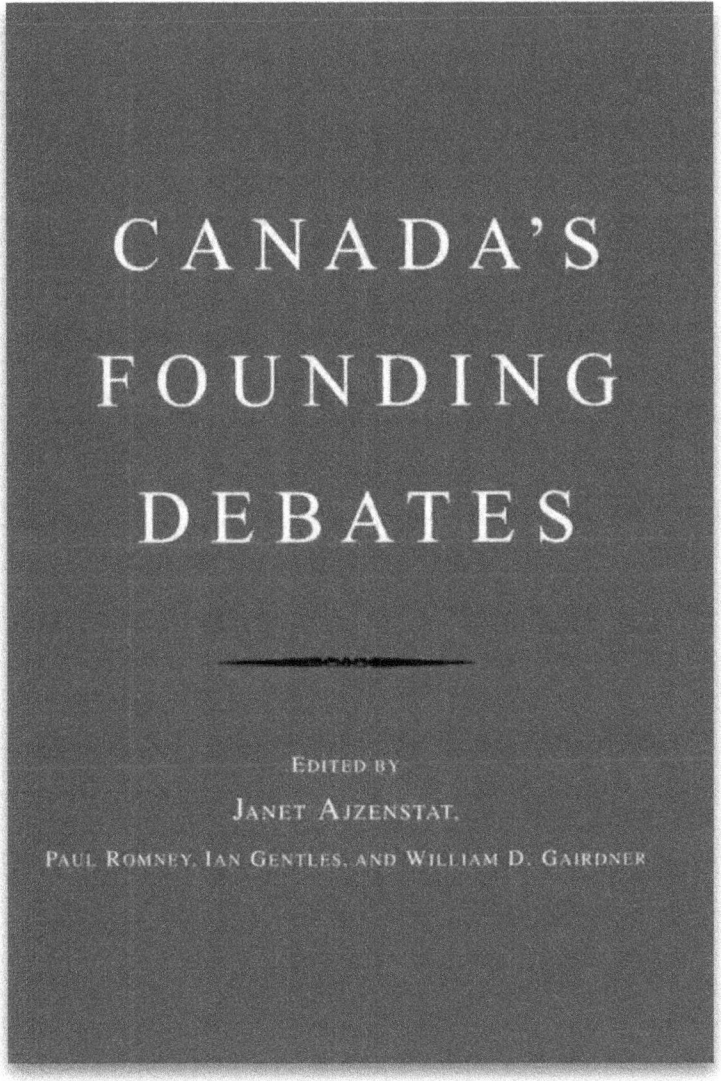

## CANADA'S FOUNDING DEBATES
## – A GIFT TO MY COUNTRY

After Dad died in spring of 1996 a great sadness descended upon me, and all motivation fled. So, I stopped writing for a while to spend time thinking. Mostly, about this strange system we call "democracy." What is it today? What was it in ancient times? In the European Middle Ages? In the so-called Age of Enlightenment (which was actually a kind of darkness that inarguably spawned so many bloody modern revolutions)? For that matter, what was it in Early America, and Canada? Most of all, I still don't understand how any democracy resolves the deepest conundrum of all, to which there is no answer: the fact that in a democracy, the vote of a fool cancels the vote of a wise man. I was deeply curious, but rather ignorant on these matters.

*The American Federalist Papers*, a collection of wonderful essays composed over a period of six months in 1787 by three of America's most influential thinkers — Madison, Hamilton, and Jay — argued for and against the need for a Constitutional Founding of America to settle the strife and chaos then present between the 13 colonies so recently untethered from Mother England. To inform myself, I began more intense reading and making notes for an eventual book I might try to write on democracy. I went to libraries and bookstores, asking: "Where's Canada's equivalent of the *Federalist Papers*?" The question drew only blank stares, time and again. So, after a few months when my contemplative mourning let up a bit, I called my excellent friend Ian Gentles, a Professor of History at York University: Where are Canada's *Federalist Papers*? Has Canada never collected and published its own founding debates, as the Americans, and every other nation even remotely proud of its own existence, seems to have done? It seemed unbelievable that we hadn't.

Ian, also "a Canadianist," informed me that he had an out-of-print copy of "the Quebec debates" that led to our BNA Act in 1867. But "No. Canada has nothing equivalent to the *Federalist Papers*. And, if you dip into the Quebec speeches, you will see why. Very few pearls, and a lot of sand. A lot of dry stuff about wheat, and railways. Nothing very stirring."

But I drove to Ian's home and picked up that old book anyway. One thousand pages of small print. Surely, they must have had *something* to say about … democracy? I wondered … The debates about creating Canada took place during and just following the American Civil War — a democratic bloodbath. And 70 years or so after the still-painful memory of the French Revolution — which produced unprecedented bloody violence in the name of the so-called "General Will" of the people. Some Will. Some bloodbath. Surely Canada's Founders had expressed a fear of unfettered democracy in their deliberations?

Months later, when time sprang me from my melancholy, I reached for the fat volume of sand and flipped it open. And there, I read the most rousing speech by George-Etienne Cartier, one of our Founders, defending the idea that a Parliamentary system in the English style was far superior to American democratic republicanism, because the Monarch is a symbol of all the people, and out of reach of politics, whereas a President, is not:

How was the head of the United States government chosen? Candidates came forward, and of course, each one was abused and vilified as corrupt, ignorant, incapable, and unworthy by the opposite party. One of them attained the presidential chair; but even while in that position he was not

Against The Tide

respected by those who had opposed his election, and who tried to make him appear the most corrupt and contemptible being in creation. Such a system could not produce an executive head who would command respect. Under the British system, ministers might be abused and assailed; but that abuse never reaches the sovereign."

"The most corruptible and contemptible being in creation?"

This was not sand! It was rousing stuff. A passionate defense of the superiority of Canada's Parliamentary system. Flipping further, I stumbled on more such speeches. Here is another rousing speech by the Quebecois Étienne Pascal Taché, illustrating how deeply the French of that day appreciated the durability of liberty under English constitutional government: "The last cannon which is shot on this continent in defence of Great Britain, will be fired by the hand of a French Canadian!"

You won't hear that today! But at this point, very excited, I called Ian back. "There are wonderful speeches here. We just have to get rid of the sand. What do you think about trying to put a book together — the title sprang to mind — of 'Canada's Founding Debates?' We just need a team of historians and constitutional scholars. It shouldn't be hard to find a publisher for such an important project, should it?"

But it was hard. I asked Jack Stoddart four or five times. Needled him. Pushed the dream of the contribution this would be to Canadian political history, and constitutional studies. He would be applauded. But Jack said "No," every time. Too expensive to risk. At the time, Jack was up to his corporate armpits in government handouts, and as his most conservative free market author I had already warned him he was being bought by the state. *Chapters*, a bookseller business that appeared overnight as a national, big-box books and cutesy-paraphernalia merchandiser, was so big they delayed paying Jack indefinitely for books he had shipped to their stores months prior.

So, no. No founding debates book, Bill.

"What if I find money?" That got Jack smiling.

As the Managing Editor of this project, I organized a dinner at our home with three political scientist/historian Professors: Ian Gentles from York, Janet Ajzenstat from McMaster, and Paul Romney, then teaching at an American University. I even made a special bottle of red wine for that night with a special label announcing our *Canada's Founding Debates* Dinner. They all came, and there was some immediate disagreement. How in the world was I going to get three scholars with different views to do this book without infighting?

My answer was, "We will search out and publish all the most important debates from every province that entered Confederation. That will be the body of this book. But if any of you wish to comment, whether on the debates or on each other's views, you can do that at the bottom of any page, in a note. So, let's consider this project "A Conversation with The Founders." Oh, that did it. On a fine evening. And it was a deeply satisfying moment for Canadian history in the making.

But I needed to find some money to pay them, along with Jeffrey McNairn, a grad-student researcher. So … with Janet's help I drafted a proposal for Heather McLean, Executive Director of the Donner Canadian Foundation, asking for a grant of $50,000, and made an appointment to see her. To make a long story short, she pitched the Donner family and officers, and they loved the idea. So, then I went to Jack and told him we now had money to help with publication and he happily produced a (gold-plated) contract for the book. Everyone was paid with Donner money for work on that book — except me. I didn't want the money. The only thing I insisted on was owning the copyright.

Our grad student searched out microfilm of all original debates about Confederation, in the legislative libraries of every province and Janet masterfully cut, edited, wrote about, and supervised the scholarly aspects of this grand project. Email letters were crisscrossing the country as our team engaged in lots of conversation, not only over what the Founders actually said, but what we thought they meant, and why they said what they said. It was wonderful fun. And all the while, Stoddart's Don Bastian got deeply involved coordinating production of what turned out to be an exceedingly handsome publication.

## A PUBLISHING POTHOLE

Along the way, very close to final production, I got a call from an itinerant political writer named Patrick Luciani, who at the time was doing consulting working for Donner, and whom I knew vaguely from a few of his occasional newspaper pieces. Would I join him for a light lunch? Sure. But why the invite?

Dark-haired, shirt-and-tie Patrick, aquiline Italian features carefully composed in executive manner, was in a somber mood and a bit unfocused, but near the end of our lunch, after managing to get his dollop of civil conversation over with, his eyes narrowed, very narrow, and he told me why I was there. It was a bombshell.

"Something came up at the Donner Board. One of the members is … she's … I mean, she's a pretty radical feminist, and she … *she doesn't want your name on the book.*"

"Pardon?" I was stunned, then immediately angry. "Let me get this straight, Patrick. For the first time in Canada's history. For the first time in more than

*Against The Tide*

a 130 friggin' years of existence, an ordinary citizen. Not a specialist. Not an historian. Not someone you might have thought *ought* to have done this by now, right? has organized a team of expert scholars, found a publisher, and raised the funding to publish our founding debates … and you don't want *what*?"

"It's not me. It's the Board. I mean, she's an influential member. She's … alright, someone with deep pockets. You know. She wants the book done, of course. But doesn't want your name, uh, *associated* with it." Patrick was staring now, as if in expectation of a violent emotional reaction, staring at his empty cup of soup.

"What does 'associated' mean, Patrick?"

"She just doesn't want your name on the book."

"Who is *she*?"

"I can't say." I stared him down.

"Well, okay. Sondra Gottlieb. She's the wife of Alan Gottlieb, the, uh, Donner Chairman."

With a pretended nonchalance — that's all I could manage — I thanked him for lunch, told him it was an upsetting demand, and "I would have to think about it," but realized there was no point in shooting the messenger.

Sondra Gottlieb was a well-known Rosedale denizen and gossip columnist with a brash attitude and sharp tongue, who couldn't shut up. The one who, as the irreverent wife of a very distinguished man said, in response to an American comment about the dullness of Canada: "Maybe we should invade South Dakota." That was pretty amusing, actually, and when it hit the news, it drew even more guests to her house parties.

At a 1986 dinner that she hosted for Prime Minister Brian Mulroney and US Vice-President George H.W. Bush, she was caught-in-the-act by a news reporter slapping her social-secretary Connie Connors, right across the face. Some feminist. This got around Toronto as "the slap flap" and made dinner at the Gottlieb's with Sondra even more desirable. It was a kind of slap in the face that she wanted me to disappear. In truth, I mostly just wanted the book published before another century went by, and if I had to step back for that, well, perhaps …

After a calming hour's run on a lovely forest trail, but still agitated, I called Ian and told him what Patrick had said. Like me, he was flabbergasted. I told him I didn't want to lose Donner funding just because my political ideas had irritated one of their Board members, so could he call Janet, and get her to write a little copy for the Acknowledgements page, inside the book, explaining to readers that the entire project originated … with me? He did, and she did.

She wrote:

*Canada's Founding Debates* is a William D. Gairdner production. The conception, choice of researchers, and the energy behind the project are entirely his. He wrote the Donner Canadian Foundation: "There is a book of passionate, interesting material to be assembled by scholars who know how to tease out the spirits of Montesquieu, Rousseau, Burke, Locke, and others who haunt these pages and point to the fascinating conflicts of political, constitutional, economic, and social opinion that were common fare in our founders' day and that echo still."

From the beginning he envisaged the commentary as a "conversation with the founders" … Throughout, our objective has been the one Bill expressed originally: "to bring the debates alive," to recapture the "vital vision that shaped our beginning. We live at a time when Canada has perhaps never been so threatened by its lack of unity and purpose," he wrote in that first letter; "I suggest one of the reasons is that we have forgotten our founding arguments."

I don't think Sondra would have understood a word of that, but it went a long way to calming me down. A day later, I called Don Bastian, and told him: "Be sure to put my name on the cover of the book, and to hell with Donner's mouthy feminist. But not in first position, because although I was the Founder and Managing Editor of this whole project, Janet was the Research Editor and did all that heavy lifting. So, her name should be first."

The book cover can be seen on page 371.

So handsome. I still love it. Stoddart did a great job designing and editing, and out of the gate it was very well-reviewed as a long-overdue classic. I am deeply proud to say that no one can be a constitutional scholar or historian of Canada today, without having this important book on their shelf. After it was released, I went back to Donner and managed to get another $12,000 to have the book translated into French, and published by Laval University as *Débats sur la fondation du Canada* so that Canada's francophones would have access to our founding debates in their mother tongue.

Not least of my motivations in producing this important book was the realization that in terms of political discourse Canada had already been drifting relentlessly leftward for a half century. But like the infamous frog that gets boiled to death in slowly heated water before ever thinking about trying to jump out, citizens, largely unaware of their intellectual entrapment by the growing tentacles of the Nanny State, just sit there, like the frog. Canadians are getting parboiled — and they haven't noticed.

Against The Tide

Froggy passivity is especially true of young students. At the time I had heard professors give lectures justifying Canada's growing statism as if it were the final realization of our Founders' dreams. But it was, and is, no such thing. Our Founders argued for morally and politically ordered liberty and a decentralized federalism, against wrap-around Statism, and perhaps the last important politician voicing this truth was Canada's seventh Prime Minister Wilfred Laurier, who declared: "*Canada is free, and Freedom is its nationality.*" How very rousing, and how forgotten! Has any Prime Minister said such a thing since? None. But until this book appeared, there was simply no easy way for students to check for themselves what our Founders *actually* said, as distinct from what a professor with a warped agenda might have said they said. But no longer. Just so, *Canada's Founding Debates* is a profoundly conservative book, and its publication a profoundly conservative act (as was the original Constitution our Founders created). Unless this book gets banned someday, or burned (statues of that marvelous Founder, John A. Macdonald, who figures so prominently in this book, and to whom we owe so much, have recently been smeared with paint, knocked down, or decapitated) it remains potent ideological ammunition for the never-ending war against big government.

But the book died shortly after it appeared, when I got a call from Don to say that Stoddart was declaring bankruptcy and closing its doors, for good. That was an unexpected torpedo that blew up my book; all my books, of which this was the sixth of seven published by Stoddart. The last with Jack was called *The Trouble With Democracy*, which I wrote while doing the founding debates book. I watched 2,500 copies roll up to Jack's warehouse in a big transport trailer, just before he closed the doors. With no marketing or publicity support it died, too, and Jack sold almost the entire stock to jobbers for a few bucks a book.

I had warned him not to put his fawning thanks to various governments in my first book, because he could go bankrupt someday if he structured his business with dependency on government handouts. But he didn't stop. He couldn't. No Canadian publisher today can compete without government grants. The whole industry stinks that way, and Canada is awash with grant-seeking authors and titles that wouldn't survive a day in a true free market for books and ideas. That's okay for some books that ought to be published regardless of markets. That's why we have academic presses. But it shouldn't be true for all books. In the end, grants and subsidies are how governments attract ideological conformity — and votes — from authors and publishers. But a change of governments can mean a change of grants, so it's a dangerous game. It wasn't just that, though. Chapters, a huge chain by then, had failed to pay for truckloads of stock with which Jack had long since supplied them. A million dollars' worth, Don said. Bye-bye Stoddart. And bye-bye to my beautiful book. I suffered the grief of a true patriot.

So, the next day I went hunting for an academic press, because university presses don't go bankrupt, and landed on Professor Peter Russell, a big man on the Board of the University of Toronto Press, a distinguished political writer, and, I suspected, a dyed-in-the-wool leftist like all his colleagues. So, I just hoped he didn't know who I was. But he actually answered the phone himself, so I told him of the team of professors that I had pulled together for this (he had been Janet's Ph.D. Thesis Supervisor, so that helped), what a fine book it was, and that alas, no sooner had it seen the light, than Stoddart crashed.

He listened but was perhaps understandably skeptical. "Well," he began — sounding a little haughty — "We don't publish books just because their authors think they're good!"

"Of course. I understand, Sir. But it's not just a good book. It's a *great* book. And the first book on our founding debates ever done — more than a century after our founding. But Stoddart closed its doors almost as soon as it got published. I don't want to see all the publicity and marketing momentum wasted. We need to get it back into production right away. So, I am searching for a good university press: you at U of T, or McGill, or UBC."

There was a long silence, "I'm heading to Europe tomorrow, for two weeks."

"I'll send you a copy today, by speedy courier." With it, I sent a handwritten letter of appreciation, telling him I was offering it to him first, but if he declined, I would take it to a competitor university press.

Back in Canada two weeks later, Professor Russell called to say "You're right. It's a beautiful book. We'd be happy to publish it." So, we had a deal, and I had relief.

That book is a gift to my country, my children, and their children. My name did get on the cover, none of the Donner feminists came out of the closet, and I own the sole copyright for the book. On my suggestion, U of T even produced a special edition for Canada's 150th Anniversary in 2017. And, once in a while ... they send me a royalty cheque.

Among the many glowing and appreciative reviews and comments on that book, I received the following most interesting letter by email from MP Jason Kenney, whom I had known for some time as a member of a society called *Civitas Canada* (my second gift to my country), of which I will speak below. It is an understatement to say that the thoughts evinced in Jason's letter betoken an extremely active and curious mind, attuned to the most profound conundrum of our time, which is the question of how we reconcile a polity devoted to liberty and forced equality at the same time, as the latter obviously cancels the former.

Against The Tide

My answer to Jason's question was worked out much later in *The Great Divide: Why Liberals and Conservatives Will Never, Ever Agree* (2015). And the short story, is as follows. All the liberal democracies of the Western world eventually found themselves in an impossible philosophical and moral contradiction because by the early part of the twentieth century, they had mutated from polities resting on a foundation of liberty, to polities resting far more on a foundation of substantive equality, or government-mandated equal outcomes. And as one goes up, the other must go down. The fascinating solution to this problem (and to Jason's question) was the near-unconscious creation of an entirely new kind of polity I have called "libertarian socialism." It is perfectly neither of those two contradictory things. But it's enough of each that what we now have is our original body-politic split into two bodies, one private, the other public. The private body is the realm of the individual who by now has countless private rights to enjoy every imaginable bodily pleasure and liberty: drugs, abortion, homosexual acts, euthanasia, easy divorce, and more. The public body, on the other hand, is the realm of state action where egalitarian rights and benefits for all to programs such as "free" (pre-paid via the tax system) medical care, pensions, public schooling, access to a myriad of grants for literally thousands of government-funded programs and services and the like, are showered on all citizens equally. You are more free than ever as a private individual; but trapped, dependent, and regulation-bound as a citizen. In this way, private conduct has been largely subtracted from public concern, which is to say, removed from the realm of public moral judgement or shame, while all public benefits have been roughly equalized, coast-to-coast. It has been a kind of rearguard action designed by no one in particular, to accommodate the looming national contradiction between boasts of liberty, and forced equality, and to justify the flight from true community that always entails whenever a polity subtracts private individual behaviour from public scrutiny. A larger state is always the residue, and the beneficiary. Perhaps a national citizen anti-statist movement aimed at open and broad discussion and remedies for such a situation was needed?

## CIVITAS CANADA – "A SOCIETY WHERE IDEAS MEET."

David Frum is currently editor of *The Atlantic* magazine, and prior to this was for many years an elegant conservative-minded pundit. Recently, in a mood of high dudgeon, he has come out as an enraged never-Trumper, and many of his most conservative colleagues feared he had lost it. In 1996, however, in his crisply conservative phase he joined forces with Ezra Levant — a sometimes far more abrasive, if more distinctly right-wing, pundit — to mount a "Winds of Change" conference in Calgary, to which I was invited.

The underlying intent of that conference, not effectively realized until much later by Stephen Harper (at the time mostly a freelance adviser to Preston Manning), was to "Unite the Right" by ending the division in the conservative camp caused by the existence of two conservative parties: the so-called Progressive Conservative party (perceived by many of its own members, and many of the public as too left), and the Reform Party (perceived by many of the public and some members, as too right). This conference was in effect the first-ever gathering of the most influential Canadian authors, journalists, academics, and media mavens of a conservative, libertarian, classical liberal, and generally free-market, anti-big government bent. I had never met, and had nothing to do with any of them, and was likely invited only because of the nationwide success of *The Trouble With Canada*, which appealed greatly to many of a conservative and libertarian bent at this conference. *War Against the Family* was also doing well at the time, but it lost me a lot of fans — mostly the so-called "fiscal conservatives," because they were insufficiently educated in the history of political thought to understand that all true conservatives (think of the patriarchs of modern conservatism, such as Edmund Burke and David Hume) are social by nature, or they are not conservatives at all. *War* appealed powerfully to many then prominent social conservatives because it was a wrap-around critique of the progressive attack on the traditional family. Settle in, Bill, was my mood now. Just meet, greet, and listen.

From the get-go, it was apparent that a lot of the people at this historic gathering knew each other by name but had never actually met, and all seemed anxious for their reputations. As if to say, what if someone sees me shaking hands with David Frum, or Michael Coren, or that fellow William Gairdner? You could *feel* latent anxiety in the room. But, as more hands got shook, anxieties eased, and Winds of Change ended as both a success and a flop. A flop because the idea David and Ezra had was to organize small discussion groups of a half-dozen or so and send them off to discuss political and social problems that had festered for decades, then after a couple of hours of this ask them to vote on possible solutions. It was a neophyte notion almost as shallow in conception as the speculations of fevered Jacobins. In other words, nothing got united, but some lasting relationships were engendered, and I don't know why, but I ended up proposing the most lasting thing of all.

The exact moment of conception came when I realized that here, for the first time, all the warm bodies to go with the well-known names from the invisible side of Canada's political spectrum were gathered in one room. These people were the voices of the Canada's too-oft silenced, majority. There must

Against The Tide

be a way to give them a voice and keep this going. Within minutes I found myself jotting down an outline of a possible new Canadian organization on the back of an index card. Eager to try the idea on someone much younger, I made a beeline for David Frum, congratulated him on this *Winds* event, and asked directly: Is there a plan to repeat this? Will there be other *Winds* meetings? Is there an organizational structure in place that could reproduce such an event? If not, would you consider creating one? Then I handed him my sketch for such a national organization. He glanced at it and quickly handed it back faster than I had given it to him.

His answer to all my questions was a decorously polite negative. I would have to find someone else to bring this idea to life. Well, pushing 56 at the time, I was reluctant to do it myself. But the idea wouldn't go to sleep. So, I soon found myself telephoning various think tanks and other organizations to ask how and why they were set up as they were? There was warm response from most of them, and immediate assistance (including all their organizational minutes and financial statements) from such as the American Professor and author Stanton Evans, then the President of The Philadelphia Society. I also remember helpful chats with Michael Walker and Herb Grubel, of The Fraser Institute, once again revising my notes.

Finally, in the fall of 1996 I asked three people: David Frum, for the reasons mentioned above; Michael Coren, then a catholic conservative media personality who had written good books on important figures such as G.K. Chesterton and C.S. Lewis, and who had already done a number of TV interviews with me; and Bill Robson, Head of the distinguished Toronto economic think-tank, the C.D. Howe Institute. Could they come to my farm in King City to discuss how to keep this going?

I still defend the general premise that "politics is downstream from culture," and that because Canada (and so many other democracies) had by then been in the process of moral collapse for almost half a century, it would not be able to save itself until and unless the culture was changed. And it cannot be changed from outside. The only effective long-term change, if ever, will have to be in the minds and hearts of the people as a whole — a kind of secular form of The Great Awakening of the early 18th century, when a dying religion was revived across America by aroused citizens travelling from village to village preaching against enlightenment nihilism and secularism. To help effect such a change, I envisioned this new organization as a membership of important thinkers who would gather once a year to network, share, and spark ideas and, most importantly, who would take up the role of pushing back against the closing of the Canadian mind in their books, interviews, newspaper articles, and conference talks.

As mentioned — with no aim to self-aggrandize — in the hundreds of interviews I have done (which in my eighties have slowed down considerably, but not stopped), call-in guests often ask: "Why haven't you ever run for politics?" Or (this one is embarrassing): "You should be Prime Minister!" Oh dear, here we go. My reply is always the same: If I were handed the keys to power and managed to get Canada to where I thought it should be through legislation within say, ten years, but absent any deep change in the culture, I think that when the keys were handed back to the next government, the country would simply snap like an elastic band back to where it was. Canada's parties have been engaged for a long time in a kind of "pendulum politics," caught up in a "swing left, then swing right" process that cannot change without a fundamental change of the underlying culture. By "culture" I refer to our basic political and moral assumptions about the sanctity of liberty, equality before the law (only), the centrality of marriage and the family, of civil order, minimal government, free enterprise, and dedication to sustaining a common moral community and the Common Good — a phrase that has fallen out of fashion. How, and why we departed from such standards and the damaging ideological reasons for this departure, was thoroughly outlined in all my books and essays.

So, when David pulled up to our farm in his Mercedes, Michael on his noisy, smoky motorcycle, and Bill in his economical something or other, I had already drafted corporate articles, an organizational structure, and the purpose statement still in use today, namely:

> "To promote and deepen understanding through the exchange of a wide range of political, economic, social, religious, cultural, and philosophical ideas concerning the principles and traditions of a free and ordered society."

We had a fine and spirited meeting, agreeing to organize an initial national conference for spring of 1997 in Toronto. This was great fun and rather exciting, but we couldn't yet think of a name. Nevertheless, we left with a sense of high excitement coupled with the feeling we were embarking on our own reactionary revolution of sorts. But how would other well-known thinkers feel about being linked to a new organization which as yet had no defining personality? After all, what each of us individually stood for could be distorted or tainted in a flash by some stupid public comment that escaped our upcoming conference. How would we control the quality of membership? What if left-wing troublemakers crashed our first conference next spring (which a few did)? Imagine the hysterical headlines and apoplexy at *The Toronto Star*, and the CBC as they rolled up with cameras ready to our

Against The Tide

door! Should we close the whole proceeding to media? Well, it was a dicey but exciting time, and any number of such worries had to be stick-handled to avoid blowing the whole idea up.

But in the weeks following, we knew we couldn't start without a name, and one day Bill Robson called to propose *Civitas*, which met with the silence of approval. It was a politically neutral, but noble feel-good name that was sufficiently high-toned. We had it. Next was the job of assembling a founding Board of Directors so that we would appear sufficiently established to attract a membership. (We had decided that we only wanted a limited number — I think 250 came to mind). But first we needed a founding Board. That took a lot of phone calls from me, personal persuasion, and a bit of, well ... manipulation.

Many of the initial reactions to my calls for Board members were such as: "Well, if you can get so-and-so to agree, then I'm in, but otherwise, I'm not." So, I had to call so-and-so, and tell him or her that the other so-and-so I had just spoken with had already agreed to serve ... if they would. And on it went. The crowning moment was when all the founding Directors but one, agreed. I was still working on him. After listening to the names of all the others, and keenly aware of the reputational risks to himself, he said with a tone of astonishment: "You go all *those people* to agree?" When he heard their names reconfirmed, he said "Okay," and I put down the phone with a "Yes"! We had just delivered a baby that has thrived by now for more than a quarter of a century.

Soon afterward, I was on the phone to Mark Magner, the fellow who had invited me to speak to my first sold-out Reform Party meeting in Markham in 1990, and whose justifiable reputation as an organizer I knew well. Mark leapt into action, and we soon had the logo (let's use a classical Roman font!), print-work for letterhead and banners, a bank account, and above all, we were up to our elbows organizing the spring conference, visiting hotels to find an appropriate location, and so on. Then Mark called to say we needed a cutline for *Civitas*, because people seeing the name would have no idea what it meant. As if descended from heaven, the words "*A Society Where Ideas Meet*" popped into my mind, and we used it: this would be a fellowship for the enjoyment of ideas.

The first evening of that first conference Andrew Coyne, a prominent Canadian journalist, walked up somberly to the door, notepad in hand, and I got indigestion. We had decided that everything should be run according to Chatham House rules: only *Civitas* Members and their guests could attend, and no member would be allowed to publish the speeches heard, nor any remarks made by members. The reasoning was that we wanted our speakers to feel free to speak their true minds, to tell us what they were *really* thinking,

\text{\textit{(signature)}}

as distinct from only what they thought it safe to think and say. But here was Andrew Coyne, five feet away, looking like a contestant at a chess match stymied over his next move, but very intent on scooping a story about what he likely thought was a strange-seeming right-wing cult meeting.

This was exactly why I never wanted to go in for politics. I blurted, "Andrew, this conference is for members only. I don't think you're a member, and we don't allow reporting on speeches, or on comments from members. So … *I have to ask you to leave.*" Oh Jeez, it was so embarrassing to have to say that. It made me regret ever having put the conference together, as I escorted Andrew to the exit. It was the lowest moment.

But the Conference took off in high spirits that night with super speeches by a lot of distinguished Canadian, and two American, speakers followed by lots of questions from engaged members. It was a grand success from the first moment. I vividly recall the comment made by Alan Carlson of the Rockford Institute, Illinois, then publisher of *Chronicles* magazine, who gave a stirring speech on the breakdown of the family. I asked him, "How have you enjoyed the conference?" He replied: "I love coming to these inaugural events, because they're usually the last one!" After writing these words I found him online and called him to say, "*Civitas* has been going steady for a quarter-century now." He laughed and cheered. At any rate, getting back to our first conference the next morning, Andrew Coyne showed up, with the shy smile of a kid caught with his hand in the cookie jar, as a guest of David Frum, seemed to enjoy himself a lot, never reported a word, and since then has been an excellent guest-speaker himself at a few *Civitas* conferences.

Ten years later, our *Civitas* conference was held in Ottawa. It was a special time. We were at the heart of the government beast now, with 10th Anniversary gold pins on hand. And … Stephen Harper, who had been a *Civitas* member for many years, was now Prime Minister of Canada! That night, he made a surprise visit to our Conference, low-lying security guys in black suits and wired earpieces in tow, ever watchful. Stephen was watchful, too. As our eyes met, it was "Hi Bill," with a comforting handshake. I knew, and he knew, what his visit meant to all of us: "You must feel gratified to see *Civitas* thriving like this." You bet, Sir.

It felt good for an older man like me to call young Stephen "Sir" in salute to his office, and watch him work the room, for our movement was a small part of how he got there. Unlike other politicians, who seem incapable of concentrating on the person they are speaking to without looking around to see who might now be looking at *them*, Stephen stayed fully glued, eye to eye, for his every conversation. It was impressive. Many of the *Civitas* members in that Ottawa room, such as Monte Solberg, Scott Reid (the kid — now a serious

Against The Tide

politician — who was sitting at that desk beside me, in Saskatoon), and Jason Kenney ("by the time I finished *Trouble*, I was converted!") who were now MP's. I swear that during Stephen's tenure as Prime Minister from 2006 to 2015 you could turn on the TV news almost any night and see two or three *Civitas* members speaking, being mentioned, praised, critiqued, or interviewed. It was indeed a great awakening, before the democratic pendulum swung leftward, once again, with the son of the Prime Minister who was the main reason I wrote my protest as *The Trouble With Canada* in the first place.

Here is its handsome home page, the sight of which still has me beaming with pride.[21]

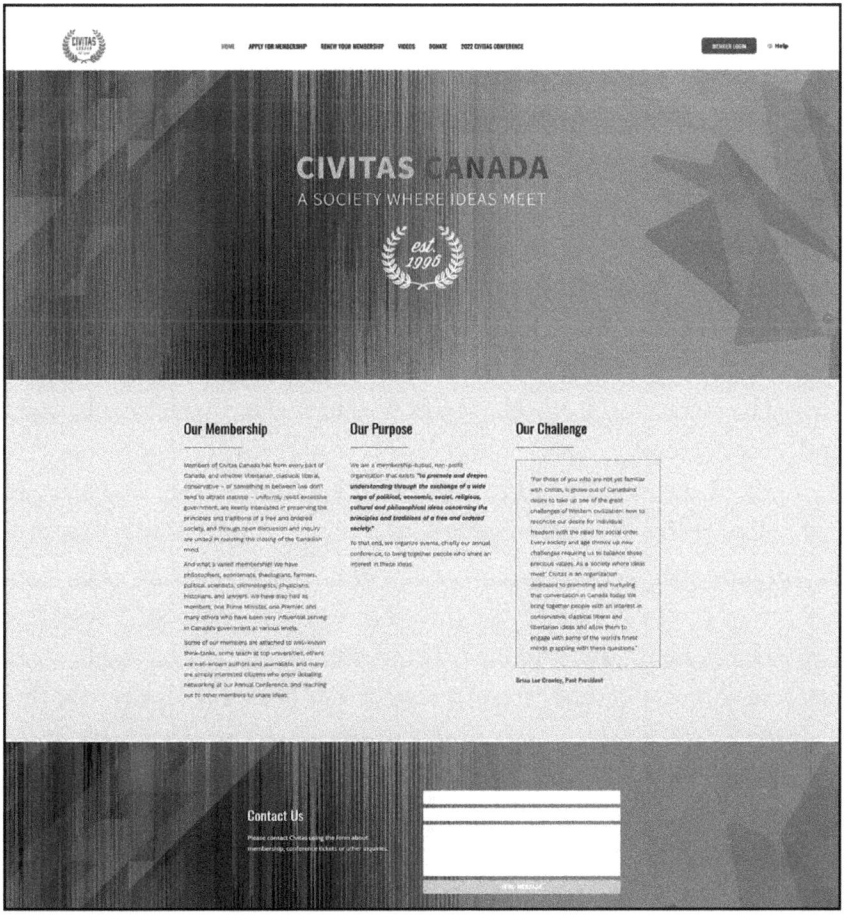

Notwithstanding the pendulum, there is considerable satisfaction in knowing for certain from the fact (excuse the flagrant self-promotion) of so many of my own books purchased, from so many gratifying personal communications received over these past decades, and from the many millions of citizens touched every year by the books, articles, media talks, interviews, podcasts, and teachings of hundreds of *Civitas* members, that public discussion in Canada has been definitively reset, altered, modified, checked, and rebalanced — perhaps permanently.

## A FEW FINAL THOUGHTS

So, this memoir has come to an end, and I am in the deep winter of a blessed and fortunate life. In searching for one of the red threads — for what made my life what it was — I'd say I have spent a lot of it dreaming; or rather, yearning, to be free. Of what? Of need? No. Like most Canadians I haven't ever been truly needy. It was more like a deep need to be free of contingency, of slavery to mundane work and control by the demands of others. So, I chose the life of a professor and writer. And though I loved teaching, and still do (a book is a kind of teaching), the world of literature as a romantic springboard into the free life of a novel writer turned out to be a crushing personal disappointment. How was it possible to be so self-deceived? To misjudge my own passions and talents so badly?

Fortunately, by the time the fiction-failure was weighing on me, a personal world of moral and political ideology was awakening. Soon, I felt like Kant when he said the philosopher David Hume "woke me from my dogmatic slumber." The transition from literary fiction to the enormous canvas of political and moral ideology (and fiction), was a natural transition because the history of civilization is a kind of enormous mixture of fact and fiction — a story we tell ourselves, about ourselves, that includes our truths, lies, and self-deceptions, and it woke me up.

So, when family called and the business world beckoned? I wondered at once, could this be it? My way out? Could this be the key to intellectual and authorial freedom? Could I, should I, turn my back on all my training, on the teaching I love, hold my nose, and throw myself into this mess of a brute commercial world, to maybe save the business, then maybe, possibly, sell it for enough money to be free to say and write whatever I pleased? For the rest of my life? That was a huge risk and gamble, and a possible deception, too. For it might have failed. And in fact, as told in Part III, we were at one time a week or so from bankruptcy.

But there was something powerfully attractive about one day becoming a writer of serious public opinion beholden to no one: not to a government, a university, a corporation, a political party, or a media network. Imagine! Outside of a totalitarian regime, where you may easily be imprisoned or assassinated for speaking out as boldly as I have done, how many human beings

Against The Tide

in all of history have ever been wholly free to say and write whatever they believe? And maybe get paid a little for it, too? So when, in October of 1988 at just 48 years of age I concluded the sale of the business and went for a long run in the forest around my home, now a young, retired man, wholly free at last to think, and write, it felt as if my heart was running all by itself along those beautiful sunlit forest trails.

Looking back, I would say that every life necessarily reflects its beginnings, in action and reaction. Early childhood illness — long periods of feeling well, then suddenly, sick once again (for no reason!), was both a curse and a blessing. As a kid, the randomness of illness — why me? — seemed without meaning. Is life really meaningless? What's the plan? After all, I could have been born someone else; been some other kid. This entailed long periods of confusion and sinking into myself over the Why? But I found only arbitrariness, and so had to create my own meaning; like, as a sick boy in bed, drawing those pictures of Tarzan leaping with glinting knife onto the back of a menacing lion. And when I got well, fleeing from who I was. Running, half-naked through the forests around home, hunting rabbits so very seriously with my self-fashioned spear, or bare-chested (sure to have peeled off my shirt to brave more pain), charging in a private test of courage through a swarm of very dry, very sharp scotch-thistles. If the Apache Cochise could do it, I could do it. I was running, I see now (though incoherently then), from the absence of an answer to the Why. Thus began a lifelong feeling that random illness, or plain bad luck, for whomsoever (but especially for me, of course), is offensive, because arbitrary. And arbitrariness in matters of life and death surely pointed to an absence of meaning in the grand scheme of things, and so, ultimately (if you really think about it: can there really be no grand scheme?), to an absence of God. Or at minimum, to a *deus absconditus*. God has left the building. Now you can love an absent God or get upset at the absence — it's a defining choice. I have been torn between love and upset for a long time.

My worry about the possibility of an unseen underlying chaos has lingered all my life. Hence the search for meaning. During a cruise off the coast of Morocco in 2015 we disembarked on Tenerife, one of the Canary Islands and trekked through a field of tortuous rocks spewed from a volcanic eruption in 1909. To me, at least (it didn't seem to bother anyone else) this was a deeply terrifying, profoundly unsettling sight that suddenly made me feel sick. Rocks twisted, torqued, slashed, smashed, ejected, spewed, from some invisible fiery cauldron in a hot spume high into the sky, only to fall and cool in exactly these tortured, mangled, meaningless shapes. To think of that scene even now gives me chills. Oh, I know, there was the logic of physics, the laws of nature. The rocks had to land the way they did because that's how they came flying out of the earth to encounter forces, cooling temperatures, wind, gravity, impact, etc. etc. But what a random — and deeply meaningless — mess.

It's okay for rocks spewed without reason or warning from the devil's cauldron — surely there are no proper gods down there? — to have random shapes, because we don't think of volcanoes or rocks as alive, as having a moral nature. But humans are not rocks; we have moral feelings about things just, and unjust. So, it's natural for a child to believe everyone ought to get what they deserve, no? But they seldom do. In the just world under a just and loving God of which I was reassured (a notion that still lurks as a possibility, I admit), I figured only very bad people would get diseases and (justly) suffer or die of them. That would have made some sense. And much later, while at Stanford reading Dostoevsky, I was gratified to see he felt my same anguish over the injustice of a single innocent child suffering and dying in agony — a twisted human shape, a tormented human rock.

At any rate, the job of perfecting the frail powers of my own young body, yearning as I was for strength and wholeness, was really a personal search expressed in running, racing (and latterly, in cycling, and cross-country skiing). Those activities were and are still a kind of physical medium in my lifelong struggle for meaning part of a fight against the arbitrary collapse of my own body. There's a lion. Prepare yourself. Jump, and stab. You can create yourself as a purpose-driven, non-arbitrary being.

That sequence seamlessly mutated. In youth it was about fixing myself and my poor health through devotion to sport. In adulthood, it changed to fixing the sick body of my country with ideas and argument. With respect to the latter, the marching order was to analyze each topic; get the history and the facts; formulate solutions; express them as honestly, carefully, and clearly as possible, and publish them in books and articles in the hope of turning what seemed like the randomly chaotic, arbitrary world outside myself into something that made sense. Your body is collapsing? Fix it. Your country is collapsing? Fix it. I yearned to expose in the clearest possible detail how and why for more than half a century the political and moral world that became the wonderful country we call Canada was now under relentless attack from within, due to its own corrosive ideological commitments.

Accordingly, I think of all my books as prods to the nation of an earnest gadfly meant to awaken fellow citizens with the deepest and most incisive questions, facts, and arguments I could possibly imagine, find, or create. As such they stand as my best epitaph, and an unsolicited gift to my country, my children, and their children.

Against The Tide

# ENDNOTES

1   The official Olympic film of the Tokyo 1964 Olympic Games can be seen at https://www.youtube.com/watch?v=WHt0eAdCCns. (page 18)

2   The Gairdner Foundation, established in 1957, is dedicated to fulfilling James A. Gairdner's vision to recognize major research contributions to the treatment of disease and alleviation of human suffering. See https://gairdner.org. (page 25)

3   *Radisson Feuilleton d'aventures* (titled *Tomahawk* in American markets) was a Canadian adventure television series which aired on CBC Television and Radio-Canada from 1957 to 1958. See https://www.youtube.com/watch?v=4fSskmM97X8. (page 60)

4   May 29, 1959 USA-USSR Track & Field meet USA runner Bob Soth goes out. See https://www.youtube.com/watch?v=ypn6TzuD4hM. (page 93)

5   My article in *The Epoch Times*. See https://www.theepochtimes.com/the-charter-at-40-how-canada-got-re-colonized_4179647.html. (page 144)

6   The complete Tokyo 1964 Olympics film, see https://www.youtube.com/watch?v=WHt0eAdCCns. (page 165)

7   *Judoka* by Doug Rogers, is a documentary about the experiences of living and training in Japan in 1964. Doug won many important tournaments and trained with Masahiko Kimura. See https://www.youtube.com/watch?v=CBFx1a4L2ig and https://en.wikipedia.org/wiki/Doug_Rogers_(judoka). (page 176)

8   Rossotti's Alpine Inn in Portola Valley. See https://www.alpineinnpv.com. (page 199)

9   The mens 440 yards Hurdles, 1966 Comonwealth Games in Jamaica. I am in lane three. See https://www.youtube.com/watch?v=F6mbRo1120A. (page 204)

10  The 1966 Commonwealth Games 440 Hurdles, see https://www.youtube.com/watch?v=F6mbRo1120A. (page 206)

11  Manifesto of the Front de libération du Québec. See https://english.republiquelibre.org/Manifesto_of_the_Front_de_lib%C3%A9ration_du_Qu%C3%A9bec. (page 239)

12  The World Masters Cross-Country Ski Association. Today, more than forty years after the first meeting, the WMA has 30 member nations, and every Masters World Cup, rotated between those three regions of the world as originally planned, regularly draws about 1,000 international competitors. You will see a lot of happy faces! See https://www.world-masters-xc-skiing.com/en/about-us/history.html. (page 285)

13  Big Jim painting a scene near his fishing lodge on Blue Lake, in northern Quebec. James A. Gairdner was, indeed, a larger than life figure. See https://www.gairdner.org/who-we-are/our-history. (page 308)

14  I wrote *The Book of Absolutes: A Critique of Relativism and a Defence of Universals* (McGill-Queens, 2008). You can hear the interview on the book with the CBC's house historian Paul Kennedy, at https://www.williamgairdner.ca/wp-content/themes/totalpress-child/audio/CBC_ideas_March30.mp3. (page 323)

15  Firing Line with William F. Buckley Jr.: The Economics and Politics of Race. Episode S0573, recorded on November 3, 1983 with guest Thomas Sowell. See https://www.youtube.com/watch?v=TEBPCOG5RHs. (page 328)

16 After several refusals, the CBC's Peter Gzowski, host of the popular national program "Morningside", finally agreed to do this interview when my book *"The Trouble With Canada"* (1990) had sold over 50,000 copies and hit #1 in Canada. See https://www.youtube.com/watch?v=y65nMMNSuMw&t=185s. (page 337)

17 William Gairdner: The unelected Senate offers a check on the tyranny of the majority. See https://nationalpost.com/opinion/william-gairdner-the-unelected-senate-offers-a-check-on-the-tyranny-of-the-majority. (page 352)

18 William Gairdner: *The Trouble with Canada ... Still* — Jan 19, 2011. One of Canada's most persistent conservative gadflies talks about why he believes the country is still headed in the wrong direction. See https://www.youtube.com/watch?v=8G6cQBpdODo&t=22s. (page 359)

19 My testy interview with Steve Paikin the host of TVO's The Agenda on *"The War Against The Family"* (1993). See https://williamgairdner.ca/interview-with-steve-paiken-host-of-tvo-on-my-book, T*he War Against The Family* 1993. (page 359)

20 My testy interview on TVO's Between The Lines with host Steve Paikin about *"The War Against The Family"* (1993). See https://www.youtube.com/watch?v=sBxpRMJGfcA&t=1618. (page 362)

21 The homepage of our *Civitas Canada* website, see https://www.civitascanada.ca/. (page 385)

# PUBLICATIONS BY WILLIAM D. GAIRDNER

1. *The Critical Wager* (ECW Press, 1982)

2. *The Trouble With Canada* (Stoddart, 1990, BPS Books, 2007 and KD Books, 2023)

3. *The War Against the Family* (Stoddart, 1992, BPS Books, 2007 and KD Books, 2023)

4. *Constitutional Crack-Up* (Stoddart, 1994)

5. *On Higher Ground* (Stoddart, 1996)

6. As Editor, and Contributor, *After Liberalism* (Stoddart, 1998)

7. *Canada's Founding Debates* (Stoddart, 1999)

8. *The Trouble With Democracy* (Stoddart, 2001, BPS Books, 2007 and KD Books, 2023)

9. As Editor, Alphonse Juilland, *Rethinking Track and Field* (SEP Editrice, 2002)

10. *Canada's Founding Debates* (University of Toronto Press, 2003)

11. *The Book of Absolutes* (McGill-Queen's University Press, 2008)

12. *OH, OH, Canada* (BPS Books, 2008)

13. *The Trouble With Canada ... Still!* (Key Porter Books, 2010, and KD Books, 2023)

14. *The Great Divide: Why Liberals and Conservatives Will Never, Ever Agree* (Encounter Books, 2015).

15. *The French Traveler*, A Translation by William Gairdner of Joseph Delaporte, *Le Voyageur Français* (1768), with Notes and Commentary (KD Books, 2019)

16. *Nightlost: Poetry, Painting, and Sculpture* (KD Books, 2021)

17. *Disruptive Essays: There Are No Safe Spaces In This Book* (KD Books, 2019)

18. *Beyond the Rhetoric* (A collection of In-Depth Essays published in *Epoch Times*, 2020)

19. *Beyond The Rhetoric: Expanded Edition* (KD Books, 2023)

www.ingramcontent.com/pod-product-compliance
Lightning Source LLC
Chambersburg PA
CBHW041135120626
46547CB00020B/2999